CLIMATE CHANGE IN THE MIDWEST

CLIMATE CHANGE IN THE MIDWEST

Impacts, Risks, Vulnerability, and Adaptation

Edited by S. C. Pryor

INDIANA UNIVERSITY PRESS

Bloomington and Indianapolis

This book is a publication of

Indiana University Press
601 North Morton Street
Bloomington, Indiana 47404-3797 USA

iupress.indiana.edu

Telephone orders   800-842-6796
Fax orders   812-855-7931

♾ The paper used in this publication meets the
   minimum requirements of the American National
Standard for Information Sciences—Permanence of
Paper for Printed Library Materials, ANSI Z39.48-1992.

Manufactured in the United States of America

Library of Congress Cataloging-in-Publication Data

Climate change in the Midwest : impacts, risks, vulnerability, and adaptation / edited by S.C. Pryor.
      p. cm.
   Includes bibliographical references and index.
   ISBN 978-0-253-00682-0 (cloth : alk. paper)
ISBN 978-0-253-00774-2 (eb) 1. Climatic changes—
Middle West. 2. Climatic changes—Environmental
aspects—Middle West. 3. Climatic changes—Risk
assessment—Middle West. 4. Plants—Effect of global
warming on—Middle West. 5. Vegetation and climate.
6. Middle West—Climate. 7. Water levels—Great Lakes
(North America) I. Pryor, S. C., [date]
   QC984.M53C55 2012
   363.738'740977—dc23

                                                    2012017798

               1 2 3 4 5 18 17 16 15 14 13

For Barbara Pryor, with love always.

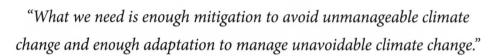

"What we need is enough mitigation to avoid unmanageable climate change and enough adaptation to manage unavoidable climate change."

—John Holdren, U.S. Presidential Science Advisor (2010).
Presentation to the 2010 Kavli Prize Science Forum, Oslo, Norway

Contents

Color plates appear after pages 78 and 174.

Preface

Informing effective responses to climate change is predicated on (1) advancement of fundamental understanding of climate science, including development of projections at scales suitable for impact assessments; (2) mitigation activities designed to limit the magnitude of climate change; and (3) efforts to understand the risks, vulnerabilities, and opportunities posed by climate change and thus to develop optimal adaptation strategies. Research presented in this volume is focused on identifying and quantifying the major vulnerabilities to climate change as manifest in the midwestern United States and thus lays the foundation for addressing the "adaptation gap" (i.e., the difference between the scale of efforts to mitigate anthropogenic forcing of climate and the likely scale and magnitude of climate change). We provide state-of-the-art, spatially disaggregated information regarding the historical, current, and possible future climate states within the region with a particular focus on extremes, and we undertake assessments of the risks and vulnerabilities of critical socioeconomic and environmental systems in the region to climate change and variability. Key sectors discussed herein are agriculture, human health, water resources, energy, and infrastructure, each of which exhibits current vulnerability to climate variability that may be amplified under current climate change trajectories. Challenges and opportunities in developing local and regional strategies for addressing the risks posed by climate change are discussed in the context of developing an integrative policy for the region.

Acknowledgments

Funding for this volume was provided by the Center for Research in Environmental Science at Indiana University and by the National Science Foundation (grant 1019603).

Abbreviations and Acronyms

AMO   Atlantic Multi-decadal Oscillation

AO   Arctic Oscillation

AOGCMs   Atmosphere-Ocean General Circulation Models

AR4   Fourth Assessment Report (of the IPCC)

ASOS   Automated Surface Observing System

AWEA   American Wind Energy Association

BTU   British Thermal Units (a traditional unit of energy equal to about 1055 joules)

CCSP   Climate Change Science Plan

CDC   Centers for Disease Control and Prevention

CDD   Cooling Degree Days

CCCMA   Canadian Centre for Climate Modelling and Analysis

CH_4 Methane

CI   Confidence Intervals

CMAQ   Community Multiscale Air Quality Modeling System

CMIP3   Coupled Model Intercomparison Project phase 3

CNA   Central North America

CNRM   Centre National de Recherches Météorologiques

CO   Carbon monoxide

CO_2 Carbon dioxide

CO_2-eq CO_2-equivalents   The total GHG burden converted into a radiative forcing using the functionally equivalent amount or concentration of CO_2 (i.e., CO_2-equivalent concentration is the concentration of CO_2 that would cause the same amount of radiative forcing as a given mixture of CO_2 and other forcing components)

COOP   CO-OPerative observer network

CRCM   Canadian Regional Climate Model

CRU   Climatic Research Unit (at the University of East Anglia)

CSIRO   Commonwealth Scientific and Industrial Research Organization

CUM_HEAT   Cumulative Heat Index

DoE   Department of Energy

DTR   Diurnal Temperature Range

ECMWF   European Center for Medium Range Weather Forecasts

EHE   Extreme Heat Events

EIA   Energy Information Administration

ENSEMBLES   Ensemble-Based Predictions of Climate Changes and their Impacts (a European Project)

ENSO	El Niño–Southern Oscillation	INCA	Interagency National Climate Assessment Task Force
Energy intensity	A measure of the energy intensity of the economy. Use of energy in BTU per dollar of Gross Domestic Product	IPCC	Intergovernmental Panel on Climate Change
EPA	Environmental Protection Agency	IPSL	Institut Pierre Simon Laplace
ERA-40	Forty-year reanalysis data set issued by ECMWF	kWhr	Kilowatt hour (a unit of energy equal to 1000 watt hours or 3.6 megajoules)
ESD	Empirical/Statistical Downscaling	KS	Kansas
ESM	Earth System Models	KY	Kentucky
FEMA	Federal Emergency Management Agency	LST	Land Surface Temperature
		MAO	Multidecadal Atlantic Oscillation
FHA	Federal Highways Administration	MGA	Midwest Governors Association
FRIS	USDA Farm and Ranch Irrigation Survey	MI	Michigan
		MIP	Model Intercomparison Projects
GCM	General Circulation Model or Global Climate Model	MIROC	Model for Interdisciplinary Research on Climate
GDD	Growing Degree Days	MIUB	Meteorologischen Instituts der Universität Bonn
GDP	Gross Domestic Product		
GFDL	Geophysical Fluid Dynamics Laboratory	MMWR	Morbidity and Mortality Weekly Report
GHCN	Global Historical Climatology Network	MN	Minnesota
		MO	Missouri
GHG	Greenhouse Gases	MPI	Max Plank Institute
GISS	Goddard Institute for Space Studies	MRI	Meteorological Research Institute of Japan
GPP	Gross Primary Productivity	MRCC	Midwest Regional Climate Center
GWP	Global Warming Potential	N_2O	Nitrous oxide
HDD	Heating Degree Days	NAAQS	National Ambient Air Quality Standards
HFCs	Hydrofluorocarbons		
HHWS	Heat/Health Watch Warning System	NAM	Northern Annular Mode
		NAO	North Atlantic Oscillation
HRM3	Hadley Center Regional Climate Model (third generation)	NARCCAP	North American Climate Change Assessment Program
HTCI	Human Thermal Comfort Index	NASA	National Aeronautics and Space Administration
IA	Iowa		
IAM	Integrated Assessment Models	NBS	Net Basin Supply
IL	Illinois	NCAR	National Center for Atmospheric Research
IN	Indiana		

NCDC	National Climatic Data Center	$PM_{2.5}$	Particulate Matter of less than 2.5 microns diameter
NCEP	National Center for Environmental Prediction	PM_{10}	Particulate Matter of less than 10 microns diameter
ND	North Dakota		
NDMC	National Drought Mitigation Center	PNA	Pacific/North American
		PRISM	Parameter-elevation Regressions on Independent Slopes Model
NDVI	Normalized Difference Vegetation Index	RCM	Regional Climate Model
NE	Nebraska	RegCM3	Regional Climate Model (third generation)
NEPA	National Environmental Policy Act		
NFIP	National Flood Insurance Program	Resp	Respiration
		RISA	Regional Integrated Sciences and Assessments
NIDIS	National Integrated Drought Information system	RPS	Renewable Portfolio Standard
NOAA	National Oceanographic and Atmospheric Administration	RR	Rate Ratio
		SD	South Dakota
NNR	NCEP/NCAR Reanalysis	SECC	Southeast Climate Consortium
NO	Nitric oxide	SF_6	Sulfur hexafluoride
NO_2	Nitrogen dioxide	SLP	Sea Level Pressure
NOx	Oxides of nitrogen (NOx = NO + NO_2)	SO_2	Sulfur dioxide
		SOC	Soil Organic Carbon
NPP	Net Primary Productivity	SOM	Self-Organizing Maps
NPS	Non-Point Source	SoVI	Social Vulnerability Index
NREL	National Renewable Energy Laboratory	SPEI	Standardized Precipitation Evapotranspiration Index
NWRS	National Wildlife Refuge System	SPI	Standardized Precipitation Index
NWS	National Weather Service	SRES	Special Report on Emissions Scenarios (of the IPCC)
O_3	Ozone		
OECD	Organization for Economic Cooperation and Development	SWAT	Soil Water Assessment Tool
		Td	Dew point temperature
OH	Ohio	Tmax	Maximum daily temperature
PAR	Pressure and release model	Tmin	Minimum daily temperature
PCDMI	Program for Climate Model Diagnosis and Intercomparison	UMRB	Upper Mississippi River Basin
		UEA	University of East Anglia
PCM	Parallel Climate Model	UHI	Urban Heat Island
PDO	Pacific Decadal Oscillation	UKMO	United Kingdom Meteorological Office
PDSI	Palmer Drought Severity Index		
PFC	Perfluorinated Compounds	UNFCCC	United National Framework Convention on Climate Change
PM	Particulate Matter		

USACE	U.S. Army Corps of Engineers	VOC	Volatile Organic Compounds
USDA	U.S. Department of Agriculture	WCRP	World Climate Research Programme
USDM	U.S. Drought Monitor		
USGCRP	U.S. Global Change Research Program	WI	Wisconsin
		WTI	Waterway Traffic Index
USGS	U.S. Geological Survey		

CLIMATE CHANGE IN THE MIDWEST

1. Climate Change Impacts, Risks, Vulnerability, and Adaptation: *An Introduction*

S. C. PRYOR

Global Climate Change

There is an overwhelming preponderance of evidence to suggest that human activities have, and are, modifying the global atmospheric composition sufficiently that anthropogenic climate change is already being experienced (Bernstein et al. 2007). Further, it is now inevitable that the global climate system will continue to change as a consequence of both past and future emissions of greenhouse gases (GHG) (Bernstein et al. 2007) and may achieve conditions that lie outside the range of climate states that humans have experienced (Solomon et al. 2009). Although "No-one can predict the consequences of climate change with complete certainty; . . . we now know enough to understand the risks" (Stern 2007). Substantiating evidence for these assertions may be drawn from the following major findings from the Fourth Assessment Report from the Intergovernmental Panel on Climate Change (IPCC) (see Table 1.1 for information regarding the IPCC definitions used to articulate confidence or likelihood):

- We have *"very high confidence* that the global average net effect of human activities since 1750 has been one of warming, with a radiative forcing of +1.6 [+0.6 to +2.4] W m^{-2}" (Solomon et al. 2007).
- "Warming of the climate system is unequivocal. Palaeoclimatic information supports the interpretation that the warmth of the last half century is unusual in at least the previous 1,300 years. . . . Most of the observed increase in global average temperatures since the mid-20th century is *very likely* due to the observed increase in anthropogenic greenhouse gas concentrations" (Solomon et al. 2007).
- "For the next two decades, a warming of about 0.2°C per decade is projected for a range of SRES emission scenarios. Even if the concentrations of all greenhouse gases and aerosols had been kept constant at year 2000 levels, a further warming of about 0.1°C per decade would be expected . . . Continued greenhouse gas emissions at or above current rates would cause further warming and induce many changes in the global climate system during the 21st century that would *very likely* be larger than those observed during the 20th century" (Solomon et al. 2007).

1

• "Observational evidence from all continents and most oceans shows that many natural systems are being affected by regional climate changes, particularly temperature increases (*very high confidence*)" (Parry et al. 2007).

• "Global mean temperature changes of 2°C to 4°C above 1990–2000 levels would result in an increasing number of key impacts at all scales (*high confidence*), such as widespread loss of biodiversity, decreasing global agricultural productivity. Global mean temperature changes greater than 4°C above 1990–2000 levels would lead to major increases in vulnerability (*very high confidence*), exceeding the adaptive capacity of many systems (*very high confidence*)" (Parry et al. 2007).

• "There is still *high confidence* that the distribution of climate impacts will be uneven, and that low-latitude, less-developed areas are generally at greatest risk. However, recent work has shown that vulnerability to climate change is also highly variable within individual countries. As a consequence, some population groups in developed countries are also highly vulnerable." (Parry et al. 2007)

• Between 1970 and 2004, global emissions of CO_2, CH_4, N_2O, HFCs, PFCs and SF_6, weighted by their global warming potential (GWP), have increased by 70 percent (24 percent between 1990 and 2004), from 28.7 to 49 gigatonnes of carbon dioxide equivalents ($GtCO_2$-eq) (Metz et al. 2007).

• The "span of energy-related and industrial CO_2 emissions in 2100 across baseline scenarios . . . is very large, ranging from 17 to around 135 $GtCO_2$-eq. . . . The majority of scenarios indicate an increase in emissions during most of the century. However, there are some

Table 1.1. Terminology used in the *IPCC Fourth Assessment Report* to convey the level of confidence and likelihood in the correctness of a result.

Terminology	Degree of confidence
Very high confidence	At least 9 out of 10 chance of being correct
High confidence	About 8 out of 10 chance
Medium confidence	About 5 out of 10 chance
Low confidence	About 2 out of 10 chance
Very low confidence	Less than 1 out of 10 chance

Terminology	Likelihood of occurrence
Virtually certain	>99% probability
Very likely	>90% probability
Likely	>66% probability
More likely than not	>50% probability
About as likely as not	33%–66% probability

baseline (reference) scenarios both in the new and older literature where emissions peak and then decline (*high agreement, much evidence*)"[1] (Metz et al. 2007).

Table 1.1 and the discussion above illustrate a key challenge in formulating and communicating effective policy to respond to climate non-stationarity: how to effectively convey the degree of confidence in climate change scenarios and impacts. As shown in Figure 1.1, non-numeric probability statements evoke very different responses in different individuals when mapped onto a numeric probability scale. For this reason, the IPCC and other similar bodies and agencies have increasingly sought to clarify terminology. These measures are a key component of efforts to correct misconceptions. However, confusion and failure to understand the scientific underpinning of climate change research stems not only from use of imprecise (or poorly understood) terminology and language, but also from the large divergence between discourse in the scientific community and U.S. press coverage (Boykoff and Boykoff 2004). A key source of the perceived need to present a "balanced" depiction of (1) the scientific consensus regarding the causes/magnitude and likely impacts of climate change and (2) the views of "climate change skeptics" in the popular press derives from misconceptions regarding the meaning of scientific uncertainty. Further, in this discourse, uncertainty has often been invoked to "inspire inaction" (Boykoff and Boykoff 2004)

The vignettes from the IPCC reports also speak to two other key components of the task of enabling decision makers to manage climate-related risks/opportunities: the need for reliable detection and attribution of changes in climate and their effects (Hegerl et al. 2010). Detection refers to identification of a change in a biological or physical process at some level of confidence, while attribution refers to statistical confidence in assigning responsibility to a given forcing mechanism (e.g., anthropogenic change of the atmospheric composition). Improved understanding of drivers of the climate system and the response of the climate system to those drivers derived from robust detection and attribution analyses naturally lead to greater confidence in projections of possible future climate states (Santer et al. 2009) and will thus greatly benefit the development of robust climate change policies.

Climate Change Mitigation and Adaptation

Informing effective responses to climate change and variability is predicated on three linked activities: (1) advancing fundamental understanding of climate science, including developing climate projections targeted at the scales at which the impacts are likely to be manifest, (2) mitigation activities designed to limit the magnitude of future climate change, and (3) efforts to understand the risks, vulnerabilities, and opportunities posed by climate change and thus to develop optimal adaptation strategies. Adaptation and mitigation are thus two policy responses to climate change, which can be "complementary, substitutable or independent of each other" (Metz et al. 2007). In many cases there are clear symbioses between climate change mitigation (i.e., actions designed to reduce the atmospheric concentration of GHG) and adaptation measures (i.e., actions designed to exploit beneficial opportunities or moderate negative effects associated with climate change) (Coffee et al. 2010), and naturally, necessary adaptation measures will in part be determined by the degree of investment in mitigation (Warren 2010). Despite these symbioses, mitigation and adaptation differ with respect to the dominant players. Mitigation policies are often focused at the national or international level (e.g., the Kyoto agreement), while policy measures focused on adaptation are often enacted (and the benefits reaped) at the local level (Hallegatte 2009). "Mitigation of greenhouse gases can be viewed as a public good, adaptation to climate change is a private good benefiting only the country or the individual that invests in adaptation" (Hasson et al. 2010). Further, at least in some regions, thresholds for damaging impacts from climate change are likely to change, and thus the degree of desired climate change mitigation may be raised by implementation of adaptation measures. Some adaptation options may either ultimately be maladaptive (e.g., increase vulnerability to climate change) or increase GHG emissions (offsetting mitigation efforts) (Barnett and O'Neill 2010). Thus there is a substantial benefit to be gained from coordinating adaptation and mitigation activities, and while this volume is focused on improved understanding of the risks, vulnerabilities, and opportunities poised by climate change with a focus on providing the basis for developing optimal adaptation strategies, where appropriate, the link with climate change mitigation is also discussed.

There are two types of adaptation. The first may be termed "autonomous" and refers to actions unmanaged or "naive" systems responding in an instinctive way based on their experience of recent and current conditions. The second is referred to as "planned" or prescriptive adaptation based on information regarding anticipated climate change. Planned adaptation typically involves conscious human intervention to protect or enhance desirable traits of the system (Pittock and Jones 2000, Smit et al. 2000). Thus the latter is predicated, in part, on reliable climate

projections and articulation of vulnerability, exposure, and risk. Indeed, I assert that clear identification of the primary sources of risk associated with climate change and variability, articulated in the context of changing socioeconomic and environmental conditions, is a necessary prerequisite to identifying suitable adaptation mechanisms that can be implemented to ensure that disruption and damage to society, the economy, infrastructure, and the environment are minimized and that possible opportunities associated with these changes can be realized. This book is designed to achieve these goals with a focus on the midwestern region of the United States of America.

Article 2 of the United National Framework Convention on Climate Change (UNFCCC) requires the prevention of dangerous interference with the climate system and hence the stabilization of atmospheric GHG concentrations at levels and within a time frame that would achieve this objective. Defining "dangerous" climate change is a judgment cast in the sociopolitical context and is necessarily contingent upon the acceptable level of risk. "The criteria in Article 2 that specify (risks of) dangerous anthropogenic climate change include: food security, protection of ecosystems and sustainable economic development" (Metz et al. 2007). Despite Article 2 of the UNFCCC, global climate will likely evolve to surpass 2°C of warming and enter a realm that many consider dangerous (Parry et al. 2009). Even if full-scale climate change mitigation options are implemented, and the predicted rise in energy-related carbon emissions (of 45% by 2030) are not realized (Helm 2009), it now seems inevitable that there is "an adaptation gap"—that the scale and magnitude of climate change will exceed efforts to mitigate anthropogenic forcing of climate (Parry et al. 2009, Parry 2010) (Figure 1.2). Thus it is imperative to quantify the risks and opportunities posed by climate change and the vulnerability of society to climate change and to enact measures to increase resilience to evolution of the climate system. Accordingly, adaptation is a key component of post-2012 international climate policy negotiations. For example, according to the December 2009 Copenhagen Accord, by 2020, developed countries will provide US$100 billion per year to address the needs of developing countries, including adaptation (Ciscar et al. 2011)

Although the founding assumptions of analyses, such as those presented in the Stern Report on the "Economics of climate change" (Stern 2007), have been subject to considerable critique (Weyant 2008, Yohe and Tol 2008), there is evidence to suggest that actions to both mitigate climate change and adapt thereto will yield benefits in excess of the costs of doing so (Stern 2007). One recent study of the cost effectiveness of hazard mitigation programs in the United States found benefit-cost ratios of 3:1 to 7:1 for individual flood projects, and further estimated that the federal treasury saved $3.64 of future discounted expenditures or lost taxes for every dollar spent (Rose et al. 2007, Whitehead and Rose 2009). Fur-

ther, some have suggested that strategies enacted to manage risks associated with climate change (and to adapt thereto) can, if managed well, promote other desirable outcomes (Costello et al. 2011). Further, in the content of agricultural systems, there are many potential adaptation options available that require only fairly marginal change of existing agricultural systems, at least some of which are variations of existing climate risk management. In one recent analysis, implementation of these options was shown to "likely have substantial benefits under moderate climate change" and in wheat cropping systems led to an increase in yields of 18 percent in the temperate latitudes (Howden et al. 2007).

Purpose of this Volume

In the previous volume within this series (*Understanding Climate Change: Climate Variability, Predictability, and Change in the Midwestern United States*), we provided a regionally comprehensive synthesis of historical and projected climate change and variability in the Midwest, plus an overview of specific climate hazards (Pryor 2009). Here we focus on the potential impacts and vulnerability of the midwestern United States to climate evolution, and specifically to the changing frequency, magnitude, or intensity of extreme events. For a national perspective, the reader is directed to the forthcoming 2013 National Climate Assessment report from the U.S. Interagency National Climate Assessment (INCA) Task Force, or prior reports therefrom (National

Assessment Synthesis Team 2000). Additional sources of information regarding the scientific basis of climate projections and framing concepts for impact analyses and evaluation of adaptation and mitigation options may be found in recent reports from the National Research Council (National Research Council 2010a,b,c,d,e).

Many definitions of key terms have been proposed within the climate change adaptation literature (Füssel 2007). Herein we adopt the following (drawn in part from National Research Council (2010a) and Dawson et al. (2011)):

- Adaptation: Adjustment in natural or human systems to a new or changing environment that exploits beneficial opportunities or moderates negative effects.
- Adaptive capacity: The ability of a system to adjust to climate change (including climate variability and extremes), to moderate potential damages, to take advantage of opportunities, or to cope with the consequences.
- Exposure: The extent of climate change likely to be experienced at a locale. Thus exposure is a function of both the rate and magnitude of the change.
- Resilience: A capability to (1) anticipate, (2) prepare for, (3) respond to, and (4) recover from significant multi-hazard threats with minimum damage to social well-being, the economy, and the environment.
- Risk: A combination of the magnitude of the potential consequence(s) of climate change impact(s) and the likelihood that the consequence(s) will occur.
- Sensitivity: The degree to which the survival/performance/persistence of a system is dependent on the prevailing climate.

- Vulnerability: The degree to which a system is susceptible to, or unable to cope with, adverse effects of climate change, including climate variability and extremes.

There are major and multiple challenges in assessing the impacts and vulnerabilities of climate change and implications for risk and adaptation. Not least among these is the challenge of decision-making in the context of uncertainty. There is an uncertainty cascade from translation of socioeconomic and demographic data into GHG emission and concentration projections, through climate modeling at the global and regional scale, to impact analyses and vulnerability and adaptation assessments (Wilby and Dessai 2010). Exhaustive efforts to characterize at least parts of the uncertainty are becoming tractable and are resulting in illumination of research foci to reduce uncertainty (Hawkins and Sutton 2009, Pryor and Schoof 2010, Pryor et al. 2012). While uncertainty is and will remain a key component of any assessment exercise, we assert that identification of optimal adaptation options to increase resilience to climate variability and change is greatly facilitated by first quantifying the vulnerability and risk associated therewith. Key components of this analysis are:

- Severity of the impact and degree of benefit of adaptation measures.
- Immediacy of the required intervention/response.
- Need to change current operating procedures and the practicality of the intervention.
- Potential co-benefit and possibility of a measure to address multiple cross-sectoral issues.

• Distribution and equity of perceived benefits of a given adaptation strategy.

A key theme in this book is quantification of midwestern vulnerability to climate change. Defining vulnerability as "the degree to which a system is susceptible to, and unable to cope with, adverse effects of climate change, including climate variability and extremes" (Parry et al. 2007), it is clear that vulnerability is a function of the character, magnitude, and rate of climate change and variation to which the system is exposed, in addition to the sensitivity and adaptive capacity of that system. While some adaptation measures designed to reduce human vulnerability to climate change may generate social benefits under all future climate scenarios (Heltberg et al. 2009), prioritizing resources to be applied to adaptation will likely benefit from high-resolution and robust climate projections. It should be acknowledged that the skill associated with climate projections generally increases with the degree of spatial aggregation, while their value for quantifying risk and vulnerability is greatest at smaller spatial scales. Equally, projections from climate models are generally most robust for the central tendency of geophysical variables, while the impacts are generally greatest for the low-probability but high-intensity events (National Research Council 2010b). Nevertheless, given the importance of extreme events in determining climate change impacts and the importance of providing high-resolution (both in time and space) information to decision makers, herein we provide both regional syntheses and sub-regional analyses.

In this volume, we provide the state-of-the-art spatially disaggregated information regarding the historical, current, and possible future climate states within the Midwest with a particular focus on extremes and undertake assessments of the risks and vulnerabilities of critical socio-economic and environmental systems in the Midwest to climate change and variability. In taking a regional perspective, we seek to address the following in a single, focused volume:

(i) Identify the regions biophysical, socio-economic and institutional context and articulate key socioeconomic and environmental sectors, their vulnerabilities, and opportunities.
(ii) Summarize past and possible future climate states.
(iii) Quantify key impacts of past and possible future climate conditions.
(iv) Briefly document current regional efforts aimed at climate change mitigation and adaptation.

Using the conceptual framework of the process of adaptation to climate change shown in Figure 1.3, this volume is focused on providing a sound basis for components 1 and 2;

1. Identification and quantification of current and future climate states
2. Assessment of vulnerabilities and risks in key sectors

We further propose initial steps toward defining appropriate foci for initial adaptation measures (step 3). This volume is thus designed to inform effective responses to climate change and to provide the necessary basis to build resilience and identify and begin the process of implementing optimal adaptation strategies in the Midwest and across the United States.

Evaluation of appropriate mechanisms to reduce the risk posed by climate change must be informed by the many non-climatic stressors that face decision makers within the Midwest. Even in the absence of an evolving climate, it has been suggested that North America needs to invest $6.5 trillion between 2005 and 2030 on infrastructure associated with water and power supply, road and rail transport, and air- and seaports to modernize obsolete systems (Doshl et al. 2007). Thus, herein non-climatic stressors are identified to provide a proper context for the current focus on vulnerabilities and opportunities arising from climate change and variability, and also in direct acknowledgement that many environmental and societal stressors may intersect to reduce/increase resilience to climate change.

Structure of This Volume

The structure of this book is as follows. Chapter 2 provides an overview of the socioeconomic context and physical climate of the Midwest. The third chapter provides a counterpoint to the Midwest by providing a case study of climate change risk and adaptation analyses drawn from the southeastern United States. Using monetary damages to assess risk and consequences neglects socially contingent consequences (Tol and Yohe 2007), but

in the fourth chapter of this volume we present an overview of economic perspectives on risk reduction. Inactivity in the face of an evolving climate and associated risk is explicable in the context of potentially large upfront costs and delayed (and sometimes highly uncertain) benefits, particularly within a cost-benefit framework applied with heavy discounting of future benefits. These challenges are discussed in chapter 4, along with potential strategies that could be adopted to address them. The following chapters are focused on the Midwest and are presented around the themes of the risks and impacts associated with climate extremes focused on three key impact sectors: agriculture, human health, water resources, energy, and infrastructure. Each section is preceded by an introduction to the topic under study that highlights and synthesizes prior research to contextualize the contributions contained herein. The individual chapters that follow present unique research focused on a variety of impact sectors and climate hazards. We conclude the volume by synthesizing information provided herein, discussing existing mitigation and adaptation measures being enacted in the region and articulating a road-map for future research and prioritized action items.

ACKNOWLEDGEMENTS

Funding for the workshop from which this volume evolved was provided by the Indiana University Center for Research in Environmental Science (CRES).

NOTES

1. In the Climate Change 2007: Working Group III: Mitigation of Climate Change report, the de-

gree of agreement is the relative level of convergence of the literature as assessed by the authors.

REFERENCES

Barnett J, O'Neill S (2010). Maladaptation. Global Environmental Change 20:211–213

Bernstein L, Bosch P, Canziani O, Chen Z, Christ R, Davidson O, Hare W, Huq S, Karoly D, Kattsov V, Kundzewicz K, Liu J, Lohmann U, Manning M, Matsuno T, Menne B, Metz B, Mirza M, Nicholls N, Nurse L, Pachauri R, Palutikof J, Parry M, Qin D, Ravindranath N, Reisinger A, Ren J, Riahi R, Rosenzweig C, Rusticucci M, Schneider S, Sokona Y, Solomon S, Stott P, Stouffer R, Sugiyama T, Swart R, Tirpak D, Vogel C, Yohe G (2007). Climate change 2007: Synthesis report summary for policymakers. Cambridge, UK: Cambridge University Press.

Boykoff MT, Boykoff JM (2004) Balance as bias: global warming and the U.S. prestige press. Global Environmental Change-Human and Policy Dimensions 14:125–136

Ciscar J, Szabo L, Van Regemorter D, Soria A, Iglesias A, Feyen L, Dankers R, Amelung B, Moreno A, Nicholls R, Watkiss P, Christensen OB, Garrote L, Goodess CM, Hunt A, Richards J (2011). Physical and economic consequences of climate change in Europe. Proceedings of the National Academy of Sciences of the United States of America 108:2678–2683.

Coffee JE, Parzen J, Wagstaff M, Lewis RS (2010). Preparing for a changing climate: The Chicago climate action plan's adaptation strategy. Journal of Great Lakes Research 36:115–117

Costello A, Maslin M, Montgomery H, Johnson AM, Ekins P (2011). Global health and climate change: moving from denial and catastrophic fatalism to positive action. Philosophical Transactions of the Royal Society a-Mathematical Physical and Engineering Sciences 369:1866–1882.

Dawson TP, Jackson ST, House JI, Prentice IC, Mace GM (2011). Beyond predictions: Biodiversity conservation in a changing climate. Science 332:53–58.

Doshl V, Schulman G, Gabaldon D (2007). Lights! water! motion! Strategy+Business, 46:Spring 2007.

Füssel H-M (2007). Vulnerability: A generally applicable conceptual framework for climate change research. Global Environmental Change 17:155–167.

Hallegatte S (2009). Strategies to adapt to an uncertain climate change. Global Environmental Change-Human and Policy Dimensions 19:240–247.

Hasson R, Lofgren A, Visser M (2010). Climate change in a public goods game: Investment decision in mitigation versus adaptation. Ecological Economics 70:331–338.

Hawkins E, Sutton R (2009). The potential to narrow uncertainty in regional climate projections. Bulletin of the American Meteorological Society 90:1095–1107.

Hegerl GC, Hoegh-Guldberg O, Casassa G, Hoerling MP, Kovats RS, Parmesan C, Pierce DW, Stott PA (2010). Good practice guidance paper on detection and attribution related to anthropogenic climate change. In: Stocker TF, Field CB, Qin D, Barros V, Plattner G-K, Tignor M, Midgley PM, K.L. E (eds) Meeting report of the intergovernmental panel on climate change expert meeting on detection and attribution of anthropogenic climate change. IPCC Working Group I Technical Support Unit. Bern, Switzerland: University of Bern.

Helm D (2009). Climate-change policy: Why has so little been achieved? In: Helm D, Helpburn C (eds) The economic and politics of climate change. Oxford, UK: Oxford University Press, 9–35.

Heltberg R, Siegel PB, Jorgensen SL (2009). Addressing human vulnerability to climate change: Toward a "no-regrets" approach. Global Environmental Change-Human and Policy Dimensions 19:89–99.

Howden SM, Soussana JF, Tubielloe FN, Chhetri N, Dunlop M and Meinke H (2007). Adapting agriculture to climate change. Proceedings of the National Academy of Sciences of the United States of America 104:19691–19696.

Metz B, Davidson OR, Bosch PR, Dave R, Meyer LA (eds) (2007). Climate change 2007: Mitigation of climate change. Contribution of working group iii to the fourth assessment report of the intergovernmental panel on climate change, vol. Cambridge, UK: Cambridge University Press.

National Assessment Synthesis Team (ed) (2000). Climate change impacts on the United States—Overview report: The potential consequences of climate variability and change, vol. Available from www.usgrcp.gov/usgrcp/Library/nationalassessment/. Cambridge, UK: Cambridge University Press.

National Research Council (2010a). Adapting to the impacts of climate change, Washington, DC: The National Academies Press,

National Research Council (2010b). Advancing the science of climate change. Washington, DC: The National Academies Press.

National Research Council (2010c). America's climate choices. Washington, DC: The National Academies Press.

National Research Council (2010d). Informing and effective response to climate change. Washington, DC: The National Academies Press.

National Research Council (2010e). Limiting the magnitude of future climate change. Washington, DC: The National Academies Press.

Parry M (2010). Copenhagen number crunch. Nature Reports Climate Change 4:18–19.

Parry M, Lowe J, Hanson C (2009). Overshoot, adapt and recover. Nature 458:1102–1103.

Parry ML, Canziani OF, Palutikof JP, van der Linden PJ, Hanson CE (eds) (2007). Climate change 2007: Impacts, adaptation and vulnerability. Contribution of Working Group II to the Fourth Assessment Report of the Intergovernmental Panel on Climate Change, Cambridge, UK: Cambridge University Press.

Pittock AB, Jones RN (2000). Adaptation to what and why? Environmental Monitoring and Assessment 61:9–35

Pryor SC (ed) (2009). Understanding Climate Change: Climate variability, predictability and change in the Midwestern United States. Bloomington: Indiana University Press.

Pryor SC, Barthelmie RJ, Clausen NE, Drews M, MacKellar N, Kjellstrom E (2012). Analyses of possible changes in intense and extreme wind speeds over northern Europe under climate change scenarios. Climate Dynamics 38:189–208

Pryor SC, Schoof JT (2010). Importance of the SRES in projections of climate change impacts on near-surface wind regimes. Meteorologische Zeitschrift 19:267–274

Rose A, Porter K, Dash N, Bouabid J, Huyck C, Whitehead J, Shaw D, Eguchi R, Taylor C, McLane T, Tobin LT, Ganderton PT, Godschalk D, Kiremidjian AS, Tierney K, West CT (2007). Benefit-Cost Analysis of FEMA Hazard Mitigation Grants. Natural Hazards Review 8:97–111

Santer BD, Taylor KE, Gleckler PJ, Bonfils C, Barnett TP, Pierce DW, Wigley TML, Mears C, Wentz FJ, Bruggemann W, Gillett NP, Klein SA, Solomon S, Stott PA, Wehner MF (2009). Incorporating model quality information in climate change detection and attribution studies. Proceedings of the National Academy of Sciences of the United States of America 106:14778–14783.

Smit B, Burton I, Klein RJT, Wandel J (2000). An anatomy of adaptation to climate change and variability. Climatic Change 45:223–251.

Solomon S, Plattner GK, Knutti R, Friedlingstein P (2009). Irreversible climate change due to carbon dioxide emissions. Proceedings of the National Academy of Sciences of the United States of America 106:1704–1709.

Solomon S, Qin D, Manning M, Chen Z, Marquis M, Averyt KB, Tignor M, Miller HL (eds) (2007). Climate change 2007: The physical science basis. Contribution of Working Group I to the Fourth Assessment Report of the intergovernmental Panel on Climate Change. Cambridge, UK: Cambridge University Press.

Stern NH (2007). The economics of climate change. Cambridge, UK: Cambridge University Press.

Tol RSJ, Yohe GW (2007). Infinite uncertainty, forgotten feedbacks, and cost-benefit analysis of climate policy. Climatic Change 83:429–442.

Wallsten TS, Budescu DV, Rapoport A, Zwick R, Forsyth B (1986). Measuring the vague meanings of probability terms. Journal of Experimental Psychology-General 115: 348–365.

Warren R (2010). The role of interactions in a world implementing adaptation and mitigation solutions to climate change. Philosophical Transactions of the Royal Society a Mathematical Physical and Engineering Sciences 369:217–241.

Weyant JP (2008). A critique of the stern review's mitigation cost analyses and integrated assessment. Review of Environmental Economics and Policy 2:77–93.

Whitehead JC, Rose AZ (2009). Estimating environmental benefits of natural hazard mitigation with data transfer: Results from a benefit-cost analysis of Federal Emergency Management Agency hazard mitigation grants. Mitigation and Adaptation Strategies for Global Change 14:655–676.

Wilby RL, Dessai S (2010). Robust adaptation to climate change. Weather 65:180–185.

Yohe GW (2010). "Reasons for concern" (about climate change in the United States). Climatic Change 99:295–302.

Yohe GW, Tol RSJ (2008). The Stern Review and the economics of climate change: An editorial essay. Climatic Change 89:231–240.

2. The Midwestern United States:
Socioeconomic Context and Physical Climate

S. C. PRYOR AND R. J. BARTHELMIE

Socioeconomic Overview

The terms "midwestern United States" and "Midwest" have been applied to a range of sub-regions of the contiguous United States. The Census Bureau defines the Midwest region as comprising 12 states (listed from northwest to southeast): North Dakota, South Dakota, Nebraska, Kansas, Minnesota, Iowa, Missouri, Wisconsin, Illinois, Michigan, Indiana, and Ohio. The U.S. Global Change Research program excludes the four most westerly states (North Dakota, South Dakota, Nebraska, and Kansas). The Midwestern Governors Association is an alliance of 10 states; Illinois, Indiana, Iowa, Kansas, Ohio, Michigan, Minnesota, Missouri, South Dakota, and Wisconsin. Thus there is no universally accepted definition of the region. In this chapter we provide data for the most inclusive definition of the Midwest—the thirteen states listed in Table 2.1 and shown in Figure 2.1. Using this domain definition, the Midwest has a combined population of about 71 million people, around 23 percent of the U.S.

total population, and a total land area of approximately 505 million acres, which is about 22 percent of the U.S. total. Agriculture continues to be a key economic sector in the region. Accordingly, the percentage of the population defined as "urban" by the U.S. Department of Agriculture ranges from 46 percent in South Dakota to 87 percent in Illinois, the latter being the only state in the region that has a higher fraction of the population that is urban than the national average (Table 2.1). However, the Midwest is also home to a number of major metropolitan areas (including Chicago, Illinois; Detroit, Michigan; Indianapolis, Indiana; and St Louis, Missouri).

INFRASTRUCTURE AND TRANSPORTATION

Although the precise needs vary from location to location, there is evidence that critical infrastructure will be put under increasing strain by demographic, socioeconomic and potentially climate shifts (Stern 2007). Globally, damage associated with natural catastrophes increased from

Table 2.1. Overview of the states comprising the Midwest. Data pertaining to the population and land cover/land use are drawn from the US Department of Agriculture Economic Research Service (data source: http://www.ers.usda.gov/). The contribution of agriculture to GDP for 2008 was derived from data from the Bureau of Economic Analysis (http://www.bea.gov/regional/) by combining the total for two categories—Agriculture, Forestry, Fishing, and Hunting with Crop and Animal Production (Farms)—and dividing that by the state GDP. Greenhouse gas (GHG) emissions in million metric tonnes of carbon dioxide (CO_2) equivalent were taken from the World Resources Institute CAIT-US for 2007 (http://cait.wri.org). The GHG emissions include carbon dioxide, methane, nitrous oxide, and fluorine gases and exclude contributions from land-use change.

State	State abbreviation	Approximate total land area (acres) (2007) (1 hectare = 2.24 acres = 0.01 square kilometer).	Percentage of land designated as farm-land (2007)	Population (2009)	Percentage of population designated as urban (2007)	Percentage of state GDP from agriculture (2008)	GHG emissions (2007) (million metric tonnes CO_2-eq per year) (state rank in parentheses)	GHG emissions per capita (2007) (metric tonnes per person) (state rank in parentheses)
Illinois	IL	35,529,619	75.4	12,910,409	87.1	2.1	288.0 (6)	22.5 (27)
Indiana	IN	22,924,685	64.4	6,423,113	78.4	3.0	274.6 (7)	43.3 (7)
Iowa	IA	35,747,594	86.0	3,007,856	56.7	12.3	127.0 (21)	42.6 (8)
Kansas	KS	52,320,102	88.6	2,818,747	64.1	7.6	114.0 (25)	41.1 (11)
Kentucky	KY	25,275,577	55.4	4,314,113	57.8	2.9	180.6 (12)	42.4 (10)
Michigan	MI	36,176,779	27.7	9,969,727	81.6	1.7	212.0 (10)	21.1 (31)
Minnesota	MN	50,906,881	52.9	5,266,214	73.3	5.0	125.3 (22)	24.1 (24)
Missouri	MO	43,974,665	66.0	5,987,580	73.9	3.1	169.1 (15)	28.6 (19)
Nebraska	NE	49,168,368	92.5	1,796,619	58.9	13.5	75.2 (36)	42.5 (9)
North Dakota	ND	44,161,773	89.8	646,844	48.9	19.9	64.1 (37)	100.5 (2)
Ohio	OH	26,149,825	53.4	11,542,645	80.8	1.3	310.2 (3)	26.9 (21)
South Dakota	SD	48,511,810	90.0	812,383	46.4	19.5	31.6 (43)	39.6 (13)
Wisconsin	WI	34,655,459	43.8	5,654,774	73.1	3.7	124.4 (23)	22.2 (28)
United States		2,260,994,361	40.8	307,006,550	83.6	2.1	6303.6	—

$3.9 billion in the 1950s to $40 billion per year in the 1990s, with about a quarter of the losses being associated with direct damage to infrastructure components (Freeman and Warner 2001). The Midwest is home to a range of critical infrastructure. For example, there are a number of major transportation hubs and links (Figure 2.1). According to data from the Federal Aviation Authority (FAA), Chicago O'Hare ranked second in the nation in terms of passenger embarkations (boarding) in 2009 with 31,135,732 people. The regions' next busiest airport was Minne-apolis with 15,551,206 recorded boardings (ranked 15th in the nation), and then Detroit with 15,211,402 passenger embarkations (ranked 17th in the nation).

The Midwest is also a major center for freight transportation by road, rail, and waterways. The Mid-America Freight Coalition was established to provide a regional organization to cooperate in the planning, operation, preservation, and improvement of transportation infrastructure and freight distribution in ten states (Illinois, Indiana, Iowa, Kansas, Kentucky, Michigan, Minnesota, Missouri, Ohio, and

Wisconsin) that share key interstate corridors, rail infrastructure, and inland and Great Lakes waterways. Data from that organization and the U.S. Department of Transportation Federal Highways Administration (FHA) indicate that the interstate highways I-290, I-90, and I-94 around Chicago had the highest freight congestion rankings in the United States in 2009, while I-70 and I-64 in St Louis, Missouri, ranked 6th for congestion. According to a study by the FHA, adverse weather accounted for 15 percent of all highway delays with heavy precipitation accounting for about 70 percent of the weather-related delays, followed by snow and high winds (U.S. Department of Transportation 2007). Nationally, the cost of weather-related delays to trucking companies is estimated to range from about $2.2 to $3.5 billion annually (US Department of Transportation 2007).

ENERGY

Like the United States as a whole, the Midwest has a highly energy-intensive economy. For example, per capita energy consumption in Indiana in 2005 was 464 million BTU (British Thermal Units), while the national average was 339 million BTU (Table 2.2). At the national level the energy intensity of the United States in 2007 (expressed as energy use per dollar of gross domestic product generated (GDP)) was approximately 7.9 thousand BTUs per US$1 of GDP, while the European average was 5.5 thousand BTU/US$ (US Energy Information Administration 2010). Expressing these data in SI units,

the energy intensity of the United States is 2.32 kWhr/US$1, while that of Europe is 1.62 kWhr/US$1. Calculations for 2008–2009 indicate that of the midwestern states, only Illinois has an energy intensity index below the national average (Table 2.2). Accordingly, the states that comprise the Midwest have, for the most part, relatively high emissions of both total and per capita emissions of greenhouse gases (GHG) (Table 2.1). Ohio, Illinois, and Indiana rank in the top 10 states when the GHG emissions are expressed as a total for the state, while Nebraska, North Dakota, and South Dakota are ranked in the lowest 15 states. However, on a per capita basis, North Dakota ranks second (after Wyoming), and none of the midwestern states rank in the lowest 20 states for GHG emissions.

Fossil fuels dominate energy consumption in most of the midwestern states, accounting for more than 70 percent of energy consumption in every state (Figure 2.2). However, there are marked differences in the state-by-state energy mix and particularly the penetration of non-fossil-carbon fuels. Fossil fuels provide over 96 percent of energy consumed in both Kentucky and Indiana, but renewable sources comprise over 25 percent of energy consumed in South Dakota, and nuclear energy contributes nearly 20 percent of the energy used in Illinois.

Electricity transmission within the Midwest as defined herein is served by the PJM Interconnection and Midwest Independent System Operators (ISO). These ISO, which also serve markets to the east (PJM) and the north (MISO), had a combined generation capacity of over 294,000

Table 2.2. Overview of energy use during 2008 in the states comprising the Midwest. Data pertaining to the energy consumption and interstate flows are from United States Energy Information Administration (data source: http://www.eia.gov/state/seds/). The "Net interstate flow of electricity is the difference between the amount of energy in electricity sold within a State (including associated losses) and the energy input at the electric utilities within the state. A positive number indicates that more electricity (including associated losses) came into the State than went out of the State during the year." Data for the state GDP in 2009 was provided by the Bureau of Economic Analysis (data source: http://www.bea.gov/regional/gdpmap/GDPMap.aspx). The "Net interstate flow of electricity is the difference between the amount of energy in electricity sold within a State (including associated losses) and the energy input at the electric utilities within the state. A positive number indicates that more electricity (including associated losses) came into the State than went out of the State during the year."

State	Energy consumption (trillion BTU)	Net interstate flow of electricity/losses (trillion BTU)	GDP in 2009 (millions $)	Energy intensity (thousand BTU/$1 of GDP)
Illinois	4,089	−512.3	630,398	6.5
Indiana	2,857	−171.4	262,647	10.9
Iowa	1,414	−55.5	142,282	9.9
Kansas	1,136	−78	124,921	9.1
Kentucky	1,983	−25	156,553	12.7
Michigan	2,918	−47.8	368,401	7.9
Minnesota	1,979	151	260,692	7.6
Missouri	1,937	−24	239,752	8.1
Nebraska	782	−29.8	86,439	9.0
North Dakota	441	−229.8	31,872	13.8
Ohio	3,987	163.4	471,264	8.5
South Dakota	350	44.6	38,308	9.1
Wisconsin	1,862	111.1	244,370	7.6
United States	99,382		14,150,826	7.0

MW in 2005 (Joskow 2006). By 2010, the Midwest region had electricity generation capacity of over 250,000 MW, with the majority of the generation capacity located in the east of the region (Figure 2.3). The Midwest thus was home to nearly one-quarter of the total national generation capacity (Joskow 2006). The net state interflow of electricity/losses (Table 2.2) is negative in most Midwestern states indicating electricity export. Indeed in North Dakota electricity export accounts for more than half its net energy consumption. The spatial variation in wholesale electricity prices over the eastern portion of the United States as documented in a

2006 report from MISO indicate prices are almost half as much in Iowa than across much of the eastern seaboard (Midwest ISO 2006). This implies that with increased grid capacity to facilitate interstate transfer there could be potential for growth particularly of the renewable energy sector (e.g., the wind energy industry) within the Midwest since the resource is displaced from the demand locations (Midwest ISO 2007). Accordingly, the Midwestern Governors Association identified the need for regional transmission planning and investment as a key regional priority (Midwestern Governors Association Advisory Group 2009).

The energy sector composes approximately two-thirds of global total GHG emissions (Sims et al. 2007, Neufeldt et al. 2010), and more than 80 percent of U.S. GHG emissions are in the form of carbon dioxide (CO_2) from fossil fuel combustion (National Research Council 2010b). Thus the energy sector, in the Midwest and elsewhere, is an obvious candidate for mitigation efforts designed to reduce GHG emissions (Wang et al. 1999). Key among the renewable energy resources accessible within the Midwest are the good wind resources that can be harnessed by wind turbines (Figure 2.4) and substantial existing and potential for expanded bio-fuel production. A brief review of these technologies, their implementation in the Midwest and the characteristics of those supplies relevant to adaptation is given below.

In the case of a typical wind turbine, the energy payback period for the entire life cycle is approximately 4 or 5 months, or 2 percent of a 20-year expected lifetime (Martinez et al. 2010). Further, life-cycle GHG emissions from wind turbines are estimated to be about 1 percent of those from a coal-fired power station when expressed in gCO_2-eq per kWh of electricity produced (Weisser 2007). While this comparison neglects issues of spinning-reserve necessary for use with intermittent resources at high penetration levels (but is minimal at current levels of penetration (Georgilakis 2008)), it is indicative of a positive contribution to emission reductions if properly managed (e.g., used with high-resolution forecasting (Barthelmie et al. 2008), integrated into a plan for greater

transmission capacity or with expansion of fast-response thermal or hydro units (Denny et al. 2010)). The 2008 U.S. Department of Energy report *20% Wind by 2030* proposes that by 2030, 20 percent of the U.S. electricity supply could readily derive from wind turbines, and indeed recent growth in the industry re-emphasizes the feasibility of such predictions (NREL 2008). New wind projects installed in the United States during 2007 represented an investment of $9 billion, while those installed during 2008 represent an investment of $17 billion and created 35,000 jobs despite the economic downturn (AWEA 2009). The years 2007–2010 were record years of increased installed capacity (AWEA 2009). During these years the installed capacity grew by 5.4 GW, 8.5 GW, and 10 GW, respectively, increasing the installed wind-generated electricity capacity to > 40 deriving from over 33,000 wind turbines (AWEA 2011). To provide a context for these figures, national new electricity generation capacity added between 1997 and 2004 totaled 200 GW (Joskow 2006). Wind power is thus a growing player in the U.S. energy market. Indeed, during 2008, wind developments accounted for over one-third of all new electrical generation capacity within the contiguous United States (Lu et al. 2009). As of the end of 2010, 33 percent of the national wind energy installed capacity was within the Midwest (http://archive .awea.org/projects/). The installed wind energy capacity in Iowa is 3.7 GW ranking the state second in the nation. Illinois, Minnesota, and Indiana also rank in the top 10 states. Of the 13 states in the region, only Ohio and Kentucky have less than 100 MW of installed wind capacity, in keeping with the generally lower wind speeds in these states (see Figure 2.4). Further expansion of the wind energy installed capacity for electricity generation could be facilitated by a range of policy options, such as adoption of a Renewable Portfolio Standard (RPS). As of December 2010, only 5 midwestern states (Minnesota, Wisconsin, Iowa, Illinois, and Missouri) have enacted an RPS, but there seems to be public support for such measures in the other midwestern states. For example, a recent poll conducted by the research firm Public Opinion Strategies found that 77 percent of Indiana voters support legislation creating a requirement for 10 percent renewable energy by the year 2020 (http://www.awea.org/newsroom/pressreleases /release_022811 _02.cfm).

Agriculture accounted for an estimated emission of "5.1 to 6.1 $GtCO_2$-eq/yr in 2005 (10%–12% of total global anthropogenic emissions of GHG). Methane (CH_4) contributes 3.3 $GtCO_2$-eq/yr and nitrous oxide (N_2O) contributes 2.8 $GtCO_2$-eq/yr. Of global anthropogenic emissions in 2005, agriculture accounts for about 60% of N_2O and about 50% of CH_4" (Smith et al. 2007). Agricultural systems afford tremendous mitigation potential, and one study concluded that the global mitigation potential from agriculture (excluding fossil fuel offsets from biomass) was ~ 5,500–6,000 $MtCO_2$-eq/yr in 2030. "Economic potentials are estimated to be 1500–1600, 2500–2700, and 4000–4300 $MtCO_2$-eq/yr at carbon prices of up to 20, 50 and 100 US\$/tCO_2-eq, respectively" (Smith et al. 2007). Agricultural soils emit about 50 percent of the global flux of N_2O attributable to human influence, mostly in response to nitrogen fertilizer use. Specific to the Midwest, one study found that corn (maize) cropping in the Midwest emits approximately 268 tCO_2-eq per tonne of grain produced, with 59 percent deriving from N_2O evolved from applied N fertilizer and 11 percent from loss of soil organic carbon (Grace et al. 2011) However, the precise management techniques for tillage, crop residues and fertilizer application can greatly modify emissions of GHG (Al-Kaisi and Yin 2005, Alvarez 2005. See also chapter 7 of this volume for an analysis of projected soil organic carbon pool trends under reasonable climate change scenarios).

The U.S. Energy Independence and Security Act of 2007 mandated a goal of 36 billion gallons of renewable fuels by 2022 (Blanco and Isenhouer 2010), and the Midwest is playing a major role in the development and production of biofuels. Most biodiesel produced in the United States derives from soybean, rapeseed, or palm oils (Demirbas 2011), with the former being a major crop from the Midwest. As of February 2011, biodiesel annual production capacity in the midwestern states exceeded 1,000 million gallons, which is over 40 percent of the national total biodiesel generation capacity (Figure 2.5). U.S. ethanol production is also reaching unprecedented levels, with 180 operational ethanol production facilities in the United States with over 10 billion gallons of annual capacity (http://www.ethanol.org/).

Ethanol-gasoline blends now comprise 70 percent of gasoline sold within the United States, most as E10 (10 percent ethanol, 90 percent unleaded gasoline) (http://www.ethanol.org/). Although a wide variety of fuel stocks are being evaluated (Demirbas 2011), corn still dominates ethanol production (Crago et al. 2010), and in 2007, 20.8 percent of the U.S. corn crop was used for ethanol production (data from http://www.ethanol.org/). The top 12 ethanol-producing states are all in the Midwest, and ethanol production capacity from the 13 midwestern states is 87.5 percent of the national total (Figure 2.5). Thus, agricultural activities in the Midwest are being molded in part by mandates to reduce use of fossil fuels and develop biofuel alternatives. While many consider use of biofuels to be a key component of any climate change mitigation strategy, with the bio-economy gaining momentum, additional stress will be placed on water resources (Mubako and Lant 2008) and agricultural yields in the region (Wang et al. 1999, McNew and Griffith 2005), which may change the resilience of food production within the Midwest to climate change and variability. Further, increased fertilizer use to increase yields would have to be considered carefully in light of the large equivalent-CO_2 GHG emissions from current corn production in the region (see above).

AGRICULTURE

Agricultural lands (lands used for agricultural production: cropland, managed grassland, and permanent crops, including agro-forestry and bio-energy crops) occupy about 40–50 percent of the Earth's land surface (Smith et al. 2007). Agriculture also dominates land use within the Midwest (Table 2.1). Over two-thirds of the land area of the Midwest is designated as farmland (although this fraction is highly variable by state, see Table 2.1). Indeed, the 357 million acres of land within the Midwest that is designated as farmland comprises about 39 percent of the national total. Agriculture is, therefore, a major economic sector within the region, as indicated by the contribution of agriculture and farming to state gross domestic product (GDP) (Table 2.1). For example, based on these estimates agriculture accounts for nearly one-fifth of the state GDP for both North and South Dakota. Key crops within the region are corn (maize) and soybeans (Figure 2.6). Together the thirteen states listed in Table 2.1 produced 90 percent of U.S. corn (defined as a percentage of US$ receipt) and 83 percent of soybeans.

Agricultural yields across the United States and indeed worldwide have greatly increased over the last few decades primarily as a result of technological innovation. This is also true within the Midwest (see, for example, chapter 5 of this volume). However, agricultural yields remain highly dependent on climate variables (Rosenzweig et al. 2001, Lobell et al. 2011). The impact of climate extremes on agricultural productivity is critically dependent on nature, timing, and duration of the stress (Cutforth et al. 2007). For example, specific to corn and soybeans, the following events are particularly important at different stages of crop development (Rosenzweig et al. 2001):

- Soil temperatures > 35°C cause death of soybean seedlings. Flooding at this juvenile stage causes seedling death in both corn and soybeans.
- Air temperatures > 36°C during the reproductive stages will cause loss of corn pollen viability and reduce yields of soybeans.
- Corn is particularly sensitive to soil moisture deficits during the reproductive stage. As discussed further below, at the national level 18 percent of corn and 10 percent of soybean crops are grown on land that is irrigated.
- Soil saturation during the plant mature phase can lead to increased disease damage (e.g., by common smut in corn), while water deficits (associated with hot, dry summers) can lead to excess buildup of aflatoxins (which are considered carcinogenic) in corn.

One economic study of weather impacts on agriculture in the western Midwest indicated that climate change impacts on agriculture could generally be positive if projections indicating warmer wetter climate are realized (Kelly et al. 2005). Another study projected decreases in soybean yields in the southern United States but increases in yields in the Midwest under climate change because of the balance between yields and climate parameters, external stressors and the fertilization impact of increased CO_2 concentrations (Hatfield et al. 2010).

A key consideration in climate-agriculture interactions is water supply. The USDA Farm and Ranch Irrigation Survey (FRIS) in 2008 found that US farmers and ranchers irrigated 54.9 million acres in 2008, which was up by 4.6 percent from 2003 (http://www .agcensus.usda.gov/Publications/2007/). The total quantity of water used for horticultural irrigation in the 28,881 operations increased by 5 percent over the same period to 112.5 cubic kilometers of water. Indeed, over the whole United States, agricultural withdrawals accounted for 41 percent of total freshwater withdrawals in 2000 (Gollehon and Quinby 2006).

Relatively little agricultural land in the Midwest is subject to irrigation (Gollehon and Quinby 2006) (Table 2.3). Irrigation use across the Midwest for corn and soybeans is highly variable but broadly follows the pattern of precipitation across the Midwest—with the states that are characterized by high annual precipitation and high frequency of precipitation exhibiting lowest penetration of irrigation. When an analysis is conducted for farms that have implemented irrigation on some or all of their land, the use of irrigation is highest in Nebraska, with an average of over three-quarters of the land being irrigated, while Ohio and Kentucky have less than 14 percent of the land under these crops being irrigated. Despite the relatively abundant precipitation over much of the Midwest, the 2008 FRIS clearly demonstrates the yield benefits of irrigation, even within the Midwest, to enhanced yields of corn and soybean (Table 2.3). Indeed, according to some estimates increased agricultural yields due to use of irrigation contributed $50 billion to the national economy (Clemmens et al. 2008), leading to suggestions that expanded use of irrigation could facilitate enhanced yields necessary to meet joint food and energy provision goals and potentially reduce interannual variability of yields due to climate variability. However, the degree to which increased water use can be sustained is uncertain particularly in the face of other growing demands even in the relatively "water-rich" Midwest (Dominguez-Faus et al. 2009; see also discussion in chapters 12 and 17).

Animal husbandry is also common within the Midwest. Iowa and Wisconsin have largest numbers of cattle, and Iowa ranks number one both for chickens kept for egg production for and hogs and pigs (U.S. Census of Agriculture 2007, data available from http://www.agcensus.usda.gov/Publications/2007/Full_Report/index.asp). Climate stresses on livestock are moderated by confined production facilities and provision of shelters for animals in non-confined facilities. However, this component of the agricultural sector may be affected by changes in insect and disease prevalence (Wall et al. 2011) and demand for energy for cooling of facilities as a result of regional climate change.

ECOSYSTEMS

Although not a focus of this book, ecosystem services provided by non-cropland are also vulnerable to climate change, and natural resource managers are increasingly invoking climate change science into plans to build and maintain resilience (Benson and Garmestani 2011, Alid 2011). According to some assessments, climate

change may be the largest challenge ever faced by the U.S. National Wildlife Refuge System (Griffith et al. 2009). Accordingly, the U.S. National Wildlife Refuge System (NWRS) has developed a strategy to manage climate change effects, as these will impact the United States, including the 54 NWRS sites in the Midwest (Griffith et al. 2009). Considering the main issues as biome shifts, changes in hydrology, sea level rise, invasive species, and disease and parasites, the NWRS has considered adaptation measures focused on "increase the resilience of the refuges to a changing climate" (Griffith et al. 2009).

Forest management with the Midwest may need to be altered in light of changing fire, drought, and pest scenarios. One analysis of the impact and responses of forests in Missouri that employed a forest-gap model found that if no management response is assumed, "average forest biomass in the region declines by 11% within ten years, primarily due to moisture-stress induced mortality" (Bowes and Sedjo 1993). Further, altered hydrology of rivers and lakes in the region will also have profound implications for management of fish, migratory waterfowl and habitat quality. Climate change can affect organisms both directly (e.g., via their physiology, growth, and behavior) and indirectly (e.g., through effects on ecosystem structure and function), leading to concerns about the persistence of species (terrestrial, aquatic (freshwater and marine)), particularly in light of the rapidity of possible changes. Rising air temperatures will act to increase water temperatures in many streams and rivers,

Table 2.3. The percentage of irrigated cropland in 2007 (http://www.ers.usda.gov/StateFacts/). Also shown is a summary of the use of irrigation by state for two of the major crops from midwestern farms. The data are for 2008 and were taken from the USDA Census of Agriculture—2008 Farm and Ranch Irrigation Survey (data source: http://www.agcensus.usda.gov/Publications/2007/Online_Highlights/Farm_and_Ranch_Irrigation_Survey/index.asp). The data show for those farms that had implemented irrigation, how much acreage was under irrigation, the yield from that land, and data from those farms for the non-irrigated area of the farms.

	Percentage of irrigated cropland	Corn for grain or seed (2008 Farm and Ranch Irrigation Survey)				Soybeans for beans (2008 Farm and Ranch Irrigation Survey)			
		Acres harvested—irrigated	Average yield per acre (bushels)—irrigated	Acres harvested—not irrigated	Average yield per acre (bushels)—not irrigated	Acres harvested—irrigated	Average yield per acre (bushels)—irrigated	Acres harvested—not irrigated	Average yield per acre (bushels)—not irrigated
Illinois	2.0	309,187	190	409,642	177	90,497	52	258,230	46
Indiana	3.1	244,574	176	459,093	159	102,279	52	303,862	43
Iowa	0.7	107,979	171	205,225	163	48,946	48	160,680	44
Kansas	9.7	1,368,126	191	475,908	84	396,613	53	281,995	36
Kentucky	0.8	14,099	174	64,366	136	6,173	49	67,550	37
Michigan	6.4	248,790	175	258,096	130	73,986	51	191,470	33
Minnesota	2.3	254,960	174	272,178	147	100,513	45	259,803	36
Missouri	7.3	361,275	172	140,825	142	488,319	48	461,362	39
Nebraska	39.3	5,058,195	184	1,230,756	129	2,272,944	57	957,491	43
North Dakota	0.8	90,271	156	162,710	131	18,939	40	153,189	32
Ohio	0.3	7,260	162	33,585	127	1,702	60	33,423	39
South Dakota	1.9	175,593	173	301,760	134	79,296	44	277,566	35
Wisconsin	3.7	105,890	166	153,058	127	30,410	45	89,440	31

and studies of thermal effects on stream fishes in northern parts of the Midwest have generally indicated loss of viable stream length for key cold- and cool-water species (Lyons et al. 2010). Climate change may alter the location of optimal habitat for given freshwater organisms. However, their ability to relocate may be hampered by obstacles, some of which are "natural" (e.g., seasonal drying of waterways), and others, anthropogenic. As discussed in chapter 12 volume, there are tens of thousands of dams, diversions, and impassable road culverts in the United States, including approximately 80,000 large dams and an estimated 2.5 million or more small impoundments (Graf 2006), all of which may inhibit the ability of freshwater fish to undertake "autonomous" adaptation and disperse into more favorable surroundings. This has prompted calls for managed relocation to preserve the viability of key (climate sensitive) species, although such measures would have to be undertaken carefully to avoid unintended effects in the recipient ecosystems (Olden et al. 2011).

WATER

Water usage by thermoelectric power stations exceeded 39 percent of the national total for the first time in 2000 (Gollehon and Quinby 2006). Primary uses of fresh water in the United States in 2005 were irrigation (128,000 million gallons per day, or 37 percent) and thermoelectric power (143,000 million gallons a day, or 41 percent) (Table 2.4). Equivalent figures for the Midwest indicate thermoelectric power uses 66 percent of freshwater withdrawals,

while irrigation accounts for 16 percent. However, this partitioning between use-sectors and the total water withdrawals exhibit tremendous variability across the midwestern states (Figure 2.7). Freshwater withdrawal varies from a minimum of 500 million gallons a day in South Dakota to 15,200 million gallons a day in Illinois. In accord with analysis presented in other sections of this chapter, thermoelectric power is the major user of freshwater (between 61% in Minnesota and 82% in Illinois) in all states except South Dakota (1%), Nebraska (28%) and Kansas (12%). In the latter three states irrigation is the largest user accounting for between 58 percent of freshwater withdrawals in South Dakota and 72 percent in Kansas. Public and domestic water withdrawals are fairly consistent around the average of 11 percent with the notable exceptions of 3 percent in Nebraska and 22 percent in South Dakota. Livestock and aquaculture use is 4 percent or less in every state except South Dakota (16%). The only states where more than 10 percent of freshwater withdrawals are attributed to industry and mining are Indiana (25%) and Minnesota (14%).

The Midwest is also home to Lakes Superior, Huron, Michigan, Ontario, and Erie (the Great Lakes), which contain 20 percent of the world's fresh water, supplies drinking water for 40 million people, and support "a $4 billion sport fishing industry, plus $16 billion annually in boating, 1.5 million U.S. jobs and $62 billion in annual wages" (Fortner and Manzo 2011). The ecology of the Great Lakes is subject to a plethora of environmental stressors (Niemi et al. 2009), including climate change

Table 2.4. Total freshwater withdrawals by water-use categories for 2005 (Kenny et al. 2009) (million gallons per day). Saline contributions to water withdrawals are very small in the Midwest and have been disregarded (but should be included for the total US water withdrawals).

State	Public supply	Domestic	Irrigation	Livestock	Aquaculture	Industrial	Mining	Thermo-electric power	Total freshwater withdrawals
Illinois	1700	101	504	38	9	364	86	12,400	15,200
Indiana	676	124	151	39	1	2,200	100	6,050	9,340
Iowa	398	35	33	116	16	190	47	2,530	3,370
Kansas	403	15	2,740	108	5	42	15	459	3,790
Kentucky	558	35	19	46	20	186	37	3,430	4,330
Ohio	1,430	149	43	24	9	703	174	8,930	11,500
Michigan	1,140	251	308	20	65	629	95	9,150	11,700
Minnesota	537	78	244	60	113	139	426	2,450	4,040
Missouri	831	60	1,370	76	156	81	35	6,180	8,790
Nebraska	330	52	8,460	108	83	11	10	3,550	12,600
North Dakota	67	9	151	23	6	15	6	1,060	1,340
South Dakota	100	8	292	48	33	4	11	5	500
Wisconsin	552	87	402	73	82	471	33	6,900	8,600
Sum of Midwest	8,722	1,004	14,717	779	598	5,035	1,076	63,094	95,100
United States	44,200	3,830	128,000	2,140	8,780	17,000	2,310	143,000	349,000

and variability. As discussed in chapter 15 of this volume, historical changes in lake level due in part to climate variability have been associated with substantial ecological damage and economic impacts. Future changes, and particularly decreased water levels, may greatly impact the viability and health of wetland ecosystems (Mortsch 1998).

AIR QUALITY

The Clean Air Act of 1970 (and subsequent amendments) requires the Environmental Protection Agency (EPA) to set National Ambient Air Quality Standards (NAAQS) for six common (criteria) air pollutants: carbon monoxide (CO), lead (Pb), nitrogen dioxide (NO_2), ground-level ozone (O_3), sulfur dioxide (SO_2) and particles

(PM). With respect to the latter, the EPA regulates exposure to atmospheric particles into two both size classes: particulate matter with a diameter of ≤ 2.5 µm ($PM_{2.5}$) and particulate matter with a diameter of ≤ 10 µm (PM_{10}). Several of these pollutants are emitted by combustion of fossil fuels or are formed in the atmosphere from precursor gases associated in part with combustion products. For example, O_3 is formed in the lower atmosphere (i.e., near ground level) by reactions between volatile organic compounds (VOCs, a class of chemicals that will readily evaporate into the atmosphere and contain carbon) and oxides of nitrogen (NO_x). As might be expected from the energy-intensive nature of the Midwest economy, the midwestern states exhibit relatively high emissions of these air pollutants (Figure 2.8), with the spatial patterns of emissions of oxides of nitrogen and sulfur dioxide closely mirroring the distribution of major electricity generating plants (Figure 2.3).

Exposure to elevated concentrations of these criteria pollutants has been demonstrated to cause human mortality (premature death) and morbidity (excess illness). According to some estimates, 811,000 people worldwide die prematurely each year from exposure to elevated concentrations of PM (Russell and Brunekreef 2009). Despite progress made in the last 30 years (Lefohn et al. 2010), millions of people across the United States still live in counties that experience concentrations of one or more of the criteria pollutants above the NAAQS. For example, in 2008, approximately 127 million people nationwide lived in counties where the concentrations of at least one of the criteria pollutants exceeded the NAAQS (www.epa .gov/air/airtrends). At the national level, and in the Midwest, the majority of the unhealthful conditions were associated with high concentrations of either ground-level O_3 or particulate matter. In the Midwest in 2008, over 26 million people lived in counties that failed the NAAQS for $PM_{2.5}$, and over 24 million lived in counties that failed the NAAQS for O_3 (Figure 2.9). Since not all counties have air quality measurement stations in place, these data must be considered a lower bound on the actual number of counties that violate the NAAQS.

Relatively high air pollution levels also have implications for agricultural yields. For example, O_3 enters plant leaves through the stomata and acts to produce byproducts that reduce the efficiency of photosynthesis. A recent modeling study estimated that current near-surface O_3 concentrations are responsible for global relative yield losses of 7 to 12 percent for wheat, 6 to 16 percent for soybean, 3 to 4 percent for rice and 3 to 5 percent for corn (maize) (Van Dingenen et al. 2009). "Translating these assumed yield losses into total global economic damage for the four crops considered, using world market prices for the year 2000, we estimate an economic loss in the range $14–$26 billion" (Van Dingenen et al. 2009). According to some estimates, the value of corn and soybean production in Iowa, Illinois, Indiana, and Nebraska during 1990 totaled nearly $30 billion. Associated yield losses due to O_3 exposure was over $1 billion, and may have been as high as $2 billion (Murphy et al. 1999).

Given that emissions of air pollutants such as VOCs show a temperature dependence as do many of the chemical reactions that lead to the formation of secondary pollutants such as PM and O_3 (Seinfeld and Pandis 1998), further deterioration of air quality is possible under moderate climate change projections (Leung and Gustafson 2005, Jacob and Winner 2009, Tai et al. 2010). This tendency may also be amplified by changes in synoptic-scale meteorological regimes, and specifically the tendency for stagnation (Leibensperger et al. 2008). Indeed, some studies have indicated increased air pollution concentrations under climate change scenarios even in the absence of changes in precursor emissions (Bell et al. 2007). One recent model study used the CMAQ Modeling System driven by changes in meteorology from the GISS Global Climate Model and compared projected O_3 and PM derived mortality in 2050 and compared the results to those for a reference year of 2001. Their results indicate "climate change driven air quality-related health effects will be adversely affected in more than ⅔ of the continental U.S. . . . Nationally the analysis suggests approximately 4000 additional annual premature deaths due to climate change impacts on $PM_{2.5}$ and 300 due to climate change-induced ozone changes" (Tagaris et al. 2009). A large fraction of the increased mortality in this study derives from increased pollution concentrations in the midwestern states.

Climatological Norms, Historical Tendencies, and Future Projections

Information regarding the current climate state and historical tendencies therein is critical to providing a context for projected climate states and to assessing vulnerabilities and resilience to climate extremes. In the following, we briefly synthesize the midwestern climate and trends that have been derived from observational data and present a summary of climate projections for the region.

THERMAL REGIMES

Historical temperature observations across the midwestern United States exhibit strong north-south temperature gradients and high seasonality (Figure 2.10) (Pryor and Takle 2009). Although there

is tremendous inter-annual variability in regional temperatures, and there are multiple break points in temperature data sets (Ivanov and Evtimov 2010), historical tendencies for the Midwest region as a whole are toward increased temperatures (Figure 2.11). As with the recent increase in the global rate of temperature increase, according to the CRUTEM3 data set (Jones et al. 1999), which is a homogenized data set with spatial resolution of $5° \times 5°$ (Brohan et al. 2006), the annual mean temperature over the Midwest increased by approximately 0.067°C per decade when the period 1900–2010 is considered, increasing to 0.12°C per decade for the period 1950–2010, and 0.23°C per decade for the period 1979–2010. This is consistent with the increase in the rate of global carbon dioxide emissions that increased by the fastest growth rate (of 3.3%/year) in the early to mid-2000s. The estimate of temperature change for 1900–2010 over the Midwest are comparable to, but of lower magnitude than, estimates of 0.072°C–0.089°C per decade for the entire Northern Hemisphere land mass for 1902–2005 (Trenberth et al. 2007). As discussed below, this may be in part due to the presence of a "warming hole" centered along the Iowa–Nebraska–South Dakota border (Pan et al. 2009).

Historical temperature tendencies over the Midwest are not uniform in space or time. For example, the warming trend is of largest magnitude during winter (Schoof 2009). Based on data from the CRUTEM3 data set, the temporal trend in the mean temperature in January is approximately 0.24°C/decade when calculated for 1950–2010, while for July it is 0.056°C/decade (Figure 2.12). Nighttime minimum temperatures in the Midwest have risen more than daytime maximum temperatures, leading to a reduced diurnal temperature range (DTR). This effect is entirely consistent with expectations for increased counter-radiation due to increased GHG concentrations, but has been amplified by changing land use and soil moisture (Bonan 2001, Zhang et al. 2009). Analyses of historical temperatures since 1900 and reconstructed cropland extent show a negative temporal correlation between land use and cooling indicating land use transitions, "especially clearing of forest for agriculture and reforestation of abandoned farmland, are an important cause of regional climate change" (Bonan 2001). The "warming hole" (i.e., decline of summertime maximum temperatures) in the southwest of the Midwest also appears to be associated with changes in cloudiness and precipitation that can be directly linked to changes in land practices and increased use of irrigation (Pan et al. 2009).

Ensemble average regional projected temperatures based on direct output from ten Global Climate Models (GCM) from the IPCC Fourth Assessment Report indicate increases of 3°C–5°C by the end of the 21st century (Figure 2.13), with the magnitude of the changes being determined by the GHG emission scenario (SRES). The ensemble mean temperature anomaly in the middle and end of the 21st century are 2.1°C and 3.2°C above the 1961–1990 mean for the SRES B1 scenario, while those for the A1B scenario are 2.9°C and 4.3°C, and for the A2 SRES they are 2.8°C and 4.7°C

(Figure 2.13). The global GHG emissions associated with these three scenarios of socioeconomic future states are as follows: For the B1 SRES the annual emissions in 2030 are ~ 52 Gt CO_2-eq., and in 2100 they are ~ 23 Gt CO_2-eq.. For the A1B SRES the annual emissions in 2030 are ~ 63 Gt CO_2-eq., and in 2100 they are ~47 Gt CO_2-eq.. For the A2 SRES the annual emissions in 2030 are 67 Gt CO_2-eq., and in 2100 they are ~110 Gt CO_2-eq. (Metz et al. 2007). The warming for a constant composition scenario equates to about 1°C.

It is unlikely that temperature changes will be uniform across the region or across the seasons. Thus Figure 2.14 gives illustrative examples of projected changes in the probability distribution of air temperatures from Regional Climate Model (RCM) simulations. Although these projections derive from only one GCM-RCM coupling, they illustrate the complexity of addressing a key question within climate science: how will the probability distribution of air temperatures at a given location change? Will the change be principally characterized by a shift in the mean (toward higher temperatures) while the variance around the mean remains the same? Or will the variance increase as the mean increases? (Meehl et al. 2000) Accurate simulation of temperature variability is a stringent challenge of climate models, and the relationships between the mean and variance of geophysical parameters are complex (Meehl et al. 2000). However, at least for the simulations shown in Figure 2.14 it appears that the principal change in the probability distributions is an increase in the mean air temperature in the winter and summer, while the variability around the mean remains relatively constant. The implications of changes in the probability distribution of air temperature for human health are provided in chapters 9–11 of this volume, while the implications for energy demand and supply are a focus of chapter 12. One feature evident in the model simulations for Fargo (Figure 2.14a), which is also common to surrounding grid cells, is the indication of an increase in winter temperatures, which causes a greatly increased propensity for near-freezing temperatures during the winter and thus increased risk of icing (see chapter 16 of this volume).

There is strong evidence across the Northern Hemisphere of phenological tendencies and increased duration of the growing season (Schwartz et al. 2006). Consistent with these phenological changes toward lengthening of the growing season, one feature of historical temperature records across the Midwest is a tendency towards longer frost-free seasons during the latter part of the 20th century, due in large part to negative trends in the date of the last spring freeze (Schoof 2009). Analysis of changes in the length of the growing season derived from satellite-measured normalized difference vegetation index indicate the change in growing season length seems to be more strongly related to warming in the June–September period before the end of the season, than to pre-season warming prior to the start of the growing season (Jeong et al. 2011). While net primary productivity (NPP, net carbon uptake) by forests is a result of complex interactions between meteorological and

soil conditions over the course of the year, there is evidence for recent expansion of the period of the year characterized by carbon uptake, leading to greater removal of CO_2 from the atmosphere in midwestern forests (Dragoni et al. 2010).

Results of transient 21st century Global Climate Model simulations downscaled using a statistical approach indicate a further increase in frost-free season length by approximately two weeks by mid-century (2046–2065) and more than four weeks by 2081–2100 (Schoof 2009). As a caveat to this finding, as shown in the examples given in Figure 2.14, overlain on a general warming trend is a continued tendency for cold air outbreaks (incursions of cold polar air into lower latitudes). Such events are relatively frequent over parts of the Midwest in the historical record (Vavrus et al. 2006), and while the frequency decreased in an analysis of output from GCMs, these events remain a feature of the midwestern climate through the current century (Vavrus et al. 2006) which is consistent with results in Figure 2.14. This, coupled with changes in hydrologic regimes, has ramifications for agricultural yields within the region as discussed further in chapters 5–8 and for cycling of soil organic carbon (chapter 7).

PRECIPITATION AND HYDROLOGICAL REGIMES

The climatological pattern for precipitation over the Midwest exhibits strong spatial gradients in annual accumulations, with east-west gradients on its western boundary (separating the semi-arid or steppe climate to the west from the temperate continental climate over the Midwest) and north-south gradient throughout (separating the subtropical humid climate to the south from the temperate continental Midwest) (Figure 2.15). Annual precipitation accumulation in the Midwest is highly sensitive to extreme precipitation events. Over much of the domain 40 percent of annual total precipitation derives from the top 10 wettest days, despite the fact that over much of the domain precipitation is observed on approximately 1 day in 3 to 7 days (Pryor et al. 2009b, Pryor et al. 2009c). Instrumental records of precipitation exhibit very high inter-annual variability, but 24 percent of stations across the Midwest experienced increased annual total precipitation over the 20th century, with trends of over 2 percent per decade at some stations. Much of the change in precipitation derived from increases in the sum of precipitation on the top 10 wettest days in a year (Pryor et al. 2009c). Extreme (100-year return period) daily precipitation exhibits a similar spatial tendency to that shown in Figure 2.15, increasing from approximately 100 mm in parts of North Dakota to approximately 200 mm in southern Missouri, and has also been shown to have exhibited weak upward tendency over the last 75 years (Villarini et al. 2011).

Making climate projections for precipitation, and specifically intense and extreme precipitation, is very challenging. One recent study applied a probabilistic downscaling approach to 10 GCMs to generate station specific projections of pre-

cipitation regimes across the contiguous United States for the middle and end of the 21st century (Schoof et al. 2010). Precipitation occurrence (the number of wet days) and precipitation intensity (the amount of precipitation on wet days) were downscaled separately to allow investigation of the relative roles of occurrence and amount of precipitation in changing the overall hydroclimate. This empirical statistical downscaling approach (ESD) was applied to 963 stations across the contiguous United States based on predictors derived from output of 10 CMIP3 AOGCMs (BCCR BCM2.0, CCCMa CGCM3.1, CNRM CM3, CSIRO Mk3.0, GFDL CM2.0, GISS Model E Russell, IPSL CM4, MIUB ECHO G, MPI ECHAM5, and MRI CGCM2.3.2a) driven by the A2 SRES for 2046–2065 and 2081–2100. The ESD method applied used first-order Markov chains to simulate precipitation occurrence, the gamma probability distribution to quantify wet-day amount, and used regionally specific large-scale predictors drawn from a suite that included specific humidity, temperature and flow components at 700 and 500 hPa, and sea-level pressure. Projections developed by Schoof et al. (2010) from each individual AOGCM and each station exhibit a high degree of variability, but the ensemble average projections synthesized across all AOGCMs and all stations within seven regions are shown in Figure 2.16.

The results for the Midwest (Figures 2.16, 2.17, and 2.18) from the ESD analysis of Schoof et al. (2010) indicate four clear tendencies:

a) Stations that are characterized by projected increases in seasonal total precipitation typically exhibit increased precipitation intensities. Conversely, those stations for which the future scenarios indicate negative changes in precipitation totals typically have projections characterized by large changes in small precipitation intensities with relatively little change in large events.

b) There is a tendency for increased cool season (defined as NDJFM) precipitation. Over two-thirds of stations within the region exhibit a tendency towards increased cool-season total precipitation (Figure 2.18). However, it should be acknowledged that there are stations within the region (particularly in the northwestern states) for which the ensemble average projection is toward declining values.

c) Although there is an almost equal number of stations indicated increases and declines in warm-season precipitation in the 2046–2065 period, over the course of the entire 21st century the tendency is toward area-averaged increases in total warm-season precipitation, due principally to an increase in the magnitude of intense events. However, the results also indicate important sub-regional signals. For example, while the region as a whole indicates a tendency toward increased warm-season precipitation, projections for the majority of stations in the southwest of the region indicate declining warm-season precipitation (Figure 2.17).

d) There is evidence that intense precipitation events are likely to either maintain their current frequency or increase in frequency regardless of the sign of changes in total precipitation. This tendency toward increased magnitude of high intensity events even in locations with declining overall precipitation receipt is consistent with historical tendencies in precipitation regimes. Tendencies toward increases in high magnitude events are also frequently accompanied by positive tendencies in indicators of summer drought (Schoof et al. 2010).

The positive tendency in historical precipitation over much of the Midwest described above has been accompanied by positive tendencies in runoff (Dai 2010). The overall trend in the Palmer Drought Severity Index (PDSI) over the historical period (1950–2008) has not indicated a consistent drying trend, though future projections of the PDSI through 2030–2039, 2060–2069 and 2090–2099 using a 22-model ensemble mean appear to indicate more of a drying trend focused on the south of the region (Dai 2010).

Further information regarding how changing precipitation regimes may impact key economic sectors in the Midwest is contained in multiple chapters within this volume, including chapters 13 and 14, which discuss analyses, and possible consequences, of changing drought and flood frequency and/or intensity.

ATMOSPHERIC CIRCULATION AND FLOW REGIMES

The Midwest is characterized by frequent passages of synoptic-scale transient systems. Much of the region has cyclone counts in excess of 13 per month in the ERA-40 reanalysis data set (Coleman and Klink 2009). This and the large seasonality of the climate is associated with both the behavior of the polar jet stream and the relative intensity of several semipermanent pressure systems, including the subtropical (Bermuda) high (often located within or to the east/southeast of the study area) and the sub-polar (Hudson) low (often located within or to the north/northeast of the study area) (Schoof and Pryor 2006). Variations in the intensity of these pressure systems and the tracking and intensity of synoptic scale phenomena have been linked to internal modes of climate variability and larger pressure oscillations (or teleconnection patterns)— most notably the North Atlantic Oscillation (NAO), the Pacific/North American (PNA) index and indices of the El Niño Southern Oscillation (ENSO) (Pryor and Takle 2009, Schoof and Pryor 2009). Given the importance of these internal modes to the cyclone climates in the mid-latitudes, and the long-term periodicities in many of these indices, it is difficult to identify robust historical tendencies in the synoptic-scale regimes and cyclone numbers or intensities (Pryor et al. 2012) or to attribute them to anthropogenic forcing of the climate system. For example, one study found a long-term decline in cyclone number over the eastern United States during the summer of −0.15 per year over the period 1948–2006 based on the NCEP/NCAR reanalysis, but this tendency was not manifest in the NCEP/DOE reanalysis data set (1979–2006) (Leibensperger et al. 2008).

The hemispheric-scale modes of climate variability described above are also strongly linked to surface temperature, precipitation, and wind speeds in the study region via synoptic scale circulation patterns (Sheridan 2003). For example, the NAO accounts for 31 percent of the variance in mid-latitude winter mean surface air temperatures (Hurrell 1996). The PNA accounts for as much as 40 percent of the variance in surface air temperature during winter season (Leathers et al. 1991). Positive phase PNA is associated with lowering of the upper percentiles of the wind speed probability distribution (at 850 hPa) over the Midwest, while positive phase NAO is associated with increased wind speeds at this level (Pryor and Ledolter 2010). These associations indicate the importance of internal modes and causes of climate variability and need to be accounted for in both analysis of historical data and interpretation of climate projections (Guentchev et al. 2009).

Due, in part, to the high frequency of cyclone passages, the Midwest experiences comparatively high wind speeds and thus has a moderate-to-good wind resource (see Figure 2.4) (Pryor and Barthelmie 2011). Wind speed magnitudes and historical tendencies across the Midwest are difficult to quantify from direct observations because of numerous problems with station moves and other data inhomogenities (Pryor et al. 2009a). Further information regarding projections of the wind resource is provided by Pryor and Barthelmie (2011), while projections of extreme and intense wind speeds are provided in chapter 16 of this volume.

The summary of midwestern climate-related impacts in the recent National Research Council reports (National Research Council 2010a) included early snowmelt, degraded air quality, urban heat islands, heat waves, droughts, and extreme rainfall with flooding. As indicated by Tables 2.5 and 2.6, a range of key climate related hazards have been responsible for over 400 Presidential Disaster Declarations within the states that comprise the Midwest over the last few decades. The weather-related losses in these major disasters in the Federal Emergency Management Agency (FEMA) regions V and VII (which cover the majority of the Midwest) during 1953–2009 are estimated at approximately $12 billion, and comprised over 99 percent of the total losses associated with events that prompted Presidential Disaster Declarations. In the midwestern states, the primary sources for the Presidential Disaster Declarations are floods, snow and ice storms, tornado and severe storms. These events are discussed in more detail in the following sections and form much of the focus of the subsequent chapters.

FLOODING

Between 1971 and 1995, floods affected more than 1.5 billion people worldwide and caused about 40 percent of all economic damage globally deriving from extreme weather events (Pielke and Downton 2000). Specific to the United States, FEMA considers flooding "America's number one natural hazard." Flooding ranks third in terms of the economic losses that prompted Presidential Disaster Declarations (Tables 2.5 and 2.6), and estimates from the National Weather Service (NWS) indicate flooding caused an average of $4.5 billion in property damage and 98 deaths per year in the United States between 1983 and 2000 (Table 2.7). While other estimates of average annual cost of floods in the United States range from $2–$3 billion (current U.S. dollars) (Ntelekos et al. 2010), it is clear that flooding represents a significant natural hazard in the United States. The federal government has assumed responsibility for mitigating the impacts of flooding through the creation of the National Flood Insurance Program (NFIP), which provides subsidized flood insurance (Ntelekos et al. 2010). Due to increased flood costs during the past two decades, the NFIP is operating at a deficit, and some flood projections indicate that annual flood costs in the United States will increase to $7–$19 billion (current US dollars) under reasonable climate, economic, and GHG emission scenarios (Ntelekos et al. 2010). While many of the high-impact events are linked to flooding associated with tropical cyclones in the southeastern United States, the widespread flooding of the Midwest during 1993 led to damage to over 40,000 square kilometers of crops and over $3 billion in losses (Rosenzweig et al. 2001). During the May–June 2008 midwestern floods, total accumulated precipitation between May 21 and June 13 exceeded 400 mm in some parts of the Midwest in locations (e.g., eastern Iowa) that have historically exhibited annual average accumulations of approximately 900 mm. The excess precipitation caused

Table 2.5. Estimated economic losses (in thousands of 2009 dollars) associated with Presidential Disaster declarations, 1953–2009. Only weather-related sources are identified explicitly while the totals reflect the total from all sources. The FEMA regions that include states within the Midwest are: Region 4 (IV) (Kentucky, Tennessee, Mississippi, Alabama, Georgia, Florida, South Carolina, and North Carolina); Region 5 (V) (Minnesota, Wisconsin, Illinois, Indiana, Michigan, and Ohio); Region 7 (VII) (Nebraska, Kansas, Iowa, and Missouri); Region 8 (VIII) (Montana, North Dakota, South Dakota, Wyoming, Utah, and Colorado). The data were obtained from http://www.peripresdeceusa.org/mainframe.htm. Note the inflation factors used to convert historical data to 2009 dollars equivalent are provided on the aforementioned website.

Region	Flood & tornado	Coastal storm	Drought	Flood	Freezing	Hurricane/ typhoon	Severe ice storm	Snow	Tornado	Severe storm(s)	Total
I	0	$61,539	$767	$547,907	0	$262,905	0	$165,225	$9,738	$536,068	$1,602,422
II	0	0	$12,479	$2,082,648	0	$5,671,691	0	$446,536	0	$1,990,154	$20,717,915
III	$93,703	$1,826	$846	$2,666,139	0	$835,614	0	$185,416	$73,996	$1,011,000	$4,906,594
IV	$1,081,442	$17,140	0	$1,579,663	0	$32,793,547	$15,265	$632,135	$498,541	$2,568,750	$39,230,901
V	$868,661	0	0	$2,191,928	0	0	$28,399	$378,859	$561,772	$1,915,198	$5,955,101
VI	$587,080	0	0	$1,067,593	0	$37,015,376	$107,693	$883,377	$371,577	$3,161,046	$43,305,903
VII	$203,202	0	0	$1,658,078	0	0	$211,986	$439,514	$281,514	$3,014,553	$5,808,849
VIII	$171,706	0	0	$933,662	0	0	0	$282,070	$9,017	$971,053	$2,386,059
IX	$248,202	0	$16,349	$2,748,732	$10,872	$2,103,172	0	$20,418	0	$2,259,393	$21,196,771
X	0	0	0	$1,071,179	0	0	0	$57,362	0	$859,149	$2,841,282
Total	$3,253,996	$80,506	$30,442	$16,547,529	$10,872	$78,682,305	$363,344	$3,490,910	$1,806,156	$18,286,363	$147,951,797

Table 2.6. Estimated number of Presidential Disaster declarations 1953–2009. The data were obtained from http://www.peripresdeceusa.org/mainframe.htm.

Region	Flood and tornado	Coastal storm	Drought	Flood	Freezing	Hurricane/ typhoon	Severe ice storm	Snow	Tornado	Severe storm(s)	Total
I	0	5	1	45	0	20	0	10	3	38	128
II	0	0	4	45	0	23	0	10	0	33	119
III	6	1	2	71	0	19	0	12	5	40	158
IV	49	1	0	84	0	69	1	27	36	71	342
V	39	0	0	94	0	0	1	14	31	48	229
VI	31	0	0	105	0	28	1	14	34	50	269
VII	13	0	0	71	0	0	4	8	21	53	170
VIII	5	0	0	54	0	0	0	15	4	33	115
IX	1	0	3	71	1	58	0	1	0	22	204
X	0	0	0	58	0	0	0	8	0	34	123
Total	144	7	10	698	1	217	7	119	134	422	1,857

major flooding that was sustained for approximately 24 days over parts of Iowa, southern Wisconsin, and central Indiana (Budikova et al. 2010). Overall, losses resulting from the flooding were estimated to be $15 billion, including about $8 billion in agricultural losses and 24 deaths (Budikova et al. 2010). Floods are also a substantial threat to infrastructure. One analysis of the 2008 spring-summer floods found that within Illinois (the busiest rail area of the United States), flooding caused the closure of 56 rail lines. "The damaged tracks led to eight train wrecks and nine bridges were ruined. The damage costs to the 15 railroads affected were $85 million; the revenues lost totaled $69 million; and the total of $154 million rates as one of the major rail losses on record" (Changnon 2009a). Early estimates of losses associated with Mississippi River flooding from the spring/summer 2011 excess precipitation that fell over the Midwest are $3.0– $4.0 billion (http://www.ncdc.noaa.gov/sotc/hazards/2011/5#flooding).

Naturally, it is difficult to establish cause-effect relationships between changing precipitation regimes and flooding due to confounding factors such as population growth and exposure, economic development, and changes in infrastructure. A study of human and climate impacts on four watersheds in the Midwest states that "the long-term trend of baseflow recession is mainly caused by human interferences" (Wang and Cai 2010). Nevertheless, there is some evidence that historical shifts in precipitation regimes, and specifically changes in the intensity of extreme events and seasonality of precipitation, have been linked to increased flood risk (see chapters herein).

As mentioned above, assigning monetary value to flood impacts is uncertain. As one example, in Table 2.7, we summarize flood damage estimates for each of the midwestern states from two sources. Some of the discrepancy manifest in these estimates derives from comparison of annual median versus annual mean flood

Table 2.7. Flood damage estimates for the midwestern states from two data sources. The first two data columns ("Mean annual total damages (millions 2007 US$)" and "Mean annual total wealth-adjusted damages (millions 2007 US$)") are based on data from the National Center for Atmospheric Research (http://www.sip.ucar.edu/sourcebook/) and are based on estimated flood damage from 1955 to 2007. The damage estimates have been normalized to their values in 2007 dollars. The last two columns ("Median annual damage from all years of data (millions 1995 US$)" and "Maximum damage in any year (millions 1995 US$)"), are from http://www.flooddamagedata.org/. Data in these columns are based on 1955–1978 and 1983–1999 and are corrected to represent the value in 1995 dollars. Note: In these estimates, years with missing damage estimates are assumed to be zero; thus these damage estimates are likely negatively biased.

State	Mean annual total damages (millions 2007 US$)	Mean annual total wealth-adjusted damages (millions 2007 US$)	Median annual damage from all years of data (millions 1995 US$)	Maximum damage in any year (millions 1995 US$)
Illinois	132	219	15.31	2,754
Indiana	50	106	19.29	310
Iowa	218	329	17.18	5,987
Kansas	54	92	8.61	575
Kentucky	63	125	17.67	453
Michigan	25	38	0.21	528
Minnesota	102	168	2.4	1,006
Missouri	158	271	25.42	3,577
Nebraska	36	68	13.89	307
North Dakota	123	175	0.41	3,280
Ohio	73	124	22.06	313
South Dakota	52	88	0.51	796
Wisconsin	58	83	1.61	943

damage in highly non-Gaussian data, and also from comparison of damages normalized to US dollars in 1995 and 2007. Further, as discussed in chapter 14 of this volume, de-convoluting the roles of social versus physical causes and consequences is highly complex. Many rivers within the United States have been extensively modified by human activities and/or are regulated for navigation and power generation (see chapter 12). For example, in Idaho the worst damage directly from precipitation and streamflow is estimated at $120 million, while the maximum damage of $1,507 million (in 1995 $) was caused by failure of the Teton Dam in 1976. This, and other similar catastrophes, has led to in-

creased integration of climate projections into dam design and operation (Yao and Georgakakos 2001).

Despite uncertainties in costing flood losses, it is clear that flooding represents a significant financial burden to the midwestern states, both in terms of infrastructure damage, disruption of transportation and agricultural losses. One study of the impact of heavy precipitation on U.S. corn production found that yield losses associated with plant damage due to excess soil moisture, which is already a substantial source of losses, "may double during the next thirty years, causing additional damages totaling an estimated $3 billion per year" (Rosenzweig et al. 2002). In addition to the direct losses in crop yields, excess water can lead to increased pathogen outbreaks (Jacobsen et al. 1995, Munkvold and Yang 1995), further suppressing agricultural productivity. Insect pests coupled with pathogens may be associated with economic losses at the national scale of approximately $1.5 billion each year (National Research Council 2010a). Extreme precipitation and flooding potentially increase the incidence of waterborne diseases and hence also represent a potential risk to human health. The toxic algal bloom in Lake Erie during 2011 was linked (in part) to excess wash-off of phosphorus from the surrounding land by spring rains. Concentrations of *Microcystis* toxins nearly 50 times those associated with moderate recreational risk from contact (World Health Organization) were measured in the lake. Overflow of urban storm water associated with extreme precipitation events can also cause significant degradation of water quality (Goulding et al. 2010). The Great Lakes serve as a drinking water source for more than 40 million people. Flood events can lead to overflow of sewers in neighboring cities and excess pollutant discharge into the lakes, which could contaminate the water supply for the region (Patz et al. 2008. See further discussion in chapter 12). Thus there may be considerable benefit to application of adaptation measures designed to reduce exposure of humans and critical economic sectors and infrastructure to flood damage and the risks associated therewith. If the risk associated with floods and societal vulnerability is projected to be amplified as a result of climate change, then the need

to develop and implement such plans becomes even more important.

DROUGHT

In the broadest context, drought is caused by a prolonged negative anomaly in precipitation receipt (meteorological drought), which when coupled with positive anomalies in air temperature leads to soil moisture depletion and thus reduced streamflow (hydrological drought) and water stress in agricultural lands and decreased plant productivity (agricultural drought) (Mishra and Cherkauer 2010). For example, primary productivity (carbon uptake) by vegetation across Europe was suppressed by 30 percent due to the persistent heat wave and associated drought conditions during 2003 (Ciais et al. 2005, Vetter et al. 2008).

Given the lack of penetration by irrigation technologies across much of the Midwest (see Table 2.3), crop yields within the region are strongly coupled to drivers of agricultural drought. Retrospective analyses of the importance of drought to corn and soybean yields indicate:

• Droughts that occurred in the 1930s (and specifically influenced the growing seasons of 1930, 1931, 1934, and 1936) influenced over 90 percent of Illinois and Indiana (Mishra and Cherkauer 2010) and reduced national wheat and corn yields by up to 50 percent (Warrick 1984).
• Drought frequency has been lower during the last few decades, and the droughts of the 1930s were matched in severity only by the 1988 drought (Mishra and Cherkauer 2010). Nevertheless, research reported in Mishra and Cherkauer (2010) suggested that reduced crop

yields across the United States due to droughts and heat waves has led to losses of approximately $145 billion over the last three decades.

• The 1988 drought reduced national corn production by about 30 percent, and led to $3 billion in government direct relief payments to farmers (Rosenzweig et al. 2001). This drought was also associated with outbreaks of crop-pests, which further suppressed soybean yields in the Midwest. "The damage occurred during the critical flowering, pod-development and pod-filling growth stages. Approximately 3.2 million hectares were sprayed with insecticide to control mites across the region, and estimated losses to Ohio farms were $15 to 20 million" (Rosenzweig et al. 2001).

• Corn and soybean yields in Illinois and Indiana over the last 30 years are negatively correlated with the average daily maximum temperature during June–August (r = –0.80 and –0.64, respectively for corn and soybean) and positively correlated with a standardized precipitation index (r = 0.61 and 0.48 for corn and soy, respectively) (Mishra and Cherkauer 2010).

It has been proposed that to safeguard yields under a warming climate, it may be desirable to shift the North American Corn Belt into Canada, but this "vacates high-quality prairie soils for less productive soils farther north" (Ainsworth and Ort 2010). Thus increased use of irrigation may be a preferable strategy to avoid agricultural drought but may come at considerable cost and lead to competition with other end-users (see Table 2.4).

EXTREME HEAT

Virtually all climate scenarios for the Midwest indicate a warming trend (e.g.,

Figures 2.13 and 2.14). One analysis of the United States suggested that at the national level the increased electricity consumption for cooling will lead to increased net American energy expenditure, "resulting in welfare damages that increase as temperatures rise. For example, if the U.S. warms by 5°C by 2100 we predict annual welfare losses of $57 billion" (Mansur et al. 2008).

Generally, the Midwest experiences more heating degree days (HDD) than cooling degree days (CDD) (Pryor and Takle 2009) (Table 2.8). However, with projected tendencies toward warming, there may be a shift in the seasonal demand curve for energy. Over 40 percent of the 500 billion liters of freshwater used in the United States each day is used to cool power plants (Pryor and Takle 2009). Most power plants within the Midwest are not situated on the Great Lakes (Figure 2.3) but rather are adjacent to rivers and draw the water required for cooling purposes from those rivers (see water withdrawals by state and category in Table 2.4 and Figure 2.7). Given that periods of extreme heat within the Midwest are frequently associated with low precipitation (and even drought), these power stations and the electricity network they supply are potentially vulnerable to reductions in streamflow and thus water scarcity like those responsible for loss of significant power generation potential in France during the 2003 heat wave (Hightower and Pierce 2008).

Heat or anomalously hot weather that lasts for several days—"heat waves"—have clear impacts on society, including a rise

Table 2.8. Climate normal heating degree days (HDD) and cooling degree days (CDD) for the capital cities of the thirteen midwestern states. These indices are based on data for 1971–2000 derived from the National Climate Data Center (NCDC) and were calculated using a reference temperature of 65°F. (Data source: http://cdo.ncdc .noaa.gov/climatenormals/).

Capital city	HDD	CDD
Springfield, Illinois	5,569	1,165
Indianapolis, Indiana	5,521	1,042
Des Moines, Iowa	6,436	1,052
Topeka, Kansas	5,225	1,357
Frankfurt, Kentucky	5,129	994
Lansing, Michigan	7,098	558
St Paul, Minnesota	7,606	715
Jefferson City, Missouri	5,158	1,261
Lincoln, Nebraska	6,242	1,154
Bismarck, North Dakota	8,802	471
Columbus, Ohio	5,492	951
Pierre, South Dakota	7,282	919
Madison, Wisconsin	7,493	582

in mortality and morbidity (Hayhoe et al. 2010). Recent heat waves have been observed in multiple locations across North America (Gosling et al. 2009), for example:

- California (2006) (Knowlton et al. 2008, Margolis et al. 2008).
- Eastern United States (including the Midwest) (1980, 1988, 1995, and 1999) (Applegate et al. 1981, Changnon et al. 1996, Kunkel et al. 1996, Semenza et al. 1996, Whitman et al. 1997, Smoyer 1998, McGeehin and Mirabelli 2001, Naughton et al. 2002, Ebi et al. 2004).

During July 2011, 132 million people across the US were under a heat alert. During this period, over 1,000 records for minimum, maximum, and dew point temperature were broken and, for example, on

July 20 the majority of the Midwest experienced temperatures of over 100°F.

Depending on location and implementation of strategies to reduce the severity of heat stress, the intensity and human toll extracted by heat waves may increase (Kovats and Hajat 2008). Extreme heat events are reported to be the single largest cause of weather-related mortality, causing over 3,442 deaths in the United States between 1999 and 2003 (Luber and McGeehin 2008). The summer heat wave of 1980, which extended with only minor breaks from middle of June to middle of September, was one of the deadliest weather events in U.S. history. Nationwide the events resulted in over 1,300 premature deaths, with Missouri alone experiencing 311 deaths (Morgan and Moran 1997). Increased mortality, especially among the elderly, due to extreme heat has been attributed to cardiovascular illness (13%–90%), stroke (6%–52%) and respiratory systems (up to 14%) (Knowlton et al. 2009). While mortality is the more visible outcome of extreme heat, morbidity associated with extreme heat affects a broader cross-section of the population, and a much larger number of people. For example, during a heat wave in 2006 there were 140 deaths in California, but 16,166 excess visits to emergency rooms and 1,182 excess hospitalizations (Knowlton et al. 2009).

Extreme heat not only causes negative human health outcomes, but also places strains on infrastructure and agriculture (power, water, and transport).

Recent heat waves have raised questions regarding whether anthropogenic forcing of climate will lead to an increase in heat wave occurrence and/or intensity (see executive summary of the Health Sector in the USA National Assessment of 2000 (Patz et al. 2001) and 2007 (O'Neill and Ebi 2009)). Studies based on output from climate models have suggested that historical anthropogenic forcing of climate had doubled the risk of heat waves in Europe by 2003 relative to the start of the instrumental record (mid-19th century) (Stott et al. 2004). Other research conducted in the United States suggests a significant (at the 99% confidence level) increase in the frequency of heat waves in both the eastern and western United States between 1949 and 1995 (Luber and McGeehin 2008). One recent study developed projections of multiple metrics to find a tendency towards increased frequency and intensity of heat waves at least in the Chicago metropolitan area under a range of climate change projections (Hayhoe et al. 2010). This research, along with high-profile assertions of likely future increases in heat wave occurrence and intensity (Meehl and Tebaldi 2004, Tebaldi et al. 2006, Battisti and Naylor 2009), has focused attention on the need to improve understanding of the mechanisms of heat wave occurrence, their possible changes under climate change scenarios and health outcomes (McGeehin and Mirabelli 2001), and mitigation/adaptation measures (Luber and McGeehin 2008). For example, historical heat waves have prompted development of heat watch warning systems for a number of cities (including some within the Midwest) (Ebi et al. 2004). The 1995 heat wave resulted in over 700 deaths throughout the central United States, but

87 percent of the fatalities (approximately 700 deaths) were in the Midwest and 65 percent were in the city of Chicago (Kunkel et al. 1996). This event caused 1,072 excess hospital admissions in Chicago alone (Semenza et al. 1999) and over 3,000 excess emergency room visits (Vavrus and Van Dorn 2010). A significant factor in determining health outcomes (and specifically mortality) associated with this event was access to air conditioning (Semenza et al. 1996). Thus increased access to air conditioning will undoubtedly reduce future death tolls from extreme heat but is a possible example of maladaptation since the increased electricity demand may be met with increased use of fossil fuels. Description of vulnerability analyses, heat wave mitigation measures and projected heat wave frequency are provided in chapters 9–11 of this volume.

STORMS

The Midwest episodically experiences a range of severe weather, including that deriving from instability and deep convection (e.g., thunderstorms and the associated lightning, hail, and tornadoes), snow and ice storms, and non-tornadic high winds (Kunkel and Changnon 2009). The "super derecho" that occurred on May 8, 2009, caused multiple wind gusts of over 35 m s^{-1} and damaged buildings, utility lines, and trees over an area extending from Kansas to eastern Kentucky (Corfidi et al. 2010). Southern portions of the region experience over 40 days with thunderstorms each year (Changnon 2001) and over seven tornadoes per year (Kunkel and Changnon 2009). The average number of deaths from lightning strikes within the region exceeds 158 per year (Kunkel and Changnon 2009). These and other such extreme events are also associated with substantial economic losses (see Table 2.5).

Despite the importance of deep convection and the associated meteorological hazards, such events are not described in detail herein because of the difficulty in establishing robust climate projections of phenomena that are characterized by scales and physical processes generally not resolved in climate models. Correct representation of deep convection is another stringent test of Regional Climate Models (RCMs), and convective intensity is highly variable with parameterization scheme (Zanis et al. 2009). There is some evidence in North America of a recent increase in the frequency of severe hail events, which may be symptomatic of an increase in the intensity of deep convection (Cao 2008). One recent study that sought to examine deep convection in possible future climate scenarios used a "perfect-prog" approach to "estimating the potential for surface-based convective initiation and severity based upon the large-scale variables well resolved by climate model simulations" and found that when applied over the contiguous United States, using a single AOGCM and SRES, "relative to inter-annual variability, the potential frequency of deep moist convection does not change, but the potential for severe convection is found to increase east of the Rocky Mountains and most notably in the 'tornado alley' region of the U. S. Midwest" (Van Klooster and Roebber 2009).

In this volume we focus on large-scale, or synoptic-scale, systems that are responsible for the majority of damaging wind events, icing, and snowstorms in the Midwest, are likely to be manifest on larger spatial scales (Changnon 2007, 2009b), and are likely to be better reproduced by climate models (see chapter 16).

Concluding Remarks

This chapter is designed to provide information about the socioeconomic context of the Midwest, the climate thereof, and some indications regarding the principal risks, vulnerabilities, and impact sectors of climate change and variability. The chapters that follow provide further specifics to inform decision makers regarding effective responses to and mechanisms for adapting to climate change as it will be manifest at the regional and local levels.

ACKNOWLEDGEMENTS
Funding for the research presented herein was provided by the Indiana University Center for Research in Environmental Science (CRES), the National Science Foundation (grant 1019603), and the International Atomic Energy Authority.

REFERENCES
Ainsworth EA, Ort DR (2010). How do we improve crop production in a warming world? Plant Physiology 154:526–530.

Al-Kaisi MM, Yin XH (2005). Tillage and crop residue effects on soil carbon and carbon dioxide emission in corn-soybean rotations. Journal of Environmental Quality 34:437–445.

Alid RJ (ed) (2011). Effects of climate change on natural resources and communities: A compendium of briefing papers. US Department of Agriculture, Forest Service, Pacific Northwest Research Station. Portland, OR.

Alvarez R (2005). A review of nitrogen fertilizer and conservation tillage effects on soil organic carbon storage. Soil Use and Management 21:38–52.

Applegate WB, Runyan JW, Brasfield L, Williams ML, Konigsberg C, Fouche C (1981). Analysis of the 1980 heat-wave in Memphis. Journal of the American Geriatrics Society, 29:337–342.

AWEA (2009). 2008: Another record year for wind energy installations. Available from: http://www.awea.org/la_pubs.cfm.

AWEA (2011). AWEA: Year end 2010: market report. Available from: http://www.awea.org/.

Barthelmie RJ, Murray F, Pryor SC (2008). The economic benefit of short-term forecasting for wind energy in the UK electricity market. Energy Policy 36:1687–1696.

Battisti DS, Naylor RL (2009). Historical warnings of future food insecurity with unprecedented seasonal heat. Science 323:240–244.

Bell ML, Goldberg R, Hogrefe C, Kinney PL, Knowlton K, Lynn B, Rosenthal J, Rosenzweig C, Patz JA (2007). Climate change, ambient ozone, and health in 50 US cities. Climatic Change 82:61–76.

Benson MH, Garmestani AS (2011). Can we manage for resilience? The integration of resilience thinking into natural resource management in the United States. Environmental Management 48:392–399.

Blanco L, Isenhouer M (2010). Powering America: The impact of ethanol production in the Corn Belt states. Energy Economics 32:1228–1234.

Bonan GB (2001). Observational evidence for reduction of daily maximum temperature by croplands in the Midwest United States. Journal of Climate 14:2430–2442.

Bowes MD, Sedjo RA (1993). Paper 3. Impacts and responses to climate change in forests of the mink region. Climatic Change 24:63–82.

Brohan P, Kennedy JJ, Harris I, Tett SFB, Jones PD (2006). Uncertainty estimates in regional and global observed temperature changes: A new data set from 1850. Journal of Geophysical Research 111: D12106 , doi:10.1029/2005JD006548.

Budikova D, Coleman JSM, Strope SA, Austin A (2010). Hydroclimatology of the 2008 Midwest floods. Water Resources Research 46:W12524, doi:12510.11029/12010WR009206.

Cao ZH (2008). Severe hail frequency over Ontario, Canada: Recent trend and variability. Geophysical Research Letters 35:L14803, doi:14810.11029/12008gl034888.

Changnon SA (2001). Damaging thunderstorm activity in the United States. Bulletin of the American Meteorological Society 82:597–608.

Changnon SA (2007). Catastrophic winter storms: An escalating problem. Climatic Change 84:131–139.

Changnon SA (2009b) Temporal and spatial distributions of wind storm damages in the United States. Climatic Change 94:473–482.

Changnon SA (2009a) Impacts of the 2008 floods on railroads in Illinois and adjacent states. Transactions of the Illinois State Academy of Science 102:181–190.

Changnon SA, Kunkel K, Reinke B (1996). Impacts and responses to the 1995 heat wave: A call to action. Bulletin of the American Meteorological Society 77:1497–1506.

Ciais P, Reichstein M, Viovy N, Granier A, Ogee J, Allard V, Aubinet M, Buchmann N, Bernhofer C, Carrara A, Chevallier F, De Noblet N, Friend AD, Friedlingstein P, Grunwald T, Heinesch B, Keronen P, Knohl A, Krinner G, Loustau D, Manca G, Matteucci G, Miglietta F, Ourcival JM, Papale D, Pilegaard K, Rambal S, Seufert G, Soussana JF, Sanz MJ, Schulze ED, Vesala T, Valentini R (2005). Europe-wide reduction in primary productivity caused by the heat and drought in 2003. Nature 437:529–533.

Clemmens AJ, Allen RG, Burt CM (2008). Technical concepts related to conservation of irrigation and rainwater in agricultural systems. Water Resources Research 44: W00E03, doi:10.1029/2007WR006095.

Coleman JSM, Klink K (2009). North American atmospheric circulation effects on midwestern USA climate. In: Pryor SC (ed) Understanding climate change: Climate variability, predictability and change in the midwestern

United States. Bloomington: Indiana University Press, 156–168.

Corfidi SF, Coniglio MC, Kain JS (2010). Environment and early evolution of the 8 May 2009 "Super Derecho" *preprints*, 25th Conference on Severe Local Storms, Denver, CO, p 11.

Crago CL, Khanna M, Barton J, Giuliani E, Amaral W (2010). Competitiveness of Brazilian sugarcane ethanol compared to US corn ethanol. Energy Policy 38:7404–7415.

Cutforth HW, McGinn SM, McPhee KE, Miller PR (2007). Adaptation of pulse crops to the changing climate of the northern Great Plains. Agronomy Journal 99:1684–1699.

Dai A (2010). Drought under global warming: A review. Wiley Interdisciplinary Reviews: Climate Change 2:45–65.

Demirbas A (2011). Competitive liquid biofuels from biomass. Applied Energy 88:17–28.

Denny E, Tuohy A, Meibom P, Keane A, Flynn D, Mullane A, O'Malley M (2010). The impact of increased interconnection on electricity systems with large penetrations of wind generation: A case study of Ireland and Great Britain. Energy Policy 38:6946–6954.

Dominguez-Faus R, Powers SE, Burken JG, Alvarez PJ (2009). The water footprint of biofuels: A drink or drive issue? Environmental Science & Technology 43:3005–3010.

Dragoni D, Schmid HP, Wayson CA, Potter H, Grimmond CSB, Randolph JC (2010). Evidence of increased net ecosystem productivity associated with a longer vegetated season in a deciduous forest in south-central Indiana, USA. Global Change Biology 17:886–897.

Ebi KL, Teisberg TJ, Kalkstein LS, Robinson L, Weiher RF (2004). Heat watch/warning systems save lives—Estimated costs and benefits for Philadelphia, 1995–98. Bulletin of the American Meteorological Society 85:1067–1073.

Fortner RW, Manzo L (2011). Great lakes literacy principles. EOS 92:109–110.

Freeman P, Warner K (2001). Vulnerability of infrastructure to climate variability: How does this affect infrastructure lending policies? Report commissioned by the Disaster Management Facility of the World Bank and ProVention Consortium, Washington, DC.

Georgilakis PS (2008). Technical challenges associated with the integration of wind power into power systems. Renewable & Sustainable Energy Reviews 12:852–863.

Gollehon N, Quinby W (2006). Irrigation resources and water costs. In: agricultural resources and environmental indicators, 2006 edition / EIB-16 Economic Research Service/ USDA, chapter 2.1, 24–32.

Gosling SN, Lowe JA, McGregor GR, Pelling M, Malamud BD (2009). Associations between elevated atmospheric temperature and human mortality: A critical review of the literature. Climatic Change 92:299–341.

Goulding G, Barrack B, Jaligoma G, Muneer A, Narayanaswamy K, Radhakrishnan V (2010). Urban wet-weather flows. Water Environment Research 82:941–996.

Grace PR, Robertson GP, Millar N, Colunga-Garcia M, Basso B, Gage SH, Hoben J (2011). The contribution of maize cropping in the Midwest USA to global warming: A regional estimate. Agricultural Systems 104:292–296.

Graf WL (2006). Downstream hydrologic and geomorphic effects of large dams on American rivers. Geomorphology 79:336–360.

Griffith B, Scott JM, Adamcik R, Ashe D, Czech B, Fischman R, Gonzalez P, Lawler J, McGuire AD, Pidgorna A (2009). Climate change adaptation for the US National Wildlife Refuge System. Environmental Management 44:1043–1052.

Guentchev GS, Piromsopa K, Winkler JA (2009). Estimating changes in temperature variability in a future climate. In: Pryor SC (ed) Understanding climate change: Climate variability, predictability and change in the midwestern United States. Bloomington: Indiana University Press, 66–75.

Hatfield JL, Boote KJ, Kimball BA, Ziska LH, Izaurralde RC, Ort D, Thomson AM, Wolfe D (2010). Climate impacts on agriculture: Implications for crop production. Agronomy Journal 103:351–370.

Hayhoe K, Sheridan S, Kalkstein L, Greene S (2010). Climate change, heat waves, and mortality projections for Chicago. Journal of Great Lakes Research 36:65–73.

Hightower M, Pierce SA (2008). The energy challenge. Nature 452:285–286.

Hurrell JW (1996). Influence of variations in extratropical wintertime teleconnections on Northern Hemisphere temperatures. Geophysical Research Letters 23:665–668.

Ivanov MA, Evtimov SN (2010). 1963: The break point of the Northern Hemisphere temperature trend during the twentieth century. International Journal of Climatology 30: 1738–1746.

Jacob DJ, Winner DA (2009). Effect of climate change on air quality. Atmospheric Environment 43:51–63.

Jacobsen BJ, Harlin KS, Swanson SP, Lambert RJ, Beasley VR, Sinclair JB, Wei LS (1995). Occurrence of fungi and mycotoxins associated with field mold damaged soybeans in the Midwest. Plant Disease 79:86–89.

Jeong S-J, Ho C-H, Gim H-J, Brown ME (2011). Phenology shifts at start vs. end of growing season in temperate vegetation over the Northern Hemisphere for the period 1982–2008. Global Change Biology 17:2385–2399.

Jones PD, New M, Parker DE, Martin S, Rigor IG (1999). Surface air temperature and its changes over the past 150 years. Reviews of Geophysics 37:173–199.

Joskow PL (2006). Markets for power in the United States: An interim assessment. Energy Journal 27:1–36.

Kelly DL, Kolstad CD, Mitchell GT (2005). Adjustment costs from environmental change. Journal of Environmental Economics and Management 50:468–495.

Kenny JF, Barber NK, Hutson SS, Linsey KS, Lovelace JK, Maupin MA (2009). Estimated use of water in the United States in 2005. Report No. Circular 1344, ISBN 978-1-4113-2600-2. Reston, VA: U.S. Department of the Interior, U.S. Geological Survey.

Knowlton K, Rotkin-Ellman M, King G, Margolis HG, Smith D, Solomon G, Trent R, English P (2009). The 2006 California heat wave: Impacts on hospitalizations and emergency department visits. Environmental Health Perspectives 117:61–67.

Knowlton K, Rotkin-Ellman M, King G, Margolis HG, Smith D, Solomon G, Trent R, English P (2008). The 2006 California heat wave: Impacts on hospitalizations and emergency department visits. Epidemiology 19:S323-S323.

Kovats RS, Hajat S (2008). Heat stress and public health: A critical review. Annual Review of Public Health 29:41–55.

Kunkel KE, Changnon SA (2009). Severe storms in the midwestern USA. In: Pryor SC (ed) Understanding climate change: Climate variability, predictability and change in the midwestern United States. Bloomington: Indiana University Press, 225–235.

Kunkel KE, Changnon SA, Reinke BC, Arritt RW (1996). The July 1995 heat wave in the midwest: A climatic perspective and critical weather factors. Bulletin of the American Meteorological Society 77:1507–1518.

Leathers DJ, Yarnal B, Palecki MA (1991). The Pacific/North American teleconnection pattern and the United State climate. Part I: Regional temperature and precipitation associations. Journal of Climate 4:517–528.

Lefohn AS, Shadwick D, Oltmans SJ (2010). Characterizing changes in surface ozone levels in metropolitan and rural areas in the United States for 1980–2008 and 1994–2008. Atmospheric Environment 44:5199–5210.

Leibensperger EM, Mickley LJ, Jacob DJ (2008). Sensitivity of US air quality to mid-latitude cyclone frequency and implications of 1980–2006 climate change. Atmospheric Chemistry and Physics 8:7075–7086.

Leung LR, Gustafson WI, Jr. (2005). Potential regional climate change and implications to US air quality. Geophysical Research Letters 32: L16711, doi:10.1029/2005GL022911.

Lobell DB, Schlenker W, Costa-Roberts J (2011). Climate trends and global crop production since 1980. Science 333:616–620.

Lu X, McElroy MB, Kiviluoma J (2009). Global potential for wind-generated electricity. Proceedings of the National Academy of Sciences of the United States of America 106:10933–10938.

Luber G, McGeehin M (2008). Climate change and extreme heat events. American Journal of Preventive Medicine 35:429–435.

Lyons J, Stewart JS, Mitro M (2010). Predicted effects of climate warming on the distribution of 50 stream fishes in Wisconsin, U.S.A. Journal of Fish Biology 77:1867–1898.

Mansur ET, Mendelsohn R, Morrison W (2008). Climate change adaptation: A study of fuel choice and consumption in the US energy sector. Journal of Environmental Economics and Management 55:175–193.

Margolis HG, Gershunov A, Kim T, English P, Trent R (2008). 2006 California heat wave high death toll: Insights gained from coroner's reports and meteorological characteristics of event. Epidemiology 19:S363-S364.

Martinez E, Jimenez E, Blanco J, Sanz F (2010). LCA sensitivity analysis of a multi-megawatt wind turbine. Applied Energy 87:2293–2303.

McGeehin MA, Mirabelli M (2001). The potential impacts of climate variability and change on temperature-related morbidity and mortality in the United States. Environmental Health Perspectives 109:185–189.

McNew K, Griffith D (2005). Measuring the impact of ethanol plants on local grain prices. Review of Agricultural Economics 27: 164–180.

Mearns LO, Gutowski W, Jones R, Leung R, McGinnis S, Nunes A, Qian Y (2009). A regional climate change assessment program for North America. EOS 90:311–312.

Meehl GA, Tebaldi C (2004). More intense, more frequent, and longer lasting heat waves in the 21st century. Science 305:994–997.

Meehl GM, Karl T, Easterling DR, Changnon S, Pielke Jr R, Changnon D, Evans J, Groisman PY, Kutson TR, Kunkel KE, Mearns LO, Parmesan C, Pulwarty R, Root T, Sylves RT, Whetton P, Zwiers F (2000). An introduction to trends in extreme weather and climate events: Observations, socioeconomic impacts, terrestrial ecological impacts, and model projections.

Bulletin of the American Meteorological Society 81:413–416.

Mesinger F, DiMego G, Kalnay E, Mitchell K, Shafran PC, Ebisuzaki W, Jovic D, Woollen J, Rogers E, Berbery EH, Ek MB, Fan Y, Grumbine R, Higgins W, Li H, Lin Y, Manikin G, Parrish D, Shi W (2006). North American regional reanalysis. Bulletin of the American Meteorological Society 87:343–360.

Metz B, Davidson OR, Bosch PR, Dave R, Meyer LA (eds) (2007). Climate change 2007: Mitigation of climate change. Contribution of Working Group III to the Fourth Assessment Report of the Intergovernmental Panel on Climate Change. Cambridge, UK: Cambridge University Press.

Midwest ISO (2006). 2006 Midwest ISO-PJM Coordinated System Plan (CSP). Available from: http://www.electricity-tool.com/doc/212078/downloaddo.

Midwest ISO (2007). Growing the grid. Available from: http://nocapx2020.info/wp-content/uploads/2009/07/ex-mtep07_report_10-04-07_final.pdf.

Midwestern Governors Association Advisory Group (2009). Midwestern energy security and climate stewardship roadmap. Lombard, IL: Midwestern Governors Association.

Mishra V, Cherkauer KA (2010). Retrospective droughts in the crop growing season: Implications to corn and soybean yield in the midwestern United States. Agricultural and Forest Meteorology 150:1030–1045.

Morgan MD, Moran JM (1997). Weather and people. Upper Saddle River, NJ: Prentice Hall.

Mortsch LD (1998). Assessing the impact of climate change on the Great Lakes shoreline wetlands. Climatic Change 40:391–416.

Mubako S, Lant C (2008). Water resource requirements of corn-based ethanol. Water Resources Research 44:W00A02, doi:10.1029/2007WR006683.

Munkvold GP, Yang XB (1995). Crop damage and epidemics associated with 1993 floods in Iowa. Plant Disease 79:324–324.

Murphy JJ, Delucchi MA, McCubbin DR, Kim HJ (1999). The cost of crop damage caused by

ozone air pollution from motor vehicles.
Journal of Environmental Management
55:273–289.

National Research Council (2010a). Adapting to
the impacts of climate change. Washington,
DC: The National Academies Press.

National Research Council (2010b). Limiting the
magnitude of future climate change. Washington, DC: The National Academies Press.

Naughton MP, Henderson A, Mirabelli MC, Kaiser R, Wilhelm JL, Kieszak SM, Rubin CH,
McGeehin MA (2002). Heat-related mortality
during a 1999 heat wave in Chicago. American
Journal of Preventive Medicine 22:221–227.

Neufeldt H, Jochem E, Hinkel J, Huitema D,
Massey E, P. W, McEvoy D, Rayner T, Hof A,
Lonsdale K (2010). Climate policy and inter-
linkages between adaptation and mitigation.
In: Hulme M, Neufeldt H (eds) Making cli-
mate change work for us. Cambridge, UK:
Cambridge University Press, 413.

Niemi GJ, Brady VJ, Brown TN, Ciborowski JJH,
Danz NP, Ghioca DM, Hanowski JM, Hollen-
horst TP, Howe RW, Johnson LB, Johnston
CA, Reavie ED (2009). Development of ecological indicators for the US Great Lakes
coastal region—A summary of applications
in Lake Huron. Aquatic Ecosystem Health &
Management 12:77–89.

NREL (2008). 20% wind energy by 2030: Increasing wind energy's contribution to US electricity
supply. Report No. DOE/GO-102008-2567,
NREL.

Ntelekos AA, Oppenheimer M, Smith JA, Miller
AJ (2010). Urbanization, climate change and
flood policy in the United States. Climatic
Change 103:597–616.

O'Neill MS, Ebi KL (2009). Temperature extremes and health: Impacts of climate
variability and change in the United States.
Journal of Occupational and Environmental
Medicine 51:13–25.

Olden JD, Kennard MJ, Lawler JJ, Poff NL (2011).
Challenges and opportunities in implementing
managed relocation for conservation of freshwater species. Conservation Biology 25:40–47.

Pan ZT, Segal M, Li X, Zib B (2009). Global
climate change impact on the Midwestern
USA—A summer cooling trend. In: Pryor SC
(ed) Understanding climate change: Climate
variability, predictability, and change in the
midwestern United States. Bloomington: Indiana University Press, 29–41.

Patz JA, McGeehin MA, Bernard SM, Ebi KL,
Epstein PR, Grambsch A, Gubler DJ, Reiter
P, Romieu I, Rose JB, Samet JM, Trtanj J
(2001). The potential health impacts of climate
variability and change for the United States—
Executive summary of the report of the health
sector of the US National Assessment. Journal
of Environmental Health 64:20–28.

Patz JA, Vavrus SJ, Uejio CK, McLellan SL (2008).
Climate change and waterborne disease risk
in the Great Lakes region of the US. American
Journal of Preventive Medicine 35:451–458.

Pielke RA, Downton MW (2000). Precipitation
and damaging floods: Trends in the United
States, 1932–97. Journal of Climate 13:3625–
3637.

Pryor SC, Barthelmie RJ (2011). Assessing climate
change impacts on the near-term stability of
the wind energy resource over the USA. Proceedings of the National Academy of Sciences
of the United States of America 108:8167–8171.

Pryor SC, Barthelmie RJ, Clausen NE, Drews M,
MacKellar N, Kjellstrom E (2012). Analyses
of possible changes in intense and extreme
wind speeds over northern Europe under climate change scenarios. Climate Dynamics
38:189–208.

Pryor SC, Barthelmie RJ, Young DT, Takle ES,
Arritt RW, Flory D, Gutowski Jr WJ, Nunes A,
Road J (2009a). Wind speed trends over the
contiguous USA. Journal of Geophysical Research 114 D14105, doi:10.1029/2008JD011416.

Pryor SC, Howe JA, Kunkel KE (2009b). How
spatially coherent and statistically robust are
temporal changes in extreme precipitation in
the contiguous USA? International Journal of
Climatology 29:31–45.

Pryor SC, Kunkel KE, Schoof JT (2009c). Did
precipitation regimes change during the

twentieth century? In: Pryor SC (ed) Understanding climate change: Climate variability, predictability, and change in the midwestern United States. Bloomington: Indiana University Press, 100–112.

Pryor SC, Ledolter J (2010). Addendum to: Wind speed trends over the contiguous USA. Journal of Geophysical Research 115: D10103, doi:10.1029/2009JD013281.

Pryor SC, Takle GS (2009). Climate variability, predictability and change: An introduction. In: Pryor SC (ed) Understanding climate change: Climate variability, predictability and change in the midwestern United States. Bloomington: Indiana University Press, 1–18.

Rosenzweig C, Iglesias A, Yang XB, Epstein PR, Chivian E (2001). Climate change and extreme weather events: Implications for food production, plant diseases, and pests. Global Change and Human Health 2:90–104.

Rosenzweig C, Tubiello FN, Goldberg R, Mills E, Bloomfield J (2002). Increased crop damage in the US from excess precipitation under climate change. Global Environmental Change—Human and Policy Dimensions 12:197–202.

Russell AG, Brunekreef B (2009). A focus on particulate matter and health. Environmental Science & Technology 43:4620–4625.

Schoof JT (2009). Historical and projected changes in the length of the frost-free season. In: Pryor SC (ed) Understanding climate change: Climate variability, predictability, and change in the midwestern United States. Bloomington: Indiana University Press, 42–54.

Schoof JT, Pryor SC (2009). Teleconnection and circulation patterns in the Midwestern United States. In: Pryor SC (ed) Understanding climate change: Climate variability, predictability and change in the midwestern United States. Bloomington: Indiana University Press, 196–206.

Schoof JT, Pryor SC (2006). An evaluation of two GCMs: Simulation of North American teleconnection indices and synoptic phenomena. International Journal of Climatology 26:267–282.

Schoof JT, Pryor SC, Suprenant J (2010). Development of daily precipitation projections for the United States based on probabilistic downscaling. Journal of Geophysical Research 115: D13106, doi:10.1029/2009JD013030.

Schwartz MD, Ahas R, Aasa A (2006). Onset of spring starting earlier across the Northern Hemisphere. Global Change Biology 12:343–351.

Seinfeld J, Pandis S (1998). Atmospheric chemistry and physics: from air pollution to climate change, Wiley Interscience.

Semenza JC, McCullough JE, Flanders WD, McGeehin MA, Lumpkin JR (1999). Excess hospital admissions during the July 1995 heat wave in Chicago. American Journal of Preventive Medicine 16:269–277.

Semenza JC, Rubin CH, Falter KH, Selanikio JD, Flanders WD, Howe HL, Wilhelm JL (1996). Heat-related deaths during the July 1995 heat wave in Chicago. New England Journal of Medicine 335:84–90.

Sheridan S (2003). North American weather-type frequency and teleconnection indices. International Journal of Climatology 23:27–45.

Sims REH, Schock RN, Adegbululgbe A, Fenhann J, Konstantinaviciute I, Moomaw W, Nimir HB, Schlamadinger B, Torres-Martínez J, Turner C, Uchiyama Y, Vuori SJV, Wamukonya N, Zhang X (2007). Energy supply. In: Metz B, Davidson OR, Bosch PR, Dave R, Meyer LA (eds) Climate change 2007: Mitigation. Contribution of Working Group III to the Fourth Assessment Report of the Intergovernmental Panel on Climate Change. Cambridge, UK: Cambridge University Press, 251–322.

Smith P, Martino D, Cai Z, Gwary D, Janzen H, Kumar P, McCarl B, Ogle S, O'Mara F, Rice C, Scholes B, Sirotenko O (2007). Agriculture. In: Metz B, Davidson OR, Bosch PR, Dave R, Meyer LA (eds) Climate change 2007: Mitigation. Contribution of Working Group III to the Fourth Assessment Report of the Intergovernmental Panel on Climate Change. Cambridge, UK: Cambridge University Press.

Smoyer KE (1998). A comparative analysis of heat waves and associated mortality in St. Louis, Missouri—1980 and 1995. International Journal of Biometeorology 42:44–50.

Stern NH (2007). The economics of climate change. Cambridge, UK: Cambridge University Press.

Stott PA, Stone DA, Allen MR (2004). Human contribution to the European heatwave of 2003. Nature 432:610–614.

Tagaris E, Liao KJ, Delucia AJ, Deck L, Amar P, Russell AG (2009). Potential impact of climate change on air pollution-related human health effects. Environmental Science & Technology 43:4979–4988.

Tai APK, Mickley LJ, Jacob DJ (2010). Correlations between fine particulate matter (PM2.5). and meteorological variables in the United States: Implications for the sensitivity of PM2.5 to climate change. Atmospheric Environment 44:3976–3984.

Tebaldi C, Hayhoe K, Arblaster JM, Meehl GA (2006). Going to the extremes: An intercomparison of model-simulated historical and future changes in extreme events. Climatic Change 79:185–211.

Trenberth KE, Jones PD, Ambenje P, Bojariu R, Easterling D, Klein Tank A, Parker D, Rahimzadeh F, Renwick JA, Rusticucci M, Soden B, Zhai P (2007). Observations: Surface and Atmospheric Climate Change. In: Solomon S, Qin S, Manning M, Chen Z, Marquis M, Averyt KB, Tignor M, Miller HL (eds) Climate change 2007: The physical science basis. Contribution of Working Group I to the Fourth Assessment Report of the Intergovernmental Panel on Climate Change. Cambridge, UK: Cambridge University Press.

US Department of Transportation (2007). Freight performance measurement: Travel time in freight-significant corridors. Washington, DC: US Department of Transportation, Federal Highways Administration.

US Energy Information Administration (2010). International Energy Outlook 2010. Washington, DC: US Energy Information Administration, Office of Integrated Analysis and Forecasting, U.S. Department of Energy.

Van Dingenen R, Dentener FJ, Raes F, Krol MC, Emberson L, Cofala J (2009). The global impact of ozone on agricultural crop yields under current and future air quality legislation. Atmospheric Environment 43:604–618.

Van Klooster SL, Roebber PJ (2009). Surface-based convective potential in the contiguous United States in a business-as-usual future climate. Journal of Climate 22:3317–3330.

Vavrus S, Van Dorn J (2010). Projected future temperature and precipitation extremes in Chicago. Journal of Great Lakes Research 36:22–32.

Vavrus S, Walsh JE, Chapman WL, Portis D (2006). The behavior of extreme cold air outbreaks under greenhouse warming. International Journal of Climatology 26:1133–1147.

Vetter M, Churkina G, Jung M, Reichstein M, Zaehle S, Bondeau A, Chen Y, Ciais P, Feser F, Freibauer A, Geyer R, Jones C, Papale D, Tenhunen J, Tomelleri E, Trusilova K, Viovy N, Heimann M (2008). Analyzing the causes and spatial pattern of the European 2003 carbon flux anomaly using seven models. Biogeosciences 5:561–583.

Villarini G, Smith JA, Baeck ML, Vitolo R, Stephenson DB, Krajewski WF (2011). On the frequency of heavy rainfall for the Midwest of the United States. Journal of Hydrology 400:103–120.

Wall R, Rose H, Ellse L, Morgan E (2011). Livestock ectoparasites: Integrated management in a changing climate. Veterinary Parasitology 180:82–89.

Wang D, Cai X (2010). Comparative study of climate and human impacts on seasonal baseflow in urban and agricultural watersheds. Geophysical Research Letters 37:L06406, doi: 10.01029/02009GL041879.

Wang M, Saricks C, Wu M (1999). Fuel ethanol produced from Midwest US corn: Help or hindrance to the vision of Kyoto? Journal of the Air & Waste Management Association 49:756–772.

Warrick RA (1984). The possible impacts on wheat production of a recurrence of the 1930s drought in the United States Great Plains. Climatic Change 6:5–26.

Weisser D (2007). A guide to life-cycle greenhouse gas (GHG) emissions from electric supply technologies. Energy 32:1543–1559.

Whitman S, Good G, Donoghue ER, Benbow N, Shou WY, Mou SX (1997). Mortality in Chicago attributed to the July 1995 heat wave. American Journal of Public Health 87:1515–1518.

Yao H, Georgakakos A (2001). Assessment of Folsom Lake response to historical and potential future climate scenarios 2. Reservoir management. Journal of Hydrology 249:176–196.

Zanis P, Douvis C, Kapsomenakis I, Kioutsioukis I, Melas D, Pal J (2009). A sensitivity study of the Regional Climate Model (RegCM3). to the convective scheme with emphasis in central eastern and southeastern Europe. Theoretical and Applied Climatology 97:327–337.

Zhang JY, Wang WC, Wu LY (2009). Land-atmosphere coupling and diurnal temperature range over the contiguous United States. Geophysical Research Letters 36:L06706, doi: 10.01029/02009GL037505.

3. Vulnerability and Adaptability of Agricultural Systems in the Southeast United States to Climate Variability and Climate Change

K. T. INGRAM, J. W. JONES, J. J. O'BRIEN,
M. C. RONCOLI, C. FRAISSE, N. E. BREUER,
W. L. BARTELS, D. F. ZIERDEN, AND D. LETSON

Introduction

Climate change is a global phenomenon, but its impacts are not uniform across the globe. Thus, the impacts of climate change, as well as vulnerabilities and appropriate adaptation measures, must be addressed on a local or regional scale. Agricultural systems have great adaptive capacity but are highly sensitive to climate change. Prior research has suggested that climate change is more likely to adversely affect agriculture in the southern parts of the United States than in the north (Adams et al. 1999). Here, we focus on vulnerability and adaptation in the context of climate change over the southeast United States (SE), thus providing a counterpoint to the midwestern focus of this book and articulating some successful strategies that might be adopted within the Midwest.

In contrast to the Midwest, where agriculture is dominated by relatively few commodities (see chapter 2), agriculture in the SE states of Alabama, Georgia, Florida, and North and South Carolina is far more diverse. These five states have 41 million acres in agriculture with total sales in 2007 exceeding $31 billion (NASS 2007). Poultry and eggs represent the sector with highest income in all states except Florida, for which fruits and tree nuts have the highest economic impact. For all of the states, cattle and nursery commodities are among the top earners. Other important crops include cotton, peanuts, pecans, swine, tobacco, diverse fruits and vegetables, corn, soybeans, and sugarcane. In addition, the region has significant aquaculture and extensive managed forests, though the National Agricultural Statistics Reports do not include forests.

Application of climate information to the management of risk in agriculture is a complex undertaking. Herein we present a case study of activities of the Southeast Climate Consortium (SECC) that focus on quantifying and mitigating risk posed by climate change. Most examples are drawn from the agricultural sector, but the SECC is now applying these methods to other sectors. Thus, in this chapter we review research and extension programs that the SECC has conducted over the past decade—programs that have improved our understanding of the climate systems of the SE, identified climate information needs and interests of agricultural decision makers, and explored opportunities for managing climate risks at various time-scales.

Overview of the Southeast Climate Consortium

The mission of the SECC is to use advances in climate sciences, including improved capabilities to forecast seasonal and long-term climate change and to provide scientifically sound information and decision support tools for agricultural ecosystems, forests, and other terrestrial ecosystems and coastal ecosystems of the SE United States. As a multidisciplinary, multi-institutional team, the SECC conducts research and outreach to a broad community of users and forms partnerships with extension and education organizations to ensure that SECC products are relevant, reliable, and delivered to the public through these organizations through their networks and mechanisms.

In order to understand how the SECC reached its current status, it is important to understand its history. Late in 1996, a multidisciplinary team of scientists from Florida State University (FSU), University of Florida (UF), and University of Miami (UM) established the Florida Climate Consortium (FLC 2001). A central premise of the FLC was that climate forecasts alone would be of little utility to decision and

policy makers if they were not produced in the context of a broader information system. With funding from the National Oceanic and Atmospheric Administration (NOAA), the FLC conducted end-to-end research to develop and apply seasonal climate forecasts based on the El Niño Southern Oscillation (ENSO) phase to manage climate related risks to agriculture in Argentina. An end-to-end approach addresses the flow of work from development and analysis of information to its extension and application by information users, which in this case was the agricultural community of Argentina.

In 1998, the FLC shifted its focus towards the SE United States, initially targeting agriculture in the state of Florida, to capitalize on their earlier experience. When NOAA established the Regional Integrated Sciences and Assessments (RISA) program (McNie et al. 2007), the FLC became part of this program. Sociologists and anthropologists within the FLC conducted assessments that have greatly enhanced our understanding of the role of climate information in decision making and users' perception of climate. This research has helped researchers from all fields to understand the information needs and constraints of, and has helped to inform, decision makers.

As it became clear that the climate information needs in the region were far greater than what could be provided with NOAA RISA funding alone, the FLC sought additional funding. With additional funding beginning in 2002 from the partnership agreement with the USDA Risk Management Agency to develop a web-based decision support system that would help farmers and ranchers to manage climate-related risks, the FLC added the University of Georgia to its members and renamed itself the SECC. The USDA Cooperative State Research, Education, and Extension Services (CSREES) provided funding to the SECC through a federal administrative research grant, which allowed the SECC to add Auburn University and the University of Alabama–Huntsville in 2003, North Carolina State University in 2007, and Clemson University in 2008. The decision to include these additional universities in the SECC was based on the similarity of agricultural systems and a common, well-characterized ENSO signal. Both USDA RMA and CSREES (now NIFA) have continued to support SECC activities, and we have continued to diversify our support base by attracting competitive funding to address special needs. Members of the SECC include the land-grant universities of five member states as well as the state climatologists of all states except South Carolina, where the state climatologist is not associated with a university.

SECC research and extension activities focused mostly on the agricultural sector until 2004, when we started activities to develop climate information for water resource managers. Then, following the publication of the Stern Review (Stern 2006) and IPCC AR4 (IPCC 2007), demands for climate change information has grown rapidly. These demands have come not only from the agricultural sector, but also from local governments, public health agencies, environmental engineering firms, and others. A common challenge to meet-ing these requests is the need for reliable, probabilistic information at the local level regarding climate change.

An important factor contributing to SECC success in agriculture has been a strong partnership with Cooperative Extension Service, which provides a boundary organization to link research to users for broad applications. Much of the climate information that the SECC produces is based on integrated models and analyses that address the needs expressed by these stakeholders. Stakeholders need climate forecasts over multiple time scales and climate change scenarios that are specific to their local and regional enterprises. Using results of stakeholder assessments, multidisciplinary groups will develop climate forecasts and climate change scenarios downscaled to local scales for use in vulnerability assessments and adaptive management of water resources, coastal ecosystems, and agricultural systems. For example, based on information from growers and extension agents, SECC investigators recommended a delay of planting tomatoes during El Niño years to avoid probable crop injury (Messina et al. 2006). The SECC process of engaging stakeholders in the development of decision support systems is shown in Figure 3.1.

Attitudes, Concerns, and Interests of Farmers and Other Decision Makers

As implied above, the prime motivation for SECC programs derives from our understanding of end user needs, which we identify through social science assessments. Leiserowitz et al. (2008, 2010) identified

Table 3.1. Results of two surveys on public attitudes and perceptions of climate change. Data show the percentage of respondents in each of six categories. Source: Leiserowitz et al., 2010.

Year	Alarmed	Concerned	Cautious	Disengaged	Doubtful	Dismissive
2008	18	33	19	12	11	7
2010	10	29	27	6	13	16

six categories to describe the spectrum of public opinions on climate change (Table 3.1). About two-thirds of the public fall into one of the three categories—alarmed, concerned, and cautious—that indicate an acknowledgement that climate change is an issue, whereas about one-third fall into the three opinion categories that indicate climate change is not a significant concern—disengaged, doubtful, and dismissive. From 2008 to 2010, a period that coincided with a U.S. and global economic recession, there were significant changes in the numbers of people that have the most extreme opinions, with a 8-point drop in those who are alarmed and a 9-point increase in those who are dismissive. On the other hand, the general balance between the three groups who considered climate change a real risk and the three groups who did not remained nearly unchanged.

SECC assessments of farmers and extension agents in the SE indicate their opinions fall across the full spectrum expressed by the general public. However, there appears to be a larger proportion of farmers and extension agents in the SE that would fit into the three categories that do not consider climate change to be a significant risk than Leiserowitz (2010) found for the population at large. Farmers and extension agents in the SE that do not con-

sider climate change to be a significant risk will often say that they "do not believe in global warming," a statement that reflects the political, social, and environmental context for their opinions. To the extent possible, the SECC strives to provide information of value to decision makers across this entire spectrum of public opinion. We do not advocate for one side or the other in the climate change polemics but rather emphasize the importance of using the best information available to support decisions.

Climate variability over the SE is strongly linked to a number of climate "modes" that manifest through teleconnection for various climate indices, such as the El Niño Southern Oscillation (ENSO), North Atlantic Oscillation (NAO), and Multidecadal Atlantic Oscillation (MAO) (Katz et al. 2003). The ENSO phenomenon in particular exerts a strong influence on seasonal variability of climate parameters, vegetation indices (Peters et al. 2003), and crop yields (Hansen et al. 1998). During the past five years, farmers and extension agents have become more familiar with El Niño and its impact on seasonal climate in the SE (Breuer et al. 2010). Thus, when discussing climate information needs and interests with farmers, SECC researchers often open conversations with discussions of weather and seasonal climate. In general, farmers do not distinguish between weather and seasonal climate information. Rightly, they perceive climate and weather to be part of a continuum, and they want to receive weather and climate information in a seamless, unified format. All farmers express an interest in receiving seasonal climate outlooks and forecasts, yet it is difficult to ascertain how they incorporate this information into the complex of factors that they consider in their decisions. Farmers report that the following have the greatest influence their management decisions: (1) markets, in the form of prices for various commodities and inputs; (2) farm and energy policies, especially those in the farm bill (http://www.ers.usda.gov/FarmBill/); and (3) local infrastructure, such as access to cotton gins, packing and processing plants, and irrigation. Climate forecasts and outlooks become part of the information environment, but certainly not a dominant component. Another obstacle to the use of seasonal climate outlooks and forecasts is their probabilistic nature. While farmers generally understand probabilities and risks, they often want concrete advice. To meet this need, the SECC works in partnership with extension specialists to translate climate outlooks into agricultural outlooks that are posted regularly on *AgroClimate* (Fraisse et al. 2006), a web-based decision support system (e.g., http://agroclimate.org/forecasts/Agricultural_Outlook.php).

When we discuss historical climate with farmers, we often solicit their recollections of seasons with extreme conditions, whether extremely cold or hot,

wet or dry. Farmers rely heavily on their experience and have requested quantitative historical data, including those that assess historical crop productivity with climate. In response to such requests, we have developed a tool for *AgroClimate* that displays yields of different crops sorted by ENSO phase at a county level based on historical data (http://agroclimate.org/tools/countyYield/). Interestingly, when farmers view such historic data it often leads to discussions of climate change. They first use the data to explain historic observations—for example, a southward migration of citrus production in the SE that has been related to incidents of killing freezes (Winsberg et al. 2003). Similarly, many farmers report that they have delayed planting because spring temperatures have cooled. Note that these reports of historical climate and adaptations are related to cooling rather than warming, which will be further discussed in the following section on adaptation challenges in the SE.

Once farmers have started discussing historical climate changes, they often begin to question how climate will develop in the future. The time scales for climate that interest them most are as follows: (1) seasonal (up to 6 months), the period for which they would make crop management decisions such as crop and variety selection, crop insurance purchases, pasture stocking rates, and hay sales; (2) near-term (2 to 5 years), the period of information needed to inform decisions about equipment purchases or new annual crops, which often require new equipment; and (3) long-term (10 to 20 years), the period that concerns decisions about land and agribusiness investments, including orchard crops, construction of processing or packing plants.

Whether or not they "believe in global warming," farmers and extension agents often request information that is related to climate change. Examples include:

- Carbon footprint calculators. Strawberry farmers in Florida have expressed a desire to improve the energy efficiency of their production systems in order to increase profits and enhance marketability compared with competitors from other regions that would have greater carbon emissions related to transportation. Organic farmers in Georgia have requested a carbon footprint calculator so they can monitor their emissions and strive to be carbon negative—that is, to capture more carbon than they emit.

- Information on carbon markets. Both farmers and forest managers have expressed an interest in participating in carbon markets through selling carbon credits. Some farmers have stated that they do not agree that we should have policies that regulate carbon emissions, but if we do, then they want to be able to benefit through sequestering carbon and selling carbon credits.

- Biofuels. Many farmers are interested in production of biofuels, which represent a new market opportunity for them. In contrast to the Midwest (see chapter 2 of this volume), to date, there is only one operational corn ethanol plant in the SE, located in southern Georgia. Farmers in the area produced corn for the swine and poultry industries before the construction of the ethanol plant, so it has been relatively easy for them to increase (or recently

to decrease) corn production for the ethanol plant based on the prices offered. Farmers are also carefully watching the ongoing construction of a cellulosic ethanol plant in Florida and will undoubtedly consider providing feedstock for that plant.

Challenges to Climate Change Adaptation in the Southeast United States

Key issues in assessing climate risk and vulnerability in SE derive from:

(i) The key role of internal climate modes in dictating interannual variability.

(ii) The absence of warming tendencies in the historical record.

As described above, the climate of the SE is strongly influenced by ENSO phase, and thus ENSO phase is useful to predicting seasonal climate—especially during the fall and winter months. The SECC has been very successful in developing tools and information systems that extension agents, crop consultants, and farmers can use to manage risks related to seasonal climate variability. Through workshops and demonstrations, extension personnel have become well accustomed to using climate information to guide seasonal crop decisions (Breuer et al. 2010). Using a seasonal forecast to manage risks is a short-term form of adaptation upon which researchers, extension agents, and farmers can together build to address issues of longer-term adaptation (Fraisse et al. 2009).

Historical temperature trends in the SE show a distinct difference between rural and urban areas, indicating a key role of land use/land cover in influencing local climate. As one example of this, we contrast herein trends in data from an observing station in Fort Myers with analysis of data from within Arcadia. The Fort Myers station is near downtown, in the middle of an area that has undergone tremendous urban development over the past 40 years. Fort Myers is in Lee County, which has grown in population from 60 thousand to more than half a million over the past 40 years. By contrast, Arcadia is a small town less than 50 miles (75 km) north of Fort Myers that is surrounded by pastures, citrus orchards, pine groves, and wetlands. The station is located next to a water treatment plant in the city limits. With a population of about 10,000, Arcadia has grown little over the past 40 years. From 1925 through 2005, annual average maximum temperatures increased by about 1.5°F (0.8°C) in Fort Myers and decreased by about 1°F (0.6°C) in Arcadia (Figure 3.2). Trends similar to those from Fort Myers were observed for all urban climate stations in the database, and trends were also similar to Arcadia for all rural climate stations. Results are similar for the annual average minimum temperatures. Clearly, land use/land cover has a strong impact of on historical temperatures. The increases in temperatures in urban areas could be attributed to anthropogenic increases in atmospheric GHG, but they can also be attributed to the heat island effect of urban areas (Zhou and Shepherd 2010). The temperature decreases observed in rural areas may be explained by increases in irrigation (Kuep-

pers et al. 2007). On average, temperatures have changed little in the SE over the past century, which is in accord with conclusions presented in IPCC (2007), though it is clear that even within a region, climate changes are not uniform. Historical observations appear to align with conclusions from global circulation models (GCMs), most of which suggest that temperatures in the SE are likely to increase from 0°C to 2°C over the next century (IPCC 2007). This projected increase is far less than the current estimates of global warming by the year 2100, which forecast a rise in the global average temperature on the order of 2°C to 4°C (IPCC 2007). Historic observations of precipitation for the SE do not show significant trends. Similarly, projections from the suite of the GCMs used in the IPCC assessment do not indicate large precipitation changes in the SE, though they suggest that there may be changes in precipitation distribution such that their rain events are more intense, but less frequent, which would result in both more frequent floods and more frequent short-term agricultural droughts (IPCC 2007). Whether considering how vulnerable agriculture is to climate change or how agriculture might adapt to climate change, we first need to understand how climate is likely to change in a particular location, in this case the SE. The SECC is following four approaches to improving our understanding of how climate is likely to change in our region and how to respond to that change:

1) Statistical downscaling of climate model projections (Vrac et al. 2007).

2) Dynamical downscaling using a nested regional model (Lim et al. 2007).

3) Analysis and extrapolation of trends in historical data.

4) Development of scenarios for climate variables based on analog data (Zorita and von Storch 1999).

We are using data from methods 1, 2, and 4 to serve as inputs to crop simulation models from the Decision Support System for Agrotechnology Transfer (DSSAT) family (Jones et al. 2003) and in order to assess the vulnerability of agriculture in the SE and to evaluate alternative adaption options.

Overall, agricultural stakeholders in the SE express greatest concern about future changes in the frequency of extreme events, including tropical storms, freezes, heat waves, droughts, and floods. It is often very difficult to develop robust climate projections for such extreme events, and they are often beyond the scope of adaptation options. Modern agricultural systems have sufficient resilience to withstand occasional crop failures that arise from extreme events, but there is great uncertainty regarding whether they can withstand the increased frequency of crop failures that would result if extreme events become more common.

Adaptation Frameworks

Adaptation is an important complement to mitigation of anthropogenic climate change (Easterling et al. 2004). Adaptation to climate change is not synonymous with avoidance of all harm or loss. Moreover,

some systems and sectors are likely to benefit from climate change. The potential for adaptation to climate change depends on magnitudes of both average climate and climate extremes for a given location. Most importantly, proactive adaptation research can help inform decisions by farmers, agrobusiness, and policy makers with implications over a range of timescales (Adams 1999).

Howden et al. (2007) presented a framework for adaptation to climate change that suggests that as the magnitude of climate change increases, necessary adaptation will follow a progression from incremental changes in farm management, to system changes that might include diversification or changes in production chains, to transformative changes that would include changes in land use and new products. In general, incremental adaptation actions maintain the existing basic farming practices and build on existing technologies. Incremental adaption may be either reactive or proactive, but they are usually implemented at the local scale. In contrast, transformative adaptation involves major changes in agricultural enterprises, land use, and capital. To be successful, such adaption actions likely need to be proactive and strategic, and generally span spatial scales. In the SE, because climate changes are likely to be relatively small over the next 5 to 10 decades, it is likely that incremental adaptation actions will be sufficient—that is, as long as extreme events do not increase drastically. On the other hand, it is only a matter of time before transformative adaptations are necessary.

Vulnerability to climate change increases with potential exposure and decreases with adaptive capacity. While incremental adaptation allows maintenance of current agricultural systems, it has the potential of increasing future vulnerability to climate change because incremental adaptation reaches a threshold beyond which they do not provide additional adaptive capacity (Howden et al. 2007). Discrepancies between global causes and local impacts also affect vulnerability. For the SE, where temperature trends are likely to be of smaller magnitude than the global temperature increases, this discrepancy is likely to reduce vulnerability of agriculture in the SE, at least for several decades. On the other hand, the SE would have to adapt to changes in national agriculture policies independently of local and regional climate conditions.

As should be the emphasis in other regions, priorities for adaption in the SE are those that contribute to mitigation within a "no regrets" context. A "no regrets" action is one that should benefit agriculture today as well as decrease vulnerability to climate change. Examples would include management systems that reduce net greenhouse gas emissions, either through improved energy efficiency or enhanced carbon sequestration. If other factors are constant, many farmers have expressed an interest to implement energy efficiency measures based on the cost savings alone, and thus there are "no regrets" to such adaptations. While there are many examples of adaptations that would contribute to both adaptation and mitigation, they tend to have relatively small benefits to profit-

ability and may not be adopted unless the policy environment provides incentives (e.g., through opportunities to sell carbon credits or to derive economic benefits from ecosystem services).

In addition to pursuit of "no regrets" incremental adaptations, because the frequency and intensity of extreme events are likely to increase, research on adaptation for agricultural systems in the SE should begin to focus on transformative adaptation options as soon as possible. One example of a transformative system adaptation that has been suggested to improve resilience to a greater frequency of agricultural droughts (see Figure 2.16) is the construction and use of off-stream reservoirs, which are already being tested in Alabama (J. Christy, personal communication 2010). Such systems withdraw from streams during the fall and winter months, when streamflows in the SE are generally high, and store this water in reservoirs that farmers can use during spring and summer months to supplement rainfall and prevent crop injury from drought. Ultimately, the long-term sustainability of agriculture in the SE will depend on the development of a suit of such transformative adaptations that are appropriate for crops and locations within the region.

Concluding Remarks

In summary, the application of climate information to managing risk in agriculture is a complex undertaking that challenges the traditional roles of research and extension in land-grant institutions. Assessing the vulnerability of agriculture to climate change and identifying adaptation options is more challenging, as there is little information available on how climate is likely to change at local and regional spatial scales over the next 10 to 30 years, the timescale for which most agricultural stakeholders have expressed the greatest interest.

Since the late 1990s, the SECC has been working to develop information products and decision support tools to help agricultural decision makers better manage climate-related risks. First addressing climate risks arising from seasonal climate variability and more recently addressing risks associated with climate change at decadal timescales, we have found that the successful application of climate information to managing risks requires collaborative, multidisciplinary research that is integrated with extension and engages stakeholders throughout the research and development process. This participatory process of co-learning is necessarily iterative and evolutionary, with regular interactions among researchers, extension experts, and stakeholders, whereby each learns from the others as partners. Since 2004, the SECC has partnered with extension in the development of *AgroClimate*, an information delivery and decision support web site that focuses largely on managing seasonal climate variability. The SE has a particular advantage over most of the rest of the nation in that seasonal climate in the SE is strongly affected by the El Niño–Southern Oscillation (ENSO) phase. Thus there is direct evidence of the importance of climate variability and, by extension, of the risk posed by climate change. The SECC is undertaking an effort to provide information relevant to risk, vulnerability, and adaptation with a two-pronged approach:

1) Develop and vet local and regional climate change scenarios over the decadal timescales. Throughout the United States, there has been great interest in downscaling climate change projections from the Intergovernmental Panel on Climate Change (IPCC) . The SECC is working on three projects to develop and use downscaled scenarios as inputs to crop simulation models to assess climate change vulnerability and potential adaptation strategies. One project uses statistically downscaled data, one uses dynamically downscaled data, and the third uses historical analog data.

2) Engage stakeholders, including researchers, extension agents, and farmers, in the development and evaluation of new climate information and climate change scenarios. Stakeholder engagement uses a combination of working groups, telephone interviews, and focus groups to bring decision makers into the research enterprise.

REFERENCES

Adams, RM, Hurd BH, Reilly J (1999). Agriculture and global climate change. Arlington, VA: Pew Center on Global Climate Change.

Breuer NE, Fraisse CW, Cabrera VE (2010). The Cooperative Extension Service as a boundary organization for diffusion of climate forecasts: A 5-year study. Journal of Extension (on line) 48:4RIB7.

Easterling, WE, Hurd BH, Smith JB (2004). Coping with global climate change: the role of adaptation in the United States. Arlington, VA: Pew Center on Global Climate Change.

Fraisse CW, Breuer N, Bellow JG, Cabrera VE, Hatch U, Hoogenboom G, Ingram KT, Jones JW, O'Brien JJ, Paz J, Zierden D (2006). AgClimate: A climate forecast information system for agricultural risk management in the southeastern USA. Computers & Electronics in Agriculture 53:13–27.

Fraisse CW, Breuer NE, Zierden D, Ingram KT (2009). From climate variability to climate change: challenges and opportunities to extension. Journal of Extension (online), 47: Article 2FEA9.

Hansen JW, Hodges AW, Jones JW (1998). ENSO influences on agriculture in the southeastern United States. Journal of Climate 11:404–411.

Howden, SM, Soussana JF, Tubiello FN, Chhetri N, Dunlop M, Meinke H (2007). Adapting agriculture to climate change. Proceedings of the National Academy of Sciences of the United States of America 104:19691–19696.

IPCC (2007). Climate change 2007: The physical science basis. Contribution of Working Group I to the Fourth Assessment Report of the Intergovernmental Panel on Climate Change. Solomon S, Qin D, Manning M, Chen Z, Marquis M, Averyt KB, Tignor M, Miller HL (eds). Cambridge, UK: Cambridge University Press.

Jones, JW, Hoogenb G, Porter CH, Boote KJ, Batchelor WD, Hunt LA, Wilkens PW, Singh U, Gijsman AJ, Ritchie JT (2003). The DSSAT cropping system model. European Journal of Agrononmy 18,235–265.

Katz RW, Parlange MB, Tebaldi C (2003). Stochastic modeling of the effects of large-scale circulation on daily weather in the southeastern US. Climatic Change 60:189–216.

Kueppers, LM, Snyder MA, Sloan LC (2007). Irrigation cooling effect: regional climate forcings by land-use change. Geophysical Research Letters 34: L03703, doi: 10.1029/2006GL028679.

Leiserowitz, A, Maibach E, Roser-Renouf C (2008). Global warming's "six Americas." Fairfax, VA: Center for Climate Change Communication, George Mason University.

Leiserowitz, A (2010). The six Americas. Available from: http://environment.yale.edu/uploads/SixAmericasJan2010.pdf.

Lim, YK, Shin DW, Cocke S, LaRow T, Schoof J, O'Brien JJ, Chassignet E (2007). Dynamically and statistically downscaled seasonal simulations of maximum surface air temperature over the southeastern United States. Journal of Geophysical Research—Atmospheres 112:D24102, doi:10.1029/2007JD008764.

McNie, E, Pielke Jr. R, Sarewitz D (eds) (2007). Climate science policy: Lessons from the RISAs. Science Policy Assessments and Research on Climate—Reconciling Supply and Demand. Report from a workshop held August 15–17, 2005, in Honolulu, Hawaii. Available from: http://cstpr.colorado.edu/sparc/research/projects/risa/risa_workshop_report.pdf.

Messina CD, Letson D, Jones JW (2006). Tailoring management of tomato production to ENSO phase at different scales. Transactions of the ASABE 49:1993–2003.

National Agricultural Statistical Service (2007). Census of Agriculture. U.S. Department of Agriculture. Available from: http://www.agcensus.usda.gov/Publications/2007/index.asp.

Peters AJ, Ji L, Walter-Shea E (2003). Southeastern US vegetation response to ENSO events (1989–1999). Climatic Change 60:175–188.

Stern N (2006). Stern Review on the economics of climate change. Office of Climate Change. HM Treasury, UK.

Vrac M, Stein M, Hayhoe K (2007). Statistical downscaling of precipitation through non-homogeneous stochastic weather typing. Climate Research 34:169–184.

Winsberg MD, O'Brien JJ, Zierden DF, Griffin M (2003). Florida weather. Second edition. Gainesville: University Press of Florida.

Zhou Y, Shepherd JM (2010). Atlanta's urban heat island under extreme heat conditions and potential mitigation strategies. Natural Hazards 52:639–668.

Zorita E, von Storch H (1999). The analog method as a simple statistical downscaling technique: comparison with more complicated methods. Journal of Climate 12:2474–2489.

4. Uncertainty and Hysteresis in Adapting to Global Climate Change

J. ZHAO

Global climate change is one of the greatest environmental challenges facing our civilization, and despite efforts in mitigating emissions of greenhouse gases (GHGs), global temperature is likely to rise, possibly significantly (Bernstein et al. 2007, also chapter 1 of this volume). Recognizing this challenge, the global community is increasingly focused on adapting to climate change. These measures include research and development (R&D)—such as downscaling global circulation models (GCMs) to support development of local adaptation strategies—and international assistance and cooperation in adaptation. America's Climate Choices devoted an entire report to adaptation in the United States (National Research Council 2010), and the United Nations Climate Change Conference's (UNFCCC) sixteenth Conference of the Parties (COP) held in Cancun, Mexico, declared that "adaptation must be addressed with the same priority as mitigation" (COP-16 2010).

In this chapter, I define adaptation as a set of activities through which economic, technological, institutional, and demographic resources are reallocated on a large scale across economic sectors, geographical regions, and time periods in response to long-term significant environmental changes. It includes mitigation activities, technological and institutional innovation and adoption, and environmentally driven mass migration. As documented in Orlove (2005), human society has a long history of responding to major environmental shocks, including climate and weather variations. Prominent among the responses are technological and institutional innovations (e.g., the development and diffusion of irrigation technologies in response to droughts and the private-public partnerships in Colonial India in response to floods). However, if local responses fail to be adequate or effective, environmental changes can lead to mass migration and population decline (e.g., the rise and fall of Easter Islands) (Diamond 2005). Unlike the many environmental shocks that have occurred in history, global climate change is characterized by the unique combination of the following features:

59

- It occurs on a global scale, impacting every region of the world.
- While mitigation of climate change is a global common property problem (i.e., reduced atmospheric GHG concentrations will benefit a large portion of the global population), adaptation to climate change is largely local and benefits the locality itself.
- The entire adaptation process is characterized by large uncertainty, in the costs and benefits of various adaptation strategies, in the actions of other nations/regions when collective actions are needed, and in linking GHG emissions to the environmental impacts.
- Scientific research on climate change and adaptation strategies is significantly advanced relative to concrete government policies and mitigation/adaptation activities that have been adopted.

Since scientific research is largely leading policy development, there will be many opportunities to obtain new information and adjust policies and activities in response to the new information. Proactive instead of reactive policies could be developed in anticipation of future environmental consequences and provision of new information. Such proactive approaches to adaptation make it possible to adopt transformative strategies incorporating entirely new ways of thinking about human-nature interaction and of moving beyond incremental adaptations that operate under existing institutional paradigms.

Adaptation activities in response to large environmental changes share several features: high degrees of uncertainties in the associated costs and benefits, signifi-

cant sunk costs (i.e., costs that are hard to be recouped if the activities fail to generate the expected benefits), and the opportunities of learning about these uncertainties. Under these conditions, a rational decision maker has incentive to delay the adoption of adaptation activities until more information is gathered in order to avoid losses from incurring the sunk costs if the activities turn out to be ineffective. This kind of hysteresis is optimal when individual decisions have no externalities, but when information is shared and there is learning from others, the delay in adaptation is socially suboptimal (Zhao 2007).

In this chapter, I argue that the theoretical and practical paradigm of climate change adaptation has to fully account for the unique combinations of the uncertainties, learning, and transaction costs. I will present a real options framework based on these features, review applications of this framework to two important cases of adaptation, and, finally, discuss the lessons learned and the next steps. The cases include water market trading and farmers' decisions to grow dedicated energy crops in the upper Midwest region.

Theoretical Framework

Choosing an optimal adaptation strategy is similar to choosing optimal investment or policy in that there are costs and benefits associated with the choices. A standard economic approach in studying such choices is cost-benefit analysis (i.e., the chosen strategy should be "optimal" in that it maximizes the (expected) net benefit, or benefit net of costs) (Mishan and Quah 2007). In the United States, the National Environmental Policy Act (NEPA) was enacted with a goal of promoting "enhancement of the environment" (Bronstein et al. 2005, Caldwell 1999). It mandates cost-benefit analysis for federal government policies and programs, and major environment and resource projects, such as water projects, under the authorities of the Army Corps of Engineers or the Bureau of Reclamation have to pass the cost-benefit test. However, I assert that traditional cost-benefit analysis methods are not well equipped to handle new institutions, policies, rules, and technologies in climate change adaptation, as they do not adequately account for uncertainty, learning, and adjustment costs.

To illustrate the inadequacy of the traditional cost-benefit methods, consider a simple example of an investment project illustrated in Figure 4.1. The project incurs a onetime cost of $84 and in the first year generates an income of $10. Future returns are uncertain, depending on, say, a legislation currently being debated. Based on the current information, there is a 50 percent chance that the legislation will be favorable, in which case future returns will be $15 per year. There is also a 50 percent probability that the legislation will be unfavorable, in which case the future returns will be $5 per year. The discount rate applied to future revenues is 10 percent, and for simplicity, the decision maker is assumed to be risk neutral. It should be noted that the theoretical framework still applies when the decision maker is risk averse, by using risk-adjusted discount rates or working with concave utility functions.

Given the uncertainties, the future expected return is $15 × 0.5 + $5 × 0.5 = $10 per year, and the expected net present value of the project is $10 / 0.1 = $100. Thus, the net expected return is $100 − $84 = $16. Since the net expected return is positive, traditional cost-benefit analysis would indicate that the investment should be undertaken. That is, the project would pass the cost-benefit test.

Consider, however, postponing the investment decision for one year, by which time the outcome of the legislation will be known. If it turns out that the legislation is favorable, future returns will be $15 per year, and the net return of investment *from the perspective of the next year* would be $15 / 0.1 − $84 = $66. If the legislation turns out to be unfavorable, the annual return of $5 amounts to a net present value (in next year) of $50, which is lower than the cost of $84. In this case, the investment will not be undertaken, resulting in a net return of zero. Given the equal probabilities of the two cases, the *expected* return from the perspective of the next year is $66 × 0.5 + 0 × 0.5 = $33, and discounting this to the current period, the net expected return is $33 / 1.1 = $30. This is higher than the net return if the investment is undertaken now ($16), and the optimal decision is thus to wait until the next year when the outcomes of the legislation are known.

This simple example focuses solely on economic benefits but nevertheless illustrates deep insights about decision making under uncertainty, learning, and transaction costs. By waiting for one year, information obtained about the underlying uncertainty helps avoid a bad investment (when the legislation is unfavorable). The decision maker always has the *option* of investing in the project, but the return from *exercising* the option (i.e., from undertaking the investment) depends on the available information as well as future learning opportunities. The act of investing effectively "kills" the option, and doing so is desirable only when the return is sufficient to overcome not only the investment cost but also the option value.

There are several conditions required for the investment option to have positive value. First, there must be uncertainties about the net returns. Second, there must be future learning opportunities about the underlying uncertainties. It is obvious in our example that if there are no uncertainties or learning (i.e., if nothing can be learned about the legislation in future years, waiting has no value—it can only reduce the net return of the project). Third, the investment needs to be *irreversible*, or reversing the investment needs to be costly. Otherwise, if the project can be freely reversed (e.g., the cost of $84 can be completely recouped after the investment takes place), the decision maker should invest now and de-invest if the legislation turns out to be unfavorable. Although the example assumes absolute irreversibility, the results still hold when the investment decisions can be reversed but at a cost (e.g., the equipment can be resold at scrap value that is much lower than the original investment cost).

When these factors are present, a decision maker has an incentive to delay the investment decision until more favorable conditions arise. This kind of hysteresis has been found in many real-world situations. Many profitable technologies are not adopted or are diffused slowly because of uncertainty and sunk costs (Sunding and Zilberman 2001). The incentive to gather information in this case plays an important role; Besley and Case (1993) found that farmers have the incentive to gather information from other adopters (by waiting for the latter to adopt first) when uncertainties are present. Zhao (2007) showed that the incentive to delay and learn can lead to the S-shaped diffusion curve observed for many technologies.

To overcome the hysteresis, a sufficient amount of information needs to be gathered or provided, or an extreme event is needed to trigger investment. For instance, large-scale adoption of irrigation technologies usually happens after severe droughts (Sunding and Zilberman 2001). Safety measures (e.g., traffic lights) are undertaken after accidents occur (Birkland 1998). Government policies respond more readily to large-scale disasters (e.g., homeland security measures after terrorist attacks).

These observations of hysteresis are relevant for designing institutions that facilitate adaptation to climate change since, as argued above, adaptation decisions are characterized by uncertainty, learning, and adjustment costs. The real options framework provides an extremely useful paradigm in thinking about adaptation choices. Below I discuss two examples to illustrate how the real options framework can be used to facilitate institutional support for adaptation decisions.

Water Market Trading: Role of Flexible Mechanisms

The ability of modern agriculture to adapt to higher temperatures, especially extreme temperatures, depends critically on the availability of water, either naturally supplied or through irrigation (Schlenker et al. 2007). However, in 1995, nearly 1,400 million people lived in water-stressed watersheds, and climate change may cause increases in water resource stresses. For example, the Colorado River has the most complete allocation of resources in the United States and is heavily regulated (Christensen et al. 2004). Water apportionment rights were allocated after a period of abnormally high flows and thus water resources are over-allocated. Climate change projections for the Colorado River basin are indicative of reduced flow and thus further exacerbation of the demand to supply deficit (Christensen et al. 2004).

Historical water use governance structures have led to inefficient water allocations to its various uses. For instance, prior appropriation water rights in the western United States have restricted the allocation of water to its highest marginal uses. As a response, water markets have been adopted, but with varying degrees of success (Chong and Sunding 2006). When trading involves the selling of entire water rights, there have been fewer trades than expected. Subsequently, flexible leasing schemes have been designed to reduce the hysteresis involved and promote smooth trading. Such schemes include, for instance, callable water use options that allow buyers (e.g., cities) to lease water from sellers (farmers) under certain drought conditions, and water leasebacks in which farmers can lease the sold water back under certain conditions (Chong and Sunding 2006).

Prior work on commitment costs (Zhao and Kling 2001, Zhao and Kling 2004, Carrigan et al. 2008, Kling et al. 2012) explains why flexible trading mechanisms perform better than trading of entire water rights. Consider the decision of a farmer to sell their water rights without any buyback options, two perspectives of which appear below:

- The farmers' perspective. Although the selling price is certain, the foregone future agricultural output and thus profit are uncertain due to yield and agricultural price shocks. Thus, there is uncertainty about the net benefit from selling their water rights. Given that the water trade is irrevocable, the farmers have an incentive to gather more information about future yield and prices, as argued by the real option theory. However, if the farmers are asked to trade *now* based on the current information, they forego the opportunity to obtain more information in the future. They would agree to trade *now* if, *and only if*, the selling price is high enough to compensate them not only for the expected lost profits, but also the lost option value from gathering more information to make a more informed trade. That is, the asking price will be higher than the farmers' true willingness to sell, and the difference between the two values is the commitment cost.

- The buyers' perspective. The buyers of water rights face the risk that the purchased water is less valuable under certain conditions. Since the trade is irrevocable, the buyers' bid (the price at which they are willing to purchase the water right) is less than their willingness to pay for the water right, since by purchasing the water right now, the buyers forego the opportunity to gain more information and thus the associated option value. That is, there is a commitment cost on the buyer side as well, and this commitment cost reduces the bid of the buyers. Such commitment costs can be significant, accounting for 25–57 percent of the bid prices in an application evaluating the willingness to pay for improved water quality (Carrigan et al. 2008).

The two commitment costs imply that even when the intrinsic values of the buyer and the seller are such that there should be trade, water trading might not occur. That is, even if the buyer's willingness to pay exceeds the seller's willingness to sell, the buyer's bid, which equals their willingness to pay *minus* their commitment cost, might be lower than the seller's ask price, which equals their willingness to sell *plus* the seller's commitment cost. The rigidity of trading entire water rights without any flexible buyback options can preclude welfare-improving trading that would otherwise take place.

Thus, the reason that the flexible mechanisms (leasing and buyback options) promote water trading is that they reduce the adjustment costs involved in the trading decisions. Without uncertainty, such reductions in adjustment costs would not have affected water trading at all. I assert that it is the existence of uncertainty and future information that makes the flexible mechanisms particularly useful. In a similar fashion, the real options

and commitment cost theories would predict that information provision about future prices and outputs will facilitate trading as well, especially if the information is provided during early stages of the negotiation process. Greater initial information reduces the value of gaining more information and thus reduces the option value of waiting for future information.

This illustrative example points to some important lessons in designing institutions that promote adaptation to climate change:

- Lower levels of commitment by decision makers will promote adaptation. Reduced commitment can be achieved by flexible institutions that reduce the transaction costs (e.g., sunk costs or adjustment costs) or that make the adaptation actions more reversible in response to new information.

- Information is critical at early stages of decision making. This observation calls for the involvement of stakeholder groups in early stages of scientific discovery, so that useful information can be generated early to assist adaptation decisions.

- If new technologies are invented for adaptation, technologies that do not involve significant front sunk costs are more likely to be adopted than expensive technologies involving high sunk costs. Stakeholder input in scientific research will help researchers identify technologies that are more amenable to adoption and diffusion.

Dedicated Energy Crops: Unintended Consequences of Policies

The next example shows how well-intended policies that encourage climate change adaptation and mitigation might have unintended consequences when uncertainty and adjustment costs are important. The policies considered are designed in part to achieve climate change mitigation and specifically the reduction of GHG emissions—development of biofuels. In the United States and European Union, government policies exist that subsidize the development of renewable energies including dedicated energy crops as a climate change mitigation measure (see chapter 2 of this volume) and for energy security purposes (Rajagopal and Zilberman 2007, Burer and Wustenhagen 2009). For instance, in the United States, federal and state governments provide subsidies of up to 75 percent of the establishment costs of energy crops and provide tax exemptions for biofuels (Feng et al. 2010). The mechanism seems intuitive and straightforward: the subsidies should encourage more land to be converted to energy crops. But is this true when farmers face adjustment costs in converting? Assuming that economic strategies are pursued as mechanisms to promote ethanol production, which form of subsidies will work the best?

Using data from the United States, in the following we examine questions regarding a range of government subsidy policies on the decision of a representative farmer in the Midwest (Illinois, Indiana, Iowa, Michigan, Minnesota, Missouri, Ohio, and Wisconsin) to convert land in corn-soybean (the dominant crops in the Midwest—see chapter 2 of this volume) to switchgrass (Feng et al. 2010, Feng et al. 2011). The corn-soybean return is char-acterized by two stochastic processes, geometric Brownian motion and mean-reverting processes, and historical return data from the USDA are used to estimate the parameters of the corn-soybean processes. The return of switchgrass is constructed using ethanol price data and estimated switchgrass yields.

A farmer can convert their land from corn-soybean to switchgrass at a cost that is sunk (e.g., costs of planting switchgrass and obtaining necessary farm equipment). For simplicity, we do not distinguish between the two costs, thus implicitly assuming that the equipment can still be used if the land is converted into switch-grass again in the future. Converting from switchgrass to corn-soybean is also costly. Given uncertainties in both corn-soybean and switchgrass returns, the farmer will convert out of corn-soybean only if the switchgrass return is *much higher* than the corn-soybean return, after accounting for the conversion costs. Similarly, to convert from switchgrass to corn-soybean, the return from corn-soybean needs to be much higher than that of switchgrass. In principle, the farmer can convert between the two land uses multiple times, depending on the observed returns. Thus, the option value associated with converting from corn-soybean to switchgrass depends on the option value of converting from switchgrass to corn-soybean and vice versa: the farmer knows that if they convert to switchgrass, the future benefits depend not only on the switchgrass return, but also on the corn-soybean return since they have the option of converting the land back to corn and/or soybean.

Figure 4.2 shows an example of a land conversion decision under this setup. The two lines represent the "conversion boundaries": the upper line indicates that for a corn-soybean grower to convert to switchgrass, the required return from switchgrass more than doubles that of corn-soybean. Similarly, the lower line represents the conversion boundary to corn-soybean: the required corn-soybean return almost doubles that of switchgrass in order for the farmer to make the conversion.

I consider four subsidy policies: constant subsidy that pays switchgrass growers a fixed amount of money each year; variable subsidy that pays switchgrass growers at a rate proportional to their switchgrass returns, akin to a tax exemption policy; insurance against switchgrass returns falling below a certain threshold level; and cost sharing for establishing switchgrass. The four subsidy levels are calibrated so that they have the same expected government expenditure under net present value rules. That is, if the farmer makes their land use decision based on the traditional cost-benefit approach, the four policies are equivalent: they raise the acreage in switchgrass by the same amount. However, once hysteresis is taken into consideration, the four policies perform differently. Figure 4.3 shows the proportion of land in switchgrass over a period of 30 years under the four subsidy policies and the case of no subsidy (solid line). In this example, from the perspective of encouraging switchgrass acreage, insurance subsidy performs the best and variable subsidy is the least effective. Cost

sharing is almost as ineffective as variable subsidy.

To understand the inferences that may be drawn from this scenario example, consider the case of the cost-sharing subsidy. Although the subsidy makes it easier to convert into switchgrass, it also reduces the *degree of irreversibility* of converting out of switchgrass. In particular, a farmer is more willing to convert out of switchgrass since the subsidy makes it easier to revert their decision (i.e., converting back into switchgrass) when appropriate market conditions arise. The two incentives work in opposite directions and in this case almost cancel each other out by year 30. The results are particularly striking in that the four policies are equally costly (in expected terms) to the government.

Unlike the case of water markets, reducing the transaction cost does not effectively promote adaptation in the case of land use choices. Instead, insurance that reduces the downside risks is much more effective. Careful design of institutions is thus case specific, and the real options framework provides a useful approach to finding the effective institutions for specific cases.

Concluding Remarks

Traditional institutional design approaches developed for static decisions will not necessarily work when the decisions are dynamic and when uncertainties and adjustment costs are present. Hysteresis is a rational response of decision makers to uncertainties and adjustment costs. To promote adaptation to global climate change, institutions should be designed to ameliorate factors that increase the degree of hysteresis. Such institutions should emphasize flexibility, initial information provision, reduction of transaction costs, and, in certain cases, insurance coverage of downside risks.

Implementing the real options framework requires data that go beyond static cost-benefit analysis. In addition to the basic cost and benefit values, the framework needs data characterizing uncertainties and learning. Typically long time series data of relevant variables (e.g., returns of corn-soybean) are used to estimate uncertainties, and continuous learning can be estimated using time series data of decisions made (e.g., past land use choices). Discrete learning from extreme events is harder to estimate (e.g., information gained from extreme weather events). Econometric estimations such as those described herein do not always work in this case, and calibration of key parameters might be necessary.

The real options framework calls for more organic linkages of behavioral models with physical process models in studying adaptation to climate change. Key uncertainties in adaptation arise from those associated with; future emission scenarios, the causality from GHG emissions to future climate, and the effects of climate change on agriculture and other sectors of the global economy. For real options models to formally incorporate these uncertainties, probability estimates of the uncertainties are needed from physical process models. Institutional design for adaptation calls for modeling approaches that truly couple behavioral models with physical process models.

REFERENCES

Bernstein L, Bosch P, Canziani O, Chen Z, Christ R, Davidson O, Hare W, Huq S, Karoly D, Kattsov V, Kundzewicz K, Liu J, Lohmann U, Manning M, Matsuno T, Menne B, Metz B, Mirza M, Nicholls N, Nurse L, Pachauri R, J. P, Parry M, Qin D, Ravindranath N, Reisinger A, Ren J, Riahi R, Rosenzweig C, Rusticucci M, Schneider S, Sokona Y, Solomon S, Stott P, Stouffer R, Sugiyama T, Swart R, Tirpak D, Vogel C, Yohe G (2007). Climate change 2007: Synthesis report summary for policymakers. Cambridge, UK: Cambridge University Press.

Besley T, Case A (1993). Modeling technology adoption in developing countries, American Economic Review 83:396–402.

Birkland TA (1998). Focusing events, mobilization and agenda setting. Journal of Public Policy 18:53–74.

Bronstein DA, Baer D, Bryan H, DiMento JF, Narayan S (2005). National environmental policy act at 35. Science 307:674–675.

Burer MJ, Wustenhagen R (2009). Which renewable energy policy is a venture capitalist's best friend? Empirical evidence from a survey of international cleantech investors. Energy Policy 37:4997–5006.

Caldwell LK (1999). The National Environmental Policy Act: An agenda for the future. Bloomington: Indiana University Press.

Carrigan, J, Kling C, Zhao J (2008). Willingness to pay and the cost of commitment: An empirical specification and test. Environmental and Resource Economics 40:285–298..

Chong H and Sunding D (2006). Water markets and trading. Annual Review of Environment and Resources 31:11.1–11.26.

Christensen NS, Wood AW, Voisin N, Lettenmaier DP, Palmer RN (2004). The effects of climate change on the hydrology and water resources of the Colorado River basin. Climatic Change 62:337–363.

COP-16 (2010). Outcome of the work of the Ad Hoc Working Group on long-term cooperative action under the convention. United Nations Framework Convention on Climate Change. Available at http://unfccc.int/resource/docs/2010/cop16/eng/07a01.pdf#page=2.

Diamond JM (2005). Collapse: How societies choose to fail or survive. New York: Penguin.

Feng S, Zhao J, Swinton S (2010). Alternative land use policies: real options with costly reversibility. Working paper, Michigan State University.

Feng S, Zhao J, Swinton S (2011). Switching to perennial energy crops under uncertainty and costly irreversibility. American Journal of Agricultural Economics 93:768–783.

Kling C, List J, Zhao J (2012). A dynamic explanation of the willingness to pay and willingness to accept disparity. Economic Inquiry (in press) doi:10.1111/j.1465-7295.2011.00368.x.

Mishan EJ, Quah E (2007). Cost-benefit analysis. Fifth edition. New York: Routledge.

National Research Council (2010). Adapting to the impacts of climate change. Washington, DC: National Academies Press.

Orlove B (2005). Human adaptation to climate change: a review of three historical cases and some general perspectives. Environmental Science & Policy 8:589–600.

Rajagopal D, Zilberman D (2007). Review of environmental, economic, and policy aspects of biofuels. World Bank Policy Research, working paper WPS4341. Available from; http://econ.worldbank.org.

Schlenker W, Hanemann WM, Fisher AC (2007). Water availability, degree days, and the potential impact of climate change on irrigated agriculture in California. Climatic Change 81:19–38.

Sunding D, Zilberman D (2001). The agricultural innovation process: research and technology adoption in a changing agricultural sector. Handbook of Agricultural Economics, Vol 1A: Agricultural Production. Oxford, UK: Elsevier.

Zhao J (2007). The role of information in technology adoption under poverty. In: Nissanke and Thorbecke (ed) The impact of globalization on the world's poor. Basingstoke, UK: Palgrave Macmillan.

Zhao J, Kling C (2004). Willingness-to-pay, compensating variation, and the cost of commitment. Economic Inquiry 42:503–517.

Zhao J, Kling C (2001). A new explanation for the WTP/WTA disparity. Economics Letters 73:293–300.

5. Climate-Agriculture Vulnerability Assessment for the Midwestern United States

D. NIYOGI AND V. MISHRA

Introduction

The Midwest is a breadbasket for the United States and one of the major contributors of corn and soybean production globally. Current corn yields in the Midwest are around 150 bushels per acre with a total production of about 10 billion bushels, while soybean yields in the Midwest are 45 bushels per acre with production of about 3 billion bushels. Agriculture is a major enterprise requiring investments in terms of water, landscape, energy, and human/economic resources. Projected climate and land use changes can affect the dynamics and availability of soil, water, and land resources leading to food insecurity (Lobell et al. 2008). Thus the water and land required for agricultural production are vital components of the natural resources of the Midwest. Agricultural land comprises 89 percent of the land use in the Midwest, and as documented in chapter 2 of this volume, agriculture continues to play a major role in the economy of the region.

Agriculture is both a source and sink of greenhouse gas (GHG) emissions. Photosynthesis is a significant seasonal sink, while the emissions from the soil surfaces for nitrous oxide and other gases from animal waste and fertilizers are a source term. Agriculture accounted for about 17 percent of the global GHG emissions and 7 percent of the emissions across the United States (Pryor and Takle 2009). Additionally, as documented in several chapters to follow, the agricultural sector is perhaps uniquely sensitive to climate variability and change.

The historical observations and model-based projections indicate a tendency towards higher atmospheric carbon dioxide (CO_2) concentrations with every passing decade accompanied by higher global temperatures (though regional manifestations may include cooling (e.g., Pan et al. 2009)). Analyses deriving from the Intergovernmental Panel on Climate Change (IPCC) Fourth Assessment Report (AR4) multimodel ensembles indicate a possibility of 1°C to 3°C warming in the midwestern United States in coming decades (see chapter 2 of this volume). Changes in future precipitation are somewhat uncertain; however, more intense rainfall or wetter conditions accompanying warming is expected (O'Gorman and Schneider 2009, Schoof et al. 2010). Specific to the Midwest, changes in rainfall patterns are much more variable from the models with higher rainfall potential by about 20–30 percent in spring and winter, and significant variability in the summer and fall (Charusombat and Niyogi 2011). While precipitation projections vary between the models and are likely to be refined greatly with more local-scale information and processes, the results continue to suggest that local and regional changes to the weather and hydroclimate within the Midwest are probable (Maraun et al. 2010; Hossain et al. 2011; Niyogi et al. 2011b), and such changes may have important implications for shifts in ecosystems and agricultural productivity.

An overview of key components of adaptation measures and vulnerabilities associated with agricultural production in the midwestern United States is given in Figure 5.1. These vulnerabilities and adaptation options are discussed in more detail herein.

Changes in climate that can affect the agricultural enterprise include the increasing likelihood of warmer nights and possibly days; more intense, frequent, and long-lasting heat waves; higher potential for heavier-than-normal precipitation; disproportionate increase in areas experiencing droughts or dry conditions (see chapter 2 and Charusombat and Niyogi 2011) with a shift in the rainfall patterns; and a likelihood for poor air quality and ozone stress (Leung and Gustafson Jr. 2005). As a result of these changes,

synthesis studies suggest that crop productivity can in fact show an increase for initial warming and further warming (approximately 4°C in most circumstances) would likely lead to a reduction in the yields (Schlenker and Roberts 2009). The hydrological impacts appear to be visible with temperature changes with a modification of the hydrological cycle involving changes in the snowpack for 1°C to 2°C changes and much more vigorous evaporation/transpiration feedback leading to potential reduction in the water availability in the crop growing regions.

Climate Change and Agricultural Futures in the Midwest

To assess the relationship between climatic changes and the Midwest agriculture, we evaluated historic climate variability and its impacts on corn and soybean yields for the U.S. Corn Belt. The study domain is defined by identifying states with the highest production of corn and soybean based on the National Agricultural Statistics Service (NASS 2009, crop yield and plantation data) data. This resulted in the selection of 13 states: Illinois, Indiana, Iowa, Kansas, Kentucky, Michigan, Minnesota, Missouri, Nebraska, North Dakota, Ohio, South Dakota, and Wisconsin (Figure 5.2a), and thus includes part of the Central Plains. Daily climate data including maximum and minimum temperature and precipitation were obtained from the National Climatic Data Center (NCDC) for 1920–2009. The daily station data for the climate variables were then gridded (⅛-degree spatial resolution) to remove spatial and temporal inconsistencies following the method described in Hamlet and Lettenmaier (2005). Figure 5.2 shows the time series of corn and soybean yields from the Midwest over the 20th century along with corresponding time series of growing season rainfall and temperature. These observations indicate that during the grain-filling season, wetter and cooler climate favors crop growth, while during the planting season, higher temperatures with less moisture support better yields (Mishra and Cherkauer 2010).

We selected the standardized precipitation index (SPI) (McKee et al. 1993) and the standardized precipitation evapotranspiration index (SPEI) (Vicente-Serrano et al. 2010) to further quantify differences in precipitation and air temperature that might have an effect on crop productivity. These metrics were examined in three agronomically important periods corresponding to field preparation and planting (April–May, planting), reproductive and grain filling (June–August, grain filling), and maturity and harvesting (September–October, harvesting). While SPI can represent meteorological drought or precipitation deficit, the SPEI also accounts for the combined impact of temperature and precipitation by estimating changes to potential evapotranspiration during drought and is expected to be important for the agricultural regions. We calculated SPI and SPEI annually from 1920–2009 for each of the different crop stage periods using a 2-month SPI/SPEI at the end of May to identify drought state during planting. This was followed by analysis of a 3-month SPI/SPEI at the end of August for the

grain filling period, and a 2-month SPI/SPEI to evaluate drought conditions during harvesting. Severe (SPI −1.3 to −1.5), extreme (SPI −1.6 to −1.9), and exceptional droughts (SPI <−2.0) can hamper the crop growth and yields (Svoboda et al. 2002). To understand the impacts of spatial precipitation change and droughts, annual areal extent of severe or higher category droughts were estimated for the period of 1920–2009. To understand the impacts of extreme warm temperature, we calculated a Cumulative Heat Index (CUM_HEAT) for each of the selected periods during the crop-growing season. CUM_HEAT represents the cumulative temperature when daily maximum temperature exceeds the 90th percentile of the reference temperature (1961–1990).

The co-variability of crop yields and climate indices was evaluated using the Spearman rank correlation for the period of 1980–2009 (Figure 5.3). For this analysis, both severity and area of drought and temperature extremes were evaluated. Results indicate that relatively drier (based on negative SPI/SPEI) climate conditions during the field preparation and planting period favors corn and soybean yields in the region. All three climatic indices related to temperature (mean maximum temperature, TMAX; mean minimum temperature, TMIN; and the cumulative heat index, CUM_HEAT) were positively correlated with crop yields during the planting season suggesting that higher temperatures during this period enhance crop growth (Figure 5.3a,d). Areal extents of precipitation indices (SPI_A and SPEI_A) and the cumulative heat index

(CUM_HEAT_A) during the planting period are also positively correlated with the corn and soybean yields. The reproductive and grain filling period was found to be important for determining corn and soybean yields and also the most vulnerable to climatic variability. Interestingly, while relatively drier and warmer climate conditions during the planting season favored crop yields (Figure 5a,d), wetter and cooler climate conditions were associated with increased crop yields during the grain filling period (Figure 5.3b,e).

Smaller (in areal extent) and less severe droughts or the absence of drought conditions were all associated with higher crop yields. Elevated air temperatures with high cumulative heat stress also affected the corn and soybean yields adversely during June–August. The effect was even stronger as the areal extent of heat stress increased, reducing crop yields further. Results showed that climate anomalies related to precipitation and temperature extremes are more influential on crop yields during the planting and grain filling seasons (Figure 5.3a,b,d,e); however, variability in minimum air temperature during the maturity and harvesting season is an important source of temperature induced vulnerability. Higher minimum temperatures during the harvest season were associated with increased corn and soybean yields (Figure 5.3c,f).

Trends in the regional rainfall normalized as standardized precipitation, precipitation/evaporation indices (SPI and SPEI), and temperature variables are shown in Figure 5.4. These trends were derived using a Mann Kendall trend analysis on data from the period of 1920–2009. The results indicate that the region has been trending towards having a significant wet (SPI, 0.03/decade), cool (TMAX, −0.07°C/decade), and less heat stress (CUM_HEAT, −1.1°C/decade) during the planting and reproductive crop period (JJA).

TEMPERATURE CHANGES

For the midwestern United States during the 1980–2007 period, cereal crop yields are positively correlated with daytime temperatures during the reproductive growth phase (Mishra and Cherkauer 2010). However, the question may be posed—could increased warming (as is projected for the coming decades) lead to supra-optimal photosynthesis rates that can reduce yields? Recently, Ainsworth and Ort (2010) suggest that the temperature-yield relations under the suboptimal temperature ranges may not transfer to supra-optimal temperatures. That study highlights that limitations in photosynthesis due to warming would likely reduce yields, and this will be through complex interactive feedbacks of pollen productivity, shorter growth spans, reproductive phases, and faster growth, ultimately resulting in a shorter grain fill duration which will negatively impact productivity. For example, Lawlor and Mitchell (2000) showed that a 1°C warming can reduce reproduction phase and grain filling duration by about 5 percent and proportionally decrease the yield. Further changes in the temperature stress can affect pollen-pistil interaction, fertility, graining, female gametogenesis, and possible genetic alterations that can propagate to future generations (Ainsworth and Ort 2010). Thus, the timing of the temperature stress is an important vulnerability component for the Midwest agricultural stress.

CHANGES IN GROWING SEASONS AND SHIFTS IN RAINFALL

Analyses of historical data indicate a regional tendency towards a longer frost-free period (Schoof 2009), consistent with analysis conducted by Kunkel et al. (2004) for the entire United States. The study by Kunkel et al. (2004) suggested that the nighttime temperatures may be increasing more rapidly than the daytime and contributing to this trend. While there is interannual variability, the first frost date is typically occurring later in the winter and last frost date is occurring earlier in the spring, leading to an overall longer frost-free period (Sinha et al. 2010). There is also evidence for a continuation of this tendency under climate change projections, with increased duration of the frost-free season of about two weeks by the middle of the current century relative to 1961–2000 (Schoof 2009). The impact of such a change on the planting dates is still unknown. However, there is some anecdotal evidence based on discussions with farmers and regional extension educators of earlier planting dates in the region as compared to previous decades which may be in response to the farmers' perception that recent weather is conducive to planting generally earlier in the season and thus leads to higher yields. While there is a perception that the earlier

planting date may contribute to a higher yield potential, this earlier planting is also leading to a late-season frost vulnerability among the younger crops (Gu et al. 2008).

Observed and projected shifts in the rainfall patterns and seasonality over the midwestern United States (Pryor and Schoof 2008) may also have significant impacts on agricultural productivity. The precipitation changes, discussed earlier using SPI- and SPEI-based analyses, highlights the vulnerabilities due to the extremes—heavy precipitation and flooding losses and losses due to droughts. Rosenzweig et al. (2002) analyzed the impact of these rainfall shifts on the corn production with regards to crop growth, soil moisture availability, and the potential for yield loss or crop damage. They concluded that the current crop loss due to heavy precipitation and related events is around 3 percent for maize (corn) and much higher ($\sim$ 24 percent) for other horticultural crops. The main vulnerability is not expected to be the heavy rains themselves but a result of the impacts such as excess soil moisture and the higher runoff that can affect soils. As a result, they conclude that the heavy rains based loss on the U.S. corn production could double in the next thirty years, causing damage worth $3 billion per year.

Interestingly, the causes for such rainfall changes over the Midwest seem to be more dominantly manifested by local and regional forcings (Shaw et al. 2011). Land use change including agricultural intensification and urbanization and regional aerosol loading in the Midwest may be one factor causing this intensification and the regional vulnerability to extreme precipitation events (Pielke et al. 2007a, b; Niyogi et al. 2011b).

Most of the agriculture in the Midwest is rain-fed, with about 10–15 percent of the agricultural land being irrigated in the eastern United States (see chapter 2 of this volume). However, with the shifts in the precipitation regimes, there is a possibility that more acreage may need to be irrigation-ready to reduce its vulnerability to the rainfall vagaries (Rosenzweig et al. 2004).

COMBINED INFLUENCE OF SHIFTS IN THERMAL AND HYDROLOGIC REGIMES

The interaction of changes in thermal and hydrological regimes (e.g., wet and warmer conditions versus wet and colder temperatures) and the differential vulnerability of non-irrigated versus irrigated crops can each contribute to a different vulnerability in terms of the spatial expression of potential crop yield changes in the Midwest. While multiscenario-based vulnerability assessment studies have not been reported specifically for the Midwest, the U.S. Climate Change Science Plan (CCSP) summarizes some findings that are relevant for Midwest (Hatfield et al. 2008). The CCSP summary findings suggest that soybean yield is sensitive to the mean temperature during the post-anthesis phase. For the upper Midwest, where mean soybean growing season temperatures are about 22.5°C, soybean yield may increase by 2.5 percent with a 1.2°C warming, and this can increase by

about 7.4 percent due to an increase in CO_2 levels. Meanwhile, the combined effect of warming, CO_2 increase, and irrigation availability could thus translate into a 9.9 percent increase in the soybean growth potential over Midwest. Comparatively, corn would show a reduction in yield by about 4 percent due to the warming, but the direct effect of CO_2 increase would be about 1 percent increase in yield, with the combined effect of climate change including irrigation availability indicating a 3 percent reduction in the corn yield for the Midwest region.

Niyogi et al. (2011a) summarize a modeling study for corn and soybean yield changes using the CERES-Maize and the Soygro model within the CSM-DSSAT modeling system (Jones et al. 1998). The model was calibrated against observations made in North Carolina (Booker et al. 2005), but the interactions and the kind of feedbacks that can affect crop yield are still illustrative and qualitatively transferable to the Midwest (Figure 5.5). A design of experiment approach was used (cf. Mera et al. 2006) to prescribe possible changes to radiation, precipitation, and temperature under current and doubled CO_2, as well as irrigated and non-irrigated scenarios. The results were then diagnosed using a statistical factor separation approach to extract the direct and interaction effects of these climatic changes. Generally similar direct and interaction effects were noted for corn and soybeans. Increased sunshine hours and radiation increased the yield under ambient and elevated CO_2 levels when irrigation was available, but increasing drought stress led to a lower yield under elevated CO_2 conditions. One important finding of this multivariable, interaction-explicit vulnerability assessment was that drought stress amplified the negative impacts and reduced the positive effect that enhanced CO_2 could have on the crop yield.

SOIL LOSS, PATHOGEN, AND WEEDS

Historically, soils in the midwestern United States have reportedly lost up to 40 Mg of carbon per hectare from their pre-agricultural to present day state (see chapter 7 of this volume). This loss accounts for nearly one-third to a half of the carbon and nutrient pool available in the soils (Lal 2002) and is another important vulnerability to the agricultural enterprise in the Midwest. Nearing et al. (2004) highlight that the net effect of the different climatic changes that are underway and projected for the Midwest would lead to even more significant soil loss through erosion than has been seen in the previous century. It is anticipated that the soil loss will be a function of different climatic factors involving rainfall intensity, duration, frequency, and type—along with other modulators such as regional land use, crop cover, and soil, organic, and microbial activity will all contribute to the soil loss in the region. Nearing et al. (2004) conclude that in places experiencing more intense rainfall, the impact on runoff and soil erosion will be even greater (by about 70%). In places with reduced rainfall under a changing climate, the regional adaptation

and mitigation strategies that help maintain or increase biomass production will be important in maintaining or reducing the soil loss.

The increasing threat and geographic susceptibility of pests and weeds in the agricultural and horticultural landscapes also represents a significant potential vulnerability in the Midwest (e.g., Evans et al. 2008). Weeds are expected to be at an advantage in productivity as compared to cereal crops, and thus a rapid expansion and persistence of weeds will increase competition for land resources over agricultural fields (Hatfield et al. 2008). This is occurring through the increasing susceptibility of both the roots and the leaves with more prevalent and frequent occurrence of the diseases. The infestation potential generally increases with temperature and humidity, both of which are showing an increasing trend (chapter 11). This stress is not only for the cereal crops but also for the turf industry, which is a dominant agroeconomic enterprise in the midwestern United States (Palmieri et al. 2006).

It should be cautioned that while multiple studies have indicated pathogen stress will increase under climate change scenarios, a review by Chakrobarty et al. (2000) suggests that climate change could have "positive, negative or no impact on individual plant diseases." For example, for weed interactions, changes in the temperature and rainfall patterns can alter soil microbial pests and the defense mechanisms of the plant tissue, but the changes in CO_2 levels can also stimulate soil symbionts that can contribute to enhanced productivity (Pritchard and Amthor 2005).

ECONOMIC AND POLICY CHANGES: THE EXAMPLE OF BIOFUELS

Not all changes in agricultural risk and vulnerability derive from climate forcing. Key potential mechanisms for changing vulnerability are economics and policy changes including those related to biofuel-driven growth incentive for the region (see chapter 2 of this volume). The benefits of the biofuel as a net sink of GHG (or at least as a carbon-neutral energy source) versus source of GHG is being debated (e.g., Searchinger et al. 2008), but the U.S. Environmental Protection Agency (EPA) and other federal programs have helped incentivize biofuel usage by offering tax credits (Yacobucci 2010). Widespread increases in crop usage for biofuel production may lead to agronomic stress as the acreage required to grow the biofuel stock of demand—cereal crop or switchgrass—increases, potentially affecting the regional land cover, water use, and the soil nutrient status (Tyner 2008).

Adaptability Constraints

A key question regarding vulnerability to climate change in the agricultural sector is the elasticity of the sector. That is, how quickly can agricultural practices including crop selection be adapted to climatic changes? A further key question is this: to what degree is the agricultural sector, and particularly the dominant crop types, at the limit of the climate envelope? With

respect to the latter, it appears that corn and soybeans found in the Midwest are expected to be resilient to climatic variability. Adaptation approaches may include changes in planting dates, changes in irrigation potential, using different growth genotypes, and fertilizer and pesticide use, as well as farm changes related to row crop shelters, amongst other options that may become available. On the other hand, the horticultural crops and herbs are considered prone to higher risk due to climatic change and the narrow optimal growth conditions. The fruit industry may be particularly vulnerable to climatic changes, especially when coupled with climate variability (Hatfield et al. 2008; see also chapter 8 of this volume).

Another constraint on adaptation is the competing need for land available for agriculture. The availability of agricultural landscape and even possible intensification is also an important regional climatic driver. Fall et al. (2010a,b) analyzed the dependence of the land use on temperature and humidity trends and concluded that the regions' lack of warming can be largely attributed to the greening caused by agriculture dominated landscapes. The Midwest is showing population shifts, economic changes, and growing urbanization, both from sprawling urban centers and from transformation of agricultural zones into towns with budding agroeconomic shifts. Therefore, warmer conditions can be expected over the region if the agricultural buffer diminishes or the urban zones continue expanding. Additionally, Niyogi et al. (2011b) conducted a climatological analysis of the rainfall patterns around urban areas in central Indiana and showed that thunderstorms, which contribute to the majority of summer rainfall in the Midwest, are altered because of urbanization. Thus increased urbanization may change local temperature, humidity, and rainfall patterns, which, coupled with regional changes in the agricultural landscapes, will add another challenge to understanding the dynamical feedbacks as adaptation and mitigation approaches are identified.

Studies such as Howden et al. (2007) show that the different adaptation approaches are expected to have positive impacts on the agriculture cropping systems. However, most would be suitable under "moderate" climate change and may be limited under more "severe" changes. They recommend that a risk assessment involving systematic changes in resources and targeted diversification of production systems and livelihoods will be needed in the future.

The biggest challenges still remain not in assessing the vulnerabilities and the possible adaptation approaches for the agriculture as an enterprise, but in correctly identifying the economics of the changes needed and developing realistic assessments from the past case studies (Tol et al. 1998). Yet as highlighted by Lal et al. (2004), there may be "win-win" options involving some of the mitigation strategies such as no-till farming and residue mulching that can also help with the farm economics and will continue to be possible tools. Other practices that can be potentially available include a winter rotation cover, nutrient management strate-

gies, and elimination of summer fallow. Additionally, technological options such as irrigation, drainage systems, availability of hybrid seeds, and market incentives will also need to be explored as available tools (Smither and Blay-Palmer 2001).

Concluding Remarks

Climate is a major component of the Midwest agricultural system. Some projected changes in atmospheric conditions will likely be beneficial at least initially for agricultural activity within the Midwest. For example, positive effects may include an increase in CO_2 levels that can increase the productivity as a "carbon fertilizer effect" (Leakey 2009), or increase the growing season length, allowing a wider latitude for plant growth and possibly the type of varieties and crops that can be grown. Changes in the hydrologic cycle may be either beneficial or detrimental to agricultural yields, as would the impact due to temperature changes. The drought impacts would be potentially negative, but again, the effect would largely depend on the timing of the event, while the pest and pathogen stress would have a negative impact. In some regions, the hydrological shifts might cause more soil carbon changes, including soil oxidation and salinity changes that can affect the fertility and yield dramatically.

Observations and models alike indicate that changes in climate will affect crop yields. However, changes in agricultural practices can affect regional climate and agricultural yields more dramatically. This indicates that adaption and mitigation approaches can be effective in altering the regional climate and the agricultural vulnerability and opens future opportunities. For example, the planting areas in the Midwest are changing and moving northward toward North Dakota, South Dakota, and Minnesota from the lower Midwest because of cooler planting seasons correlating with higher yields. The suitability of the soils to support the crops remains one of the challenges in this northward migration. Crop growing season is lengthening, and in the future, more area could be available for these crops if this trend continues.

Assessing crop production vulnerabilities is a key to sustained economic well-being in the Midwest. Regional-scale assessments and retrospective analyses of climate-yield relations are key to identifying both vulnerabilities and suitable adaptation mechanisms. There is currently a disconnect between simpler climate and agriculture impact studies and the actual complexity of the scale, processes, and feedback that need to be considered in order to inform optimal regional-scale agronomic decision making. Future studies need to consider adaptive opportunities available through genetic changes, agronomic changes, soil carrying capacity, and economic incentives, and each of these are still poorly known and modeled. The vulnerability assessment in this chapter highlights the viability of a simpler framework that adopts potential yield modulation by considering scenarios of forcings (e.g., temperature change, drought, heat stress, rainfall changes) and using factors to scale the yield. In the long term, controlling greenhouse gas emissions is critical, and already, a number of rulings and pieces of legislation are underway, but agricultural policies can only help create the buffer and time needed for technological advances to evolve.

ACKNOWLEDGEMENTS
The study benefited in part by grants from the USDA NIFA U2U Project and the NSF INTEROP DRINet project at Purdue University.

REFERENCES.
Ainsworth EA, Ort DR (2010). How do we improve crop production in a warming world? Plant Physiology 154:526–530.

Booker FL, Miller JE, Fiscus EL, Pursley WA, Stefanski LA (2005). Comparative responses of container versus ground-grown soybean to elevated carbon dioxide and ozone. Crop Science 45:883–895.

Chakraborty S, Tiedemann AV, Teng TS (2000). Climate change: potential impact on plant diseases. Environmental Pollution 108:317–326.

Charusombat U, Niyogi D (2011). A hydroclimatological assessment of the regional drought vulnerability: a case study for Indiana drought. Earth Interactions 15:doi:10.1175/2011EI343.1.

Evans N, Baier A, Semenov MA, Gladders P, Fitt BDL (2008). Range and severity of a plant disease increased by global warming. Journal of Royal Society 5:525–531.

Fall S, Niyogi D, GluhovskyA, Pielke Sr. RA, Kalnay E, Rochon G (2010a) Impacts of land use land cover on temperature trends over the continental United States: Assessment using the North American Regional Reanalysis. International Journal of Climatology 30:1980–1993.

Fall S, Diffenbaugh N, Niyogi D, Pielke Sr. RA, Rochon G (2010b) Temperature and equivalent temperature over the United States (1979–2005). International Journal of Climatology 30:2045–2054.

Gu L, Hanson PJ, Post WM, Kaiser DP, Yang B, Nemani R, Pallard S, Meyers T (2008). The

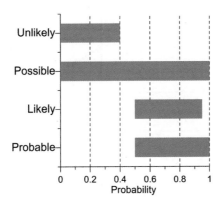

Figure 1.1. Understanding of four examples of nonnumeric probability statements from the work by Wallsten et al. (1986). The bars shown for each term indicate the range of subject evaluations of the meaning of that term when expressed in terms of numeric probability. The membership function for "Unlikely" was in the range of 0 to 0.4, and thus was interpreted by different members of the study population as being equivalent to having a probability of between 0 and 40 percent.

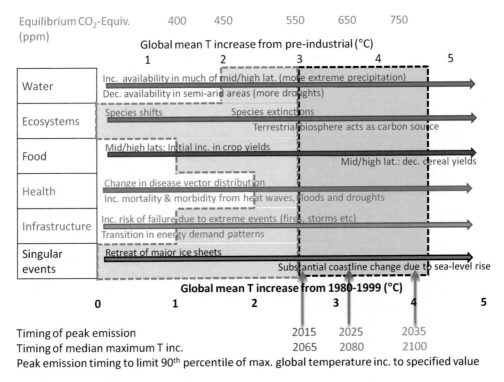

Figure 1.2. Synthesis of some major impacts of projected climate change (Parry et al. 2007; Stern 2007; Parry et al. 2009; Parry 2010; Yohe 2010) as characterized using the change in temperature (from preindustrial time and from the end of the twentieth century) for a range of greenhouse gas (GHG) stabilization levels shown by the equilibrium GHG concentration (expressed in CO_2-equivalents, ppm). The temperature increases presented are the mean value shown in Stern (2007). The area shaded in red shows the "adaptation gap" (Parry 2010) (i.e., the difference between resources allocated to adaptation (to the left), and resources allocated to reduce the magnitude of climate change (the area shaded in gray to the right)). The right-hand edge of the gray box shows the expected amount of warming under a business-as-usual, zero-mitigation scenario. The numbers at the bottom of the frame show the estimates of global mean temperature rise resulting from different CO_2 emission scenarios. The analyses are based on estimates of the timing of peak GHG emissions (2015, 2025, 2035) followed by an assumed reduction of 3 percent per year. The arrows show the 90th percentile global warming (in °C) for each scenario, while the lower figure shows the date of the maximum warming (estimates from Parry et al. 2009).

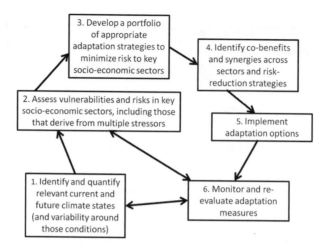

Figure 1.3. Schematic of the processes of identifying, developing, and implementing adaptation strategies designed to reduce the risk posed by climate change and to maximize opportunities presented both by a changing climate and vulnerability reduction (Figure adapted from National Research Council 2010a).

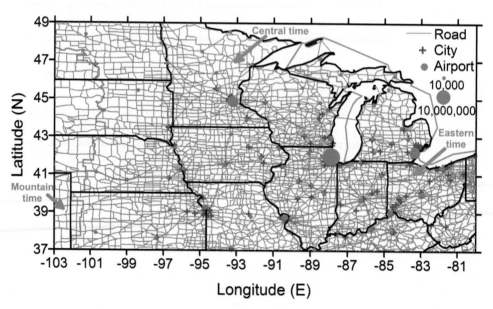

Figure 2.1. Location of the major cities, airports, and roads within the Midwest. The locations of major cities within the region are denoted by the blue plus symbols (Boundary file provided by Golden Software. Data from http://www.goldensoftware.com/public/boundary_mv7/USMiscellany/). The gray lines depict major roads (Boundary file provided by Golden Software. Source: http://www.goldensoftware.com/public/boundary_mv7/USMiscellany/). The red dots show the major commercial airports in the Midwest. (Data from http://www.faa.gov/data_research/passengers_cargo/.) The diameters of the dots scales linearly with passenger boarding numbers. Shown in pink are the boundaries of the three time zones within the Midwest. The states are denoted by the two-letter abbreviations given in the upper left-hand corner of the state.

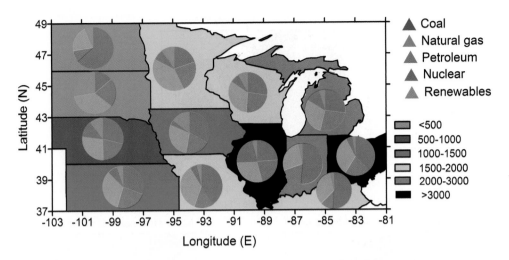

Figure 2.2. Total state energy use (shown by the state color shading) in trillion British Thermal Units (BTU) in 2008. Also shown by the pie charts for each state is the energy consumption by five sources: coal, natural gas, petroleum, nuclear energy, and renewables in 2008 (shown as a percentage of the total of those categories). Data from the US Energy Information Administration (http://www.eia.doe.gov/).

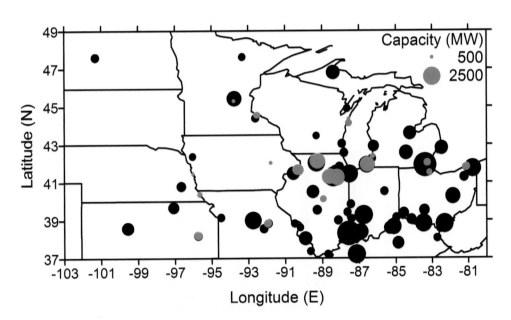

Figure 2.3. Location of major power stations in the Midwest. The red dots show the location of currently operating (2009) nuclear power plants with a capacity ≥ 500 MW, while the black dots show the location of operational fossil fuel power plants with a capacity ≥ 1000 MW. The scale for the power station generation capacity is shown in the upper right-hand corner of the map. Data for the nuclear facilities were obtained from the International Nuclear Safety Center. Data for the other power stations were obtained from Power Plant Jobs (http://www.powerplantjobs.com/).

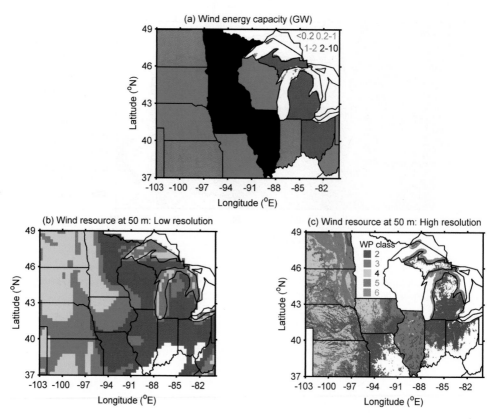

Figure 2.4. (a) Installed wind-energy-derived electricity generation (in MW of installed capacity) by state as of the end of 2010. Note the scale used to depict the wind energy installed capacity is approximately logarithmic. Frames (b) and (c) show the wind resource at 50 m in wind power classes: 2 = "marginal," wind energy density = 200–300 W m^{-2}; 3 = "fair," 300–400 W m^{-2}; 4 = "good," 400–500 W m^{-2}; 5 = "excellent," 500–600 W m^{-2}; 6 = "outstanding," 600–700 W m^{-2}. Estimates in (b) were derived primarily from observational data and have a spatial resolution of 0.25° of latitude by 0.33° of longitude. Estimates depicted in (c) are derived primarily based on modeling assessments for specific states or regions. The original raster data from which the shapefiles were derived varied in resolution from 200 to 1,000 m. States or regions with no shading indicate that the relevant data have not been made publicly available. Data plotted in (b) and (c) were developed by the National Renewable Energy Laboratory (NREL) and were obtained from the GIS data portal developed and operated by NREL (http://www.nrel.gov/gis/data_analysis.html).

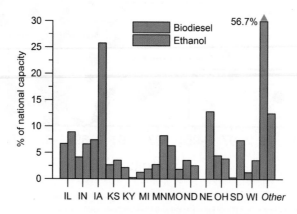

Figure 2.5. Contribution to US capacity by each of the midwestern states for biodiesel and ethanol (shown as a percentage of total national capacity). (Data from http://www.biodiesel.org/ accessed on February 10, 2011, and http://www.neo.ne.gov/statshtml/121.htm for December 2010.)

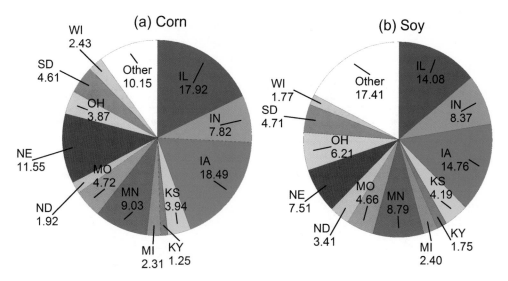

Figure 2.6. Value of US (a) corn and (b) soybeans grown in individual states shown as a percentage of the total value of these crops. The estimates are based on the value of receipts in 2008 as given by the US Department of Agriculture Economic Service. (Data from http://www.ers.usda.gov/StateFacts; accessed February 11, 2011.)

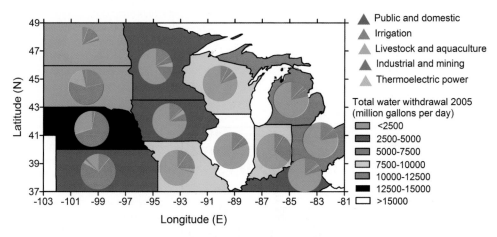

Figure 2.7. Freshwater withdrawals by state and by category for 2005 (Kenny et al. 2009). The colored shading for each state indicates the total freshwater withdrawal in millions of gallons per day. The pie chart for each state indicates the contribution of withdrawal in each of the five categories in the legend (public and domestic, irrigation, livestock and aquaculture, industrial and mining, and thermoelectric power) expressed as a percentage of the total in each state. Note that saline water withdrawals are very small in the Midwest in comparison with freshwater withdrawals and are therefore not presented here. See also Table 2.4

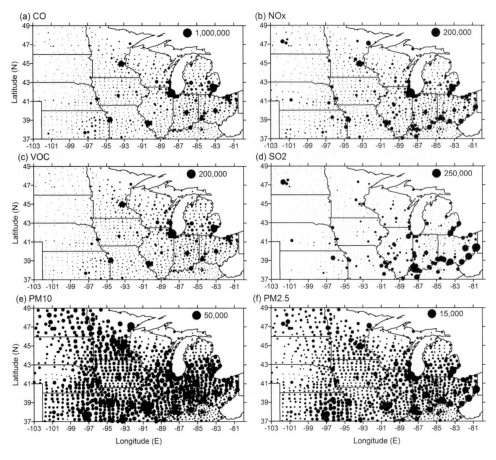

Figure 2.8. County-level emissions of the criteria pollutant or precursors thereof (in tons/year) for 2002: (a) carbon monoxide (CO), (b) oxides of nitrogen (NOx), (c) volatile organic compounds (VOC), (d) sulfur dioxide (SO_2), (e) particulate matter of diameter less than ten microns (PM_{10}), and (f) particulate matter of diameter less than 2.5 microns ($PM_{2.5}$). Data from the last complete emission inventory compile by the EPA (source: http://www.epa.gov/air/data/geosel.html). The emissions are plotted at the county center-point as indicated by the population distribution within the county as documented in the 2000 US Census (http://www.census.gov/geo/www/cenpop/county/ctyctrpg.html). The magnitude of the symbol scales with the square root of the emission magnitude. The maximum value and the size of dot that represents that value are given in the upper right hand corner of each frame.

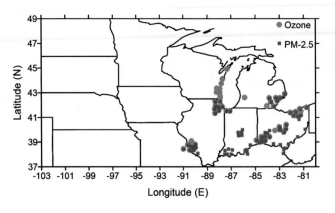

Figure 2.9. Counties in the Midwest that failed the National Ambient Air Quality Standards (NAAQS) (status updated in December 2008). All failures of the NAAQS within the region were for O_3 or $PM_{2.5}$. Data are for the last comprehensive assessment and were obtained from the Environmental Protection Agency (http://www.epa.gov/airdata/).

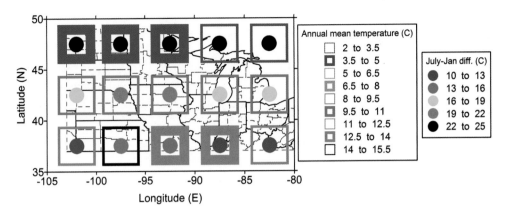

Figure 2.10. Annual mean temperature (°C) and the mean July–January temperature difference (°C) over the Midwest during 1961–90 based on data from the CRUTEM3 data set. The data have a spatial resolution of 5° × 5°. Because of the dataset spatial resolution the domain used herein is 35°N to 50°N and 105°W to 80°W, and thus extends beyond the boundaries of the Midwest region as depicted in Figure 2.1. (Data from http://www.cru.uea.ac.uk/cru/data/temperature/#datdow.) Also shown by the gray lines are the Climate Divisions used by NOAA.

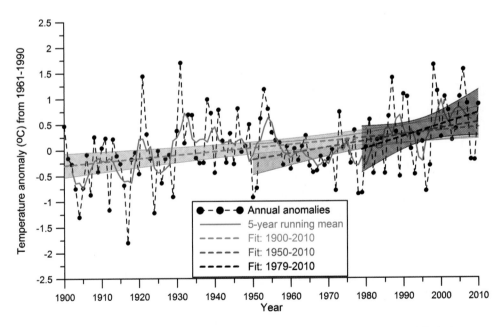

Figure 2.11. Annual temperature anomalies for the Midwest from the CRUTEM3 data set. The anomalies are relative to 1961–1990. The data have a spatial resolution of 5° × 5°, and thus the domain used to construct this figure is 35°N to 50°N and 105°W to 80°W. (Data from http://www.cru.uea.ac.uk/cru/data/temperature/#datdow.) Also shown is a 5-year running mean and linear fits to the annual data for 1900–2010, 1950–2010 and 1979–2010. The shading represents the 95 percent confidence intervals on the fits. The slopes of the region fits are equivalent to 0.067°C/decade (1900–2010), 0.12°C/decade (1950–2010), and 0.23°C/decade (1979–2010).

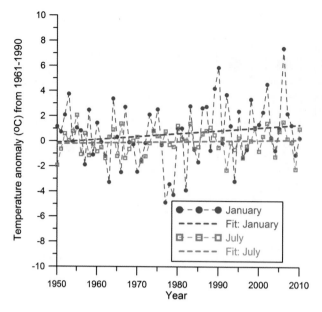

Figure 2.12. Temperature anomalies in January and July during 1950–2010 for the Midwest from the CRUTEM3 data set. The anomalies are relative to 1961–1990. The data have a spatial resolution of 5° × 5°, and thus the domain used to construct this figure is 35°N to 50°N and 105°W to 80°W. (Data from http://www.cru.uea.ac.uk/cru/data/temperature/#datdow.) The slopes of the region fits are equivalent to 0.24°C/decade for January, and 0.056°C/decade in July.

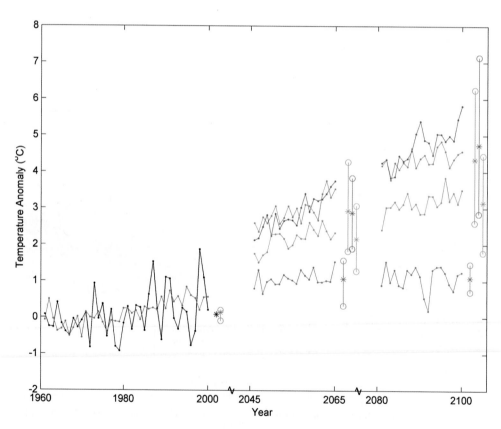

Figure 2.13. Midwestern regional temperature projections (for the domain 35°–50°N and 105°–80°W) based on a multimodel ensemble from IPCC AR4 GCMs. All values are based on anomalies from 1961–1990 means. The black line depicts observations from the CRUTEM3 gridded data (Brohan et al. 2006). The corresponding green line represents the multimodel ensemble from twentieth-century climate simulations. For the climate projections, four series are presented: the green series represent the committed climate change scenario, the magenta series is for SRES B1, the red series is for SRESA1B, and the blue series is for SRESA2. The vertical bar next to each time period indicates the range of mean values for that period among the ten GCM simulations. This figure was provided by J.T. Schoof.

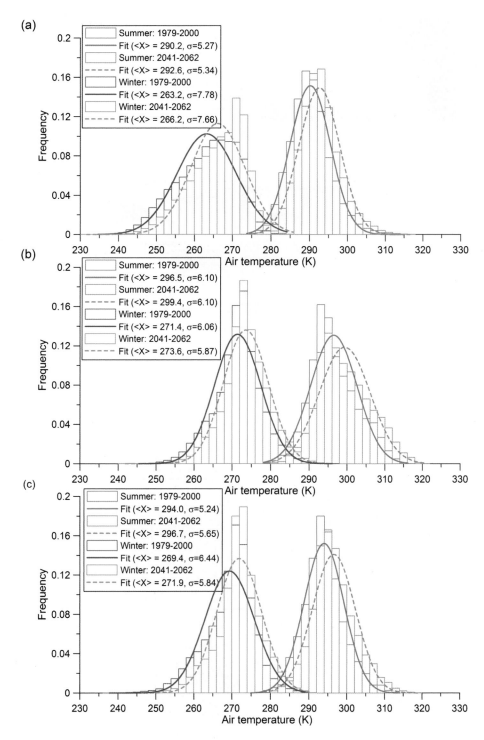

Figure 2.14. Probability distribution of summer (JJA) and winter (DJF) air temperatures for 50×50 km grid cells containing three Midwestern cities: (a) Fargo, North Dakota, (b) Kansas City, Kansas, and (c) Indianapolis, Indiana. The probability distributions are derived based on output from simulations of 2041–2062 and 1979–2000, conducted with the Canadian Regional Climate Model (CRCM) and nested within the Canadian Global Climate Model (CGCM3). The future time period equates to an SRES A1B emission scenario. The simulations were conducted as part of the NARCCAP project (Mearns et al. 2009). The bars denote the raw three-hourly output, while the lines show Gaussian distribution fits to the model output.

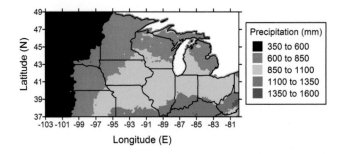

Figure 2.15. Annual average precipitation for 1971–2000 over the Midwest computed using gridded data from the PRISM Group at Oregon State University (http://www.prismclimate .org). The data have a resolution of 30 arcsec (1 arcsec of longitude equates to a distance of 20 m at a latitude of 49°).

Precipitation (mm)
- 350 to 600
- 600 to 850
- 850 to 1100
- 1100 to 1350
- 1350 to 1600

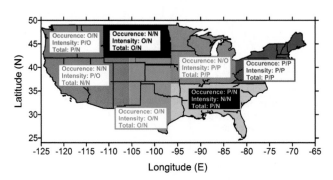

Figure 2.16. Mid-century (2046–2065) projected changes in cold-season (November–March) and warm-season (May–September) precipitation characteristics (relative to 1961–2000) based on statistical downscaling of 10 AOGCMs to 963 surface stations. For each region, the first letter denotes the change in the cold season, while the second letter shows the result for the warm season. If the letter is *P*, there is an increase in precipitation occurrence, intensity, and total seasonal receipt. Thus precipitation frequency, amount received on wet days, and/or seasonal total are higher in the future period. If the letter is *N*, there is a decrease in the given metric. Changes are only depicted where downscaled results from 8 or more climate models (out of 10 considered) exhibit the same sign of change; otherwise the letter *O* denotes a result of "no change." (Data from Schoof et al. (2010).)

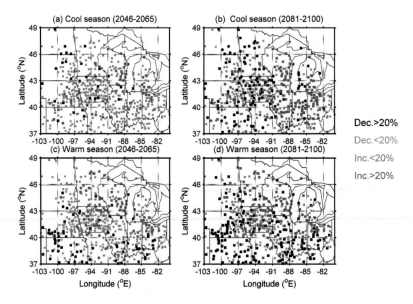

Dec.>20%
Dec.<20%
Inc.<20%
Inc.>20%

Figure 2.17. Ensemble average change in total precipitation (expressed in %) at stations across the Midwest in the cold season (November–March) for (a) 2046–2065 and (b) 2081–2100 and in the warm season (May–September) for (b) 2046–2065 and (d) 2081–2100, relative to 1961–2000 and derived from output from the empirical downscaling analysis of Schoof et al. (2010). The ensemble average is derived by computing the mean change from the 10 independently downscaled AOGCMs at each station.

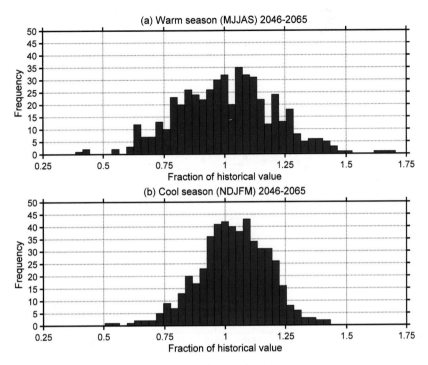

Figure 2.18. Frequency distribution of precipitation scenarios for the (a) warm season (May–September) and (b) cool season (November–March) for 2046–2065 relative to 1961–2000 and derived from output from the empirical downscaling analysis of Schoof et al. (2010). The histograms show the number of stations within the region that exhibited a change of a given magnitude. The information presented is the ensemble average from the 10 independently downscaled AOGCMs at each station, and the projected precipitation during the season for the future period is shown as a fraction of that for the historical period. Thus a value of 1 indicates the same precipitation receipt in the future and past, a value of less than 1 indicates lower precipitation in the future scenario.

Decision Support System Development Process

Phase 1	Phase 2	Phase 3	Phase 4
Conceptual Prototype	Prototype Testing	Operating Product	Open Source
Data collection & analysis	Prototype design	Transition to boundary organization operations	User adoption & boundary organization deployment
User engagement & needs assessment	User feedback & assessment	User feedback & impact assessment	Science community for research & support

Figure 3.1. The SECC approach to development of a decision support system has four phases, with user- or boundary-organization engagement or participation throughout. While the science community may initiate and motivate the first two phases, leadership is transferred to an appropriate boundary organization in phase three. By the end of the fourth phase, the appropriate boundary organization leads the effort with support from the science community.

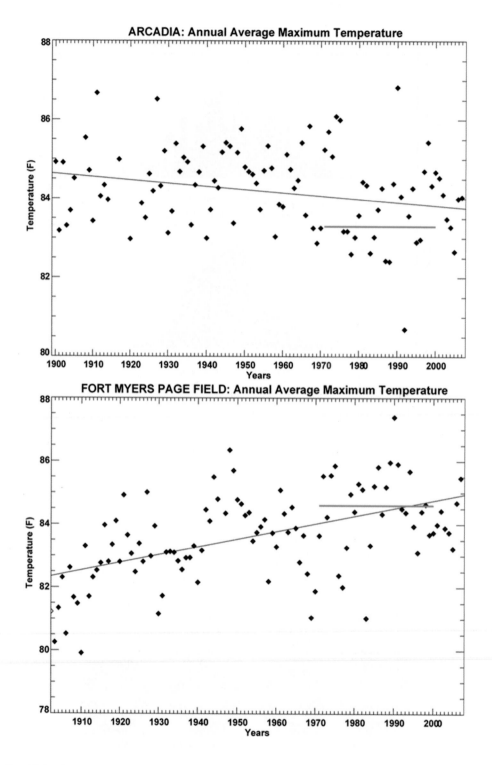

Figure 3.2. Annual average maximum temperature for Fort Myers and Arcadia, Florida. (Data from stations in the NWS Cooperative Observer Program (http://www.weather.gov/om/coop/what-is-coop.html) and analyzed by David Zierden, Florida state climatologist.) Regression lines show trends over total period of record. Horizontal bars show 30-year "normals" from the National Climate Data Center, which are recomputed at the beginning of each new decade.

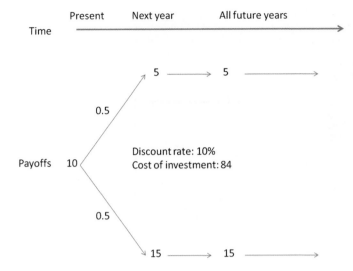

Figure 4.1. Example of a simple investment project. An investment projects costs $84 and generates an expected benefit stream of $10 per year. The uncertainty about the future benefits will be resolved the next year. With a discount rate of 10 percent, the project passes the expected cost-benefit test. However, real options theory shows that investing now is not optimal since the decision maker is better off waiting one more year until the benefit uncertainty is resolved before making investment decisions.

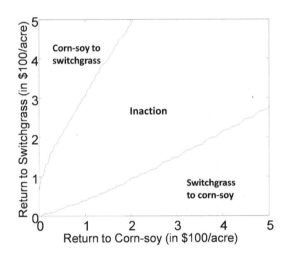

Figure 4.2. Conversion boundaries between corn-soybean and switchgrass. In order for the farmer to convert from corn-soybean to switchgrass, the switchgrass return needs to be much higher than the corn-soybean return, as indicated by the "corn-soy to switchgrass" conversion boundary. Conversely, for the farmer to convert from switchgrass to corn-soybean, the required switchgrass return is also much higher than that of corn-soybean. The two conversion boundaries show a large inaction region due to the option values.

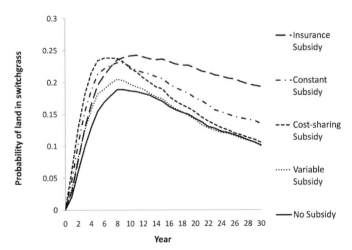

Figure 4.3. Proportion of land in switchgrass under different policy settings. Due to the low starting acreage switchgrass, land is quickly converted into switchgrass from corn-soybean under all policy scenarios. But in the long run, insurance subsidy leads to the highest percentage of land in switchgrass, followed by constant (per acre) subsidy, cost-sharing subsidy, and variable subsidy. Note that variable subsidy to switchgrass does not increase the probability of land in switchgrass at all in the long run compared with the default of no subsidy.

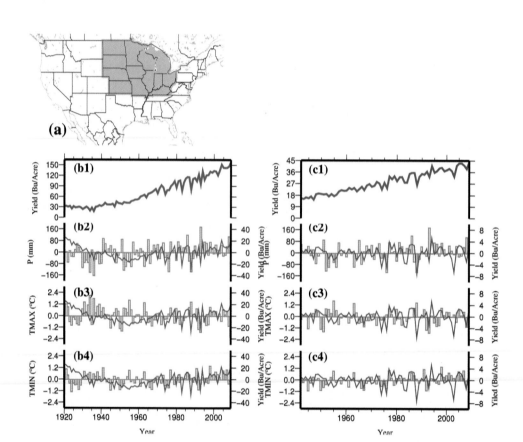

Adaptation	Agricultural Production In Midwestern U.S.	Vulnerability
Climate Change • Shift in planting dates • Increased irrigation •Change in seeds		**Climate Change** • Warming and changes in extremes • Droughts and Floods • Increase in frost-free days
Economic Policy and Change • Increased farm income • Better seed varieties		**Economic Policy and Change** • Biofuel production • Impacts on crop rotation system • Degradation of natural resources
Land Use Change • Agricultural buffers		**Land Use Change** •Urbanization causing climate change •Shift in agroecosystems

Figure 5.1. Examples of adaptation measures and vulnerabilities associated with agricultural production in the Midwestern United States.

Figure 5.2. (a) Definition of the Midwest as used here, where the gray area shows the study region. (b1) Long-term change in average corn yield for the study domain for the period of 1920–2009. (b2) Detrended corn yield (blue) and precipitation anomalies. (b3) Detrended corn yield and maximum temperature anomalies. (b4) Detrended corn yield and minimum temperature anomalies. (c1) Long-term changes in average soybean yield for the period of 1924–2009. (c2) Detrended soybean yield (blue) and precipitation anomalies. (c3) Detrended soybean yield and maximum temperature anomalies. (c4) Detrended soybean yield and minimum temperature anomalies. Precipitation and temperature anomalies were estimated with respect to the long-term mean.

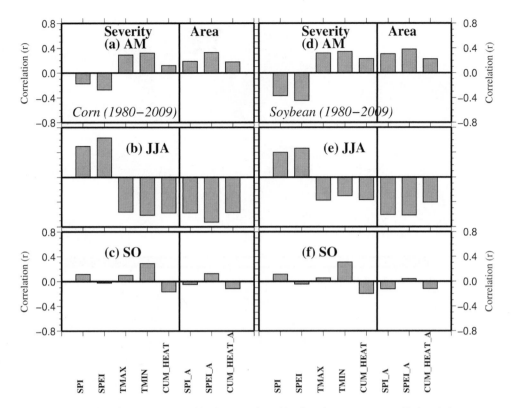

Figure 5.3. Spearman rank correlations between crop yields and severity and area of droughts and temperature extremes: (a) relationship between severity and area of drought and temperature indices during the planting season (AM) and annual corn yield; (b) same as (a), but for the grain filling and reproduction period (JJA); (c) same as (a), but for the maturity and harvest (SO) period; (d–f) same as (a–c), but for soybean. SPI_A: areal extent of severe, extreme, exceptional droughts estimated using SPI. SPEI_A: areal extent of severe, extreme, exceptional droughts estimated using SPEI,. CUM_HEAT_A: areal extent under cumulative heat stress.

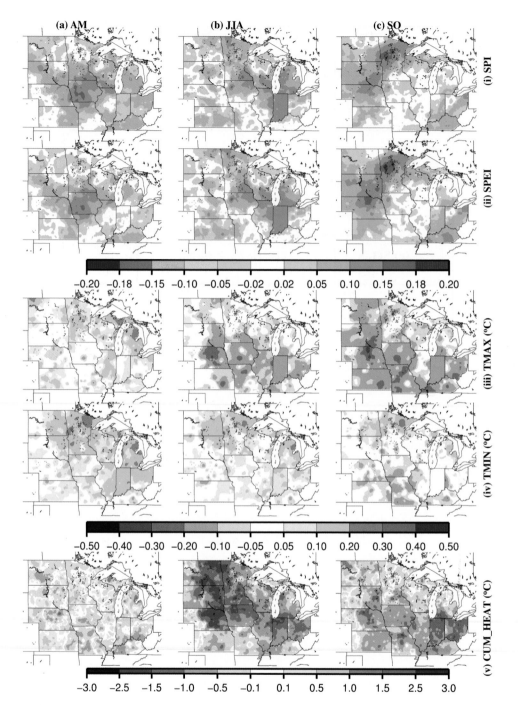

Figure 5.4. Long-term (1920–2009) spatial patterns of temporal trends for drought and temperature indices (TMAX, TMIN, and CUM_HEAT) for the selected crop growth periods: planting and field preparation (AM) (left), grain filling and reproduction (JJA) (middle), and maturity and harvest (SO) (right). Trends per decade for (i) the Standardized Precipitation Index (SPI), (ii) the Standardized Precipitation Evapotranspiration Index (SPEI), (iii) maximum temperature (°C/decade), (iv) minimum temperature per decade (°C/decade), and (iv) cumulative heat (°C/decade).

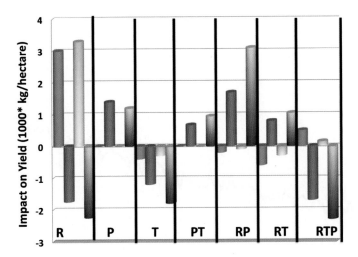

Figure 5.5. Schematic representation of crop model based individual (R, P, or T) and simultaneous (PT, RP, RT, RTP) interactions affecting soybean yield (1000*kg/ha). R, P, and T correspond to radiation, precipitation, and temperature impacts. The blue columns refer to effects involving irrigation impact, while the maroon and brown correspond to non-irrigated effects. In the series, the first two columns refer to the impacts under current or ambient carbon dioxide levels, and the remaining two refer to enhanced levels (doubling). The model results were calibrated against observations corresponding to the 1999 growing season and are adapted from Niyogi et al. (2011a).

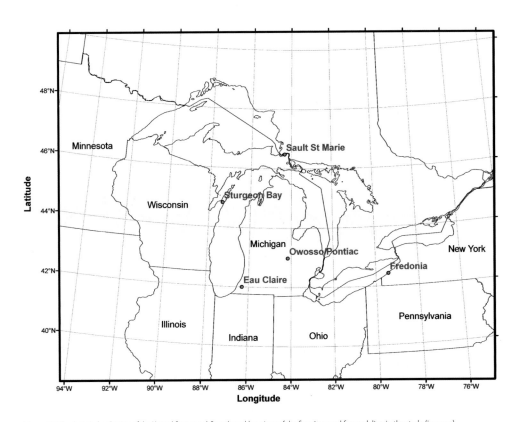

Figure 6.1. The Great Lakes Region of the United States and Canada and locations of the five sites used for modeling in the study (in green).

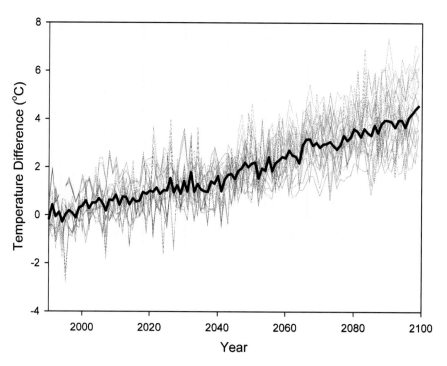

Figure 6.2a. Projected change in mean annual temperatures from the 32 climate scenarios at Owosso, Michigan, 1990–2099 relative to the 2000–2009 reference period. Red lines depict A2 emission scenarios, and blue lines are from B2 scenarios. The median of the thirty-two scenarios is plotted in the thick black line.

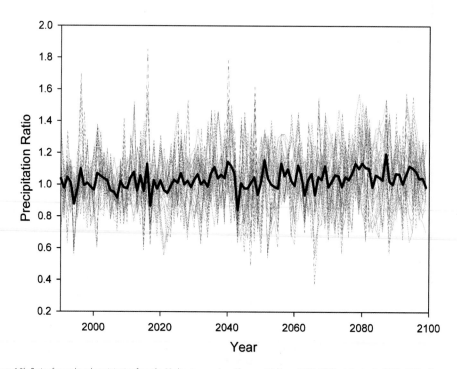

Figure 6.2b. Ratio of annual total precipitation from the 32 climate scenarios at Owosso, Michigan, 1990–2099 relative to the 2000–2009 reference period. Red lines depict A2 emission scenarios, and blue lines are from B2 scenarios. The median of the 32 scenarios is plotted in the thick black line.

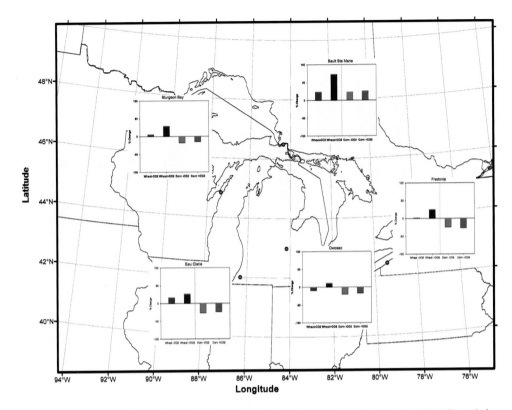

Figure 6.3. Simulated average yield changes (expressed in %) for corn (blue bars) and wheat (green bars), 2090–2099 versus 2000–2009, at each of the study sites. Changes from simulations run with constant carbon dioxide concentrations are depicted in light blue and light green (for wheat and corn, respectively), whereas changes from simulations with increasing carbon dioxide concentrations are depicted in dark blue and dark green. The y-axis in all frames extends from -100 to +100% change.

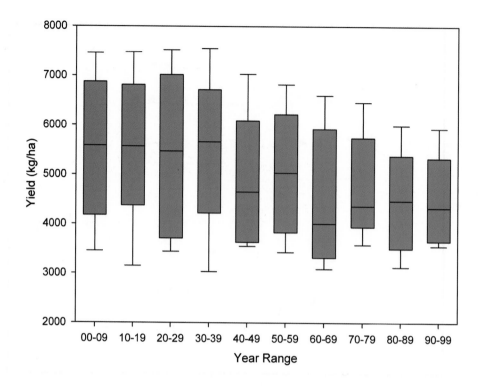

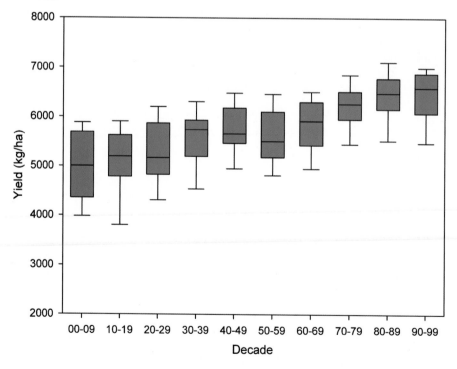

Figure 6.4. Simulated corn yields (kg ha⁻¹) at the Owosso, Michigan, site (top) and wheat yields at the Sturgeon Bay, Wisconsin, site (bottom) by decade, 2000–2099. Box and whisker plots depict median (middle line in box), 25th and 75th (lower and upper lines of the box), and 10th and 90th (bottom and top whiskers) percentiles at each of the study sites.

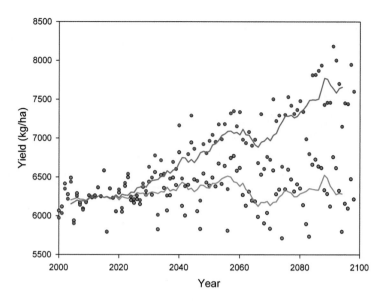

Figure 6.5. Simulated wheat yields (kg ha⁻¹) with constant CO_2 (light green) and increasing CO_2 (dark green) at Fredonia, New York, site by decade, 2000–2099. Yields are averaged across scenarios. A 9-year moving average of the individual years has been added to the plots in the thick solid lines to illustrate longer-term temporal changes.

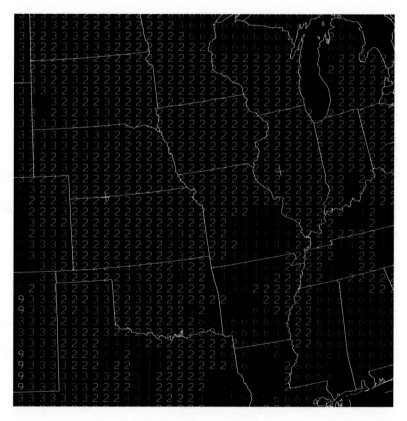

Figure 7.1. Land use categories used in DayCENT. The numbers in each grid cell depict the ecosystem type and are as follows: 2, mixed cropland; 3, short grass; 4, deciduous forest; 5, evergreen broadleaf trees; and 6, mixed woodland.

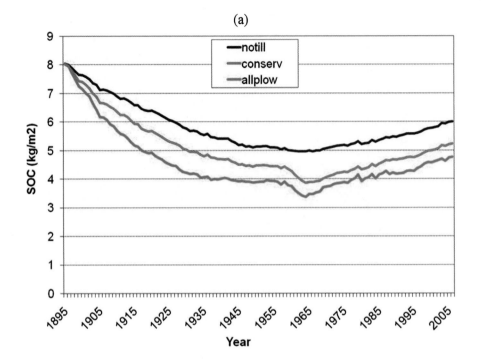

(a)

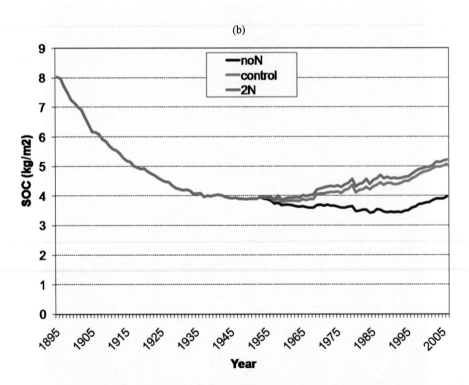

(b)

Figure 7.2. (a) DayCENT simulated time variation of soil organic carbon (SOC) within top 20 cm soil layer under different tillage schemes. "Conserv" denotes conversion tillage as defined in DayCENT; "Notill"denotes fields that are not tilled; "allplow" signifies that tillage is maximized. (b): Same as (a), but under different nitrogen application regimes. Control is default nitrogen fertilizer application; noN and 2N are no and double nitrogen applications, respectively.

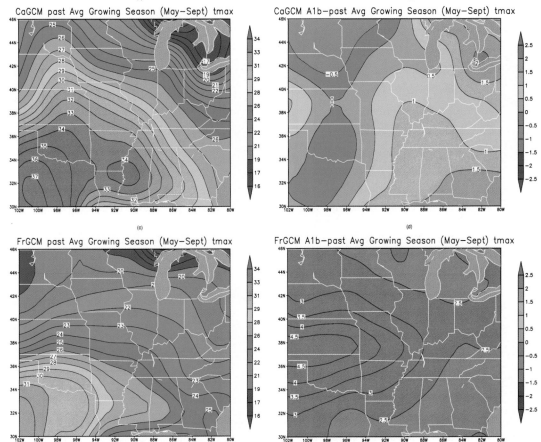

Figure 7.3. Growing-season (May–September) mean daily maximum temperature (Tmax in °C) and its change 2046–2065 versus 1961–1990 under A1B scenario (ΔTmax in °C). Thus frames (a) and (c) show the growing season Tmax during 1961–1990 from the two models ((a) CaGCM Tmax, (c) FrGCM Tmax), while frames (b) and (d) show the difference in growing season Tmax 2046–2065 versus 1961–1990 (i.e., ΔTmax) for (b) CaGCM, and (d) FrGCM.

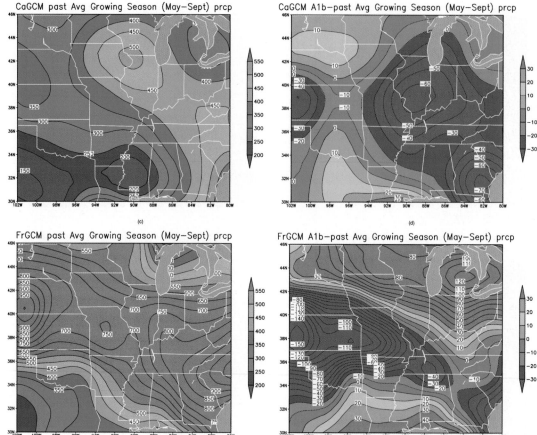

Figure 7.4. Growing-season (May–September) mean precipitation (in mm) and its change 2046–2065 versus 1961–1990 under A1B scenario (ΔPr in mm). Thus frames (a) and (c) show the growing season precipitation (in mm) during 1961–1990 from the two models ((a) CaGCM Tmax, (c) FrGCM Tmax), while frames (b) and (d) show the difference in growing season precipitation 2046–2065 versus 1961–1990 (i.e., ΔPr) for (b) CaGCM, and (d) FrGCM.

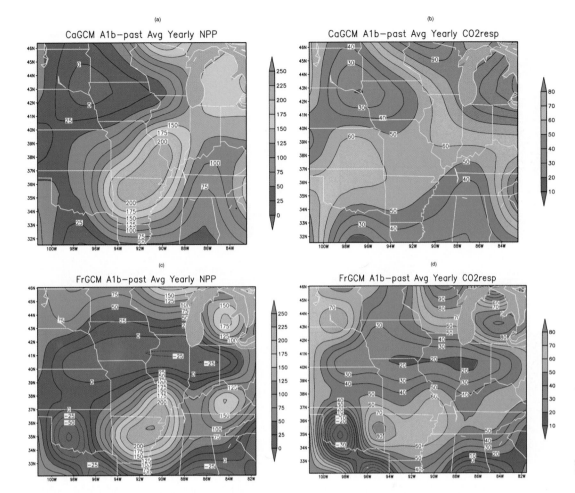

Figure 7.5. DayCENT simulated seasonal-mean weekly NPP and soil respiration change 2046–2065 versus 1961–1990 under A1B scenario (g m^{-2}) for the two models. Thus frames (a) and (c) show the change in net primary productivity (NPP) (g m^{-2}) from simulations where the climate conditions were supplied from the (a) CaGCM and (c) FrGCM output, while frames (b) and (d) show the change in respiration (g m^{-2}) for simulations forced by (b) CaGCM and (d) FrGCM.

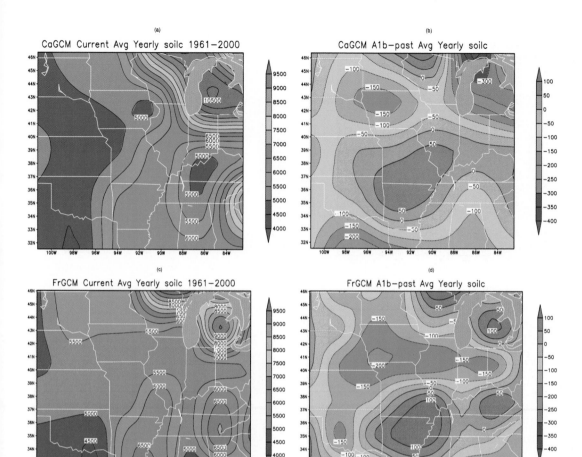

Figure 7.6. Soil organic carbon (SOC) pool in the top 20 cm soil profile (in g m⁻²) and its change 2046–2065 versus 1961–1990 under A1B scenario (g m⁻²) for the two models. Thus frames (a) and (c) show the SOC during 1961–1990 from the two models ((a) CaGCM, and (c) FrGCM), while frames (b) and (d) show the difference in SOC (ΔSOC) 2046–2065 versus 1961–1990 for (b) CaGCM, and (d) FrGCM.

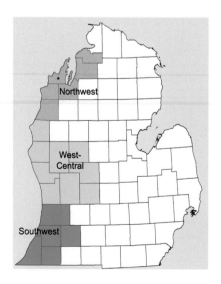

Figure 8.1. Tart cherry production areas by county in the Lower Peninsula of Michigan. The small star displayed in the northwest region is the location of Maple City, Michigan. Maple City is the example location for the analyses presented below.

Historical Tart Cherry Yield Tool

📖 Learn about this tool

Top graph displays variability in historical tart cherry yields (1944-2004) and the associated weather events as recalled by farmers who have been part of the industry since early 1940s. Blue box at the bottom shows the results from our simulation model for the same period. **We strongly recommend that you visit the** Learn About page to understand the benefits of this tool.

Graph: Weather and Tart Cherry Yields in Michigan (1944-2004)

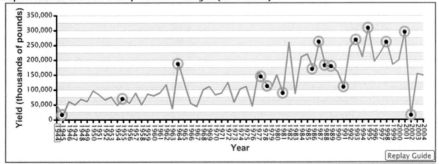

Agriculture > Historical Tart Cherry Yield Tool

Historical Tart Cherry Yield Tool

📖 Learn about this tool

Top graph displays variability in historical tart cherry yields (1944-2004) and the associated weather events as recalled by farmers who have been part of the industry since early 1940s. Blue box at the bottom shows the results from our simulation model for the same period. **We strongly recommend that you visit the** Learn About page to understand the benefits of this tool.

Graph: Weather and Tart Cherry Yields in Michigan (1944-2004)

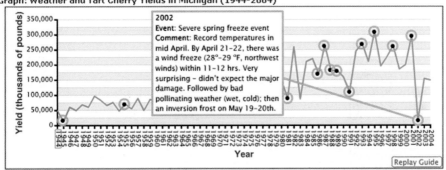

Figure 8.2. Variations in tart cherry yield for Michigan, 1944–2004 (top panel), and experienced farmers' recollections of the climate factors influencing yield in 2002 (bottom panel). The images are from the Historical Tart Cherry Yield Tool developed as part of the *Pileus Project*.

a) Wind Freeze Event

Date	Max temp (°C)	Min Temp (°C)
4/14/2002	22.22	2.22
4/15/2002	28.89	12.22
4/16/2002	30.56	20
4/17/2002	28.33	18.33
4/18/2002	27.78	5.56
4/19/2002	25	3.89
4/20/2002	6.11	0
4/21/2002	6.11	-1.67
4/22/2002	4.44	-2.22
4/23/2002	10.56	-3.33
4/24/2002	22.22	-1.11
4/25/2002	21.11	1.11
4/26/2002	6.67	-3.89
4/27/2002	7.22	-2.78
4/28/2002	6.11	0
4/29/2002	7.22	1.11
4/30/2002	10.56	3.89

You have requested information based on the following options:

Station: Maple City
Data range: 2002-04-14 to 2002-04-30

b) Inversion Freeze Event

Date	Max temp (°C)	Min Temp (°C)
5/16/2002	17.78	3.89
5/17/2002	5	1.67
5/18/2002	5.56	1.11
5/19/2002	6.67	-5
5/20/2002	8.33	-3.33
5/21/2002	13.33	-1.67
5/22/2002	20.56	5
5/23/2002	23.33	12.78
5/24/2002	21.67	3.33
5/25/2002	11.11	-1.11
5/26/2002	21.11	2.22
5/27/2002	18.89	10.56
5/28/2002	26.67	9.44
5/29/2002	26.11	11.11
5/30/2002	26.67	12.22

You have requested information based on the following options:

Station: Maple City
Data range: 2002-05-16 to 2002-05-30

Figure 8.3. Maximum and minimum temperatures (°C) reported at Maple City, Michigan, for the periods of April 14–30 and May 16–30, 2002. Anomalous warm temperatures are outlined in red and cold temperatures in blue. The observations are from the NWS Cooperative Observer Network and are displayed using the Historical Weather Tool developed as part of the *Pileus Project*.

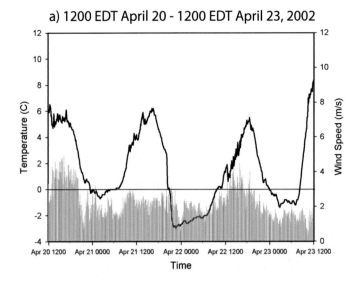

a) 1200 EDT April 20 - 1200 EDT April 23, 2002

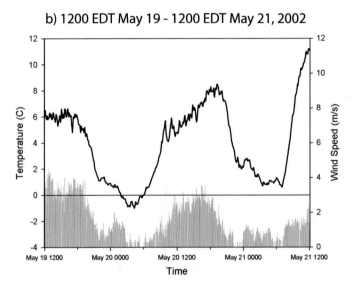

b) 1200 EDT May 19 - 1200 EDT May 21, 2002

Figure 8.4. Five-minute averaged temperature (black line) and wind speed (blue bars) for the time periods between 12:00 p.m. EDT April 20 and 12:00 p.m. EDT April 23, 2002 (top panel) and between 12:00 p.m. EDT May 19 and 12:00 p.m. EDT May 21, 2002 (bottom panel), at the Northwest Michigan Horticultural Research Station. The measurements were taken as part of the Michigan Agricultural Weather Network (MAWN).

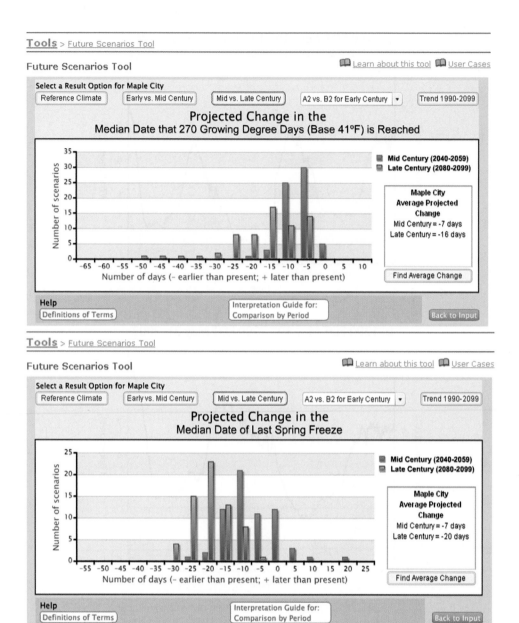

Figure 8.5. Projected future changes for Maple City, Michigan, for mid-century (2040–2059) and late-century (2080–2099) time slices in the median date that 150 growing degree days (GDDs), base 5°C (270 GDDs, base 41°F), is reached (top panel), with the median date of last spring frost defined as the last occurrence of temperatures ≤0°C (≤32°F) (bottom panel). Each panel is a screenshot from the Future Scenarios Tool developed as part of the Pileus Project and illustrates the available display options and the interpretative guides accessible to users from each screen. Note that in these displays, temperature-related quantities are provided in °F, given stakeholders' greater familiarity with the Fahrenheit temperature scale as compared to Celsius.

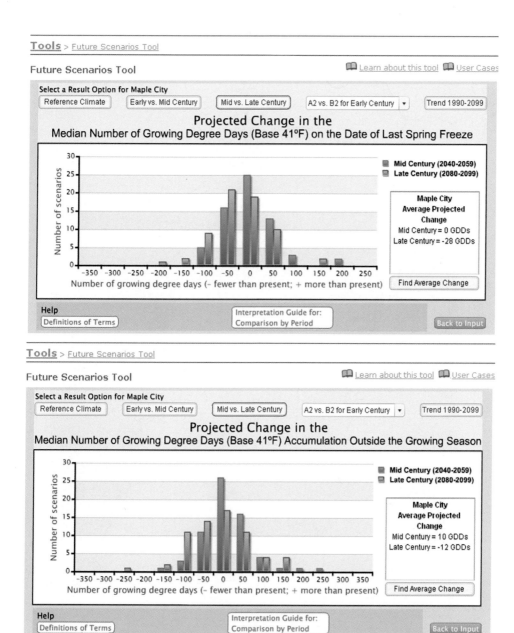

Figure 8.6. Projected future changes for Maple City, Michigan, for mid-century (2040–2059) and late-century (2080–2099) time slices in the median number of GDDs on the date of last spring frost, calculated using a 5°C (41°F) base temperature (top panel) and the median number of GDDs [base 5°C (41°F)] outside the growing season, where growing season is defined as the period between the last occurrence in spring of temperatures ≤0°C (≤32°F) and the first occurrence in fall of temperatures ≤0°C (≤32°F). Each panel is a screenshot from the Future Scenarios Tool developed as part of the Pileus Project.

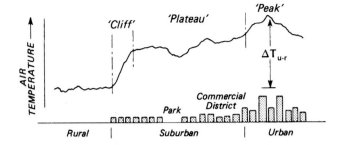

Figure 9.1. Schematic representation of the urban heat island (Figure reprinted with permission from Tim Oke). Urban (u) — Rural (r) temperature = urban heat island (UHI) intensity.

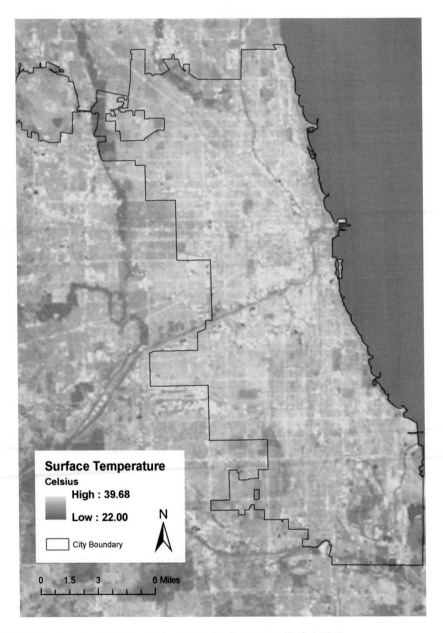

Figure 9.2. Land surface temperature during Chicago's heat wave in 1995. (Data from Johnson and Stanforth, IUPUI.)

2007 eastern US spring freeze: Increased cold damage in a warming world. Bioscience 58:253–262.

Hamlet A, Lettenmaier DP (2005). Production of temporally consistent gridded precipitation and temperature fields for the continental United States. Journal of Hydrometeorology 6:330–336.

Hatfield J, Boote K, Fay P, Hahn L, Izaurralde C, Kimball BA, Mader T, Morgan J, Ort D, Polley W, Thomson A, Wolfe D (2008). Agriculture. In: The effects of climate change on agriculture, land resources, water resources, and biodiversity in the United States. US Climate Change Science Program and the Subcommittee on Global Change Research, Washington, DC.

Hossain F, Niyogi D, Adegoke J, Pielke Sr R (2011). Making sense of the water available for future. Eos 90:144–145.

Howden MS, Soussana J-F, Tubiello FN, Chhetri N, Dunlop M, Meinke H. (2007). Climate change and food security special feature: Adapting agriculture to climate change. Proceedings of the National Academy of Sciences 104:19691–19696.

Jones JW, Tsuji GY, Hoogenboom G, Hunt LA, Thorton PK, Wilkens P, Imamura DT, Bowen WT, Singh U (1998). Decision support system for agrotechnology transfer: DSSAT v3. In: Tsuji GY, Thornton G, Hoogenboom PK (eds) Understanding options for agricultural production, Boston: Kluwer.

Kunkel, KE, Easterling DR, Hubbard K, and Redmond K (2004). Temporal variations in frost-free season in the United States: 1895–2000. Geophysical Research Letters 31:L03201, doi:10.1029/2003GL018624.

Lal R (2002). Soil carbon dynamics in cropland and rangeland. Environmental Pollution 116:353–362.

Lal R, Griffin M, Apt J, Lave L, Morgan MG (2004). Managing soil carbon. Science 304:393.

Lawlor DW, Mitchell RAC (2000). Crop ecosystem responses to climatic change: Wheat. Climate change and global crop productivity. Oxfordshire, UK: CABI Publishing.

Leakey ADB (2009). Rising atmospheric carbon dioxide concentration and the future of C-4 crops for food and fuel. Proceedings of the Royal Society B-Biological Sciences 276:2333–2343.

Leung LR, Gustafson Jr. WI (2005). Potential regional climate change and implications to US air quality. Geophysical Research Letters 32:L16711, doi:10.1029/2005GL022911.

Lobell DB, Burke MB, Tebaldi C, Mastrandrea MD, Falcon WP, Naylor RL (2008). Prioritizing climate change adaptation needs for food security in 2030. Science 319:607–610.

Maraun D, Wetterhall F, Ireson A, Chandler RE, Kendon EJ, Widmann M, Brienen S, Rust H, Sauter T, Themeß B, Venema VKC, Chun KP, Goodess C, Jones RG, Onof C, Vrac M, Thiele-Eich I (2010). Precipitation downscaling under climate change: recent developments to bridge the gap between dynamical models and the end user. Reviews of Geophysics 48:RG3003, doi:10.1029/2009RG000314.

McKee TB, Doesken NJ, Kliest J (1993). The relationship of drought frequency and duration to time scales, Proceedings of the Eighth Conference of Applied Climatology. American Meteorological Society, Anaheim, CA.

Mera RJ, Niyogi D, Buol GS, Wilkerson GG, Semazzi F (2006). Potential individual versus simultaneous climate change effects on soybean (C3) and maize (C4) crops: an agrotechnology model based study. Global and Planetary Change 54:163–182.

Mishra V, Cherkauer KA (2010). Retrospective droughts in the crop growing season: implications to corn and soybean yield in the midwestern United States. Agricultural and Forest Meteorology 150:1030–1045.

Mishra V, Cherkauer KA, Shukla S (2010). Assessment of drought due to historic climate variability and projected future climate change in the midwestern United States. Journal of Hydrometeorology 11:46–68.

National Agricultural Statistics Service USDA–NASS (United States Department of Agriculture–National Agricultural Statistics Service) (2009). National Agricultural Statistics Database. USDA NASS, Washington DC. Available from: http://www.nass.usda.gov/.

Nearing MA, Pruski FF, O'Neal ME (2004). Expected climate change impacts on soil erosion rates: a review. Journal of Soil and Water Conservation 59:43–50.

Niyogi D, Mera R, Xue YK, Wilkerson G, Booker F (2011a) The use of Alpert-Stein Factor Separation Method for climate variable interaction studies in hydrological land surface models and crop yield models. In: Alpert P and Sholokman (eds). The factor separation method in the atmosphere: Applications and future prospects. Cambridge, UK: Cambridge University Press.

Niyogi D, Pyle PC, Lei M, Arya SP, Kishtawal CM, Shepherd JM, Chen F, Wolfe B (2011b) Urban modification of thunderstorms—an observational storm climatology and model case study for the Indianapolis urban region. Journal of Applied Meteorology and Climatology 50:1129–1144.

O'Gorman P, Schneider T (2009). The physical basis for increases in precipitation extremes in simulations of 21st-century climate change. Proceedings of the National Academy of Sciences 106:14773–14777.

Palmieri R, Tredway L, Niyogi D, Lackmann G (2006). Development and evaluation of a forecasting system for fungal disease in turfgrass. Meteorological Applications 13:1–12.

Pan ZT, Segal M, Li X, Zib B (2009). Global climate change impact on the midwestern USA—a summer cooling trend. In: Pryor SC (ed) Understanding climate change: climate variability, predictability, and change in the midwestern United States. Bloomington: Indiana University Press.

Pielke RA Sr., Adegoke JO, Beltran-Przekurat A, Hiemstra CA, Lin J, Nair US, Niyogi D, Nobis TE (2007a) An overview of regional land use and land cover impacts on rainfall. Tellus B 59B:587–601.

Pielke RA Sr., Adegoke JO, Chase TN, Marshall CH, Matsui T, Niyogi D. (2007b). A new paradigm for assessing the role of agriculture in the climate system and in climate change. Agriculture and Forest Meteorology 132:234–254.

Pritchard SG, Amthor JS (2005). Crops and Environmental Change: An Introduction to Effects of Global Warming, Increasing Atmospheric CO_2 and O_3 Concentrations, and Soil Salinization on Crop Physiology and Yield. New York: Food Products Press.

Pryor SC, Schoof JT (2008). Changes in the seasonality of precipitation over the contiguous USA. Journal of Geophysical Research 113:D21108, doi:10.1029/2008JD010251.

Pryor SC, Takle GS (2009). Climate variability, predictability and change: an introduction. In: Pryor SC (ed) Understanding climate change: climate variability, predictability, and change in the midwestern United States. Bloomington: Indiana University Press.

Rosenzweig C, Francesco NT, Goldberg R, Mills E, Bloomfield J (2002). Increased crop damage in the US from excess precipitation under climate change. Global Environmental Change 12:197–202.

Rosenzweig C, Strzepek KM, Major DC, Iglesias A, Yates DN, McCluskey A, Hillel D (2004). Water resources for agriculture in a changing climate: international case studies. Global Environ Change 14:345–360.

Schlenker W, Roberts MJ (2009). Nonlinear temperature effects indicate severe damages to US crop yields under climate change. Proceedings of the National Academy of Sciences of the United States of America 106: 15594–15598.

Schoof JT (2009). Historical and projected changes in the length of the frost-free season. In: Pryor SC (ed) Understanding climate change: climate variability, predictability, and change in the midwestern United States. Bloomington: Indiana University Press.

Schoof JT, Pryor SC, Suprenant J (2010). Development of daily precipitation projections for the United States based on probabilistic downscaling. Journal of Geophysical Research 115:D13106, doi:10.1029/2009JD013030.

Searchinger T, Heimlich R, Houghton RA, Dong F, Elobeid A, Fabiosa J, Tokgoz S, Hayes D, Yu

TH (2008). Use of US croplands for biofuels increases greenhouse gases through emissions from land-use change. Science 319:1238–1240.

Shaw SB, Royem A, Riha SJ (2011). The relationship between extreme hourly precipitation and surface temperature in different hydroclimatic regions of the United States. Journal of Hydrometeorology 12:319–325.

Sinha T, Cherkauer KA, Mishra V (2010). Impacts of historic climate variability on seasonal soil frost in the midwestern United States. Journal of Hydrometeorology 11:229–252.

Smither J, Blay—Palmer A (2001). Technology innovation as a strategy for climate adaptation in agriculture. Applied Geography 21:175–197.

Svoboda M, Lecomte D, Hayes M, Heim R, Gleason K, Angel J, Rippey B, Tinker R, Palecki M, Stooksbury D, Miskus D, Stephens S (2002). The drought monitor. Bulletin of the American Meteorological Society 83:1181–1190.

Tol RSJ, Fankhauser S, Smith JB (1998). The scope for adaptation to climate change: What can we learn from the impact literature? Global Environmental Change 8:109–123.

Tyner W (2008). The US ethanol and biofuels boom: its origins, current status, and future prospects. BioScience 58:646–653.

Vicente-Serrano SM, Begueria S, Lopez-Moreno J (2010). A multiscalar drought index sensitive to global warming: The standardized precipitation evapotranspiration index. Journal of Climate 23:1696–1718.

Yacobucci BD (2010). Biofuels incentives: A summary of federal programs. Congressional Research Service 7-5700. Available from: http://digitalcommons.unl.edu/crsdocs/8/.

6. Potential Future Impacts of Climate on Row Crop Production in the Great Lakes Region

J. A. ANDRESEN, G. ALAGARSWAMY, G. GUENTCHEV,
PERDINAN, K. PIROMSOPA, A. POLLYEA,
J. VAN RAVENSWAY, AND J. A. WINKLER

Introduction

The Great Lakes region spans the U.S. states of Minnesota, Wisconsin, Illinois, Indiana, Michigan, Ohio, Pennsylvania, and New York and the Canadian province of Ontario (Figure 6.1). Agriculture ranks among the most important economic activities of the region, accounting for more than $19 billion in annual cash receipts in the U.S. states of Michigan, New York, and Wisconsin alone (USDA/NASS, 2007a). Agriculture in the region follows a south to north gradient, with intensive row crop monoculture in southern sections gradually giving way to forests and other natural vegetation across the north. Southwestern sections of the region form the northern boundary of the U.S. Corn Belt region (Hart 198).

Crop production in the Great Lakes is strongly influenced by climate and weather. Previous research has identified water availability as a key determinant of year-to-year yield variability of regional row crops. However, the amount of thermal time and growing season length was also found to be of importance, especially for annual crops in northern fringes of the region (Andresen et al. 2001). The key climate parameters of consequence for dictating crop yields within the Great Lakes region include:

- Drought: As described in chapter 2 of this volume, approximately only 3% of farmland in this region is commercially irrigated, largely for seed corn, potato, and soybean production (USDA/NASS, 2007b). Crop yields are highly sensitive to drought conditions, particularly during reproductive growth stages (Mishra and Cherkauer 2010). During extended drought periods such as 1988, large area yields for corn and soybeans were less than 50% of average trend yields (USDA/NASS, 2007b).

- Flooding: Excess water is also a source of risk to crop yields in the region, and farmers lost large portions of their crops during the extensive flooding years of 1993 and 1997, particularly in western sections of the region (Rosenzweig et al. 2002).

- Conditions in the early growing season: Early season cool, wet spells can lead to delays in planting, which require a shift to a shorter season cultivar or to a different crop such as soybeans (Schwartz 1999) and may lead to substantial crop yield and quality reductions due to plant diseases (McMullen 1997).

Crop yields in the region have increased significantly in recent decades (chapter 5 of this volume), primarily due to improvements in technology (Kucharik and Ramankutty 2005), although some of the increase was found to be also associated with concurrent trends toward wetter, less stressful growing season weather (Andresen et al. 2001).

Given the importance of thermal and hydrologic regimes to historical variability in annual crop yields—and thus the implied vulnerability of the agricultural sector to climate change—there is great interest in applying climate projections to crop models to examine possible trajectories of agricultural yields. One such study that used projected future climate scenarios from two global climate models (GCMs) and output from crop simulation models suggested that yields of soybean and alfalfa in the future may be substantially greater than those observed during the recent past, due to the effects of CO_2 enrichment and more favorable growing season weather, especially in northern sections of the region (Andresen et al. 2000). Trends for maize (corn) in the study were variable across the region, with yield decreases in some areas and minor increases in others. Similar results were obtained in a subsequent study of the midwestern

United States by Southworth et al. (2002), who also noted a strong correlation between variability of projected yields and variability of projected climate. Recent projections of future climate generally suggest warmer and potentially wetter conditions across the Great Lakes region (Karl et al. 2009). Based on known physiological and environmental constraints, Hatfield et al. (2008) concluded that crop yields in northern sections of the United States might increase with increasing temperatures during the next few decades, mostly due to the effects of CO_2 enrichment, but might decline thereafter because of continued warming of air temperatures above the optimal range of the crop species. Given the availability of updated projected climate scenarios for the Great Lakes region and the potential for increased agronomic productivity, the major objective of this study was to provide an updated characterization of the impacts of future weather and climate on regional crop production. Two representative crops commonly grown across the region were chosen for the study: corn, a C-4 crop planted in the spring, and (winter) wheat, a C-3 crop planted in the fall. Planted acreages for these crops across the eight-state Great Lakes region in 2007 were 38 million acres for corn and 4.7 million acres for wheat (USDA/NASS, 2007a).

Methodology

Estimates of crop response to the input climate conditions were obtained from deterministic crop simulation models, which are based on the underlying physiological processes governing plant growth and development. CERES-Maize and CERES-Wheat crop models, part of the Decision Support for Agrotechnology Transfer (DSSAT) model software system (Jones et al. 2003), were used for all simulations in the study. Five locations across the Great Lakes region (1 in Wisconsin, 3 in Michigan, and 1 in New York; Figure 6.1) were chosen for the study on the basis of projected climate series availability as well as geographical coverage across the region and its major land use zones. Three of the study locations were specifically chosen from northern, historically less agriculturally active areas of the region to investigate the potential for more intensive row crop production under a warmer climate.

Two sets of simulations were run for each crop to examine the relative impact of CO_2 enrichment on crop productivity: one with ambient atmospheric concentration of CO_2 held constant at 390 ppm (the approximate current level) and the second with gradually increasing levels of CO_2 up to approximately 850 ppm by 2100 based on the IPCC A2 GHG emissions scenario (Nakicenovic and Swart 2000). Most other crop and management variables in the simulations were held constant so as to isolate the effects of weather and climate. Fertility levels in all simulations were assumed to be non-limiting for crop growth and development. Other agronomic input data necessary for the crop simulations (e.g., plant populations) were chosen to reflect typical current technology and growing conditions. Crop cultivar characteristics representative of the region

were selected based on the results of a previous study (Andresen et al. 2001). Planting dates for corn were determined automatically each season by the model on the first day that met user-specified weather and soil conditions and were set at October 1 each year for wheat (following the Hessian fly free dates for the study sites). Soils data used in the simulations were based on profile data typical of agricultural soils in the vicinity of each location in the study and were obtained from laboratory pedon data available on line at the National Web Soil Survey (USDA/NRCS 2009). Total plant available water in the rooting zones of the five soils ranged from 139–259 mm.

An ensemble of scenarios for each location was created using simulations from four GCMs, each driven with two different SRES GHG emission scenarios (A2 and B2). The four GCMs used to create the scenarios were the CGCM2 model of the Canadian Climate Center, the HadCM3 model developed by the Hadley Center in Great Britain, the ECHAM4 model developed by the Max Planck Institute in Germany, and the CCSM1 model developed by NCAR in the United States. These climate scenarios are also used in chapter 8 of this volume. An empirical-dynamic downscaling approach (Winkler et al. 2012) was used to derive local climate scenarios of daily temperature and precipitation for the five locations from the coarse-scale GCM simulations. Following the method developed by Winkler et al. (1997), observed daily temperature and precipitation were empirically related to airflow and atmospheric state variables obtained from the NCEP/NCAR reanalysis (Kalnay et al. 1996). The variables used as predictors (sea-level pressure, 500 hPa geopotential height, 850 hPa specific humidity, and the u and v components of the geostrophic wind) were chosen to represent relevant dynamic and physical atmospheric processes. The transfer functions were then applied to output from the GCM simulations for the period 2000–2099. Four "variants" of the downscaling methods were employed that reflect important "user decisions" (Winkler et al. 1997) in transfer function development, most importantly the decision whether or not to adjust for biases in the GCM-simulations of the predictor variables. The transfer functions were developed separately for daily maximum temperature, minimum temperature, and liquid-equivalent precipitation. The resulting scenario suite was composed of over 60 scenarios for each location and variable, of which 32 individual projected future scenarios per site were used for this study, based on a comparison of the projected local climate variables for a control period to observed values. The 2000–2009 timeframe was used as a baseline control period for the comparisons.

In order to determine the nature of changes in the variables studied, estimates of both trend magnitude and significance were calculated for the period 2010–2099. Trend magnitude was obtained with the method of Sen (1968). This nonparametric statistic was selected due to the lack of normality for some of the variables

analyzed. The trend magnitude statistic (B), a nonparametric analogue of the least squares derived maturity slope parameter estimate, is defined as: $B = \mathrm{med}\ \{D_{ij}\}$, where $D_{ij} = (x_j - x_i)\ /\ (j - i)$ for all possible pairs (x_i, xj), $1 \leq i < j \leq n$, and n the number of observations in the series. The nonparametric Mann-Kendall or Kendall's tau statistic (Kendall 1975) was used to determine the significance of the trends. The series were analyzed with a two-sided test for trend, with H_o (i.e., no trend) of interest $(x_1, x_2, \ldots x_n)$ were a sample of n independent and identically distributed variables. The alternative hypothesis, H_1, of the two-sided test was that the distribution of x_i and x_j were not identical for all pairs of $i, j \leq n$, and $i \neq j$. The series were analyzed with a two-sided test for trend, with H_o accepted if the standard normal variate of the variable in question was less than or equal to the standard normal cumulative distribution function for a given level of significance α, $|Z| \leq z_{\alpha/2}$.

Results and Discussion

CLIMATE PROJECTIONS

Time series of the climate change projections for mean annual temperature and total annual precipitation expressed as anomalies from the 2000–2009 period for the 32 climate scenarios are shown for one representative site in Figures 6.2a and 6.2b. In general, mean annual temperatures across the region are projected to warm 2°C–6°C (relative to the 2000–2009 period) across the ensemble of projected future time series by the last decade of the century. Overall, the temperature change in simulations with the A2 scenario tended to be greater than for the B2 SRES especially between 2050 and 2099. When averaged across the GCM variants, for example, the 2090–2099 decade for the A2 emission scenario was 4.6°C warmer, while the B2 scenario average was 3.1°C warmer. There were also some consistent differences among the GCMs used in the projections, with the ECHAM4 tending to be the warmest of the four models (+4.6°C for 2090–2099 versus 2000–2009 decades on average across the eight scenario variants) with somewhat less warming on average for the HadCM3, CGCM2 and CCSM1 scenarios (+3.8°C, +3.5°C, and +3.5°C, respectively). Projected 2090–2099 annual precipitation totals in the ensembles generally remained in a range between 70–140 percent of the 2000–2009 control period totals (Figure 6.2b), with a slight overall average increase by the 2090–2099 decade (less than 10 percent at 4 of the 5 sites). There were no consistent differences between the A2 and B2 emission scenarios. Of the GCMs, the HadCM3 was the wettest of the four on average with a 15 percent increase in mean annual precipitation and ECHAM4 the driest with less than 1 percent decrease. At the majority of sites, projected future corn growing season (March through October) precipitation was similar or declined. In contrast, slight increases were noted for the wheat growing season (October through July). This pattern is consistent with a number of other more recent climate projections across the midwestern United States (Karl et al. 2009; see also Figures 2.16 and 2.17 in this volume).

PROJECTIONS OF CROP YIELDS

Simulated crop yields from the CERES-Maize and CERES-Wheat crop models run with the projected climate scenarios generally suggest overall declines in productivity for corn and increases for wheat (Figure 6.3). Corn yield differences at the five sites in the last decade and first decade of the simulations ranged from −27.3–+23.0 percent and +1.2–4.8 percent for constant CO_2 and increasing CO_2 scenarios, respectively. The same scenarios for wheat ranged from −9.3–+23.7 percent and +10.8–72.7 percent. While most of the simulated wheat yields were greater during the later decade, they were substantially greater for the CO_2 enriched runs, which is consistent with previous research concerning the potential benefit of increasing levels of CO_2 to C-3 plant species (Hatfield 2008). While late century corn yields declined at most locations, one notable exception was the Sault Sainte Marie site, where corn yields increased more than 20 percent in response to warmer, more favorable growing season conditions. Small increases in yield (generally less than 5%) were observed between the constant versus increasing CO_2 runs. No consistent differences in simulated yield were found between climate scenarios derived from different GCMs for either crop, although corn yields tended to be less for the B2 GHG SRES than for the A2 scenario, possibly due to lower average growing season precipitation totals.

Consistent with the discussion in chapter 5, changes in simulated yields over time in general were not monotonic (Figure 6.4). For the corn series at Owosso, yields remain fairly steady for the first four decades, and then decrease during the period from 2040 to 2069 before leveling off during the last three decades. Simulated wheat yields at Fredonia increase during the first three decades, decrease from 2040 to 2059, and then increase once again during the last three decades. Overall, yield variability from the corn simulations with both constant and increasing CO_2 held steady or increased during the first 60–70 years of the century, followed by a decrease during the last 30–40 years. Averaged across all sites and the 32 climate scenarios, the standard deviation of yield with constant CO_2 increased from 1,598 kg ha^{-1} during the first decade of the century to 1,853 kg ha^{-1} during the 2061–2070 decade before decreasing to 1,647 kg ha^{-1} between 2090 and 2099. Yield variability from the wheat simulations with constant CO_2 steadily decreased an average of approximately 15 percent for the first 70–80 years, followed by an increase of just over 20 percent during the last 20–30 years. The pattern for wheat with the increasing CO_2 scenarios was similar, except the increase during the last few decades was smaller. The increasing productivity of wheat with increasing concentrations of CO_2 is expected because wheat has a C-3 carbon photosynthetic pathway for which higher levels of CO_2 increase quantum ef-

ficiency and increase water use efficiency, while C-4 pathway plants generally benefit only from gains in water use efficiency (Hatfield et al. 2008).

The relative influence of increasing CO_2 concentrations on wheat yield is illustrated in Figure 6.5, which depicts yields at the Fredonia site averaged across all climate scenarios with time for both constant and increasing CO_2 concentrations. Averaged across scenarios at each of the five sites, wheat yields with CO_2 increases for the 2090–2099 decade ranged from 21–37 percent greater than yields for the constant CO_2, which is consistent with projected increases from previous studies (Amthor 2001).

Despite the non-linearity in yield response, a number of temporal trends were identified in yield and some agroclimatological output variables derived from the model simulations for the 2000–2099 study period. Trend statistics for several variables summarized by crop and site are given in Table 6.1. For corn yield, the sign of the trend statistic was negative for all sites and CO_2 scenarios except those at Sault Sainte Marie, where early-century productivity is limited by cool temperatures. The corn yield decreases were associated with decreases in growing season precipitation (at all five sites) as well as a shortening of the growing season due to warmer temperatures. In contrast to corn, the trends for wheat suggest potential increases in productivity over time, especially given increases in CO_2 concentration. Positive trends (i.e., increasing values through time) were found at all but two

Table 6.1. Trend statistics for simulated yield and agroclimatological variables at each site for corn (top) and wheat (bottom) for the period 2000–2099. Asterisks *, **, and *** denote significance at the 0.10, 0.05, and 0.01 probability levels, respectively.

Corn simulations	CO_2 scenario	Yield (kg/ha/yr)	Precipitation (mm/yr)	Evapotrans. (mm/yr)	Runoff (mm/yr)	Drainage (mm/yr)
Eau Claire	Constant	−11.6	−0.1*	−0.4	0.0	0.3**
	Increasing	−10.7		−0.3	0.0	0.3**
Fredonia	Constant	−15.6	−0.6	−0.5	0.0	0.1
	Increasing	−15.3		−0.5	0.0	0.1
Owosso	Constant	−16.2*	−0.1	−0.3	0.0	0.1*
	Increasing	−15.8		−0.3	0.0	0.1*
S.S. Marie	Constant	−12.5*	−0.5	−0.1	0.0	−0.1
	Increasing	12.7*		0.0	0.0	−0.1
Sturgeon Bay	Constant	−10.2	−0.4	−0.5	0.0	0.1
	Increasing	−10.0		−0.5	0.0	0.0

Wheat simulations	CO_2 scenario	Yield (kg/ha/yr)	Precipitation (mm/yr)	Evapotrans. (mm/yr)	Runoff (mm/yr)	Drainage (mm/yr)
Eau Claire	Constant	−1.3	0.7	0.1	0.0	0.0
	Increasing	12.2		−0.3	0.0	0.2
Fredonia	Constant	2.2	−0.1	−0.2	0.0	0.0
	Increasing	18.3		−0.5	0.0	0.3**
Owosso	Constant	−5.5	0.3	−0.2	0.0	0.0
	Increasing	7.3		−0.6	0.0	0.2**
S.S. Marie	Constant	7.7	0.5	−0.1	0.0	0.0
	Increasing	33.7*		0.1	0.0	0.0
Sturgeon Bay	Constant	1.9	0.0	0.0	0.0	−0.1
	Increasing	16.7		−0.2	0.0	0.0

of the 10 combinations for yield and three of the five sites for seasonal precipitation. Seasonal evapotranspiration for corn decreased for all but one of the ten sites and CO_2 scenario combinations, which suggests an overall reduction in plant available water with time and a possible increase in the frequency of plant water stress. Decreasing trends in evapotranspiration for wheat were consistent with the corn trends and were likely linked with conditions during the early summer in which both crops temporally overlap. Decreases in evapotranspiration were also likely to result in part from increases in water use efficiency associated with increasing CO_2 concentration, as suggested by the relatively greater negative trends (not significant) at four of the five sites for the increasing CO_2 scenarios.

It is also interesting to note that the general increases in water drainage for both crops at all but the Sault Sainte Marie site. Given general reductions in growing season precipitation, the opposite trend might have been expected. Possible causes of the increases in drainage include reductions in evapotranspiration rates (that are greater in magnitude than the reductions in precipitation), a changing seasonal distribution of precipitation (maximum precipitation rates in the region historically tend to occur during the summer months), or a change in precipitation intensity (more extreme events), although the last possibility is unlikely, given the lack of changes in the runoff variable. The tendency towards increased drainage was less frequently observed in the simulations for wheat, with positive changes at only three of the ten combinations (two of which were statistically significant).

Concluding Remarks

In this study, CERES-Maize and CERES-Wheat crop simulation models were used to identify potential future impacts of weather and climate on corn and wheat production at five sites in the Great Lakes region. The direction and magnitude of simulated impacts depended greatly on the crop and CO_2 scenario. In general, the warmer climate suggested by the climate scenarios led to decreases in average simulated maize (corn) yields and increases in wheat yields in the non-CO_2 enriched scenarios. For the increasing CO_2 scenarios, corn yields in general decreased while wheat yields increased. The decreases in corn yield were associated with decreases in (summer) growing season precipitation

and increases in growing season temperatures while the wheat yield increases appeared to be linked to steady or increasing fall and winter precipitation. Given the importance of corn to agricultural production systems in the Midwest and the importance of the Midwest region to national corn production (see chapters 2 and 5 of this volume), these scenario projections may have significant implications for food provision and the economy of the region. The impact of CO_2 enrichment was substantial for the C-3 wheat crop, with increases in yield noted for most scenarios. Largest percentage increases in yield during the 2000–2099 period were found at the northernmost study location, which suggests at least the potential for increasing agronomic productivity with time in northern sections of the region that have not been historically productive.

As estimates of crop responses to projected changes in climate, results of this study may be of use in determining potential adaptive responses by growers. At a minimum, the series of simulated agroclimatological variables developed and the techniques used in this study might serve as a baseline reference in efforts to estimate or assess the potential regional agronomic impacts. However, it is important to note that the simulations in this study did not account for the confounding influence of weeds, diseases, insect pests, or other practical, production-related factors (e.g., unlimited fertility), all of which may have profound negative (or positive) impacts on agronomic production systems in the future (Easterling et al. 2007). Our results thus likely represent an upper range of relative productivity given current levels of technology.

ACKNOWLEDGMENTS

Financial support from the Michigan State University AgBioResearch Program (Project MICL02169) and the suggestions of several reviewers are gratefully acknowledged.

REFERENCES

Amthor JS (2001). Effects of atmospheric CO_2 concentration on wheat yield: Review of results from experiments using various approaches to control CO_2 concentration. Field Crops Research, 73:1–34.

Andresen, JA, Alagarswamy G, Ritchie JT, Rotz CA, LeBaron AW (2001). Assessment of the impact of weather on maize, soybean, and alfalfa production in the Upper Great Lakes region of the United States, 1895–1996. Agronomy Journal 93:1059–1070.

Andresen JA, Alagarswamy G, Stead D, Sea WB, Cheng HH (2000). Agriculture. In: Preparing for a changing climate: The potential consequences of climate variability and change, Sousounis PJ, Bisanz JM (eds), University of Michigan, Atmospheric, Oceanic, and Space Sciences Dept., Ann Arbor.

Easterling WE, Aggarwal PK, Batima P, Brander KM, Erda L, Howden SM, A. Kirilenko A, Morton J, Soussana J-F, Schmidhuber J, Tubiello FN (2007). Food, fibre and forest products. In: Parry, Canziani, Palutikof, van der Linden and Hanso (eds) Climate change 2007: Impacts, adaptation and vulnerability. Contribution of Working Group II to the Fourth Assessment Report of the Intergovernmental Panel on Climate Change, Cambridge, UK: Cambridge University Press, 273–313.

Hart JF, (1986). Change in the corn belt. Geographical Review 76:51–72.

Hatfield J, Boote K, Fay P, Hahn L, Izaurralde C, Kimball BA, Mader T, Morgan J, Ort D, Polley W, Thomson A, Wolfe D (2008). Agriculture. In: The effects of climate change on agriculture, land resources, water resources, and biodiversity in the United States. A report by the US Climate Change Science Program and the Subcommittee on Global Change Research. Washington, DC.

Jones, JW, Hoogenboom G, Porter CH, Boote KJ, Batchelor WD, Hunt LA, Wilkens PW, Singh U, Gijsman AJ, Ritchie JT (2003). DSSAT Cropping System Model. European Journal of Agronomy 18:235–265.

Kalnay E, Kanamitsu M, Kistler R, Collins W, Deaven D, Gandin L, Iredell M, Saha S, White G, Woollen J, Zhu Y, Leetmaa A, Reynolds B, Chelliah M, Ebisuzaki W, Higgins W, Janowiak J, Mo KC, Ropelewski C, Wang J, Jenne R, Joseph D (1996). The NCEP/NCAR 40-year reanalysis project. Bulletin of the American Meteorological Society 77:437–471.

Karl TR, Melillo JM, Peterson TC (eds) (2009). Global climate change impacts in the United States. Cambridge, UK: Cambridge University Press.

Kendall, MG (1975). Rank correlation methods. Fifth edition. London: Charles Griffin and Co.

Kucharik CJ, Ramankutty N (2005). Trends and variability in US corn yields over the twentieth century. Earth Interactions, 6:1–29.

McMullen M, Jones R, Gallenberg D (1997). Scab of wheat and barley: A re-emerging disease of devastating impact. Plant Disease, 81:1340–1348.

Mishra V, Cherkauer KA (2010). Retrospective droughts in the crop growing season: Implications to corn and soybean yield in the midwestern United States. Agricultural and Forest Meteorology 150:1030–1045.

Nakicenovic, N, Swart S (2000) Emissions scenarios. A special report of Working Group III of the Intergovernmental Panel on Climate Change. Cambridge, UK: Cambridge University.

Rosenzweig, C, Tubiello FN, Goldberg R, Mills E, Bloomfield J (2002). Increased crop damage in the US from excess precipitation under climate change. Global Environmental Change 12:197–202.

Schwartz D (1999). Management strategies for delayed planting. Minnesota Crop News 5:44–45.

Sen PK (1968). Estimates of the regression coefficient based on Kendall's tau. Journal of the American Statistical Association 63:1379–1389.

Southworth J, Pfeiffer RA, Habeck M (2002). Crop modeling results under climate change for the Upper Midwest USA. In: Doering O, Randolph JC, Southworth J, Pfeiffer RA (eds), Effects of Climate change and variability on agricultural systems. Norwell, MA: Kluwer, 127–158.

USDA/NASS (2007a). USDA economics and statistics system data sets: Crops. Available from: http://usda.mannlib.cornell.edu/MannUsda/homepage.do. US Department of Agriculture, National Agricultural Statistics Service, Washington, DC.

USDA/NASS (2007b). 2007 census of agriculture. Available from: http://www.agcensus.usda.gov/Publications/2007/Full_Report/index.asp. US Department of Agriculture, National Agricultural Statistics Service, Washington, DC.

USDA/NRCS, (2009). Web soil survey. Available from: http://websoilsurvey.nrcs.usda.gov/app/HomePage.htm. US Department of Agriculture, Natural Resources Conservation Service, Washington, DC.

Winkler J, Bisanz J, Guentchev G, Piromsopa K, van Ravensway J, Prawiranata H, Torre R, Min HK, Clark J (2012). The development and communication of an ensemble of local-scale climate scenarios: an example from the Pileus Project. In: Dietz T, Bidwell D (eds) Climate change in the Great Lakes region: Navigating an uncertain future. East Lansing: Michigan State University Press.

Winkler JA, Palutikof JP, Andresen JA, Goodess CM (1997). The simulation of daily time series from GCM output. Part 2: A sensitivity analysis of empirical transfer functions for downscaling GCM simulations. Journal of Climate 10:2497–2513.

7. Vulnerability of Soil Carbon Reservoirs in the Midwest to Climate Change

Z. PAN, D. ANDRADE, AND N. GOSSELIN

Introduction

Rising atmospheric CO_2 concentrations are the main cause of recent global warming (IPCC 2007). The atmospheric CO_2 increase depends on its carbon exchange with oceans and the land that absorbs about half of anthropogenic emission into the atmosphere (Broecker et al. 1979). Soil carbon is the largest terrestrial pool, and its trends directly affect atmospheric CO_2 level. Each year the earth's terrestrial land uptakes about 60 Gt carbon through photosynthesis and at the same time it loses a similar amount of carbon by respiration (Schlesinger and Andrews 2000). Both photosynthesis and respiration are highly sensitive to temperature, precipitation, and other climate variables. The net balance between these two large opposite terms is strongly affected by climate change and is difficult to quantify accurately. Although estimates based on different techniques differ, a range of analyses indicate that North American ecosystems are significant carbon sinks and play a disproportionate role in the global carbon budget. Using an inverse modeling technique, Fan et al. (1998) estimated that the continental U.S. net carbon (C) sink in the early 1900s was 0.81 gigatonne-C per year ($Gt\text{-}C\ yr^{-1}$) (1.7 $Gt\text{-}C\ yr^{-1}$ for all North America), whereas Schimel et al. (2000) and Potter & Klooster (1999) used biogeochemical models and obtained a value of about 0.2 $Gt\text{-}C\ yr^{-1}$ over the United States. Forest inventory data have indicated that the North American forest ecosystem sequestration rate is 0.08–0.28 $Gt\text{-}C\ yr^{-1}$. Pacala et al. (2001) reconciled these somewhat divergent results by suggesting that the conterminous U.S. carbon sink is 0.30–0.58 $Gt\text{-}C\ yr^{-1}$ (Bachelet et al. 2004). To provide a context for these fluxes it is worth recalling that current anthropogenic CO_2 emissions are ~ 9 $Gt\text{-}C\ yr^{-1}$, about one-third of which is absorbed by terrestrial ecosystems (IPCC 2007).

The United States has about 130–150 million hectares of croplands, 35 percent of which lie within the Midwest (Lal et al. 1999; see also chapter 2 of this volume). The U.S. soils have lost about 5 Gt-C as a

92

result of cultivation by converting natural forests and grasses into croplands (Lal et al. 1999). It is estimated that with improved management practices U.S. cropland can potentially sequester 50 to 75 percent of the previously lost carbon over a 25- to 50-year period (Lal et al. 1999). Longer growing seasons and increased plant growth from higher levels of ambient CO_2 as a result of anthropogenic perturbation of atmospheric composition are expected to generally increase primary production and thus carbon storage in terrestrial eco-systems. However, climate variables affect primary production and respiration and, indirectly, soil carbon storage. Soil carbon over cultivated lands is projected to de-cline, partly due to increased respiration under a warmer climate (Jones et al. 2003). The release of soil carbon into the atmo-sphere under the warmer climate will in turn amplify the initial warming (Cox et al. 2000). Respiration by microbes oxidizing plant detritus, root exudates, and humified organic materials is a nonlinear function of temperature and precipitation, and thus, depending on the relative changes in thermal and hydrologic regimes, cli-mate change may be associated with either increased or decreased soil carbon in agricultural landscapes. The intense ag-ricultural operations in the Midwest will continue to have significant impacts on the size of soil carbon pool and thus CO_2 in the atmosphere. This chapter evaluates the effects of possible future climate condi-tions over the Midwest on soil carbon and assesses direction and magnitudes of soil C changes in the future climate.

Models and Data

Soil carbon pools and carbon fluxes presented herein are simulated using DayCENT, a modified version of the CENTURY model (Parton et al. 1987, Metherell et al. 1993) that uses a daily time-step. CENTURY is an ecosystem model that simulates carbon, nitrogen, phosphorus, and sulfur (C, N, P, and S, respectively) dynamics of ecosystems (in-cluding grasslands, agricultural lands, forests, and savannas) on a century time scale. The CENTURY model partitions soil organic carbon (SOC) into active (SOM1), slow (SOM2) and passive (SOM3) soil organic pools. Plant residue (stalks, stems, leaves, chaff, cobs, etc.) both above and belowground is partitioned into struc-ture and metabolic pools. Carbon is stored in three major pools based on the turn-over time: fast pool (< 1 year), slow pool (5–10 years), and inactive pool (>1000 years). The metabolic pool is further di-vided into aboveground bio-structure and belowground metabolism. The decompo-sition rates among pools are characterized by each pool's turnover time. Each Day-CENT simulation was defined in terms of a schedule, which prescribes the dates of planting and harvest, type of crop planted, and tillage, fertilization, grazing, among others, as well as the occurrence of fire and erosion.

Experimental Design

As there are few accurate measurements of soil composition and properties, we use a typical loamy soil to represent the soils across the Midwest region. The loamy soil consists of 25 percent clay, 35 percent silt, and 40 percent sand. The SOC levels in various soil pools are unknown; so default SOC contents provided with the DayCENT distribution were used. The initial SOC values are assigned according to land use categories that are mapped from the land use types in Figure 7.1. For example, crop or grasslands have an initial SOC in slow and passive pools of 3800 and 1530 g m^{-2} respectively, whereas a mixed forest has an initial SOC of 3680 and 4080 g m^{-2} respectively for the two pools. We used the same initial SOC values and DayCENT schedule files for both the current and future climates in order to isolate SOC sensitivity purely to forcing from meteorological parameters (not initial conditions). Another way of specifying initial SOC level would be spinning up of DayCENT for hundreds to thousands of years until the SOC reaches a quasi equilibrium with the assumed forcing climate. As a test run, we spun up DayCENT for 2,000 years using historical weather data for the 1894–2005 period at a single site (Ames, Iowa). The final SOC pools after the spin up were not much different from the default values. This prompted us to use default initial SOC values for subsequent simulations, which is much less computationally expensive.

Information for the future scenarios climates, including the current model climate, were extracted from the Intergovernmental Panel on Climate Change (IPCC) Fourth Assessment Report (AR4) (IPCC 2007) as archived by DOE/PCMDI (http://www-pcmdi. llnl.gov/ipcc/about _ipcc.php). Two general circulation models (GCMs) were selected to provide the climate variables used in this analysis: the Canadian Centre for Climate Modeling and Analysis model (CGCM3, hereafter called CaGCM) and the Météo-France Centre National de Recherches Météorologiques (CM3, FrGCM). These two GCMs represent a spread of model characteristics and thus their scenario climate projections also differ. Over the Midwest CaGCM climate is warm and dry relative to FrGCM (Table 7.1). For each GCM, daily temperature and precipitation were obtained under three different scenario climates under the greenhouse gas emission scenarios: B1, A1B, A2. The atmospheric CO_2 concentrations reach 550, 720, and 850 ppm by 2100 for the B1, A1B, and A2 scenarios, respectively. The CO_2 levels for the mid-21st century used herein are linearly interpolated from those values. We conducted simulations for two periods: 1961–1980 (referred to as late 20th century or current) and 2046–2065 (referred to as middle 21st century or future). We chose the future period to represent sufficiently near-term conditions to have immediate policy relevance for agricultural management.

We first examine the skill of DayCENT in simulating historical SOC changes at a site where some limited soil C data are available. Then we present climate changes in temperature and precipitation. Finally, we analyzed the carbon responses to the climate changes in terms of net primary production (NPP), respiration, and soil C.

Table 7.1. Current growing season mean climates over the Midwest (the domain is shown in Figure 7.1) from the two GCMs used herein (Canadian Centre for Climate Modeling and Analysis model (CaGCM) and Météo-France Centre National de Recherches Météorologiques (FrGCM)). Also shown are the simulated changes in the climate variables under the three emission scenarios (B1, A1B, A2) and the corresponding carbon responses (SOC = soil organic carbon, NPP = net primary productivity, Resp = respiration) for the mid-twenty-first century. The numbers shown for the climate scenarios and carbon responses indicate the difference from the historical period.

	CaGCM				FrGCM			
	Current	B1	A1B	A2	Current	B1	A1B	A2
Maximum temperature (°C)	28.2	−0.4	0.6	0.5	23.8	2.2	2.9	2.8
Minimum temperature (°C)	14.1	0.5	1.2	1.3	14.6	2.4	3.2	3.1
Precipitation (mm)	345.8	−6.1	32.1	0.0	619.6	−9.1	−1.5	−12.7
SOC (g m^{-2})	6059.0	−31.0	−59.0	101.0	5682.0	−54	−130.0	−87
Resp (g yr^{-1} m^{-2})	386.0	40.0	57.7	69.1	412.0	38.5	42.6	42.6
NPP (g yr^{-1} m^{-2})	375.0	69.1	91.0	91.0	420.0	59.8	54.6	58.2

Results

DAYCENT VALIDATION AT A SINGLE SITE

This simulation was initialized in 1895 prior to significant modification of land use by mass settlements and lasts until 2005. The meteorological data used were derived from observations at Ames, Iowa. A corn-alfalfa rotation was used prior to 1951, after which alfalfa was discontinued and corn was grown continuously. This rotation scheme was designed to match actual farming practices during the simulation period. Concurrent with the abandonment of alfalfa was the adoption of nitrogen fertilizer in 1951. Soybeans were adopted and grown in rotation with corn from 1957 until the end of the simulation. A progression of corn and soybean cultivars was used to simulate the gradual adoption of improved, high-yield varieties

through time. Simulated tillage practices included the use of a field cultivator and tandem disk in the spring, and moldboard plowing in the fall, prior to adoption of a chisel plow in 1981. A short period of no-till was used from 1991 to 1994, followed by conservation tillage through 2005. Our simulations assumed a linear increase of atmospheric CO_2 concentration from the late 19th-century level of 294 ppm to the present level of 370 ppm.

The model captured SOC trends documented in literature; the initial persistent decline from the 1890s until about the 1940s, after which SOC starts to recover as crop rotation and tillage practice improve (Figure 7.2a). The total initial SOC in the top 20 cm of the soil for simulations beginning in 1894 was assumed to be 8000 g m^{-2}, a typical value over uncultivated areas at the time (Smith 1999). This value is very close to that obtained by spinning up DayCENT simulations for

2000 years (Pan et al. 2010). The initial partitioning of carbon into the three pools (SOM1, SOM2, SOM3) was chosen to represent the loss of about half of initial SOC by the mid-20th century, and it agrees with most published works (e.g., Smith 1999). The observed climate with control management (defined as corn-soybean rotation, conservational tillage, and moderate nitrogen fertilizer) maintained a roughly steady SOC level. The model simulated a gradual decrease in SOC in the top 20 cm soil layer from 8,000 g m^{-2} in 1894 to about 4,000 g m^{-2} in early 1960s (Figure 7.2a), in close agreement with previous studies (e.g., Smith 1999). After that, SOC started to recover due to nitrogen fertilization after 1951 and the adoption of conservation tillage, started in the 1960s. At the end of the 20th century, the soil carbon recovered up to around 5,000 g m^{-2}.

Well-designed management strategies can sequester more carbon in the soil, and the tillage option is one of the most efficient conservation tools (Lal et al. 1999). To test the model sensitivity of SOC to tillage scheme and fertilizer application we performed a series of controlled experiments. The no-till scheme increased simulated SOC by about 1,200 g m^{-2} (~15%) compared to the all-plow practice, the maximum disturbance of soil structure defined in DayCENT (Figure 7.2a). Conservation tillage would also save about 500 g C m^{-2}. Doubling fertilizer application only marginally increased simulated SOC (Figure 7.2b), suggesting that the current soil nitrogen and applications are near optimum.

DayCENT biomass was also compared with observed net primary production (NPP) calculated from available crop yields. At the county level, planted acreage is roughly half corn and half soybeans in a corn-soybean rotation. To simulate this corn-soybean mixture and rotation, we ran DayCENT twice with alternated corn-soybean years and then averaged NPP for the two simulations. DayCENT simulated average NPP was 600 g m^{-2} through the period 1987–2002, when NPP data were available, compared with an observed value of 570 g m^{-2} (Prince et al. 2001). These results thus indicate surprisingly good agreement, although for individual years observed and simulated NPP varied as much as ±20 percent (not shown). The control simulation was also capable of realistically depicting the 1988 drought and the 1993 Great Flood.

CLIMATE SCENARIOS FOR THE
MIDWEST FROM THE TWO GCMS

Figures 7.3 and 7.4 show an example of the spatial patterns of temperature and precipitation over the domain and the difference between the future period and 1961–1990 for the A1B SRES. The overall spatial pattern of maximum temperatures for the Midwest as simulated by the two GCMs was similar to the observed climate (see chapter 2 of this volume), with a clear southwest-northeast gradient. However, CaGCM is 3°C–5°C warmer than FrGCM during the historical growing season (Figure 7.3). Seasonal-mean change in daily maximum temperature (ΔTmax) in the future period relative to the historical period also exhibited differences between the GCMs. The (warm) CaGCM showed only modest warming (0.5°C–1.5°C) over the eastern portion of the domain and little warming or even slight cooling in the western domain (in agreement with Pan et al. 2004). The (cold) FrGCM predicted a large warming of almost 5°C centered near the Kansas-Oklahoma border with most areas warming by 2.5°C–4.0°C in 2046–2065 relative to 1961–1990. Similar results were also found for the seasonal-mean change in mean daily minimum temperature (Tmin).

Domain average changes in Tmax and Tmin from the three scenario climates as simulated by CaGCM all fall within 1.3°C of the historical climate, and Tmax decrease slightly (0.4°C) in the B1 scenario (Table 7.1). Both Tmax and Tmin increased about 2°C–3°C in all three simulations with FrGCM. The similar future warming amplitudes for both Tmax and Tmin seem to contradict the widely reported asymmetric warming between annual Tmax and Tmin (e.g., Karl et al. 1993). However, it should be mentioned that the asymmetric diurnal asymmetric warming is smaller in the growing season than during the winter months.

During the historical period, CaGCM is dry with a rainfall total of 250–500 mm over most of the domain, whereas the cool FrGCM exhibits rainfall totals of 300–900 mm (Figure 7.4, cf Figure 2.15 of this volume). The rainfall change (ΔPr) during the growing season between the middle 21st century and the historical period ranges from −60 to +30 mm in CaGCM and −150 to +90 mm in FrGCM. Both CaGCM and

FrGCM projected west-east drying bands in the middle of the domain. The projected change in precipitation is correlated with temperature changes. For example, FrGCM predicted over 150 mm drying in western Nebraska, which roughly collocates with the severe warming center at the Kansas–Oklahoma border. Similarly, the dipole structure in both ΔT (both Tmax and Tmin) and ΔPr fields match with each other. The high correlation between ΔT and ΔPr fields in individual GCMs can be explained by dynamic constraints in the models.

The domain-average growing-season precipitation over May–September (Pr) increased in CaGCM from −6.1 under the B1 scenario to 32.1 mm in A1B scenario. The growing-season precipitation decreases slightly in FrGCM with ΔPr ranging from −12.7 (A2) to −1.5 (A1B) mm. The considerable difference in precipitation between the two GCMs may not be terribly surprising given that summer precipitation has higher spatio-temporal variability than temperature.

CARBON RESPONSE
(NPP, RESPIRATION, SOC)

Recall that NPP is equal to the difference between the rate at which the plants in an ecosystem produce useful chemical energy (GPP, gross primary productivity) and the rate at which they use some of that energy during respiration. Under the warmer scenario climate of 2046–2065, NPP increased over most of the domain in simulations conducted using climate output from both CaGCM and FrGCM (Figure

7.5)[1]. The largest increase of over 200 g m^{-2} during the period is over the Missouri-Arkansas border. Respiration simulated under the future climate increases everywhere except for isolated areas in FrGCM. NPP and respiration were well correlated in space since most increase in NPP (i.e., the increased production of biomass) are decomposed and respired into the atmosphere within the 20-year simulation period. Also both NPP and respiration responded to temperature and precipitation in similar ways.

The domain-average NPP increase was 69.1–91.0 g m^{-2} (an increase of 18.4–24.2 % relative to the historical period) in simulations driven by CaGCM and increased by 54.6–59.8 g m^{-2} (13.0%–14.2%) in DayCENT simulations using output from FrGCM (Table 7.1). These simulations thus imply that under current land use management strategies the change in climate will lead to increases in carbon uptake by vegetation. Over the whole Midwest, warming should promote vegetation growth as the maximum temperature remains under the upper limit for growth for the ecosystem types considered herein. However, most crop growth in the regions is still limited by precipitation.

Carbon release during respiration also increased, ranging from an increase in C release of 40.0 to 69.1g m^{-2} (10.4%–17.9%) in CaGCM and 38.5–42.6 g m^{-2} (9.3%–10.3%) in FrGCM (Table 7.1).

The change in soil carbon is a net-balance between C loss during respiration and carbon accumulated as NPP, both of which depend on prevailing meteorological conditions. Under the current climate,

SOC distributions simulated by DayCENT using scenarios from both GCMs were similar and largely determined by the initial SOC amount assigned to the different land use types. For example, cropland has an SOC of 5,200 g C m^{-2} in the top 20 cm soil layer whereas that for forest is 7,800 g C m^{-2} over the same profile. The ΔSOC predicted under the changing climate from the GCMs showed both increases and decreases across the domain, consistent with other studies (e.g., Jones et al. 2003). The ΔSOC ranges from −400 to +100 g m^{-2} with a maximum change of −300 g m^{-2}, roughly 1–2 percent of SOC under the current climate (Figure 7.6). Simulations using CaGCM suggest a decline in SOC almost everywhere in the domain except for a limited region centered over southern Missouri and northern Arkansas (Figure 7.6b). The largest NPP and respiration increase was over the Indiana–Missouri–Arkansas region where the dominant vegetation type is deciduous forests and result in a slight net increase of SOC. For climate projections derived from FrGCM, ΔSOC was overwhelmingly negative except for an isolated spot in the Missouri–Arkansas–Tennessee border and central Missouri (Figure 7.6d). The ΔSOC often decreases 200 g m^{-2} with localized losses exceeding 400 g m^{-2} (about 10% of the total soil organic C in the historical period). The lost soil carbon will eventually enter the atmosphere as CO_2, suggesting a positive feedback to the CO_2-induced climate change. The domain averaged SOC changes ranged from −130 to +101 g m^{-2} (−2.3%–+1.7%) among all model-scenario combinations

Table 7.2. Spatial correlation between seasonal-mean climate change variables and annual carbon response variables (NPP, respiration, and SOC) as simulated using DayCENT, based on climate parameters simulated by two GCMs: Canadian Centre for Climate Modeling and Analysis model (CaGCM) and Météo-France Centre National de Recherches Météorologiques (FrGCM).

	CaGCM			FrGCM		
	NPP	Respiration	SOC	NPP	Respiration	SOC
Maximum temperature	0.47	0.16	−0.15	−0.2	−0.13	−0.05
Minimum temperature	0.21	0.45	−0.51	−0.37	−0.11	−0.34
Precipitation	−0.55	−0.24	−0.37	0.16	0.24	−0.04

(Table 7.1). The model-scenario average SOC decrease was 77 g m^{-2} (1.3%) from the late 20th (1961–1980) to mid-21st century (2046–2065).

To diagnose which climate variables cause the largest carbon responses, we computed the spatial correlation between changes in climate variables ($\Delta Tmax$, $\Delta Tmin$, and ΔPr) and carbon response variables (ΔNPP, $\Delta Resp$, and ΔSOC, Table 7.2). In the CaGCM climate forced run, NPP was more sensitive to $\Delta Tmax$ (r = 0.47), whereas respiration had a larger response to $\Delta Tmin$ (r = 0.45), as daytime $\Delta Tmax$ controls growth, whereas nocturnal $\Delta Tmin$ determines respiration. Precipitation amount was negatively correlated with NPP (r = −0.55) and respiration (r = −0.24). The ΔSOC had a low negative correlation (r = −0.15) with $\Delta Tmax$, a strong negative correlation (r = −0.51) with $\Delta Tmin$, and moderate negative correlation (r = −0.37) with precipitation. It should be noted that the combined percentage at which the variability of SOC changes in space explained by mean $\Delta Tmax$, $\Delta Tmin$, and ΔPr is 42 percent with the remaining variance being from meteorological variable synergy, nonlinear interaction, and intra-annual and interan-

nual variability of the climate variables. Overall, correlations between changes in the climate variables and carbon responses for CaGCM were greater than for FrGCM, which is likely due to the latter having occasionally unrealistic crop failures that caused isolated local minima in NPP and SOC.

It is interesting to compare trends in temperatures and SOC between the two GCM scenario climates. The CaGCM predicted temperature changes that are three times of those of FrGCM, but the resultant SOC reduction was not substantially different between the two model climates. Why are the trends in SOC and temperature disproportionate between the two models? The SOC decline was caused by respiration, which is highly sensitive to temperature. The daytime Tmax under the current climate in CaGCM is 4.4°C warmer than FrGCM. This higher temperature would increase base respiration and its changes in future climate even though the temperature change in CaGCM is smaller than FrGCM.

Another aspect is that the domain-averaged increase in NPP as a result of climate change was projected to be greater than the increase in respiration. Under future scenario climates, NPP increase rates in projections driven by both GCMs are about 20–30 percent faster than respiration. With this result, one would expect the future SOC would increase, yet Day-CENT predicted decreases in SOC. This seeming contradiction is due to biomass removal during harvests. In the Midwest, a large portion of land use is croplands, predominately corn and soybeans. In all DayCENT simulations, we assume all the grains were removed from fields. The grain mass can contribute up to half of the aboveground NPP for these crops. The average harvest ratio defined as the portion of NPP harvested to that of non-harvested ranged between 20–30 percent for typical Midwest cropland (Pan et al. 2010).

Concluding Remarks

The DayCENT biogeochemical model was applied in the Midwest to evaluate the soil organic carbon (SOC) trends in the mid-21st century under climate change scenarios. The DayCENT model was driven by an ensemble of future climates generated by two general circulation models (Canadian GCM and French GCM) under three emission scenarios (B1, A1B, and A2). The warm/dry Canadian GCM (CaGCM) predicted growing-season (May–September) 0.6°C (scenario average) warming from the late 20th century to the mid-21st century, much smaller than the 2.8°C warming predicted by the cold French GCM (FrGCM). The difference in growing-season precipitation vary with 9 mm (2.6%) in CaGCM and −8 mm (−1.9%) in FrGCM, although both are small compared to 6 percent increase in precipitation observed for the entire United States during the 20th century (Pan and Pryor 2009). DayCENT simulations driven by these eight-member (six scenarios plus two current) ensemble climates, generate noticeable increases in net primary production (NPP) and soil respiration increases but SOC decreases under all GCM-scenario combinations. The principal results of analyses presented herein are thus:

(1) Although the magnitudes of simulated NPP changes were larger than those of respiration, a portion of increased NPP is removed from the fields as harvest, which caused the net SOC to decline. Unlike natural land use, where the balance between NPP and respiration determines the change in SOC, on highly managed croplands, fertilizer application, harvest, tillage, and other managements also impact SOC trends. Grain (and straw/stalks) harvest from croplands represents a significant portion of NPP. For corn, grain is about one-half of the total aboveground biomass.

(2) Although CaGCM simulates one-third the magnitudes of mean changes in scenario climate of those by FrGCM, the resultant changes in NPP, respiration, and SOC between the two models were of similar magnitudes. This result can be partly explained by the warmer current CaGCM climate that promotes faster respiration. Also, the temperature and precipitation variability on a daily scale might be different in the two GCMs although seasonal

means were the same, which requires analysis of not only climate means but also sub-seasonal and inter-annual variability. This analysis was not carried out in the current study. The nonlinearity in SOC change to input temperature change suggests that the errors or uncertainties contained in GCM-projected scenario climates as input may not propagate through DayCENT to generate high uncertainty in SOC (Liang et al. 2008). In other words, the uncertainty in GCM and impact models (e.g., DayCENT, hydrological moles, crop models, etc.) are, to a certain degree, quite independent. Thus non-compounding of uncertainty in climate change impact modeling provides extra confidence in assessment studies.

(3) The trends in carbon response differed from those for weather variable (e.g., temperature). The kinetics of decomposition (i.e., respiration) can be expressed by the Arrhenius equation:

$$\frac{dC}{dt} = -kC \qquad (7\text{-}1)$$

Where C represents SOC as function of time (t), and k is a reaction time constant that depends on temperature and precipitation for a given type of organic material. So, the rate of change of SOC is directly proportional to SOC itself. In climate change studies, it is widely accepted that although the projected scenario climates have errors, the trends between two time segments are more accurate because systematic errors contained in both time periods are largely canceled. (Cubasch et al. 2000). However, the assumption may not hold for SOC changes, as its rate of change is directly pro-

portional to its magnitude shown in Equation 7.1. Any errors in, for example, initial conditions for SOC will substantially affect SOC trends.

The simulations indicated that the soil carbon pool within the Midwest is vulnerable to future climate change. Under the climate scenarios and assumptions employed herein, current soil C content will not be sustained. Adaptation measures could be implemented to offset the projected SOC loss and based on sensitivity analyses presented herein might include, for example, adopting aggressive conservation tillage schemes, leaving more plant residual unharvested, and rotating crop varieties. If these alternative management strategies are not put into place, SOC will decline, which will not only affect agricultural productivity but may also increase the atmospheric CO_2 concentration, further amplifying climate change.

ACKNOWLEDGMENTS
We would like to thank Cindy Keough for CENTURY modeling support. We would also like to thank Behnjamin Zib for assisting in various technical aspects.

NOTES
1. Isolated increases (decreases) of NPP in FrGCM were caused by occasional crop failures in the current (future) climate because of FrGCM's low temperatures in some years (Pan et al. 2010).

REFERENCES
Bachelet D, Neilson RP, Lenihan JM, Drapek RJ (2004). Regional differences in the carbon source-sink potential of natural vegetation in

the US Ecological Management: 33(Supp#1)
S23-S43 doi:10.1007/s00267-003-9115-4.

Broecker WS, Takahashi T, Simpson HJ, Peng
T-H (1979). Fate of fossil fuel carbon dioxide and the global Carbon budget. Science
206:409–418.

Cox PM, Betts RA, Jones CD, Spall SA, Totterdell
IJ (2000). Acceleration of global warming due
to carbon-cycle feedbacks in a coupled climate model. Nature 408:184–187.

Cubasch U, R. Voss R, Mikolajewicz U (2000).
Precipitation: A parameter changing climate
and modified by climate change. Climatic
Change 46:257–276.

Fan S, Gloor M, Mahlman P, Pacala S, Sarmiento J,
Takahashi T, Tans P (1998). A large terrestrial
carbon sink in North America implied by
atmospheric and oceanic carbon dioxide data
and models. Science 282:442–446.

IPCC (2007). Climate change 2007: The physical
science basis. Contribution of Working Group
I to the Fourth Assessment Report of the Intergovernmental Panel on Climate Change. Solomon S, Qin D, Manning M, Chen Z, Marquis
M, Averyt KB, Tignor M, Miller HL (eds).
Cambridge, UK: Cambridge University Press.

Jones C, Cox P, Huntingford C (2003). Uncertainty in climate carbon-cycle projections associated with the sensitivity of soil respiration
to temperature. Tellus 55B:642–648.

Karl TR, Jones PD, Knight RW, Kukla G, Plummer N (1993). Asymmetric trends of daily
maximum and minimum temperature. Bulletin of the American Meteorological Society
74:1009–1022.

Lal R, Follett RF, Kimble J, Cole CV (1999). Managing US cropland to sequester carbon in
soil. Journal of Soil and Water Conservation
54:374–81.

Liang XZ, Kunkel KE, Meehl GA, Jones RG,
Wang JXL (2008). Regional climate models
downscaling analysis of general circulation
models present climate biases propagation
into future change projections. Geophysical
Research Letters 35:L08709, doi:10.1029/
2007GL032849.

Metherell AK, Harding LA, Cole VV, Parton
WJ (1993). CENTURY—Soil Organic Matter
Model (Technical Document), Agroeco-
systems Version 4.0, Great Plains Systems
Research Unit. Technical Report No. 4. U.S.
Department of Agriculture, Agricultural Re-
search Service, Ft. Collins, CO.

Pacala SW, Hurtt G, Baker D, Peylin P, Houghton
R, Birdsey R, Heath L, Sundquist E, Stallard R,
Ciais P, Moorcrft P, Caspersen J, Shevliakova E,
Moore B, Kohlmaier G, Holland E, Gloor M,
Harmon M, Fan S, Sarmiento J, Goodale C,
Schimel D, Field C (2001). Consistent land
and atmosphere-based US carbon sink esti-
mates. Science 292:2316–2320.

Pan Z, Arritt RW, Takle ES, Gutowski Jr. WJ, Anderson CJ, Segal M (2004). Altered hydrologic
feedback in a warming climate introduces a
"warming hole." Geophysical Research Letters
31:L17109, doi:10.1029/2004GL02528.

Pan Z, Pryor SC (2009). Overview: Hydrological regimes. In: Pryor SC (ed) Understanding climate change: Climate variability,
predictability, and change in the midwestern
United States. Bloomington: Indiana University Press, 88–99.

Pan Z, Andrade D, Segal M, Wimberley J,
McKinney N, Takle E (2010). Uncertainty in
future soil carbon trends at a central US site
under an ensemble of GCM scenario climates.
Ecological Modeling 221:876–881.

Parton WJ, Schimel SD, Cole CV, Ojima DS (1987).
Analysis of factors controlling soil organic matter levels in Great Plains grassland. Soil Science Society of America Journal 51:1173–1179.

Potter CS, Klooster SA (1999). Detecting a terrestrial biosphere sink for carbon dioxide:
interannual ecosystem modeling for the mid-
1980s. Climatic Change 42:489–503.

Prince SD, Haskett J, Steininger M, Strand H,
Write R (2001). Net primary production of
US Midwest croplands from agricultural
harvest yield data. Ecological Applications
11:1194–1205.

Schimel D, Melillo J, Tian H, McGuire A, Kick-
lighter D, Kittel T, Rosenbloom N, Running

S, Thornton P, Ojima D, Parton W, Kelly R, Sykes M, Neilson R, Rizzo B (2000). Contribution of increasing CO_2 and climate to carbon storage by ecosystems of the United States. Science 287:2004–2006.

Schlesinger WH, Andrews JA (2000). Soil respiration and the global carbon cycle. Biogeochemistry 48:7–20.

Smith KA (1999). After the Kyoto Protocol: Can soil scientists make a useful contribution? Soil Use and Management 15:71–75.

8. Michigan's Tart Cherry Industry:
Vulnerability to Climate Variability and Change

J. A. WINKLER, J. A. ANDRESEN, J. M. BISANZ, G. GUENTCHEV,
J. NUGENT, K. PIROMSOPA, N. ROTHWELL, C. ZAVALLONI,
J. CLARK, H. K. MIN, A. POLLYEA, AND H. PRAWIRANATA

Introduction

While commercial fruit production is a small fraction of the total agricultural output in the United States, it has major economic impacts at the local and regional level. This is particularly true for agricultural sites in the Midwest where the Great Lakes have a moderating influence on climate, allowing for commercial fruit production at relatively high latitudes for a continental location. Tart cherry production is of particular significance in the Great Lakes region. In 2009, 292 million pounds of tart cherries, or 80 percent of the national total, were produced in Michigan, New York, Pennsylvania, and Wisconsin (NASS 2010). Of this amount, 266 million pounds were produced in Michigan alone. In 2004–2008, cash receipts for Michigan tart cherries ranged from $34,697,000 to $63,030,000 (NASS 2009). Tart cherries are grown in three primary areas in the Lower Peninsula of Michigan (Figure 8.1). Over 50 percent of the statewide production occurs in the Northwest region, where tart cherries are the dominant fruit crop (Black et al. 2010). In contrast, fruit production is more diversified in the west central and southwest growing regions.

In comparison to cereal crops, the potential impacts of climate variability and change on commercial fruit production have not been as widely studied, in spite of the sensitivity of fruit trees to climate variations and the greater relative exposure of fruit production to a fluctuating climate given the perennial nature of fruit trees. In general, deciduous fruit trees lose their leaves and begin a cold hardening stage in early fall before becoming dormant in late fall. They remain dormant until early spring when the trees gradually lose their cold tolerance. Perennial fruit trees are vulnerable to cold damage at three distinct stages: (1) in the fall before the tree is adequately hardened, (2) during the winter dormant period when severe cold events can freeze flower buds and cause injury to woody tissue, and (3) during spring bloom when temperatures slightly below freezing may kill flower buds following the loss of cold hardiness (Raseira and Moore 1987). For all three of these vulnerable periods, the relative severity of consequences from a freeze event is conditionally dependent upon the weather that precedes it. Tart cherry production is also influenced by other climate factors, such as the amount of plant available moisture in the soil profile and wet and windy conditions during pollination (Zavalloni et al. 2006b, 2008). Additionally, weather conditions during the growing season contribute to the risk and development of plant diseases and insect pest populations (National Integrated Pest Management Program 2003), which also affect orchard productivity. However, of all of these potential impacts, damaging freezing springtime temperatures are considered to be the single most important climate-related risk factor for tart cherry production in the Great Lakes region (Flore 1994).

This chapter has several objectives. The first objective is to illustrate, using freeze events during spring 2002, the current susceptibility of Michigan's tart cherry production to damaging springtime temperatures. Spring 2002 is particularly interesting as two contrasting freeze events contributed to the loss of almost the entire tart cherry crop. Our second goal is to evaluate the potential impacts of projected climate change on the future risk of springtime freeze events. This analysis draws on the findings of a recently completed research effort referred to as the *Pileus Project* (Winkler et al. 2012), which investigated, with stakeholder assistance,

the influence of climate on Michigan's agriculture and recreation/tourism industries. The final goal is to provide examples of decision support tools for assessing the impacts of climate variability and change. As pointed out by Moser (2009), stakeholder groups and policymakers increasingly expect researchers to provide decision support, yet few researchers are experienced in developing, or codeveloping with stakeholders, decision support materials and instruments. The sharing of decision support products can ultimately lead to improved designs. Here we utilize images from three decision support tools developed as part of the *Pileus Project* (the Historical Tart Cherry Yield Tool, Historical Weather Tool, and Future Scenarios Tool) to both illustrate our findings and to provide examples of decision support tools for others to build and improve upon.

Spring 2002: An Example of Damaging Springtime Freeze Events

In the early stages of the *Pileus Project*, project scientists met with experienced farmers who had been part of the industry since the early 1940s to better understand the impact of weather and climate on tart cherry yield. The farmers' recollections were captured in the Historical Tart Cherry Yield Tool (available at http://www.pileus.msu.edu/growersrecdemo/index_hai1.htm). Evident from the tool is the almost total crop loss in 2002 (Figure 8.2). Farmers could not remember a similar crop loss since 1945 and attributed the loss to two contrasting freeze events and poor pollination conditions.

Table 8.1. Critical spring temperatures (°C) by phenological stage for tart cherries. Source: Dennis and Howell (1974).

	Bud swell	Side green	Green tip	Tight cluster	Open cluster	First white	First bloom	Full bloom
Possible injury (~10% buds damaged)	−9.4	−4.4	−3.3	−3.3	−2.2	−2.3	−2.3	−2.3
Severe injury (~90% buds damaged)	−17.8	−12.2	−5.6	−4.4	−4.4	−4.4	−4.4	−4.4

Springtime freeze events in Michigan are associated with either an inversion (radiation) freeze or a wind (advection) freeze. Inversion freezes, which are the most common, typically occur under calm, clear conditions when a large anticyclone (high pressure system) is located over the region. As temperatures cool during the nighttime hours, cold air that builds up near the surface flows downhill across the landscape and pools in low-lying areas, producing a low-level temperature inversion. In contrast, wind freezes are often associated with the leading edge of an anticyclone or with the passage of a cold front. The pressure gradient, and hence wind speed, are relatively strong during wind freezes. These freeze events can occur under cloudy conditions and may even be associated with precipitation, although far less is known about wind freeze conditions compared to inversion freezes.

Estimating the temperature at which damage occurs to tart cherry flower buds is challenging due to the confounding factors of growth stage and ambient conditions. Damaging temperature thresholds for different growth stages based on measurements in a controlled environment are listed in Table 8.1. These temperatures

are a more appropriate reference for inversion freezes compared to wind freezes, as damage associated with wind freezes may occur at warmer temperatures than the published temperatures, especially if the period of cold temperatures is prolonged and/or the flower buds are wet due to precipitation (Longstroth 2007).

In 2002, a wind freeze occurred on April 21–23 after a period of abnormal warmth. Temperature observations can be viewed using the Historical Weather Tool (available at http://www.pileus.msu.edu/tools/hdot/index.htm), designed to allow users to extract climate variable(s) and time period of choice (i.e., a given day or range of days for one year or multiple years) for any one of 18 stations in the Great Lakes region. At the National Weather Service (NWS) Cooperative Observer (COOP) station in Maple City (see Figure 8.1 for location), maximum temperatures exceeded 25°C for four days from April 15–18 (Figure 8.3). This warm period caused a rapid break of tree dormancy, and flower buds quickly lost their hardiness. As a result, buds were more susceptible to the following several-day period of below-freezing minimum temperatures. This period of cold temperatures was associated with wind speeds of approximately 3 m s⁻¹ as seen in the time series plot of five-minute averaged wind speed for the Northwest Michigan Horticultural Research Station (Figure 8.4), located approximately 27 km southeast of Maple City. Furthermore, the five-minute temperature measurements at the research station indicate that the coldest temperatures during the April 21–23 period occurred in the early evening of April 23, rather than in the morning as would be expected for an inversion freeze. A three-day period of similarly cold minimum temperatures was observed in May, but in contrast to the April wind freeze, the coldest temperatures occurred in the late night/early morning under near calm conditions, typical of an inversion freeze.

The two freeze events produced different damage patterns across the growing region. The "best" orchards sites are generally considered to be hilltops and slopes from which relatively cold air can flow downslope away from the orchard site. "Poor" sites are located in landscape depressions where cold air accumulates at night due to air drainage. During the April wind freeze, these "best" sites were more exposed to wind and subfreezing temperatures, and more damage was observed on hilltops and slopes compared to landscape depressions. The inversion freeze in May damaged the flower buds on trees located in the "poorer" orchard sites that had escaped damage during the earlier wind freeze. This combination of wind and inversion freeze events resulted in the almost complete crop failure as both high and low elevation orchard sites were impacted.

Projected Future Changes in Damaging Springtime Freeze Events

One goal of the *Pileus Project* was to evaluate potential future changes in the climate-related vulnerability of Michigan's agriculture and recreation/tourism industries. To accomplish this, an ensemble of local climate change scenarios of maximum and minimum temperature and precipitation was developed for fifteen locations in the Great Lakes region, including one station in each of the three tart cherry growing regions.

CLIMATE SCENARIO DEVELOPMENT

The scenario ensemble for each location was derived from simulations from four global climate models (GCMs) featured in the Third Assessment of the IPCC: the Canadian Climate Centre's CGCM2 model (Flato and Boer 2001), the HadCM3 model (Gordon et al. 2000) from the United Kingdom Hadley Center, the ECHAM4 model (Roeckner et al. 1996) from the Max Planck Institute for Meteorology in Germany, and the CSM1.2 model (Meehl and Washington 1995) developed by the National Center for Atmospheric Research in the United States. The GCM simulations were driven by the A2 and B2 greenhouse gas emissions scenarios (Nakicenovic et al. 2000; see chapter 2 of this volume for a description of these scenarios).

The coarse resolution GCM simulations were downscaled to the local scale using an empirical-dynamic approach. Empirical downscaling employs statistical methods to relate local/regional climate variables to large-scale circulation and atmospheric state variables that are chosen to represent important dynamical and physical processes in the atmosphere (Winkler et al. 2011). In this case, regression analysis was used to relate local values of temperature and precipitation (the predictands) to the large-scale circulation variables such as sea-level pressure and 500 hPa geopotential height (the predictors). The observed values of the predictor variables were obtained from the NCEP/NCAR reanalysis (Kalnay et al. 1996). Multiple variants of the downscaling procedure were employed, as earlier work had demonstrated that downscaled climate scenarios can be sensitive to quasi-subjective decisions made during their development, such as the procedures used to "debias" the GCM-simulated series of the predictor variables for deviations from observations (Winkler et al. 1997). The empirical-dynamic transfer functions were calibrated based on observations for 1970–1989 and validated for 1960–1969 and 1990–1999. The transfer functions were then applied to the GCM-simulated series of the predictor variables for 1990–2099. For each location, the resulting ensemble consisted of sixty-four scenarios of daily maximum and minimum temperature and precipitation.

FUTURE SCENARIOS TOOL

The more than 2,000 future climate scenarios were incorporated into a web-based Future Scenarios Tool (available at http://www.pileus.msu.edu/tools/t_future.htm) that allows stakeholders and other interested users to access the scenarios and view projected changes for preselected climate parameters. The parameters included in the tool were chosen based on previous literature, extensive conversations with the other *Pileus Project* researchers, and input from stakeholders. The Future Scenarios Tool was designed to provide five major graphical displays: (1) observed values for a reference climate period, (2) comparisons between early century (2010–2029) and mid-century (2040–2059) time slices, (3) comparisons between mid-century and late century (2080–2099) time slices, (4) comparisons of the scenarios developed using the A2 and the B2 greenhouse gas emissions estimates, and (5) trend analyses for 1990–2099 (Winkler et al. 2012). To assist users in appropriately interpreting the information provided, each display is accompanied by an audiovisual learning guide composed of a set of modules describing important concepts. The mid-century versus late-century displays for Maple City are used below to illustrate projected changes in the vulnerability of Michigan's tart cherry industry to springtime damaging temperatures.

CLIMATE PARAMETERS

Several parameters were employed to evaluate future changes in the risk of springtime damaging cold temperatures. The downscaled daily time series of maximum and minimum temperature were used to calculate growing degree days (GDDs) and the frequency and timing of threshold temperature events for the three future time slices. GDDs are a widely used measure of heat accumulation and are frequently employed to estimate crop development and the timing of phenological stages (e.g., Winkler et al. 2002, Zavalloni et al. 2006a,b). To assess changes in the timing of early bud development for tart cherry trees, the Baskerville–Emin (1969) method was used to calculate GDDs beginning January 1 of each year using a base value of 5°C (41°F). Early bud development is estimated to occur when approximately 150 GDDs (when temperature is measured in °C) or 270 GDDs (when temperature is measured in °F) are reached. This parameter has previously been used as a measure of early bud development for fruit trees (e.g., Winkler et al. 2002) and is used here to be consistent with these earlier studies. The projected changes in phenological development are expressed as the difference (delta) between the median dates when 150 GDDs is reached for the 20-year future periods and the median value for a control period defined as 1990–2009. The use of deltas (also often referred to as change factors) accounts, at least in part, for model error as both the future and control period temperature series were derived from the GCM simulations. To assess changes in freeze occurrence, the last occurrence of temperatures ≤ 0°C (32°F) in spring was identified from the projected time series. We used 0°C as the threshold temperature for a freeze event rather than the values shown in Table 8.1, because, as mentioned previously, damage can occur at warmer temperatures during wind freezes or during a prolonged cold period. Also, the downscaled scenarios were developed for COOP stations, and some variation is expected between the temperatures projected for the COOP stations and those at orchard sites. To take into account preceding crop development on the sensitivity of fruit buds to cold temperatures, the change in the median number of GDDs at the last occurrence in spring of temperatures ≤ 0°C was also calculated. Additionally, the projected change in the median number of GDDs outside of the frost-free period was calculated. This parameter represents the risk of the tart cherry crop being brought out of dormancy during winter.

PROJECTED CHANGES

Based on observed temperatures for 1981–2000, May 1 is the median date when 150 GDDs (base 5°C) is reached at Maple City. In the future, the median date is expected to occur earlier in the year (Figure 8.5). The average change for the 64 scenarios in the median date of early bud development is 7 days earlier than at present for the mid-century (2040–2059) time period and 16 days earlier for the late century (2060–2099) period. The spread of the scenario ensemble represents what Jones (2000) refers to as the "calibrated range of uncertainty" of the projected changes. The calibrated uncertainty range is smaller than the full, but unknown, uncertainty range and represents a lower bound on the maximum uncertainty range (Stainforth et al. 2007). For the mid-century period, the majority of scenarios suggest earlier crop development; however, a small number of scenarios suggest little change in the median date when 150 GDDs is reached. The uncertainty is considerably greater for the late century period compared to the mid-century period, although all scenarios project bud development will occur earlier in the spring with the majority implying a shift of 5 to 25 days. However, a handful of plausible scenarios project much larger future changes.

The median date of last spring freeze is also projected to occur earlier in spring than at present (the observed median date for 1981–2000 is May 25). The average projected change, calculated across the 64 scenarios, is 7 days for the mid-century period and 20 days for the late century period. The uncertainty range for the late century period is smaller than that for the projected change in the median date of early bud development, with all scenarios suggesting an earlier median date of last spring freeze. On the other hand, for the mid century period, the uncertainty range for the projected change in the median date of last spring freeze is considerably larger than that for the change in early bud development. Rather surprisingly, approximately 25 percent of the scenarios suggest little change or even a later median date of last spring freeze. The large uncertainty range is likely, at least in part, due to the relatively short temporal windows (20 years) used for calculating the median combined with the use of a strict threshold value (i.e., 0°C). Furthermore, substantial interannual variability exists in the temperature scenarios (Guentchev et al. 2009), and the magnitude of the projected changes depends in part on the choice of future time period.

Considerable uncertainty exists regarding the future susceptibility of tart cherry trees to below freezing temperatures when preceding crop development is considered (Figure 8.6). For the mid-century period, close to 40 percent of the scenarios project little change in the GDD accumulation at the time of last spring freeze, and the number of scenarios that suggest delayed crop development is similar to the number that suggest greater crop development at the time of freezing temperatures. As a reference, the observed median number of GDDs for Maple City at the time of the last occurrence of ≤0°C was 344 GDDs in 1981–1999. Although slightly more scenarios for the late century suggest less crop development at the time of last spring freeze, the projected change, when averaged over all scenarios, is very small (a decrease of 28 GDDs). Similarly, the projected changes in the median GDD accumulation outside the frost-free period (i.e., the growing season) indicate considerable uncertainty on whether tart cherries will be more or less vulnerable to cold temperatures in a perturbed future climate. For both the mid-century and late century periods, a large number of scenarios suggest little or no change, and, of the remaining scenarios, an approximately equal number suggest an increase versus a decrease in climate-related vulnerability. The findings above are in general agreement with a previous analysis (Winkler et al. 2002) prepared as part of the first U.S. National Climate Assessment, even though the studies differed considerably in terms of the number of GCM simulations used to develop local climate scenarios, the emissions scenarios used to drive the GCMs, and the downscaling methods employed. For the earlier study, only two downscaled climate scenarios were available for several locations in the lake-influenced zones surrounding the Great Lakes. These scenarios were obtained from CGCM1 and HadCM2 (earlier versions of two of the GCMs employed here), driven by the I92a (a 1% equivalent CO_2 increase per year) emission scenario. A disaggregation rather than empirical downscaling approach was used, where monthly change factors for maximum and minimum temperature, calculated as the difference between the temperatures for a future period and a control period at GCM grid points, were interpolated to a finer resolution and a weather generator was used to impose a daily time step. Winkler et al. (2002) found that although both scenarios suggested an earlier occurrence of critical growth stages and a forward shift in the date of last spring freeze, they differed in terms of the projected vulnerability to damaging cold temperatures when crop development was considered, similar to the discrepancies seen for the current analysis. The similar findings for the earlier and current studies, in spite of the large differences in scenario type and ensemble size, suggest that considerable further work is needed to better understand the reasons behind the widely varying projections between climate scenarios of future damaging springtime freeze events. An important next step is to carefully analyze the differences between GCM simulations in the projected character, frequency, and within-season distribution of the circulation patterns and airflow trajectories associated with the transport of warm and cold air masses into the Great Lakes region and how these differences are reflected in the downscaled scenarios of maximum and minimum temperature.

Next Steps: An Introduction to the CLIMARK Project

The *Pileus Project* focused on how a local/regional system may be impacted by a perturbed climate, similar to the vast majority of previous assessments of climate change impact, adaptation and vulnerability, or what Carter et al. (2007) refer to as "traditional assessments." Economic impacts usually are not explicitly considered in traditional assessments but instead are crudely estimated from projected changes in productivity or user activity (Liverman 2008). Also, other than climate, traditional assessments rarely consider the evolution in time of system components such as decision making, adaptation strategies, and policy formulation. Furthermore, traditional assessments rarely consider interactions between multiple production regions that are distributed worldwide and likely to be differentially impacted by climate change (Winkler et al. 2010). Although the need for expanded assessments that directly incorporate spatial and temporal dynamics is generally recognized (e.g., Carter et al. 2007), approaches and frameworks for conducting such assessments either do not currently exist or are not well developed.

The limitations of traditional assessments are a concern when attempting to understand the future vulnerability of

Michigan's tart cherry industry, which has been, and will continue to be, affected by changes in demand and markets. For example, after the 2002 crop failure in Michigan, tart cherries, which are primarily traded as processed products, were imported to the United States to sustain current markets, with most fruit imported from Poland. Although imports from Poland and other producing regions have since declined with improved production in Michigan and other cherry-producing states, tart cherry imports remain at a higher level than before the 2002 crop failure (Thornsbury and Woods 2005). Importation remains elevated in part because Schattenmorello, the tart cherry variety grown in Poland and several other European production regions, differs from the cultivar Montmorency primarily grown in Michigan in terms of fruit color, taste, and other physical characteristics. Thus, the two cherry cultivars are not perfect substitutes for each other. In addition, Polish cherries can be produced and shipped to U.S. markets more economically than cherries grown within the United States (J. Jensen, personal communication).

The growing international character of Michigan's tart cherry industry due to changing global markets, as well as inquiries from stakeholders on how climate change may impact worldwide tart cherry production, led to the recently initiated CLIMARK (*Climate Change Impacts on Markets*) Project. The CLIMARK research team includes climatologists, computer scientists, economists, and horticulturalists from the United States (Michigan), Germany, Hungary, Poland, and Ukraine.

The overall goal is to develop and test a framework for conducting climate change impact assessments for international market systems with long-term investments, using the international tart cherry industry as an example and proof of concept. Specific goals of CLIMARK are to assess the potential differential impact of climate change on the North American and European tart cherry production regions utilizing improved downscaling methods, evaluate regionally specific adaptation strategies to potential climate change, project changes in supply and price via the modification of international trade models to include productivity outcomes from individual decision-making models, and incorporate fine-scale landscape variability into productivity (i.e., yield) estimates for tart cherries. Although still in its early stages, the CLIMARK project will hopefully provide a more comprehensive assessment of the vulnerability of Michigan's tart cherry industry to potential climate change and a framework for conducting impact and vulnerability assessments for other international market systems.

Concluding Remarks

Michigan's tart cherry industry is vulnerable to damaging springtime cold temperatures that reduce yields, as seen in spring 2002 when a combination of an early wind freeze and a later inversion freeze contributed to the loss of the entire crop. The analyses presented here illustrate the many challenges faced when attempting to assess future changes in the frequency and magnitude of damaging springtime freeze events, particularly as flower bud suscepti-bility to cold temperatures is confounded by the growth stage, which in turn is a function of preceding weather fluctua-tions. Additionally, an ensemble of local climate change scenarios, derived from multiple climate models and emission sce-narios and employing several downscaling methods, points to a large degree of un-certainty surrounding the future timing of springtime freeze injuries with respect to flower bud development. This implies that an enhanced greenhouse climate cannot be assumed to bring more favorable con-ditions for Michigan's tart cherry industry, in spite of this production region, com-pared to others, being located in a more continental climate and at higher latitudes, which at first glance might appear to bene-fit from warming temperatures. A further complication is that Michigan's tart cherry industry is likely to be influenced by shifts in worldwide production and trade re-sulting from climate change that occurs in other production areas. Much further work is required to better understand the factors contributing to the large uncer-tainty range surrounding future climate-related vulnerability of the tart cherry industry and to develop frameworks and approaches for incorporating spatial and temporal dynamics into impact and vul-nerability assessments.

The increasing demand for decision support puts pressure on many assessment teams to develop easily accessible mate-rials and tools for stakeholder groups and policymakers. The examples provided here of three web-based tools developed for the *Pileus Project* will hopefully be of as-sistance to other assessment teams in their tool development. Of the three tools, only one—the Future Scenarios Tool—was part of the tool development plan at the onset of the project. The other two tools were developed in response to internal needs or stakeholder requests. Team members de-veloping a tart cherry yield model quickly found that the existing literature was in-sufficient to understand climate impacts on yield and sought the input of experienced farmers. The Historical Yield Tool cap-tures the farmers' recollections and pro-vides a baseline for evaluating the output of yield and other models. On the other hand, the Historical Weather Tool grew out of requests by stakeholders for tailored climate information that would allow them to assess the historical probabilities of favorable or unfavorable weather condi-tions specific to the timing of a particular farm operation (e.g., pesticide applica-tion) or crop developmental stage (e.g., pollination). These experiences in tool development point to the benefits of the coproduction of assessment outcomes, in-cluding decision support delivery systems.

ACKNOWLEDGEMENTS
This chapter was informed by research funded by the U.S. Environmental Protection Agency Project Number R83081401–0, NSF Award SES 0622954, and NSF Award CNH 0909378. It has not been subjected to peer review by these agen-cies. Any opinions, findings, and conclusions or recommendations expressed in this material are those of the authors and do not reflect the views or policies of the funding agencies. The authors are solely responsible for any errors or omissions. We thank Hannes Thiemann and Hans Luthardt from the Max Planck Institute of Meteorology for their help in obtaining the daily ECHAM4

simulations; to Lawrence Buja and Gary Strand from the National Center for Atmospheric Research, who provided the NCAR CSM1.2 daily simulations; and to David Viner at the Climate Research Unit in East Anglia, who made available the daily HadCM3 simulations. The simulations for CGCM2 were obtained from the CCCma web server. We also express our gratitude to the stakeholders of the tart cherry industry for their invaluable assistance and insights.

REFERENCES

Baskerville GL, Emin P (1969). Rapid estimation of heat accumulation from maximum and minimum temperatures. Ecology 50:514–517.

Black JR, Nugent J, Rothwell N, Thornsbury S, Olynk N (2010). Michigan production costs for tart cherries by production region. Agricultural Economics Report #639, Department of Agriculture, Food and Resource Economics, Michigan State University, East Lansing.

Carter TR, Jones RN, Lu X, Bhadwal S, Conde C, Mearns LO, O'Neill BC, Rounsevell MDA, Zurek MB (2007). New assessment methods and the characterisation of future conditions. In: Parry ML, Canziani OF, Palutikof JP, van der Linden PJ, Hanson CE (eds) Climate change 2007: Impacts, adaptation and vulnerability. Contribution of Working Group II to the Fourth Assessment Report of the Intergovernmental Panel on Climate Change. Cambridge, UK: Cambridge University Press.

Dennis FG, Howell GS (1974). Cold hardiness of tart cherry bark and flower buds. Research Report 220, Michigan Agricultural Experiment Station, Michigan State University, East Lansing.

Flato GM, and Boer GJ (2001). Warming asymmetry in climate change experiments. Geophysical Research Letters 28:195–198.

Flore JA (1994). Stone fruit. In: Schaffer B, Anderson PC (eds), Handbook of environmental physiology of fruit crops. Volume 1: Temperate crops. Boca Raton, FL: CRC Press.

Gordon C, Cooper C, Senior CA, Banks HT, Gregory JM, Johns TC, Mitchell JFB, Wood RA (2000). The simulation of SST, sea ice extents and ocean heat transports in a version of the Hadley Centre coupled model without flux adjustments. Climate Dynamics 16:147–168.

Guentchev GS, Piromsopa K, Winkler JA (2009). Estimating changes in temperature variability in a future climate. In: Pryor SC (ed) Understanding climate change: Climate variability, predictability, and change in the midwestern United States. Bloomington: Indiana University Press, 66–75.

Jones RN (2000). Managing uncertainty in climate change projections: Issues for impact assessment. Climatic Change 45:403–419.

Kalnay E, Kanamitsu M, Kistler R, Collins W, Deaven D, Gandin L, Iredell M, Saha S, White G, Woollen J, Zhu Y, Leetmaa A, Reynolds B, Chelliah M, Ebisuzaki W, Higgins W, Janowiak J, Mo KC, Ropelewski C, Wang J, Jenne R, and Joseph D (1996). The NCEP/NCAR 40-year reanalysis project. Bulletin of the American Meteorological Society 77:437–471.

Liverman D (2008). Assessing impacts, adaptation and vulnerability: Reflections on the Working Group II report of the International Panel on Climate Change. Global Environmental Change 18:4–7.

Longstroth M (2007). The 2007 Easter freeze in SW Michigan. Available from: http://www .canr.msu.edu/vanburen/feaster07.htm. Last accessed: February 6, 2011.

Meehl GA, Washington WM (1995). Cloud albedo feedback and the super greenhouse effect in a global coupled GCM. Climate Dynamics 11:399–411.

Moser S (2009). Making a difference on the ground: The challenge of demonstrating the effectiveness of decision support. Climatic Change 95:11–21.

Nakicenovic N, Alcamo J, Davis G, de Vries B, Fenhann J, Gaffin S, Gregory K, Grubler A, Jung TY, Kram T, La Rovere EL, Michaelis L, Mori S, Morita T, Pepper W, Pitcher HM, Price L, Riahi K, Roehrl A, Rogner HH, Sankovski A, Schlesinger M, Shukla P, Smith S. J,

Swart R, van Rooijen S, Victor N, and Dadi Z (2000). Special report on emissions scenarios: A special report of Working Group III of the Intergovernmental Panel on Climate Change. New York: Cambridge University Press.

NASS (2009). Michigan 2008–2009 highlights, National Agricultural Statistics Service, Michigan Field Office, Michigan Department of Agriculture, NR-09-77, issued October 8, 2009. Available from: http://www.nass.usda.gov/Statistics_by_State/Michigan/Publications/MichiganFactSheets/STHILGTS.pdf.

NASS (2010). Cherry production. National Agricultural Statistics Service, Agricultural Statistics Board, U.S. Department of Commerce, released June 17, 2010. Available from: http://usda.mannlib.cornell.edu/usda/current/CherProd/CherProd-06-17-2010.pdf.

National Integrated Pest Management Program (2003). Crop profile for tart cherries in Michigan. United States Department of Agriculture, National Information System for the Regional IPM Centers. Available from: http://www.ipmcenters.org/cropprofiles/docs/MITartCherry.pdf.

Raseira MCB, Moore JN (1987). Time of flower bud initiation in peach cultivars differing in chilling requirements. HortScience 22:216–218.

Roeckner E, Oberhuber JM, Bacher A, Chistoph M, Kirchner I (1996). ENSO variability and atmospheric response in a global coupled atmosphere-ocean GCM. Climate Dynamics 12:737–754.

Thornsbury S, Woods M (2005). Market study of the Polish tart cherry industry: Final report. Department of Agricultural Economics, Michigan State University, East Lansing. Available from: http://www.globalhort.msu.edu/docs/FinalReport_website.pdf.

Stainforth DA, Downing TE, Washington R, Lopez A, New M (2007). Issues in the interpretation of climate model ensembles to inform decisions. Philosophical Transactions of the Royal Society A 365:2163–2177.

Winkler JA, Andresen JA, Guentchev G, Kriegel RD (2002). Possible impacts of projected climate change on specialized agriculture in the Great Lakes Region. Journal of Great Lakes Research 28:608–625.

Winkler JA, Bisanz JM, Guentchev GS, Piromsopa K, van Ravensway J, Prawiranata H, Torre RS, Min HK Clark J (2012). The development and communication of an ensemble of local-scale climate scenarios: An example from the Pileus Project. In: Dietz, T, Bidwell D (eds), Climate change in the Great Lakes region: Navigating an uncertain future. East Lansing: Michigan State University Press.

Winkler JA, Guentchev GS, Perdinan, Tan P-N, Zhong S, Liszewska M, Abraham Z, Niedźwiedź T, Ustrnul Z (2011). Climate scenario development and applications for local/regional climate change impact assessments: An overview for the non-climate scientist. Part I: Scenario development using downscaling methods. Geography Compass 5/6:275–300.

Winkler JA, Palutikof JP, Andresen JA, Goodess CM (1997). The simulation of daily time series from GCM output. Part 2: A sensitivity analysis of empirical transfer functions for downscaling GCM simulations. Journal of Climate 10:2514–2532.

Winkler JA, Thornsbury S, Artavio M, Chmielewski F-M, Kirschke D, Lee S, Liszewska M, Loveridge S, Tan P-N, Zhong S, Andresen JA, Black JR, Kurlus R, Nizalov D, Olynk N, Ustrnul Z, Zavalloni C, Bisanz JM, Bujdosó J, Fusina L, Henniges Y, Hilsendegen P, Lar K, Malarzewski L, Moeller T, Murmylo R, Niedzwiedz T, Nizalova O, Prawiranata H, Rothwell N, van Ravensway J, von Witzke H, Woods M (2010). A conceptual framework for multi-regional climate change assessments for international market systems with long-term investments. Climatic Change 103:445–470.

Zavalloni C, Andresen JA, Flore JA (2006a). Phenological models of flower bud stages and fruit growth of "Montmorency" sour cherry based on growing degree-day accumulation. Journal of the American Society of Horticultural Science 131:601–607.

Zavalloni C, Andresen JA, Winkler JA, Flore JA, Black JR, and Beedy TL (2006b). The Pileus Project: Climatic impacts on sour cherry production in the Great Lakes Region in past and projected future time frames. Acta Horticulturae (ISHS) 707:101–108.

Zavalloni C, Andresen JA, Black JR, Winkler JA, Guentchev G, Piromsopa K, Pollyea A, Bisanz JM (2008). A preliminary analysis of the impacts of past and projected future climate on sour cherry production in the Great Lakes Region of the USA. Acta Horticulturae (ISHS), 803:123–130.

9. Climate Change Vulnerability and Impacts on Human Health

S. C. GRADY

Introduction

Climate change impacts on human health occur through direct and indirect exposure pathways. The most severe and long-lasting health impacts are those that result from direct exposure(s) to climate variability and changing-weather patterns, such as heat waves, winds, storms, floods, fires, and drought (see chapter 2 of this volume). Other detrimental, but somewhat more difficult to measure, impacts are those that result from indirect exposure(s), such as changes in air, water, and food quality; ecosystem disruption and the redistribution of disease vectors; economic impacts from changes in agriculture and industry; and settlement/resettlement patterns (IPCC 2007). The IPCC (2007) reports with *high confidence*, "climate change contributes to the global burden of disease and premature death." Other specific findings from this report include (see chapter 1 for a discussion of the IPCC protocols for assigning "confidence" to assertions):

- "Climate change has altered the seasonal distribution of some allergenic pollen species (high confidence); increased heat-wave-related deaths (medium confidence); and altered the distribution of some infectious disease vectors (medium confidence)."

- "Those at greatest risk in all countries are the urban poor, elderly and children, traditional societies, subsistence farmers, and coastal populations (high confidence); and adverse health impacts will be greatest in low-income countries (high confidence)."

- "Projected trends in climate change-related exposures will have mixed effects on the geographic distribution of malaria (very high confidence); increase the number of people suffering from death, disease and injury from heat waves, floods, storms, fires and drought (high confidence); increase malnutrition and consequent disorders (high confidence); increase cardio-respiratory morbidity and mortality associated with ground-level ozone (high confidence); reduce deaths from cold, although these will be outweighed by the negative effects of rising temperatures worldwide (high confidence); continue to change the range of some infectious disease vectors (high confidence); increase the burden of diarrheal diseases (medium confidence); and increase the number of people at risk of dengue (low confidence)."

- "Adaptive capacity needs to be improved everywhere; impacts of recent hurricanes and heatwaves show that even high-income countries are not well prepared to cope with extreme weather events (high confidence)."

The purpose of this chapter is to review the current state of knowledge of population vulnerability and climate change impacts on human health in the midwestern United States. Climate variability and changing-weather patterns including recent heat waves, floods, and droughts will be examined, and their direct impacts on population health will be discussed. In addition, indirect impacts of climate change on human health in the Midwest will be examined, specifically changes in air and water quality, aeroallergens, and the redistribution of disease vectors. Lastly, an assessment of public health preparedness and prevention-mitigation and adaptive strategies for climate change in the region is provided.

Heatwaves

For health surveillance the Centers for Disease Control and Prevention (CDC) defines "heat wave" as ≥ 3 consecutive days of air temperatures greater than 32.2°C (MMWR 2003). The heat index (as defined in chapter 11 in this volume) is an alternative measure that includes the influence of both temperature and humidity on the exchange of heat (evaporative and radiative) between humans and the atmosphere (Rothfusz 1990). The average core body temperature in humans is 37.0°C (Merck Manual 2011). A constant

exchange of heat between the body and environment is required to maintain core body temperature equilibrium (CDC 2011a). Prolonged or intense heat exposure prompts the thermal-regulatory system to induce vasodilatation, and sweating occurs to evaporate excess heat (Merck Manual 2011). With increasing sweat production the body must be replenished with fluids and salts to prevent dehydration and electrolyte loss and imbalance. The major health outcomes from extreme heat exposure are:

- Heat exhaustion (CDC 2011a) occurs if a person is exposed to prolonged or intense heat and in the process becomes dehydrated. The signs and symptoms of heat exhaustion include heavy sweating, muscle cramps, dizziness, headache, nausea or vomiting, fatigue, and fainting. The skin may be cool and moist, the pulse may be fast and weak, and breathing may be fast and shallow (Merck Manual 2011). The treatment for heat exhaustion includes cooling the body in air-conditioning, taking a cool shower or bath, oral rehydration, and rest (CDC 2011b). Untreated heat exhaustion for 2 to 3 days can progress to heatstroke (Merck Manual 2011).
- Heatstroke (hyperthermia) is a medical emergency that will occur if the core body temperature reaches 39.4°C for longer than 10 or 15 minutes (CDC 2011b). When humidity is high in addition to temperature, sweat will not evaporate as efficiently, causing heat to be retained in the body (Merck Manual 2011). Heatstroke occurs when the thermal-regulatory system stops functioning, and the increase in core body temperature leads to cellular dysfunction, organ system failure, and death.

Classic heatstroke generally begins as heat exhaustion and is typically seen in the elderly and/or people who are immobile, are living without air-conditioning, and whose access to fluids is limited (Merck Manual 2011). Exertional heatstroke occurs in healthy individuals when the body receives a sudden heat load and is unable to acclimatize (Merck Manual 2011). In the Midwest workers in construction, agriculture, forestry, and fishing are at increased risk of heatstroke (Adelakun et al. 1999).

- Other less severe but important heat-related illnesses include heat rash, sunburn, and heat cramps. Heat rash (red clusters of small blisters) is caused by excessive sweating and is generally observed in children, although anyone exposed to prolonged or intense heat is at risk. Heat rash most often appears on the face, neck, and upper chest, in elbow creases, under the breasts, and/or in the groin area. The treatment for heat rash is to keep the affected area(s) dry and to stay in cool environments until the symptoms subside (CDC 2011a). Sunburn can range from abnormally warm, red, and painful skin (first-degree burns) to fever, blisters, and severe pain (second-degree burns). First-degree burns may be treated by applying cold compresses, immersing the sunburned area in cool water, and applying moisturizing lotion to affected area (CDC 2011a). Second-degree burns and infants who are sunburned generally require medical attention (Merck Manual 2011). Heat cramps (muscle pain or spasms) occur as a result of excessive sweating, and muscles of the abdomen, arms, and legs become depleted of salts (Merck Manual 2011). It is important to stop all activity at the onset of heat cramps, sit quietly in a cool place, and drink fluids with salts (electrolytes) until the symptoms subside. Further exertion may lead to heat exhaustion or heat stroke. It is recommended to seek medical attention if heat cramps do not subside after one hour (CDC 2011a).

Slowly increasing the level and duration of activity during heat exposure will result in acclimatization (i.e., the amount of sweat produced for a given activity will increase, while the electrolyte content of the sweat will decrease) (Merck Manual 2011). Proper acclimatization will reduce the risk of heat exhaustion and heatstroke and is a major cause of the differential spatial vulnerability to heat waves across the United States.

People may also have impaired cooling ability, such as the elderly, who are unable to tolerate increases in cardiovascular demand associated with heat exposure, or adults with predisposing medical conditions that require the use of certain medications. Children do not have impaired cooling but are at increased risk of heatstroke because of their small body size and limited surface area to evaporate heat. Thus, the elderly, adults with predisposing medical conditions, and children have a narrower temperature tolerance range (i.e., they have less ability to acclimatize to heat as their bodies attempt to compensate for increased temperatures) (CDC 2011b). These populations, in general, are more susceptible to heat-related illnesses and thus more vulnerable to climate change. See chapter 10 of this volume for a more in-depth understanding of the complex interlinkages between physical and social environments and morbidity and mortality outcomes.

Heat-waves are typically regional in nature, but heat stress is generally observed in urban areas where air temperatures are higher than in rural areas, a phenomenon known as the "urban heat island" (UHI) effect (Figure 9.1) (Oke 1978). Urban heat islands occur because of the abundance of dark surfaces (e.g., roads, roof tops, parking lots, etc.) that absorb and reflect heat waves, a lack of vegetation to provide shade and cool the air through evapotranspiration, less wind circulating to cool the air, and less water runoff to evaporate heat (Wong et al., 2008). Residents living in urban areas are most vulnerable to heat-waves associated with climate change because of the elevated temperatures experienced in densely populated and built environments (Patz et al. 2005). Case studies of heat wave impacts on health in two midwestern urban areas are presented below.

CASE STUDY OF HEAT WAVE IMPACTS IN SAINT LOUIS AND KANSAS CITY, MISSOURI, JULY 1980

A major heat wave occurred in the Midwest in July 1980 and was centered on Saint Louis and Kansas City, Missouri (Jones et al., 1982). In Saint Louis, there were sixteen consecutive days of temperatures 37.8°C or above. In Kansas City, there were seventeen consecutive days with a maximum temperature of 38.9°C, including ten days when the temperature reached 42.2°C or above. The contribution of the urban heat island effect in these cities was 2.5°C and 4.1°C, respectively (Jones et al., 1982) The citywide heatstroke

incidence rate per 100,000 of the population at risk was 26.5 in Saint Louis and 17.6 in Kansas City (MMWR 1989). The age-specific death rate per 100,000 was highest for the elderly ≥ 65 years (121.0 in Saint Louis and 102.0 in Kansas City). Adjusting for age non-whites had a higher death rate than whites in Saint Louis (43.2 versus 15.1, rate ratio (RR) = 2.8) and Kansas City (60.7 versus 9.3, RR = 6.5), and people of low socioeconomic status had a higher death rate than people of high socioeconomic status in Saint Louis (55.8 versus 8.1, RR = 6.8) and Kansas City (36.5 versus 6.5, RR = 5.6) (Jones et al., 1992). Finally, of those persons with heat stroke, the case fatality rate was 65.2 percent in Saint Louis and 63.7 percent in Kansas City (MMWR 1989). Mortality from other causes was also enhanced in the metropolitan areas (it increased by 65.2 percent in Saint Louis and 56.8 percent in Kansas City), compared to rural Missouri (9.5 percent), which again emphasizes the vulnerability of urban populations.

CASE STUDY OF HEAT WAVE IMPACTS IN CHICAGO, ILLINOIS, JULY 1995

The heat wave of July 12–16, 1995, that affected Chicago was characterized by maximum daily temperatures ranging 33.9°C to 40.0°C (Semenza et al. 1996, Kaiser et al. 2007). From July 14 to 20 a total of 1,686 deaths occurred in Chicago. Of these, eighty (4.7 percent) deaths were attributed to "excessive heat" and 473 (28.1 percent) deaths had excessive heat as a contributing factor, with the most common underlying medical condition, cardiovascular disease, 93.7 percent, (n = 467) (Kaiser et al. 2007). On July 13, the heat index peaked at 48.3°C (119°F). In lagged temperature models a cumulative effect was observed after temperatures stayed elevated on lag days 1 and 2 (Kaiser et al., 2007). Those persons most affected from the high heat index were the elderly, males, African American residents, and residents with less than a high school education, controlling for environmental and other potential risk factors (Semenza et al. 1996), again emphasizing the key role of socioeconomic status in vulnerability.

Kaiser et al. (2007) estimated that 692 excess deaths occurred between June 21 and August 10, of which 183 deaths were displaced (i.e., there were 183 fewer deaths from other causes the week immediately after the heat wave). Of 343 excess deaths, among whites, 128 were displaced. Of 343 excess deaths among African Americans, 41 were displaced. These findings demonstrate that the overall risk of heat-related mortality was higher for African Americans. Other characteristics of populations at increased odds of mortality were people living alone, people living above ground level, and immobile persons, including those receiving home health care, mental health care, and Meals on Wheels (Semenza et al., 1996). In addition, factors that were found to significantly protect residents from heat-related death were access to an air conditioner or other source of cool shelter, living on the ground floor, being mobile, and not having preexisting medical condition(s). Figure 9.2 shows the spatial distribution of land surface temperature in Chicago and the surrounding area during the 1995 heat wave and emphasizes the spatial complexity of extreme heat exposure.

INFLUENCE OF CLIMATE CHANGE
ON HEAT WAVES IN THE MIDWEST

The Chicago heat wave in 1995 was particularly severe because of the combined high air and dew point temperatures, sustained high nighttime temperatures, and the long duration of heat intensity (Kunkel et al. 1996, Changnon et al. 1996). Hayhoe et al. (2009) show from climate change heat wave intensity scenarios that before 2040, nine urban centers in the Midwest will have a >50 percent chance of experiencing at least one heat wave with similar characteristics to those in Chicago 1995. The number of hot days (over 32.2°C) and extremely hot days (over 37.7°C) are also very likely to increase (Hayhoe et al., 2009). Ebi and Meehl (2007) estimated heat wave projections (2080 to 2099) in three Midwest urban areas—Chicago, Cincinnati, and Saint Louis—and found that there will be more and longer-lived heat waves per year (Chicago, n = 1.7 to 2.1 for 7.3 to 8.8 days; Cincinnati, n = 1.4 to 2.1 for 8.8 to 10.7 days; and Saint Louis, n = 1.4 to 1.9 for 10.3 to 14.2 days) and nighttime temperatures will increase by more that 2°C during the worst heat waves (Ebi and Meehl 2007). Measures to reduce the risk posed by the changing frequency and intensity of future heat waves are discussed further below.

Air Quality

There are six "criteria" air pollutants and 187 hazardous air pollutants that are currently regulated by the U.S. Environmental Protection Agency (EPA 2011; see discussion in chapter 2). The criteria air pollutants are carbon monoxide (CO), sulfur dioxide (SO_2), nitrogen oxides (NO_x), ozone (O_3), particulate matter (PM), and lead. Of these, ozone and PM are particularly detrimental to public health (Schwartz et al. 1996, Bernard et al. 2001, Levy et al. 2005, Jacob and Winner 2009) and are also the pollutants for which NAAQS are most frequently failed (chapter 2 of this volume). Thus these two pollutants are the focus of this review. Ozone and PM are transmitted to humans via inhalation, and thus exposure estimates are measured from air concentration levels, the duration of exposure, the average volume of air breathed per minute (ventilation rate), and the length of intervals between short-term exposures (World Health Organization 1987). In the Midwest in 2008, 84 (7.1%) counties were in nonattainment status for ozone (maximum daily 8-hour (MDA8-hr) and/or $PM_{2.5}$ annual (arithmetic mean)), according to the National Ambient Air Quality Standards (NAAQS) (Figure 9.3) (EPA 2011). These counties represented 41.6 percent of the Midwest population (n = 29,606,320); however, state-specific population percentages were substantially higher because of the large urban areas in some

states: Illinois (72.6%), Indiana (43.7%), Kentucky (28.2%), Michigan (51.2%), Missouri (34.0%), Ohio (59.7%), and Wisconsin (38.1%).

The primary health concern of elevated ozone exposure is its effect on lung function (CDC 2011b). Symptoms may include lung and throat irritation, lung inflammation, wheezing, and difficulty breathing (McDonnell et al. 1995, EPA 2006, Adams 2006); exacerbation of bronchitis, emphysema, and/or asthma symptoms (EPA 2006), especially in children requiring breathing medication (Gent et al. 2003); and increased emergency room visits and hospitalizations for asthma, chronic obstructive pulmonary disease, pneumonia, and other respiratory diseases (Mudway and Kelly 2000, Gryparis et al. 2004). Persons with respiratory and/or cardiovascular disease(s) may also be at increased risk of premature mortality (Bell et al. 2005). The number of people with selected respiratory and cardiovascular diseases in the Midwest is provided in Table 9.1.

The seasonal variation of PM is location dependent, and in the Midwest, $PM_{2.5}$ is an air quality problem year-round (Jacob and Winner 2009). The PM Supersite Program (EPA 2000) implemented in Saint Louis conducts extensive $PM_{2.5}$ surveillance to characterize particulates and assess human exposure and health outcomes (Turner and Garlock 2007). Researchers found substantial spatial variability, such as $PM_{2.5}$ "hot spots" in areas with high mobile source activities and downwind from major industrial sources (Turner and Garlock 2007). Local health effect studies found that elderly (>60 years) exposed

Table 9.1. Midwestern population by selected respiratory and cardiovascular diseases by state (Data sources: American Lung Association's State of the Air 2010 and National Center for Health Statistics 2011).

State	Pediatric asthma	Adult asthma	Chronic bronchitis	Emphysema	Cardiovascular disease	Pediatric population	Total population
Illinois	251,427	621,614	342,834	127,851	2,809,761	2,670,872	10,610,459
Indiana	109,844	316,227	150,477	57,799	1,250,605	1,166,835	4,616,202
Iowa	36,864	93,811	52,608	20,217	437,066	391,588	1,602,363
Kansas	38,395	100,996	50,324	18,691	411,889	407,875	1,571,090
Kentucky	58,893	191,010	86,873	33,682	725,460	625,618	2,608,513
Michigan	170,705	550,182	246,775	95,583	2,060,769	1,813,387	7,432,239
Minnesota	82,593	212,434	118,091	43,931	968,267	877,370	3,589,936
Missouri	80,990	225,411	117,682	45,726	984,064	860,355	3,539,658
Nebraska	25,815	55,051	32,961	11,941	266,480	274,211	1,045,281
North Dakota	5,025	14,896	7,922	2,875	64,011	53,364	239,779
Ohio	199,652	645,336	299,631	119,157	2,530,871	2,120,876	8,907,072
South Dakota	9,348	21,678	13,302	5,213	111,563	99,316	403,363
Wisconsin	94,503	299,490	141,003	54,813	1,179,247	1,003,891	4,215,143
Total	1,164,054	3,348,136	1,660,453	637,479	13,800,053	12,365,558	50,381,098
Percent	8.6	5.5	4.0	1.3	27.4		
US percent	9.6	7.7	4.4	2.2	26.5		

to increased $PM_{2.5}$ levels (interquartile increase of 8.7 μgm^{-3}) from mobile diesel sources resulted in a 24.4 percent (95% CI, 15.1–34.4) increase in subclinical pulmonary inflammation (Dubowsky et al. 2007).

PROJECTED CLIMATE CHANGE IMPACTS ON AIR QUALITY AND HEALTH IN THE MIDWEST

Wu et al. (2008) predict that increases in temperature in the Midwest will be greatest during summer months, with temperatures ranging from 38.9°C in 2000 to 41.9°C in 2050, which is consistent with increasing heat wave projections (Hayhoe et al. 2009). Future climate change may increase ground-level O_3 through increased temperatures, faster photochemical rates, and more stagnant climate conditions.

High temperatures will also enhance the emissions of the volatile organic compounds (VOCs) (Apsimon et al. 2009), which are key precursors of ozone. Ozone (MDA8hr) is expected to increase by 2–5 ppb during those high temperature events (Wu et al. 2008). Dawson et al. (2009) also predict an increase in O_3 (MDA8hr) of 2.2 ppb in the Midwest as a result of decreasing surface wind speeds and mixing heights. These findings are consistent with Hogrefe et al. (2004), who predicted increases in O_3 in the 3–5 ppb range over much of the Midwest due to climate change. Drought conditions and high temperatures will reduce plant stomata and ozone uptake, enhancing ozone levels in those areas (ApSimon et al. 2009).

Predicting climate change impacts on $PM_{2.5}$ is more complicated than for O_3

because of the diversity of $PM_{2.5}$ components (Jacob and Winner 2009) (i.e., differences in photochemical reaction rates and shifts between gas and particulate phases influenced by sunlight, humidity, precipitation, and stagnation (Liao et al. 2006, Tagaris et al. 2007, Dawson et al. 2009)). There is some evidence for increased $PM_{2.5}$ concentrations in the summer (Dawson et al. 2009), which in combination with increased O_3 concentrations may lead to increased risk of poor health, particularly in urban populations.

COST ANALYSIS OF CLIMATE CHANGE
IMPACTS ON REGIONAL AIR QUALITY

Liao et al. (2010) estimated emission reductions and associated costs required to offset future impacts of climate change on air quality. Six regions and five major cities were studied, including the Great Lakes (Illinois, Indiana, Michigan, Wisconsin, and Ohio) region and the city of Chicago in the Midwest. This research showed that estimated reductions of 24 percent in SO_2 (858 kt) and 12 percent in NO_x (431 kt) emissions in the Great Lakes region are required to offset increases in ozone and $PM_{2.5}$ levels by 2049–2051, resulting in an annual-least-cost of $579 million (1999$). Reductions in VOC emissions were not predicted to be cost-effective "because regional sensitivities of $PM_{2.5}$ to anthropogenic VOC emissions are small" (Liao et al. 2010). In Chicago a reduction of 52.3 percent in SO_2 (129 kt), 22.6 percent in NO_x (118 kt), and 14.5 percent in VOCs (47 kt) are necessary to offset increases in ozone and $PM_{2.5}$, respectively, result-

ing in an annual cost of $292 million. To offset climate effects on urban air quality in the Chicago Metropolitan Statistical Area (MSA) would require an additional $89 million dollars in cost. Based on this study, in total, the annual associated least-cost-estimate to offset future climate change on air quality in the Midwest is ~$960 million.

Aeroallergens

One in five Americans suffer from one or more allergies. Outdoor airborne allergens (aeroallergens) include pollen from trees, grasses, and weeds and mold spores. Allergic diseases include asthma, hay fever, and atopic dermatitis (Kinney 2008). Seasonal allergies in the Midwest begin in early spring (approximately March), when trees bud and begin to release pollens, followed by grass pollens in late spring to late summer and weed (ragweed) pollens in late summer and fall (approximately October) (American Academy of Allergy Asthma and Immunology (AAAI) 2011).

Relatively little research has been undertaken to examine possible climate change impacts on aeroallergens in the Midwest. Increased temperatures and carbon dioxide may cause some plants to bloom earlier (Stitt 1991), extending the pollen season and thus potentially enhancing the intensity and duration of symptoms (Haines and Patz 2004). Further, certain pollens may also become more allergenic (Beggs 2004). Projections of increased precipitation (see chapter 2) may also lead to more mold spores (Beggs 2004).

Floods and Droughts

As described in other chapters within this volume, flooding is a major natural hazard within the Midwest. The 1993 flood in the Midwest is recorded as the worst flood in U.S. history (Bell and Janowiak 1995), with rainfall totals 300–400 percent of normal during the spring and summer (Larson 1996). During June and July, heavy rains in the Upper Midwest, combined with wet soil conditions, caused severe flooding in the upper Mississippi basin, pushing the Mississippi River to a crest at Saint Louis (Larson 1996). In early July, Iowa also received record rainfalls, flooding the city of Des Moines and pushing the Mississippi River to a record high of 49 feet (Larson 1996). Farms and cropland were flooded, with 70,000 residents displaced. Fifty deaths were caused by flash flooding, in which people were washed away in heavy streamflow without warning, and river flooding, in which people drowned in motor vehicles, were electrocuted, or experienced fatal injury/injuries (Larson 1996). In Missouri, 27 deaths occurred (mean age 37.8 years, range 9 to 88 years) of which 67 percent were male. Of these, 16 deaths were directly related to flash flooding, and 11 deaths were from riverine flooding (MMWR 1993). The Midwest floods in 1993, and another in 2008, also resulted in flood-related illnesses, including gastroenteritis following the ingestion of water contaminated with disease-causing organisms, dermatitis following contact with water contaminated with abrasive chemicals, and stress-related morbidity associated with loss and displacement (MMWR

2003). Intensification of extreme precipitation events as projected under climate change scenarios (see chapter 2) may cause increased flood frequency and associated loss of life.

Droughts are periods of abnormally dry weather (i.e., elevated temperatures and suppressed precipitation) and may impact human health through reduced or contaminated water supply and dehydration, waterborne diseases, reduced agriculture and nutrition, increased forest fires, air particulate pollution, and respiratory and/or other airborne-related diseases, and decreased hydropower that may reduce the availability of electricity for air-conditioning. In the late 1980s the midwestern region experienced a 3-year drought (1987 to 1989) in which the summer of 1988 was particularly severe. The drought covered 36 percent of the United States but was focused on the North Central and Midwest regions (see chapter 2 of this volume). It had epidemiological importance due to the increase in diving-associated spinal cord injuries (n = 8) caused by victims diving into familiar bodies of water believing the water was deeper than it actually was (MMWR 1988).

Infectious Disease

Following heavy rainfall events there is often an increase in waterborne disease outbreaks following overflow of the wastewater system and mixing of untreated sewage and storm water into receiving waters (Curriero 2001, Hrudey 2003, Patz et al. 2008). If these waters (e.g., Great

Lakes or groundwater wells) are a source of the drinking water system and the contamination is insufficiently treated, people will be exposed when they consume the water (i.e., drink or eat foods washed with the water) or used for recreational activities. Following extreme precipitation these outbreaks will occur within one month of surface water contamination and 2 months of groundwater contamination. There are more than 100 different types of waterborne pathogenic bacteria, viruses, and protozoa that cause infection in humans (Patz et al. 2008). The Great Lakes are a primary water source for over 40 million people and is surrounded by a number of large cities, posing a substantial public health threat in the Midwest region. Patz et al. (2008) predicts that in the Great Lakes region, an additional 2.5 inches of rain in a single day will cause a combined sewer overflow into Lake Michigan, resulting in 50–100 percent more waterborne disease outbreaks in the region per year.

Vector-borne diseases (VBD) are infectious diseases transmitted by the bite of an infected arthropod species, such as mosquitoes, ticks, and black flies in the Midwest. VBDs are linked to climate change because of their widespread occurrence and sensitivity to climatic factors. Increases in temperature and precipitation may alter the life cycle of disease agents and multiplication rates and distribution of disease vectors (CDC 2011c). VBD surveillance, therefore, includes monitoring the level of virus activity, vector populations, infections in animal hosts, the incidence of human cases, and climate and weather factors needed to pre-

dict changes in VBD transmission cycles (CDC 2011c). The elderly and children are at greatest risk of neuroinvasive diseases (CDC 2011c).

While VBDs from mosquito and tick vectors are prevalent in the Midwest, this review focuses on five arthropod-borne viruses transmitted by mosquitoes (eastern equine encephalitis (EEE), western equine encephalitis (WEE), La Crosse encephalitis (LAC), Saint Louis encephalitis (SLE) and West Nile virus (WNV)) because of the limited treatment regimes for human-viral infections, the potential for future climate-change-induced epidemics, and the emergence of other diseases caused by arboviruses such as dengue hemorrhagic fever (Patz and Olson 2006). People bitten by an infected mosquito are generally asymptomatic or show mild flu-like symptoms (e.g., insidious or sudden onset of fever, headache, fatigue, and muscle aches, also referred to as noninvasive disease) (CDC 2011c). Infection, however, may spread to the nervous system (i.e., become invasive) resulting in encephalitis (acute inflammation of the brain), meningitis (acute inflammation of the membranes covering the brain and spinal cord) or meningoencephalitis (CDC 2011c).

• EEE is maintained in the environment by transmission between infected *Culiseta melanura* mosquitoes and bird amplifying hosts. Transmission to humans generally occurs through "bridge" mosquitoes, such as *Aedes, Coquillettidia,* and *Culex* species that also feed on bird hosts. People are considered dead-end hosts because their viremic loads are generally insufficient to infect mosquito populations (CDC 2011c). The *Cx. melanura* mosquito thrives in freshwater swamps. The incubation period (time from mosquito bite to signs and symptoms of EEE infection) is 4 to 10 days (CDC 2011c). National surveillance reports of EEE neuroinvasive disease show that 6.5 percent of cases occur in the Midwest (Table 9.2). Approximately, one-third of people with neuroinvasive EEE disease will not survive (CDC 2011c).

• WEE is transmitted by *Cx. tarsalis* mosquitoes, and birds are amplifying hosts. Many other "bridge" mosquitoes are involved in the human transmission. In Nebraska in 1997, 35 strains of WEE virus were isolated from mosquitoes (CDC 2011c). The *Cx. tarsalis* mosquito is commonly found in farming areas with irrigated fields. The incubation period for WEE is 5 to 15 days (CDC 2011c). National surveillance reports of WEE neuroinvasive disease show that 38.3 percent of cases occur in the Midwest (Table 9.2). The case-fatality rate (number of WEE deaths/number of WEE neuroinvasive case-infections) is 3.0 percent (CDC 2011c).

• SLE is the most common mosquito-transmitted pathogen in the United States (CDC 2011c). It was first recognized in Saint Louis, Missouri, in 1933 and has since been isolated in mosquitoes in 48 states (CDC 2011c). SLE is transmitted by *Cx pipien* mosquitoes, and birds are amplifying hosts. *Cx pipiens* are common suburban and urban mosquitoes and are therefore important vectors in human transmission even though "bridge" mosquitoes exist. The incubation period for SLE is 5 to 15 days (CDC 2011c). National surveillance reports of SLE neuroinvasive disease show that 41.4 percent of cases occur in the Midwest

(Table 9.2). The elderly are at highest risk of SLE neuroinvasive disease. The case-fatality rate is 5–15 percent, with deaths increasing with age (CDC 2011c).

• LAC was discovered in La Crosse, Wisconsin, in 1963 and has since been identified in several midwestern states (CDC 2011c). The transmission cycle involves the *Aedes triseriatus* mosquito, and small animals (e.g., chipmunks and squirrels) are amplifying hosts. *Ae. triseriatus* is an aggressive daytime-biting mosquito, especially in or near wood habitats of the hosts (CDC 2011c). The incubation period for LAC is 5 to 15 days (CDC 2011c). National surveillance reports of LAC neuroinvasive disease show that 68.0 percent of cases occur in the Midwest (Table 9.2). Children <16 years are at greatest risk (CDC 2011c). The case-fatality rate is 1.0 percent (CDC 2011c).

• WNV is similar to the viruses responsible for SLE and is also transmitted by the *Cx pipien* mosquito. Birds are the primary amplifying host, and chickens, horses and humans are dead-end hosts. In 2010, 22.5 percent of all U.S. cases of WNV were reported in the Midwest (Table 9.2). The incubation period is 2 to 14 days (CDC 2011c). The case-fatality rate for WNV neuroinvasive disease is 3–15 percent and death is most common among the elderly (CDC 2011c).

Following the 1993 floods in the Midwest, standing water produced large populations of *Cx. pipiens* and *Cx. tarsalis* mosquitoes, capable of transmitting arboviruses that cause SLE and WEE. Surveillance during August–September 1993 found that the risk of SLE or WEE was low in the northern part of the flood region, because flooding occurred in late summer.

Table 9.2. Prevalence of vector-borne diseases in the Midwest (Data source: Centers for Disease Control and Prevention, Division of Vector-Borne Diseases (CDC 2011c)).

State	WNV[1]	EEE[2]	WEE[2]	SLE[2]	LAC[2]	Lyme disease[3]	Tularemia[4]
Illinois	56	0	6	693	241	974	33
Indiana	12	3	1	367	143	510	10
Iowa	6	0	5	25	134	815	1
Kansas	17	0	36	127	0	174	50
Kentucky	3	0	0	68	22	225	22
Michigan	29	13	1	31	29	544	5
Minnesota	8	0	43	8	366	10,207	7
Missouri	17	0	7	76	14	476	228
Nebraska	37	0	26	14	0	80	47
North Dakota	9	0	78	18	9	51	9
Ohio	5	0	0	441	898	731	9
South Dakota	20	0	40	5	0	12	62
Wisconsin	2	1	2	5	586	15,415	6
Total	221	17	245	1,878	2,442	30,214	489
Percent US	22.5	6.5	38.3	41.4	68.0	9.7	43.2
Total US	981	260	640	4,533	3,590	311,671	1,133

Notes: [1] Includes noninvasive and invasive confirmed and probable cases, 2010. [2] Includes invasive confirmed and probable cases 1964 to 4/30/2010. [3] Includes confirmed cases, 1995–2010. [4] Includes confirmed cases, 2000–2010.

However, in the southern part of the flood region, intensive surveillance in Illinois, Iowa, Kansas, and Missouri identified a proliferation of mosquitoes. Testing of these mosquitoes revealed extremely low infectious rates for these disease agents, which was consistent with previous studies of flood-related arboviral epidemics (MMWR 1994). The cost, however, associated with mosquito surveillance and control, which must occur following flooding in case of a potential outbreak, amounted to $1.6 million (MMWR 1994).

In summary, the Midwest is endemic for arthropod viral diseases transmitted by mosquitoes and other VBDs (viral, bacterial, protozoan, and Rickettsial) transmitted by ticks (e.g., Lyme disease,

ehrlichiosis, babesiosis, and tularemia). Enzootic agent transmission may occur at low intensity in natural habitats. In rural and suburban locations these areas may remain undetected (silent zones of disease) (Meade and Emch 2010). Enzootic transmission will increase to epizootic proportions if host immunity is low, if there are abundant animal hosts (to amplify the disease), and if mosquitoes/ticks have favorable weather conditions to multiply and thrive (Moore et al. 1993). Moore et al. (1993) report that if epizootics begin early in the transmission season and/or if the epizootic foci expand into urban areas, the risk of human transmission increases. The earliest, most useful predictors of epizootic activity are climatologic factors (increased temperatures and rainfall) because they influence the size of early (season) mosquito (Moore et al. 1993) and tick populations. Climate change will likely increase the risk of VBDs in the Midwest if prevention and control measures are not implemented.

Addressing and Reducing Vulnerability

National summaries have generally resolved that climate change will increase morbidity and mortality risks from climate-sensitive health determinants, and addressing those determinants in adaptation strategies will be important (Ebi et al. 2006). Frumkin et al. (2002) outline a proactive approach to climate change using the principles of public health "prevention" and "preparedness." In an effort to be prepared for climate change, state public health systems in the Midwest will continue and expand "primary" prevention activities that prevent the onset of illnesses and injuries in individuals and populations, "secondary" prevention activities that detect disease(s) early and intervene to reduce individual and population-health burden, and "tertiary" prevention activities to limit disease progression and restore individual and population health. These public health prevention and preparedness activities are analogous to climate change mitigation and adaptation strategies. For example, primary prevention and mitigation efforts attempt to protect individuals and populations by reducing greenhouse gas emissions, and secondary and tertiary

prevention and adaptation efforts anticipate and prepare individuals and populations for climate change events in order to reduce vulnerability and minimize disease and injury. Primary prevention and mitigation efforts in the Midwest should include policies for the reduction of greenhouse gas emissions (e.g., energy efficiency, use of renewable energy sources, and forest preservation) (Haines and Patz 2004, Haines et al., 2006). Stringent emission controls to reduce ozone precursors and ozone concentrations below health-based standards (Kinney 2008) are also needed. Secondary and tertiary prevention and adaptation strategies in the Midwest will need to include continued weather forecasting and weather systems, emergency management, and disaster preparedness (Haines and Patz 2004). Heat wave warning schemes that identity and forecast heat wave events, predict potential health outcomes, and respond to high-risk populations in an effective and timely manner (Ebi and Meehl 2007) will also reduce the burden of injury and disease. Reducing the heat island effect (Patz et al. 2005) in midwestern urban areas may include reestablishing building codes (Ebi and Meehl 2007), adding trees and vegetation, green roofs, and cool roofs/pavement (Wong et al. 2008) may also be beneficial. Providing air conditioners or access to cooling environments for the elderly and adults with predisposing medical conditions during heat wave events (Semenza et al. 1996, Kaiser 2007) will also reduce morbidity and mortality, but Kinney (2008) reports that while it is important

to rely on air-conditioning as a primary
adaptive response, there will also be the
need for corresponding programs that reduce the resulting emissions from power
plants used to generate the electricity.

To reduce population vulnerability to
climate change in the Midwest there should
also be equitable access to medications for
respiratory diseases such as asthma (Kinney 2008) and education programs that inform the public on how to cope during heat
wave events and how to minimize exposure
to air pollutants and aeroallergens (Kinney
2008, CDC 2011b). There will also be the
need for increased surveillance for pollen
and mold levels (Kinney 2008) and
greater awareness of the impacts of indoor
moisture on molds on respiratory allergies (Kinney 2008). Incentives should also
be provided to shift housing development
away from flood-prone areas (Kinney
2008) and to upgrade sewage and storm
systems to decrease the potential for waterborne diseases during flood seasons (Patz
et al. 2008), especially in states boarding
the Great Lakes. There will also be the need
to monitor changes in vector-borne infectious disease rates following periods of high
temperatures and precipitation through
rapid assessment surveillance and control
activities (MMWR 1994, CDC 2011c). Importantly, the health care system, including
the education of health care practitioners
and the services provided in local hospital
and medical practices, will also need to
be assessed to ensure the heath care infrastructure in the Midwest is prepared for
future hazardous events associated with climate change (Haines and Patz 2004).

REFERENCES

Adams WC (2006). Human pulmonary responses
with 30-minute time intervals of exercise and
rest when exposed for 8 hours to 0.12ppm
ozone via square-wave and acute triangular
profiles. Inhalation Toxicology 18:413–422.

Adelakun A, Schwartz E, Blais L (1999). Occupational heat exposure. Applied Occupational
and Environmental Hygiene 14:153–154.

American Academy of Allergy, Asthma & Immunology (AAAI) (2011). Pollen and spore levels
in the Midwest. Available from: http://pollen
.aaaai.org/nab/index.cfm?region=midwest
&p=map.

American Lung Association (ALA) (2010). State
of the air. Available from: http://www
.stateoftheair.org.

Apsimon H, Amann M, Astrom S, Oxley T (2009).
Synergies in addressing air quality and climate
change. Climate Policy 9:669–680.

Beggs PJ (2004). Impacts of climate change on
aeroallergens: Past and future. Clinical & Experimental Allergy 34:1507–1513.

Bell ML, Dominici F, Samet JM (2005). A meta-
analysis of time-series studies of ozone and
mortality with comparison to the national
Morbidity, Mortality and Air Pollution Study.
Epidemiology 16:436–445.

Bell GD, Janowiak JE (1995). Atmospheric circulation associated with the midwest floods of
1993. Bulletin of the American Meteorological
Society 5:681–695.

Bernard SM, Samet JM, Grambsch A, Ebi KL,
Romieu I (2001). The potential impacts of climate variability and change on air pollution-
related health effects in the United States. Environmental Health Perspectives 109:S199–S209.

Centers for Disease Control and Prevention
(CDC) (2011a). Extreme heat: A prevention
guide to promote your personal health and
safety. Available from: http://www.bt.cdc.gov/
disasters/extremeheat/heat_guide.asp.

Centers for Disease Control and Prevention
(CDC) (2011b). National Institute of Occupational Health and Safety Ozone. Available
from http://www.cdc.gov/niosh/topics/ozone/.

Centers for Disease Control and Prevention (CDC) (2011c). National Center for Emerging and Zoonotic Infectious Diseases. Available from http://www.cdc.gov/ncezid/.

Changnon SA, Kunkel KE, Reinke BC (1996). Impacts and responses to the 1995 heat wave: a call into action. Bulletin of the American Meteorological Society 77:1497–1506.

Curriero FC, Patz J, Rose JB, Lele S (2001). The association between extreme precipitation and waterborne disease outbreaks in the United States, 1948–1994. American Journal of Public Health 91:1194–1199.

Dawson JP, Racherla PN, Lynn BH, Adams PJ, Pandis SN (2009). Impacts of climate change on regional and urban air quality in the eastern United States: Role of meteorology. Journal of Geophysical Research 114: D05308, doi:10.1029/2008JD009849.

Dubowsky Adar SD, Adamkiewicz G, Gold DR, Schwartz J, Coull BA, Suh H (2007). Ambient and micro-environmental particles and exhaled nitric oxide before and after a group bus trip. Environmental Health Perspectives 115:507–512.

Ebi KL, Mills DM, Smith JB, Grambsch A (2006). Climate change and human health impacts in the United States: An update on the results of the U.S. National Assessment. Environmental Health Perspectives 114:1318–1324.

Ebi KL, Meehl GA (2007). Heatwaves & global climate change. The heat is on: Climate change & heatwaves in the Midwest. Excerpted from the full report, Regional impacts of climate change: Four case studies in the United States. Pew Center on Global Climate Change. Available from: http://www.c2es.org/docUploads/Regional-Impacts-FullReport.pdf.

Environmental Protection Agency (EPA) (2011). National ambient air quality standards (NAAQS). Available from: http://www.epa.gov/air/criteria.html.

Environmental Protection Agency (EPA) (2011). The green book nonattainment areas for criteria pollutants. Available from: http://www.epa.gov/airquality/greenbook/index.html.

Environmental Protection Agency (EPA) (2006). Air Quality criteria for ozone and related photochemical oxidants V011–3. United States Environmental Protection Agency EPA 600 R-05/004aF.

Environmental Protection Agency (EPA) (2000). PM supersites program background. Available from: http://www.epa.gov/ttn/amtic/supersites.html.

Frumkin H, Hess J, Luber G, Malilay J, McGeehim M (2008). Climate change: The public health response. American Journal of Public Health 98:435–445.

Gent JF, Triche EW, Holford TR, Belanger K, Bracken JB, Beckett WS, Leaderer BP (2003). Association of low-level ozone and fine particles with respiratory symptoms in children with asthma. Journal of the American Medical Association 290:1959–1964.

Gryparis A, Forsberg B, Katsouyanni K, Analitis A, Touloumi G, Schwartz J, Samoli E, Median S, Anderson HR, Niciu EM, Wichmann HE, Kriz B, Kosnik M, Skorkovsky J, Vonk JM, Dortbudak Z (2004). Acute effects of ozone on mortality from the "Air Pollution and Health: A European Approach" Project. American Journal of Respiratory Critical Care Medicine 170:1080–1087.

Haines A, Patz JA (2004). Health effects of climate change. Journal of the American Medical Association 291:99–103.

Haines A, Kovats RS, Campbell-Lendrum D, Corvalan C (2006). Climate change and human health: Impacts, vulnerability and public health. Public Health 120:585–596.

Hayhoe K, VanDorn J, Naik V, Wuebbles D (2009). Climate change in the midwest projections of future temperature and precipitation. Union of Concerned Scientists. Available from: http://www.ucsusa.org/global_warming/science_and_impacts/impacts/climate-change-midwest.html.

Hogrefe CJ, Biswas BK, Civerolo K, Ku J-Y, Rosenthal J, Rosenzweig C, Goldberg R, Kinney PL (2004). Simulating regional-scale ozone climatology over the eastern United

States: Model evaluation results. Atmospheric Environment 38:2672–2638.

Hrudey WE, Payment P, Huck PM, Gillham RW, Hrudey EJ (2003). A fatal waterborne disease epidemic in Walkerton, Ontario: Comparison with other waterborne outbreaks in the developed world. Water Science & Technology 47:7–14.

Intergovernmental Panel on Climate Change (IPCC) (2007). IPCC Fourth Assessment Report: Impacts, Adaptation and Vulnerability Chapter 8: Human Health. Available from: http://www.ipcc.ch/publications_and_data/ar4/wg2/en/contents.html.

Jacob DJ, Winner DA (2009). Effect of climate change on air quality. Atmospheric Environment 43:51–63.

Jones TS, Liang AP, Kilbourne EM, Griffin MR, Patriarca PA, Wassilak SG, Mullan RJ, Herrick RF, Donnell Jr. HD, Choi K, Thacker SB (1982). Morbidity and Mortality associated with the July 1980 heat wave in St. Louis and Kansas City, Missouri. Journal of the American Medical Association 247:3327–3331.

Kaiser R, Le Tertre A, Schwartz J, Gotway CA, Daley R, Rubin CH (2007). The effect of the 1995 heat wave in Chicago on all-cause and cause-specific mortality. American Journal of Public Health 97(S1):S158-S162.

Kinney PL (2008). Climate change, air quality, and human health. American Journal of Preventive Medicine 35:459–467.

Kunkel KE, Changnon SA, Reinke BC, Arritt RW (1996). The July 1995 heat wave in the Midwest: A climatic perspective and critical weather factors. Bulletin of the American Meteorological Society 77:1507–1518.

Larson LW (1996). The Great USA Flood of 1993. Presented at the International Association of Hydrological Sciences Conference, Anaheim, CA, June 24–28, 1996.

Levy JI, Chemerynski SM, Sarnat JA (2005). Ozone exposure and mortality: An empiric Bayes metaregression analysis. Epidemiology 16:458–468.

Liao H, Chen W-T, Seinfeld JH (2006). Role of climate change in global predictions of future tropospheric ozone and aerosols. Journal of Geophysical Research 111:D12304, doi: 10.1029/2005JD006852.

Liao KJ, Tagaris E, Russell AG, Amar P, He S, Manomaiphiboon K, Woo JH (2010). Cost analysis of impacts of climate change on regional air quality. Journal of the Air & Waste Management Association 60:95–203.

Meade M, Emch M (2010). Medical Geography. Third edition. New York: Guilford Press.

McDonnell WF, Stewart PW, Andreoni S, Smith MV (1995). Proportion of moderately exercising individuals responding to low-level multi-hour ozone exposure. American Journal of Respiratory Critical Care Medicine 152:589–596.

Merck Manual Online Medical Library (2011). Available from: http://www.merckmanuals.com/professional/index.html.

Moore CG, McLean RG, Mitchell CJ, Nasci RS, Tsai TF, Calisher CH, Marfin AA, Moore PS, Gubler DJ (1993). Guidelines for arbovirus surveillance programs in the United States. Division of Vector-Borne Infectious Diseases, National Center for Infectious Diseases, Centers for Disease Control and Prevention, Fort Collins, CO.

Morbidity and Mortality Weekly Report (MMWR) (1989). Current trends heat-related deaths—Missouri, 1979–1988 June 30; 38(25):437–439.

Morbidity and Mortality Weekly Report (MMWR) (1988). Epidemiological notes and report diving-associated spinal cord injuries during drought conditions—Wisconsin, 1988. August 15; 37(30):453–454.

Morbidity and Mortality Weekly Report (MMWR) (1993). Morbidity surveillance following the Midwest flood—Missouri. October 22; 42(41):797–798.

Morbidity and Mortality Weekly Report (MMWR) (1994). Rapid assessment of vectorborne diseases during the Midwest flood—United States, 1993. July 8; 43(26):481–483.

Morbidity and Mortality Weekly Report (MMWR) (1995). Heat-related mortality—Chicago July 1995. August 11; 44(31):577–579.

Morbidity and Mortality Weekly Report (MMWR) (2003). Heat-related deaths—Chicago, Illinois, 1996–2001 and United States 1979–1999; 52(26):610.

Mudway IS, Kelly FJ (2000). Ozone and the lung: a sensitive issue. Molecular Aspects of Medicine 21:1–48.

National Center for Health Statistics (2011). FastStats. Available from: http://www.cdc.gov/nchs/fastats/default.htm.

Oke TR (1978). Boundary layer climates. London: Methuen.

Patz JA, Campbell-Lendrum D, Holloway T, Foley JA. 2005. Impact of regional climate change on human health. Nature 438:310–317.

Patz JA, Olson SH(2006). Climate change and health: Global to local influences on disease risk. Annals of Tropical Medicine & Parasitology 100:535–549.

Patz JA, Vavrus SJ, Uejio CK, McLellan SL (2008). Climate change and waterborne disease risk in the Great Lakes Region of the U.S. American Journal of Preventive Medicine 35:451–458.

Rothfusz LP (1990). The heat index "equation" (or more than you ever wanted to know about the heat index). NWS Technical Attachment SR90-23. NWS Southern Region Headquarters, Fort Worth, TX.

Schwartz JD, Dockery W, Neas LM (1996). Is daily mortality associated specifically with fine particles? Journal of Air and Waste Management Association 46:927–939.

Semenza JC, Rubin CH, Falter KH, Selanikio JD, Flanders WD, Howe HL, Wilhelm JL (1996). Health-related deaths during the July 1995 heat wave in Chicago. New England Journal of Medicine 335:84–90.

Stitt M (1991). Rising CO_2 levels and their potential significance for carbon flow in photosynthetic cells. Cell and Environment 14:741–762.

Tagaris E, Manomaiphiboon K, Liao K-J, Lenung LR, Woo J-H, He S, Amar P, Russell AG (2007). Impacts of global climate change and emissions on regional ozone and fine particulate matter concentrations over the United States. Journal of Geophysical Research 112:D14312, doi:10.1029/2006JD008262.

Turner JR, Garlock JL (2007). A conceptual model for ambient fine particulate matter over the St. Louis area. Revision 3.0. Washington University, St. Louis, MO. In St. Louis—Midwest Fine Particulate Matter Supersite. Available from: http://www.epa.gov/ttnamti1/files/ambient/super/STL-SS_FinalReport_Rev02_March2007.pdf.

Wong E, Hogan K, Rosenberg J, Denny A (2008). Reducing urban health islands: Compendium of strategies Urban heat island basics. Available from: http://www.epa.gov/heatisland/resources/compendium.htm.

World Health Organization (1987). Air Quality Guidelines for Europe. Copenhagen: WHO Regional Office for Europe.

Wu S, Mickley LJ, Leibensperger EM, Jacob DJ, Rind D, Streets DG (2008). Effects of 2000–2050 global change on ozone air quality in the United States. Journal of Geographical Research 113:D06302, doi:10.1029/2007JD008917.

10. Intra-Urban Variations in Vulnerability Associated with Extreme Heat Events in Relationship to a Changing Climate

D. P. JOHNSON, V. LULLA, AND A. C. STANFORTH

Introduction

In the developing literature on the nature of climate change and its potential impact on society, vulnerability is an emerging pervasive theme. As can be seen in chapter 1 of this volume, vulnerability, by its very nature, is a multidisciplinary and multidimensional concept and thus requires multiple levels of definition and examination (Bankoff 2001, Bankoff 2003). Vulnerability is also a term that has been recently utilized as a "catch-all" phrase and thus is in danger of losing some of its descriptive effectiveness (Cutter et al. 2008). Vulnerability is so encompassing because it stems from multiple conditions that could represent the social, health, intelligence, or economic status of an individual or location (Wisner 2004). For the present discussion, we are concerned with the vulnerability of populations to a changing climate; our definitions will focus on health and social vulnerability to extreme events, such as those that will likely punctuate climate change globally, particularly heat waves. This chapter in-tends to introduce vulnerability in the context of extreme heat and to present a case study where such an analysis of vulnerability has taken place.

Clearly, vulnerability to extreme heat, in such a complex system as an urban space, is not of the same magnitude throughout the city. Depending on where people live, their environment and socioeconomic conditions (i.e., poverty) can impact their unique vulnerability, and each area of the city may be markedly different from another. Intra-urban vulnerability (Harpham 2009, Minuci and de Almeida 2009) is increasingly being studied with remote sensing because spatial information is vital to disaster planning and mitigation (Harlan et al. 2006, Cutter et al. 2008, Johnson et al. 2009, Johnson and Wilson 2009). This type of information leads to "intelligence-led decision making" and is becoming increasingly recognized as a robust modeling framework. The examination presented in this chapter will involve the discussion of a vulnerability case study for Indianapolis, Indiana, using both demographic and environmental datasets. The current state of vulnerability in this particular location and the anticipated changes expected to occur due to a changing climate will be highlighted.

The methods for determining vulnerability can be articulated in three broad categories:

1. Vulnerability as it relates to natural processes
2. Social vulnerability
3. A mixed approach using social vulnerability in the context of extreme natural processes

Relating vulnerability to natural processes would initially appear to be a fairly straightforward undertaking. However, calculating the number of homes in Federal Emergency Management Agency (FEMA) floodplains and identifying them as vulnerable would be an oversimplification of true vulnerability. Nevertheless, purely hazard-oriented strategies published in the 1970s and 1980s (Pelling 2003) still pervade assessments of vulnerability to natural disasters. This paradigm placed increased interest in humankind's perceived technological advantages over nature and asserted that eventually we would decrease this vulnerability through use of technology alone. Thus, in this context, nature and the extreme events associated with a disaster are viewed as external to society (Wisner 2004). This context of disaster is flawed in many ways. First, people are viewed as having "bounded rationality"— that is, they are unable to make sound choices when faced with overarching risk

(Wisner 2004). Society's political, economic, and social frameworks are viewed as being detached from disasters and therefore only modifiers to the potential impacts of disaster. This approach fails to recognize the full range of people's capacity to adapt to a disaster or to their individual or societal vulnerabilities.

A second methodological approach to determining vulnerability is to examine the social fabric of a location deemed to be at-risk from a natural hazard. This is more commonly referred to as social vulnerability and takes into account many different social facets of the vulnerable location. The spectrum of social vulnerability ranges from the individual to the population level and includes such factors as an individual's age, ethnicity, and socioeconomic status to the census-based descriptors of the neighborhood in which the individuals reside. Something unique to this view, versus the more dominant natural hazard process, is the emphasis placed on reduction in social vulnerability instead of the reduction in physical damage. Further, emphasis is placed on the hazard system being open and extremely complex and not limited by bounded rationality (Enarson et al. 2003). Further development in this area is punctuated by the creation of a Social Vulnerability Index (SoVI) developed by Cutter (Cutter et al. 2008, Cutter and Finch 2008, Cutter et al. 2010). Using such approaches it is thought possible to quantify vulnerability and its spatiotemporal characteristics (Birkmann and von Teichman 2010). Predominantly in the urban environment, the urban poor are the most at risk due to their economic and social status (Moser et al. 1994). The social and economic support networks of the urban poor tend to be of slighter complexity and extent than their poor rural counterparts (Pelling 2006). The urban experience is considerably different than the rural life experience in relation to access, as goods seem to be more commodified (Moser et al. 1994). This implies that access to goods in urban settings require monetary resources, as opposed to the rural experience, where food can be readily grown and access to environmental resources may assist in a rural individual's livelihood. Urban agriculture and recycling would be exceptions to this line of thought. Additionally, there is greater social fragmentation because of higher loss of residential mobility and the loss of social networks (Hardoy et al. 2001). Further, livelihoods in urban settings are exposed to more crime and other detrimental social hazards that contribute to a decline in quality of life (McIlwaine and Moser 2001). Much of this is known as the "urban health penalty," where one may have closer access to health care but be exposed to more phenomena that would require the need for health care. Many of these issues were at the heart of the 1995 extreme heat event in Chicago, Illinois, that resulted in over 700 deaths (Browning et al. 2006, Duneier 2006).

A third approach to vulnerability attempts to mix the aspects of the natural hazard approach with that of social vulnerability. There cannot be a disaster if there are hazards but no vulnerable population, nor can there be a disaster with a vulnerable population and no hazard (Wisner et al. 2004). The argument is that risk is a function of the hazard and the number of vulnerable individuals. In this context risk and vulnerability are two separate phenomena, where vulnerability refers to the potential for loss, and risk is the probable level of loss from a natural hazard coupled with vulnerability (Alexander 2000). This risk-hazard model has inadequacies in the distinction among the variations in hazard intensity or the inclusion of vulnerable subsystems (Hewitt 1997). A more encompassing model, known as the pressure and release model (PAR), was developed to address many of the inadequacies in the risk-hazard approach. PAR is not strictly a numeric or statistical model but is similar to a paradigm of understanding two unique processes that contribute to a disaster. PAR understands a disaster to be at the intersection of the processes generating vulnerability and the natural hazard itself. The system behaves like a lever putting force on the population through the social and physical environment: the higher the pressure the greater the risk. Pressure can be released through several different means, such as a reduction in social vulnerability or in the natural phenomena leading to potential disaster. This approach has a unique and intrinsic value when considering adaptation to physical and/or social processes. Adaptation (in the context of human adaptation) implies humankind becoming more suited to the environment. Therefore, adaptation can be viewed as a potential mechanism by which pressure is released in the PAR model.

Extreme Heat Events

DETERMINING VULNERABILITY

In the context of extreme heat, as well as numerous other natural hazards, the very old, the very young, the economically disadvantaged, those with lower educational attainment, and minority populations are considered to be most at risk (Stephenson et al. 2010). Recently, there has been an increased interest in placing the social aspects of extreme heat vulnerability into models of risk for individual cities in the United States, along with meteorological components indicative of extreme heat events (Stephenson et al. 2010, Wilhelmi and Hayden 2010).

A further phenomenon that exacerbates of extreme heat vulnerability in urban locations is the presence of the urban heat island (UHI) (see chapter 9 of this volume). The UHI effect is the observed temperature differential between the urban center and its adjacent rural hinterland and can reach magnitude of 4°C–5°C (Lo et al. 1997, Weng et al. 2004). The primary driver behind the UHI effect is the built environment within the city, which contains many materials that have a higher capacity to store energy and re-emit it in the thermal wavelengths. Typically, the land surface temperature (LST) of industrial and commercial locations is warmer due to the abundance of asphalt, concrete, and metallic structures

and the lack of vegetation. Residential locations within a city that lack substantial vegetation and that contain a high density of housing are warmer than their suburban counterparts. The UHI effect is maximized at night, and thus residents do not get as much relief from the heat. Numerous studies have shown that the UHI effect within an urbanized location leads to significant enhancement of heat-related health risk (Harlan et al. 2006, Johnson et al. 2009, Johnson and Wilson 2009, Tan et al. 2010, Zhou and Shepherd 2010).

By incorporating the physical components of extreme heat along with the social vulnerability of specific locations in a PAR model, one can quickly determine the most vulnerable locations and direct resources for mitigation. Further, from such models, one can determine unique approaches to releasing pressure in the environment and moderate the intensity of the potential disaster. These methods could incorporate releases on both the social and physical environment and would need to be specific to each location, as they would likely be unique to the individual locale.

DEFINITIONS OF EXTREME HEAT EVENTS (EHE)

The first definitions of a heat wave, such as those created by the National Weather Service (NWS) (consult chapter 11 for more information on the nature of extreme heat in the Midwest), were vague and characterized heatwaves as periods of high atmosphere-related heat stress that would require the modification of lifestyles and could impact health (Robinson 2001). Heat waves were identified as warm periods where the temperature reached a predetermined level, such as 95°F, for two or more consecutive days. This method allowed local meteorologists to define heat waves but failed to account for varying climates throughout the continental United States (Changnon et al. 1996). More recent definitions have been developed and implemented in weather warning systems (Kalkstein 1991, Robinson 2001). Kalkstein's Heat/Health Watch Warning System (HHWS) uses measurements such as daily high/low temperature, wind, relative humidity, and cloud cover (Kalkstein 1991, Kalkstein et al. 1996, Kalkstein and Greene 1997, Robinson 2001, Johnson et al. 2009).

Future warning models will require integration of other data in addition to meteorological variables to improve current warning systems. For example, the Human Thermal Comfort Index (HTCI) incorporates spatial relations to heat stress and vulnerable populations (Harlan et al. 2006). The HTCI study suggests that diverse sections of a city can experience different thermal impacts. Even if a heat wave is not expected, because meteorological thresholds for a heat wave are not met, a part of the city may experience heat-related impacts. Therefore, studying the variations in community vulnerability that result from unique physical and socioeconomic factors could provide a more spatially specific heat warning system (Whitman et al. 1997, Semenza et al. 1999, Naughton et al. 2002, Cutter

et al. 2003, Harlan et al. 2006, Johnson and Wilson 2009, Johnson et al. 2009).

Case Study

In the following case study we elucidate intra-urban variations in risk to EHEs. The focus is on applying a method that incorporates both demographic information available from the U.S. Census and environmental components of the UHI effect extracted from remote sensing assets. This effectively demonstrates the spatial congruence between socioeconomic characteristics indicative of social vulnerability to extreme heat and intra-urban areas of increased land surface temperature (LST). It is thought that a combination of these effects leads to an increase in vulnerability. The application of the PAR model will demonstrate techniques that may be effective adaptation or mitigation strategies.

DESCRIPTION OF THE STUDY AREA

This case study is focused on Indianapolis, Indiana (Figure 10.1). According to the U.S. Census Bureau, Indianapolis is the 14th largest city in the United States and the 3rd most populous city in the Midwest, with a population of 807,584 in 2009. Further, the proper city boundary of Indianapolis encompasses an area of 954 sq. km. Indianapolis has a Köppen Climate Classification of Dfa (Humid Continental Climate), with four distinct seasons typical of the midwestern United States (see chapter 2 of this volume). The average summer high temperature in Indianapolis is approximately 28.6°C. According to the Marion County Health Department, the county enclosing most of Indianapolis experienced five heat-related deaths in 2000–2002, none in 2003–2004, one in 2006 and 2007, none in 2008–2009, and five or more in 2010–2011, but a recent study commissioned by the Marion County Health Department determined an extreme heat event was the most likely natural threat in Indianapolis.

DATA COLLECTION

In order to visualize the UHI effect in Indianapolis and its spatiotemporal change, Landsat 5 TM thermal imagery was collected from the U.S. Geological Survey for 1990, 2000, and 2010. The images correspond to dates of the U.S. decadal census and allow for parsimonious inclusion of demographic data for further analysis. Landsat 5 is a remote sensing satellite operated by the National Aeronautics and Space Administration (NASA) capable of sensing thermal energy in the 10.4 μm to 12.5 μm wavelengths (Markham 1985). Landsat 5 has a spatial resolution in the thermal band of 120 meters, making it sufficient enough to detect intra-urban variations in the UHI effect.

Demographic data at the block group level that are indicative of extreme heat vulnerability key (Johnson et al. 2009, Johnson and Wilson 2009) were collected from the U.S. Census Bureau for the decadal 1990 and 2000 U.S. Censuses. To account for issues in comparing data across census periods (Cutter and Finch 2008) (e.g., changes in racial definitions

or in block groups (Indianapolis had more block groups in 2000 than in 1990 due to population growth)), all selected demographic variables were standardized by total population (except median household income), converting the data values into rates. Our approach used 11 variables: less than high school education, median household income, below poverty, age 65 below poverty, age 65 and over, age under 5, white population, black population, Hispanic population, American Indian population, and other race.

METHODOLOGY

The Landsat 5 thermal data were converted to at-satellite brightness temperature (Aniello et al. 1995). Using an overlay of the block groups for Indianapolis (1990, 2000), the average temperature for each enumerated unit was calculated using a smoothing average function. This allowed for the association between the demographic variables and the LST within the block group to be determined using Principal Components Analysis (PCA) with Varimax rotation (Richman 1986). This approach effectively reduces the dimensionality of the variables into a few components that explain the most variation within the entire dataset. The Kaiser Criterion was used to select the number of final components. In theory, the first component will explain the most variance within the entire dataset and effectively discern the conditions where increased levels of demographic vulnerability spatially correspond with increased surface temperature associated with the UHI effect. This creates a metric of factor loadings that represent the scale of vulnerability (spatial correspondence between increased surface temperature and the demographic vulnerability variables), fostering the mapping of risk associated with EHEs in the study area.

RESULTS

Figure 10.2 displays the results of the conversion of each Landsat 5 TM image to LST in degrees Celsius for the Indianapolis area for 1990, 2000, and 2010. The classification scheme for the LST images utilizes quantiles (quintiles), providing an equal number of observations in each category ranging from low to high. As can be noticed from these images, the higher ranges of temperature associated with the UHI effect, LST, has shifted noticeably during the 20-year period. The extent of the UHI effect has grown throughout much of the city, but north of the central core of Indianapolis, the higher degree of LST has decreased over the time period studied. This indicates that the UHI effect has lessened to some extent but has become more geographically dispersed, indicative of the sprawl in which Indianapolis has experienced (Stone et al. 2010). The shift in the spatial extent and heterogeneous intensity of the UHI effect in the Indianapolis area is supported by numerous other studies that have utilized different sensors and techniques (Wilson et al. 2003, Weng et al. 2004, Weng and Lu 2008). This change has an impact on the level of vulnerability expected during po-

tential extreme heat events. The decrease in LST within the area north of the central core of Indianapolis can be attributed to numerous community activities (i.e., gentrification, tree-planting campaigns, etc.) (Wilson 1989, Wilson 1993, Wilson 1996, Payton et al. 2008, Peper 2008, Chapple and Jackson 2010). This area is still considerably warmer than the background rural locations, but a decrease in the more intense surface heat areas is clearly observable from Figure 10.2.

PCA was applied to examine the associations between the demographic variables and remotely sensed LST. This resulted in four components (as noted by the Kaiser Normalization), which accounted for 70.26 percent and 67.39 percent of the total variance in the original data for the years 1990 and 2000, respectively. As seen in Tables 10.1 and 10.2, in both 1990 and 2000, though there are differences in which variables contribute to vulnerability for a particular year, the important variables are UHI LST, educational attainment, household income, older population (65 and over), and Hispanic race. Urban areas within the UHI comprising people with low educational attainment and low income and considerably older populations are especially susceptible to heat-related risk. These results compare very closely with previous analyses done in Philadelphia, Chicago, and Phoenix (Harlan et al. 2006, Luber and McGeehin 2008, Johnson et al. 2009, Johnson and Wilson 2009).

Vulnerability was determined by blending the LST and demographic information (Figure 10.3) and is mapped in Figure 10.4.

Table 10.1. Component loadings matrix for 1990 vulnerability assessment

	1 (29.2%)	2 (19.2%)	3 (12.8%)	4 (9.1%)
UHI LST	0.402	−0.080	0.359	0.053
Hispanic	0.858	0.070	0.061	−0.016
Other race	0.826	0.035	−0.050	0.088
American Indian	0.556	0.191	0.055	0.038
Median household income	0.007	0.870	−0.128	0.011
White	0.391	0.790	0.170	−0.324
Age 65 and over in poverty	−0.040	−0.105	0.863	0.089
Age 65 and over	−0.084	0.545	0.652	0.063
Less than high school education	0.306	0.142	0.643	0.465
Black	−0.144	−0.132	0.107	0.903
Below Poverty	0.293	−0.126	0.485	0.661
Age under 5	0.409	0.522	0.019	0.583

Table 10.2. Component loadings matrix for 2000 vulnerability assessment

	1 (27.5%)	2 (19.4%)	3 (12.1%)	4 (8.4%)
UHI LST	0.678	0.033	0.053	0.068
Hispanic	0.535	0.227	0.672	−0.046
Other race	0.524	0.164	0.694	−0.072
American Indian	0.175	0.160	0.368	0.033
Median household income	−0.654	0.378	−0.037	−0.216
White	−0.128	0.940	−0.028	−0.029
Age 65 and over in poverty	0.045	0.050	−0.125	0.937
Age 65 and over	0.243	0.138	−0.762	0.032
Less than high school education	0.745	−0.267	−0.010	0.055
Black	0.120	−0.945	−0.046	0.041
Below poverty	0.426	−0.403	0.242	0.626
Age under 5	−0.047	−0.168	0.636	0.004

Parentheses explain how much of the variance is explained by each component individually

The vulnerability risk is displayed using the same quintile approach as the LST mappings, with equal observations in each category. The images demonstrate that in 1990 the vulnerability to extreme heat in Indianapolis was largely confined to the center of Marion County. However, over the next decade, this vulnerability went through a spatial shift to the south and spread more to the east and west. Moreover, the area north of Indianapolis's core sees a dramatic decrease in vulnerability between 1990 and 2000. Most of this shift seems due in part to the already-mentioned factors of gentrification and reforestation within these areas of the city (Payton et al. 2008, Peper 2008).

Examining the loadings matrices for the vulnerability data between 1990 and 2000 the only variable that consistently ranked in the number-one component was UHI LST. It has significantly more weight in the component matrix for 2000 than for 1990. The higher levels of risk or vulnerability indicated here correspond to areas where most of the analyzed variables have higher intensities. For example, if each variable analyzed had a high level of intensity in a single location and that particular location was common to all variables, then that locale would be considered the zone of highest risk. There appears to be a possible movement of vulnerability to be more strongly linked to educational attainment, UHI LST intensity, and household income in the 2000 data compared to the 1990 variables (more variance explained by these variables). In 1990 vulnerability appeared to be more of a result of racial groupings (disparities) and UHI LST intensity. Even though other variables were analyzed, this tendency is supported by the findings of Cutter (2008) in the SoVI groupings; arguably, educational attainment and household income are components of socioeconomic status but are not explanatory of it alone. If this tendency continues (as Cutter indicates is likely on a national level), then economic status and UHI LST intensity are likely to be primary contributors to vulnerability and to dominate over racial disparities.

Concluding Remarks

Despite the historical focus of the Midwest on agriculture, the population is increasingly urbanized (see chapter 2), possibly leading to increased vulnerability to heatwave-related mortality and morbidity even in the absence of climate non-stationarity. Some areas within Indianapolis have a demonstrated decrease in the relative intensity of LST; however, there is still considerable concern in the spatial extent of the UHI and the potential for increases in heat-related health issues (Stone et al. 2010). Another issue of concern is that it appears that the Indianapolis demographics related to vulnerability to extreme heat have shifted southward and follow a similar spatial trend to that of the demonstrated shifts in the UHI effect. Recent efforts have showed that combinations of these demographic vulnerabilities in relation to increases in UHI LST intensities can increase the risk of extreme heat mortality as much as tenfold (Johnson et al. 2009). These shifts potentially demonstrate that demographic variation within

the city, as well as intra-urban variations in UHI LST, has a duplicitous effect on vulnerability to extreme heat. Once 2010 census data becomes available, it will be imperative to examine this shift further with the growth of the UHI in Indianapolis and its southward, western, and eastern spatial shift, following procedures outlined here. Further, this suggests that as the climate changes in specific areas, vulnerability will indeed go through spatial shifts within urban locations. This could be examined further by linking urban growth models to climate models generating future scenarios. This would, of course, also need to include demographic data as presented in this chapter.

Examining both the demographic and UHI variations in a spatiotemporal framework illustrates the applicability of the PAR model to potential adaptation or mitigation strategies. Clearly, from the previous discussion of the PAR model, the demographic variables contributing to extreme heat vulnerability and the UHI effect within the city are both pressures that could initiate an extreme heat-related disaster. If pressure could be released on one or both of these external stressors, then disaster might be averted or effectively minimized. It might be exceptionally difficult or economically impossible to raise the standards of the socioeconomic conditions of the vulnerable population sufficiently to allow for the purchase of air-conditioning, which could involve rewiring of residences as well as further improvements in the structure. However, work is being done on models that might demonstrate within Indianapolis and other U.S. cities how much green space might need to be introduced into certain census block groups or census tracts in order to lower the LST (and in turn the ambient air temperature) (Payton et al. 2008, Lafortezza et al. 2009, Nagendra and Gopal 2010, Qureshi et al. 2010) sufficiently to decrease the pressure on the vulnerable population brought about by the UHI effect, thereby utilizing the PAR approach to quantify a decrease in the pressure of vulnerability. If temperatures could be lowered in census block groups that are vulnerable to extreme heat exhibited by these models to levels of block groups that are not, then this could potentially be a possible adaptation strategy. Already, cooling centers are located in numerous cities in the Midwest as possible methods of adaptation (Indianapolis included) (Bernard and McGeehin 2004, Frumkin et al. 2008, Luber and McGeehin 2008). If further impetus could be placed on sustainable "green" development with indications that it will increase the health of communities, we might be able to effectively demonstrate an action item where climatologic and social epidemiologic approaches can be blended further for effective adaptation.

REFERENCES

Aniello C, Morgan K, Busbey A, Newland L (1995). Mapping micro-urban heat islands using landsat TM and a GIS. Computers and Geosciences 21:965–967.

Alexander D. (2000). Confronting catastrophe. Hertfordshire, UK: Terra Publishing.

Bankoff G (2001). Rendering the world unsafe: "Vulnerability" as western discourse. Disasters 25:19–35.

Bankoff G (2003). Constructing vulnerability: The historical, natural and social generation of flooding in metropolitan manila. Disasters 27:15–28.

Bernard SM, McGeehin MA (2004). Municipal heat wave response plans. American Journal of Public Health 94:1520–1522.

Birkmann J, von Teichmann K (2010). Integrating disaster risk reduction and climate change adaptation: key challenges- scales, knowledge, and norms. Sustainability Science 5:171–184.

Browning CR, Wallace D, Feinberg, S, Cagney KA (2006). Neighborhood social processes and disaster-related mortality: The case of the 1995 Chicago heat wave. American Sociological Review 71:665–682.

Changnon SA, Kunkel KE, Reinke BC (1996). Impacts and responses to the 1995 heat wave: A call to action. Bulletin of the American Meteorological Society 77:1497–1506.

Chapple K, Jackson S (2010). Commentary: Arts, neighborhoods, and social practices: Towards an integrated epistemology of community arts. Journal of Planning Education and Research 29:478–490.

Cutter SL, Barnes L, Berry M, Burton C, Evans E, Tate E, Webb J (2008). A place-based model for understanding community resilience to natural disasters. Global Environmental Change-Human and Policy Dimensions 18:598–606.

Cutter SL, Boruff BJ, Shirley W (2003). Social vulnerability to environmental hazards. Social Science Quarterly 84:242–261.

Cutter SL, Burton CG, Emrich CT (2010). Disaster resilience indicators for benchmarking baseline conditions. Journal of Homeland Security and Emergency Management 7: article 51, doi:10.2202/1547-7355.1732.

Cutter SL, Finch C (2008). Temporal and spatial changes in social vulnerability to natural hazards. Proceedings of the National Academy of Sciences of the United States of America 105:2301–2306.

Duneier M (2006). Ethnography, the ecological fallacy, and the 1995 Chicago heat wave. American Sociological Review 71:679–688.

Enarson E, Childers C, Morrow B, Wisner B (2003). Vulnerability approach to emergency management. FEMA Higher Education Project, Emmitsburg, MD.

Hardoy JE, Mitlin D, Satterthwaite D (2001). Environmental problems in an urbanizing world. London: EarthScan Publications.

Harlan SL, Brazel AJ, Prashad L, Stefanov WL, Larsen L (2006). Neighborhood microclimates and vulnerability to heat stress. Social Science & Medicine 63:2847–2863.

Harpham T (2009). Urban health in developing countries: What do we know and where do we go? Health Place 15:107–116.

Hewitt K (1997). Regions of risk: a geographical introduction to disasters, Essex, UK: Longman.

Johnson D, Wilson J, Luber G (2009). Socioeconomic indicators of heat-related health risk supplemented with remotely sensed data. International Journal of Health Geographics 8:57.

Johnson DP, Wilson JS (2009). The socio-spatial dynamics of extreme urban heat events: The case of heat-related deaths in Philadelphia. Applied Geography 29:419–434.

Kalkstein LS (1991). A new approach to evaluate the impact of climate on human mortality. Environmental Health Perspectives 96:145–150.

Kalkstein LS, Greene JS (1997). An evaluation of climate/mortality relationships in large U.S. cities and the possible impacts of a climate change. Environmental Health Perspectives 105:84–93.

Kalkstein LS, Jamason PF, Greene JS, Libby J, Robinson L (1996). The Philadelphia hot weather–health watch/warning system: Development and application, summer 1995. Bulletin of the American Meteorological Society 77:1520–1528.

Lafortezza R, Carrus G, Sanesi G, Davies C (2009). Benefits and well-being perceived by people visiting green spaces in periods of heat stress. Urban Forestry and Urban Greening 8:97–108.

Lo CP, Quattrochi DA, Luvall JC (1997). Application of high-resolution thermal infrared remote sensing and GIS to assess the urban heat island effect. International Journal of Remote Sensing 18:287–304.

Luber G, McGeehin M (2008). Climate change and extreme heat events. American Journal of Preventative Medicine 35:429–435.

Markham B (1985). Spectral characterizations of the landsat thematic mapper sensors. International Journal of Remote Sensing 6:697–716.

McIlwaine C, Moser C (2001). Violence and social capital in urban poor communities: Perspectives from Columbia to Guatemala. Journal of International Development 13:1–20.

Minuci EG, de Almeida MF (2009). Birth weight intra-urban differentials in the city of Sao Paulo. Revista de Saúde Pública 43:256–266.

Moser C, Gauhurts M, Gonhan H (1994). Urban Poverty Research Sourcebook: Sub-City Level Research, World Bank Publication, Washington, DC.

Nagendra H, Gopal D (2010). Street trees in Bangalore: Density, diversity, composition and distribution. Urban Forestry and Urban Greening 9:129–137.

Naughton MP, Henderson A, Mirabelli MC, Kaiser R, Wilhelm JL, Kieszak SM, Rubin CH, McGeehin MA (2002). Heat-related mortality during a 1999 heat wave in Chicago. American Journal of Preventive Medicine 22:221–227.

Payton S, Lindsey G, Wilson J, Ottensmann JR, Man J (2008). Valuing the benefits of the urban forest: A spatial hedonic approach. Journal of Environmental Planning and Management 51:717–736.

Pelling M (2003). The vulnerability of cities: Natural disasters and social resilience. London: Earthscan Publishing.

Pelling M (2006). Measuring urban vulnerability to natural disaster risk: Benchmarks for sustainability. Open House International 31:125–132.

Peper PJ, McPherson, EG, Simpson, JR, Vargas, KE, Xiao, Q (2008). City of Indianapolis, Indiana municipal forest resource analysis. Center for Urban Forest Research, USDA Forest Service, Pacific Southwest Research Station, Indianapolis.

Qureshi S, Kazmi SJH, Breuste JH (2010). Ecological disturbances due to high cutback in the green infrastructure of Karachi: Analyses of public perception about associated health problems. Urban Forestry and Urban Greening 9:187–198.

Richman MB (1986). Rotation of principal components. International Journal of Climatology 6:293–335.

Robinson PJ (2001). On the definition of a heat wave. Journal of Applied Meteorology 40:762–775.

Semenza JC, McCullough JE, Flanders WD, McGeehin MA, Lumpkin JR (1999). Excess hospital admissions during the July 1995 heat wave in Chicago. American Journal of Preventive Medicine 16:269–277.

Stephenson J, Newman K, Mayhew S (2010). Population dynamics and climate change: What are the links? Journal of Public Health 32:150–156.

Stone B, Hess JJ, Frumkin H (2010). Urban form and extreme heat events: Are sprawling cities more vulnerable to climate change than compact cities? Environmental Health Perspectives 118:1425–1428.

Tan JG, Zheng YF, Tang X, Guo CY, Li LP, Song GX, Zhen XR, Yuan D, Kalkstein AJ, Li FR, Chen H (2010). The urban heat island and its impact on heat waves and human health in shanghai. International Journal of Biometeorology 54:75–84.

Weng Q, Lu D (2008). A sub-pixel analysis of urbanization effect on land surface temperature and its interplay with impervious surface and vegetation coverage in Indianapolis, United States. International Journal of Applied Earth Observation and Geoinformation 10:68–83.

Weng QH, Lu DS, Schubring J (2004). Estimation of land surface temperature-vegetation abundance relationship for urban heat island studies. Remote Sensing of Environment 89:467–483.

Whitman S, Good G, Donoghue ER, Benbow N, Shou W, Mou S (1997). Mortality in Chicago attributed to the July 1995 heat wave. American Journal of Public Health 87:1515–1518.

Wilhelmi OV, Hayden MH (2010). Connecting people and place: A new framework for reducing urban vulnerability to extreme heat. Environmental Research Letters 5 014021 doi:10.1088/1748-9326/5/1/014021.

Wilson D (1989). Local state dynamics and gentrification in Indianapolis, Indiana. Urban Geography 10:19–40.

Wilson D (1993). Everyday life, spatiality and inner-city disinvestment in a United States city. International Journal of urban and Regional Research 17:578–594.

Wilson D (1996). Metaphors, growth coalition discourses and black poverty neighborhoods in a US city. Antipode 28:72–96.

Wilson JS, Clay M, Martin E, Stuckey D, Vedder-Risch K (2003). Evaluating environmental influences of zoning in urban ecosystems with remote sensing. Remote Sensing of Environment 86:303–321.

Wisner B (2004). At risk: Natural hazards, people's vulnerability, and disasters. London: Routledge.

Zhou Y, Shepherd JM (2010). Atlanta's urban heat island under extreme heat conditions and potential mitigation strategies. Natural Hazards 52:639–668.

11. Historical and Projected Changes in Human Heat Stress in the Midwestern United States

J. T. SCHOOF

Introduction

Heat or anomalously hot weather that lasts for several days—"heat waves"—has clear impacts on society, including an increase in mortality and morbidity, in addition to placing strains on infrastructure and agriculture (power, water, and transport). Recent heat waves have been observed in North America, Europe, and Asia (Gosling et al. 2009). A particularly intense heat wave impacted the midwestern United States during the summer of 1995, resulting in hundreds of fatalities in Chicago (Kunkel et al. 1996). Although there are considerable challenges in computing the precise number of excess deaths attributable to each occurrence of extreme heat (Gosling et al. 2009), each of these events resulted in substantial mortality and considerable morbidity (Knowlton et al. 2009). Indeed, extreme heat events are reported to be the single largest cause of weather-related mortality, causing over 3,442 deaths in the United States between 1999 and 2003 (Luber and McGeehin 2008). These events have raised questions

regarding whether anthropogenic forcing of climate will lead to an increase in heat wave occurrence and/or intensity (see executive summary of the Health Sector in the U.S. National Assessment of 2007 (O'Neill and Ebi 2009)).

In the midwestern region of United States, high summer temperatures are often accompanied by elevated near-surface humidity, which enhances human heat stress through reduction of evaporative cooling from the skin (see the overview of temperature trends and projections in chapter 2 of this volume). The combined effect of temperature and humidity on human heat stress is usually quantified as the apparent temperature (T_a; commonly referred to as the heat index, Steadman 1984), which can be readily computed from observations:

$$T_a = -1.3 + 0.92T + 2.2e \qquad (11\text{-}1)$$

where T is the air temperature (°C) and e is vapor pressure (kPa).

As shown in Figure 11.1, apparent temperature is a linear function of air tem-

146

perature (T), but a nonlinear function of the dew point temperature (T_d), which is used to derive e using the Clausius–Clapeyron equation. Using the coefficients in Equation 11-1, it is possible to assess contributions of temperature and humidity to changes in apparent temperature. Specifically, the change in T_a scales as 0.92 of the change in temperature, and therefore, apparent temperature changes larger than 92 percent of the air temperature change can be attributed to changes in atmospheric moisture content.

Historical observations indicate that global near-surface air temperature has increased by approximately 0.74°C in the last century (1906–2005; Trenberth et al. 2007). Although temperature projections exhibit considerable uncertainty (see chapter 2 of this volume), the rate of warming is expected to accelerate this century due to additional radiative forcing from GHG. Theoretical and modeling studies have suggested that, as temperature increases, vapor pressure will change in proportion to saturation vapor pressure, resulting in roughly constant global relative humidity (Sherwood and Meyer 2006; Trenberth et al. 2007; Willet et al. 2007; Pan and Pryor 2009). It is therefore expected that stations exhibiting significant warming trends will also exhibit positive trends in dew point temperature, consistent with the expectation of increased surface evaporation. However, as noted by Bauer et al. (2002), dynamic transport and microphysical processes play an important role in near-surface relative humidity. These processes could result in differences in the magnitude of trends in temperature and dew point temperature. Therefore, on smaller spatial scales, there is greater uncertainty about the response of near-surface humidity to changes in temperature.

Dai (2006) found that from 1976 to 2004, large changes (0.5%–2.0% per decade) in surface relative humidity occurred in the central and eastern United States. Gaffen and Ross (1999) reported relative humidity trends that are weaker than specific humidity trends but are still positive for many U.S. stations and seasons. Knappenberger et al. (1996) reported only small changes in dew point temperatures in the eastern United States, while Robinson (2000) described positive dew point temperature trends for 1961–1990 for most locations. Given the importance of near-surface temperature and humidity for regulation of physical processes near the surface, including those that govern human heat stress, there is great interest in enhancing understanding of historically observed variations in these variables and in constructing projections for approaching decades.

At large scales, it has since been demonstrated that changes in both near-surface air temperature and humidity are partially attributable to anthropogenic activities (Santer et al. 2007; Willet et al. 2007). However, studies investigating future heat waves (e.g., Beniston 2004, Meehl and Tebaldi 2004) have largely ignored elevated heat stress contributions from increasing atmospheric aerosol loading, land use change, and humidity.

Previous studies (Fall et al. 2010a; Fall et al. 2010b) have demonstrated that land use change may also play an important role in the contributions of temperature and humidity to heat stress. The relative contributions of temperature and humidity changes to historical and future changes in heat stress in the midwestern United States are the subject of this chapter. Specifically, this chapter addresses four primary questions related to heat stress in this region:

(1) How have historical changes in air temperature and dew point temperature contributed to changes in apparent temperature?

(2) How sensitive are future changes in air temperature, dew point temperature, and apparent temperature to greenhouse gas forcing?

(3) What are the relative uncertainties associated with future projections of air temperature, dew point temperature, and apparent temperature?

(4) What do the best available climate projections of apparent temperatures imply about possible future heat wave risk in the Midwest?

These questions are addressed through analysis of historical climate data and statistically downscaled simulations from a range of atmospheric-oceanic general circulation models (AOGCMs) from the CMIP3 archive (Meehl et al. 2007a) used in the Fourth Assessment Report of the Intergovernmental Panel on Climate Change (IPCC).

Data and Models

HISTORICAL STATION DATA

Data from 33 stations in the midwestern United States (Figure 11.2) were chosen to quantify historical tendencies in the parameters that determine heatwave risk. This analysis, therefore, focuses on temperature and dew point temperature and uses them to compute apparent temperature during the summer (JJA) for the period 1948–2009. These stations represent a subset of the stations previously considered by Gaffen and Ross (1999), who also previously considered the impact of station moves, instrument changes, and other factors that might impact data homogeneity. Specifically, Gaffen and Ross (1999) considered the impact of changes from sling psychrometers to hygrothermometers in the 1960s and the change to dew point hygrothermometers in the 1980s. Few differences were found in the daily averages pre- and post-instrumentation changes, and daytime values were less susceptible to changes in instrumentation than nighttime values. Hourly observations from these stations were used to derive daily maximum values of air temperature, dew point temperature, and apparent temperature, hereafter referred to as T_{max}, Td_{max}, and Ta_{max}, respectively. For a daily value to be valid, at least one valid hourly observation in each 4-hour window was required. Furthermore, only summers with 90 percent of days with valid data were included in the historical analysis. Because the focus of this analysis is on heat stress, the JJA 90th percentiles of T_{max}, Td_{max}, and Ta_{max} were considered in addition to their JJA mean values for the historical analyses. The climate projections were based on downscaling of monthly mean and 90th percentile of T_{max}, Td_{max}, Ta_{max}, which were then temporally aggregated to JJA values.

REANALYSIS DATA

Near-surface variables, including those that are the focus of this study, are generally not well simulated by climate models (Wilby and Wigley 1997, Wilby et al. 1998, Huth et al. 2003). Development of projections of T_{max}, Td_{max}, and Ta_{max} therefore requires development of transfer functions that describe their relationship with large-scale climatic variables (see the description provided in the methodology section below). The historical data used to describe the large-scale climate during 1948–2009 are derived from the NCEP/NCAR reanalysis data (Kalnay et al. 1996). Because reanalysis products use a consistent modeling system throughout the historical period, the resulting data are useful for studies of climate variability and change. From the surface and upper-air reanalysis fields, a number of predictors expected to exert influence on T_{max}, Td_{max}, and Ta_{max} were extracted. Elevated apparent temperatures in the study region are often associated with high barometric pressure, southerly winds, low cloud cover, and 500 mb ridging, often associated with a subsidence inversion (see Kunkel et al. 1996 for a discussion of the role of these

factors in the historic 1995 heat wave). Predictor variables were chosen to reflect these physical controls on T_{max}, Td_{max}, and Ta_{max} and include mean sea-level pressure (SLP), specific humidity at 850 mb (Q_{850}), air temperature at 700 mb (T_{700}), meridional wind at 850 mb (V_{850}) and geopotential height at 500 mb (Z_{500}).

ATMOSPHERIC-OCEANIC GENERAL CIRCULATION MODELS (AOGCMS)

The primary tools available for producing climate projections are coupled atmospheric-oceanic general circulation models (AOGCMs or GCMs). Due to computational constraints, these models are currently run with spatial resolutions ranging from 1.5° × 1.5° to 5° × 5° and therefore require parameterization of many physical processes occurring at unresolved spatial scales. Thus, while these tools can provide realistic climate change scenarios at the seasonal timescale and continental to hemispheric spatial scales (Randall et al. 2007), they often exhibit shortcomings at smaller spatial and temporal scales. Projections from AOGCMs, based on increases in atmospheric greenhouse gas concentrations, indicate further increases in global near-surface temperature and moisture content (Held and Soden 2006), although the specific temporal and spatial manifestations of these changes, and their sensitivity to the greenhouse gas increases, remain uncertain.

Methods for extracting higher-resolution projections from AOGCMs can be broadly classified into two categories of downscaling: dynamical and statistical. Here, the focus is on statistical downscaling because it is less computationally demanding (allowing application to multiple models and greenhouse gas emissions scenarios) and has been shown to display similar skill to dynamical techniques (Kidson and Thompson 1998, Murphy 1999, Pryor et al. 2005, Lim et al. 2007, Schoof et al. 2009). While statistical downscaling has been widely applied in temperature and precipitation projection studies, such techniques have not been previously applied to AOGCM output to produce humidity projections based on increases in atmospheric greenhouse gas concentrations. Herein, output from multiple AOGCM simulations are used to provide descriptions of the large-scale climate parameters (described above) in the downscaling. Application of the transfer functions to the available AOGCM simulations will allow development of projections from a range of models and greenhouse gas scenarios (Table 11.1).

Use of multiple models, model runs, and greenhouse gas emission scenarios facilitates assessment of uncertainty and therefore addresses one of the primary objectives of this analysis. Future projections of T_{max}, Td_{max}, and Ta_{max} were developed using output from eight AOGCMs (Table 11.1) driven by three different greenhouse gas scenarios (A1B, A2, and B1 as described in the IPCC Special Report on Emissions Scenarios; Nakicenovic and Swart 2000). These scenarios differ in terms of their projections of economic development, population growth, development of new technologies, and adoption of renewable energy sources, resulting in variations in the trajectory of

Table 11.1. Number of individual simulations from each AOGCM used in the development of T_{max}, Td_{max}, and Ta_{max} projections. The column labeled "20th C" denotes the number of simulations of the historical period, while "A1B," "A2" and "B1" denote the emission scenario used in the climate projections for the twenty-first century.

Model	Time period/Emission scenario			
	20th C	A1B	A2	B1
CCCMA CGCM3	5	5	5	4
CSIRO MK3.5	2	1	1	1
GFDL CM2.0	3	1	1	1
GFDL CM2.1	3	1	1	1
MIROC3 Med	3	3	3	3
MPI ECHAM5	4	4	3	3
MRI CGCM2	5	5	5	5
NCAR PCM1	4	4	4	1

greenhouse gas emissions and concentrations in the 21st century. The scenarios do not differ substantively from one another until around 2020, and A1B and A2 are similar until around mid-century. By 2100, the B1 scenario has CO_2 concentrations that have stabilized at around 550 ppm. The A1B and A2 scenarios result in CO_2 concentrations at 2100 of approximately 720 ppm and 850 ppm, respectively. The models chosen span a range of spatial resolutions and model formulations. For the analyses conducted here, all AOGCM data were interpolated to a standard $2.5° \times 2.5°$ grid corresponding to the NCEP/NCAR reanalysis grid.

Methodology

ASSESSMENT OF HISTORICAL TRENDS IN T_{MAX}, TD_{MAX}, AND TA_{MAX}

The historical contributions of temperature and humidity to heat stress are quantified by assessing the linear trends in the JJA means and 90th percentiles of T_{max}, Td_{max}, and Ta_{max} using median of pairwise slopes regression (Hoaglin et al. 1983; Lanzante 1996). As the name implies, this approach requires computation of the slope (b_k) between each possible pair of points. For two points (x_1, y_1) and (x_2, y_2), the slope is given by:

$$b_k = \frac{y_2 - y_1}{x_2 - x_1} \qquad (11\text{-}2)$$

The median of the b_k values is the slope estimate for the regression equation. The estimate of the intercept is given by the median of the residuals. For each point (x_i, y_i), the residual is given by:

$$r_i = y_i - bx_i \qquad (11\text{-}3)$$

To assess statistical significance, a two-tailed t-test is applied to the Spearman rank-order correlation coefficient between each variable and time.

DEVELOPMENT AND APPLICATION OF THE STATISTICAL DOWNSCALING APPROACH

Statistical downscaling tools range in complexity from simple interpolation exercises to artificial neural networks and stochastic weather generators. Here, multiple regression using ordinary least squares was adopted to develop transfer functions relating the large scale variables (sea-level pressure (SLP), specific humidity at 850 hPa (Q_{850}), air temperature at 700 hPa (T_{700}), the south-north component of the

Table 11.2. Validation statistics for multiple regression-based downscaling for the historical period wherein the predictors are derived from the reanalysis data set. The mean absolute errors (MAE) are averaged across all thirty-three stations. "Validation" shows the comparison with the independent data, while 'Overall' shows the MAE for the entire data record (including data used in conditioning the transfer functions).

	JJA Mean		JJA 90th Percentile	
	Validation MAE (°C)	Overall MAE (°C)	Validation MAE (°C)	Overall MAE (°C)
T_{max}	0.66	0.66	1.02	1.08
Td_{max}	0.70	0.67	0.83	0.80
Ta_{max}	0.62	0.66	1.00	1.01

flow at 850 hPa (V_{850}) and the height of the 500 hPa level (Z_{500})) to the monthly means and 90th percentiles of T_{max}, Td_{max}, and Ta_{max}. Because the AOGCM output may exhibit bias relative to observations, all regression models were developed using monthly anomalies. This step ensures that future changes are considered in the context of individual models, not relative to the observations.

The regression equations were developed and validated using an approach in which two-thirds of the data are used to construct the model, which is then tested on the remaining one-third of independent observations. Table 11.2 shows the performance of the models when applied to the validation data and the entire time series. Although the mean absolute errors (MAE) are slightly larger for the 90th percentiles than for the means, errors for all variables and stations are much smaller than the interannual variability (defined as the standard deviation of the JJA mean or 90th percentile), suggesting that the downscaled data exhibit some skill in reproducing the observed variability (see Figure 11.3).

Results

ANALYSIS OF HISTORICAL TENDENCIES IN THE THERMAL PARAMETERS

One of the primary objectives of this work was to assess the relative contributions of changes in air temperature and dew point temperature to changes in apparent temperature. Consistent with previous findings (e.g., Pan et al. 2004), many stations in the central and southern part the region are characterized by negative (cooling) trends in summertime mean and 90th percentile values of T_{max} (Figure 11.4). However, the trends in the mean and 90th percentile of Td_{max} are generally of opposite sign to the T_{max} trends (Figure 11.4). Since apparent temperature is influenced by both parameters, the resulting trends for apparent temperature vary in sign. As temperatures have decreased at many stations, dew point temperatures have increased, partially or completely offsetting the negative contribution of air temperature to apparent temperature. The results of the trend analysis are summarized in Table 11.3 and demonstrate the importance of considering both air temperature and humidity in studies of heat stress.

CLIMATE PROJECTIONS

Application of the transfer functions described above to the available AOGCM simulations (Table 11.1) produced a large number of 21st century projections of

Table 11.3. Summary of historical trend analysis (1948–2009). Table entries indicate the number of stations with positive or negative trends for each variable. The number in parentheses indicates the number of stations with significant trends (with $\alpha = 0.05$).

	JJA mean		JJA ninetieth percentile	
	Negative trend	Positive trend	Negative trend	Positive trend
T_{max}	22 (2)	11 (0)	15 (4)	3 (0)
Td_{max}	3 (1)	30 (4)	1 (0)	20 (8)
Ta_{max}	18 (2)	15 (0)	15 (2)	17 (1)

T_{max}, Td_{max}, and Ta_{max}. To facilitate interpretation, the results are presented as decadal averages. As an example of the results generated by this process, Figure 11.5 shows the historical and future projections (A1B scenario) for T_{max} averaged over the stations in Figure 11.2. While there is not much variability among different runs from the same AOGCM, there is substantial variability in the temperature projections downscaled from the different AOGCMs. Additionally, although the late 20th century observations generally fall within the envelope of downscaled AOGCM simulations, the first decade of the 21st century is warmer in all of the downscaled AOGCM simulations than it is in the observations. Lastly, for all the greenhouse gas scenarios employed, downscaled values for the mid and late 21st century are considerably higher (warmer in the case of T_{max}, more humid in the case of Td_{max}, and more stressful in the case of Ta_{max}) than their late 20th-century counterparts.

To further facilitate analysis of the downscaled results, all of the AOGCM simulations were considered in a multi-

Table 11.4a. Regionally averaged changes (°C, relative to 1948–2000 average) in the AOGCM ensemble mean for JJA mean T_{max}, Td_{max}, and Ta_{max} for different greenhouse gas scenarios (B1, A1B, A2).

Scenario	2050–2059			2090–2099		
	B1	A1B	A2	B1	A1B	A2
T_{max}	2.3	3.7	3.0	3.1	4.7	6.2
Td_{max}	1.8	2.5	2.3	2.4	3.6	4.4
Ta_{max}	2.6	4.1	3.4	3.5	5.3	6.9

Table 11.4b. Regionally averaged changes (°C, relative to 1948–2000 average) in the AOGCM ensemble mean for JJA ninetieth percentile T_{max}, Td_{max}, and Ta_{max} for different greenhouse gas scenarios (B1, A1B, A2).

Scenario	2050–2059			2090–2099		
	B1	A1B	A2	B1	A1B	A2
T_{max}	2.3	3.6	2.9	3.0	4.6	6.1
Td_{max}	1.3	1.8	1.6	1.7	2.6	3.1
Ta_{max}	2.5	3.8	3.2	3.3	5.0	6.5

model ensemble to assess the uncertainty in the projections due to choice of greenhouse gas scenario employed. The resulting AOGCM ensemble projections are shown in Figure 11.6 and summarized for mid- and late-century periods in Table 11.4a (mean) and 11.4b (90th percentile). Consistent with the driving greenhouse gas scenarios, the A1B-, A2-, and B1-driven AOGCM projections exhibit little difference before the middle of the century but diverge considerably toward the end of the century. The largest (smallest) projected changes in T_{max}, Td_{max}, and Ta_{max} are associated with the highest (lowest) changes in greenhouse gas concentration. For each scenario considered, changes in temperature (T_{max}) are larger on average than changes in humidity (Td_{max}). However, changes in apparent temperature (Ta_{max}) are slightly larger than those for temperature, reflecting an important contribution to projected heat stress from projected increases in humidity. Using Equation 12.1, the contribution of humidity can be quantified. For the mid-century period (2050–2059), increases in humidity contribute 0.5°C, 0.7°C, and 0.6°C to the increase in the heat index for

the B1, A1B, and A2 scenarios, respectively. For the late 21st century (2090–2099), these contributions increase to 0.6°C, 1.0°C, and 1.2°C. These values correspond to 17–19 percent of the total projected change in Ta_{max}. The results of the downscaling exercise therefore suggest that (1) both the average and 90th percentile of Ta_{max} increase across all of the SRES scenarios considered and (2) changes in dew point temperature (humidity) contribute positively to changes in Ta_{max}. Divergence among results for the three SRES scenarios suggests that greenhouse gas emissions will impact the severity of heat stress during the latter half of the century. However, as shown in Figure 11.6, the range of downscaled temperatures among AOGCMs driven with the same SRES scenario is larger than the difference in ensemble means among the SRES scenarios. This result suggests that the choice of AOGCM is the single largest source of uncertainty in the projections developed here.

Concluding Remarks

Returning to the framework of assessment risk and vulnerability in the context of climate change and variability, results of climate projections presented herein suggest:

- Apparent temperature and hence heat stress in the Midwest increased across all SRES and AOGCMs over the course of the 21st century. Thus the probability of heat wave events would appear to be increased across the Midwest in the coming decades relative to the historical period.
- By considering humidity, the magnitude of increased risk is amplified relative to studies based solely on air temperature.
- Projected changes in 90th percentile apparent temperature ranged from 3°C to over 6°C relative to the end of the 20th century. This exceeds the Urban Heat Island (UHI) reported in chapter 9 in Chicago during the 1995 heat wave event. Given the elevated mortality/morbidity associated with current UHI effects during heat waves, the projections developed here raise concerns about future extreme heat events, especially in urban areas.

Naturally, the findings presented in this chapter are predicated on the quality of the models and data from which they were derived. While AOGCMs are the best available tools for understanding climate system evolution on the timescales considered here, the results are subject to several caveats. First, simple definitions of heat stress based on daily maximums of temperature and humidity have been adopted. Analysis of impacts from historical heat waves suggests that additional vulnerability results from high nighttime (i.e., daily minimum) temperatures and persistence of elevated temperature (Kunkel et al. 1996). Naturally, climate

parameters are only one component of the complex interplay of physical and socioeconomic, demographic, and policy-related factors that dictate the vulnerability and health consequences of extreme heat. For example, previous research has identified "hot spots" of heat stress vulnerability within cities and neighborhoods (see Harlan et al. 2006 and chapter 10 of this volume). The impacts of extreme heat stress events are also directly related to infrastructure and preparedness, which are difficult to assess for the future scenarios. Second, we have combined AOGCM simulations in an equally weighted ensemble although some models are likely to be better than others. There exists a need in the climate change science community to identify metrics of model performance, potentially allowing weighting of ensemble members to maximize the benefit of considering multiple models (see, for example, the recent work of Knutti et al. 2009). Third, the downscaling method is relatively straightforward. Comparison with results from other methods, including dynamical approaches, would allow further investigation of sources of uncertainty in the projections.

Despite these caveats, the downscaled projections underscore several important characteristics regarding sources of uncertainty in regional heat stress evolution. First, the magnitude of increases in all three variables considered (T_{max}, Td_{max}, and Ta_{max}) exhibits strong dependence on the driving greenhouse gas scenario during the second half of the 21st century. By the end of the 21st century, the A2 scenario produces changes in each variable that are approximately twice as large as changes produced by the A1B scenario (Table 11.4). This suggests that, although all of the scenarios considered result in increases in temperature, humidity, and heat stress, the increases could be minimized by reducing the greenhouse gas emissions. This finding is consistent with previous studies that have identified strong dependence of global and regional temperature changes on greenhouse gas emissions and concentrations (e.g., Christensen et al. 2007, Meehl et al. 2007b). Second, the scenarios developed suggest that humidity will contribute to heat stress changes beyond those expected from temperature increases. This finding underscores the need for impact and vulnerability studies to consider humidity changes in additional to the traditional focus on temperature. Lastly, the choice of AOGCM is the single largest source of uncertainty in the development of the climate change projections presented here. This finding suggests that projections derived using a single AOGCM should be treated with caution. Use of multiple models is warranted in any analysis that attempts to quantify climate system responses to changes in radiative forcing.

REFERENCES

Bauer M, Del Genio AD, Lanzante JR (2002). Observed and simulated temperature-humidity relationships: Sensitivity to sampling and analysis. Journal of Climate 15:203–215.

Beniston, M (2004). The 2003 heat wave in Europe: A shape of things to come? An analysis based on Swiss climatological data and model simulations. Geophysical Research Letters 31:L02202, doi:10.1029/2003GL018857.

Christensen, JH, coauthors (2007). Regional climate projections. In: Solomon S, Qin D, Manning M, Chen Z, Marquis M, Averyt KB, Tignor M, Miller HL (eds). Climate change 2007: The physical science basis. Contribution of Working Group I to the Fourth Assessment Report of the Intergovernmental Panel on Climate Change. Cambridge, UK: Cambridge University Press.

Dai, A (2006). Recent climatology, variability, and trends in global surface humidity. Journal of Climate 19:3589–3606.

Fall S, Diffenbaugh NS, Niyogi D, Pielke RA, Rochon G (2010a). Temperature and equivalent temperature over the United States (1979–2005). International Journal of Climatology 30:2045–2054.

Fall S, Niyogi D, Gluhovsky A, Pielke RA, Kalnay E, Rochon G (2010b). Impacts of land use land cover on temperature trends over the continental United States: Assessment using the North American Regional Reanalysis. International Journal of Climatology 30:1980–1993.

Gaffen DJ, Ross RJ (1999). Climatology and trends of US surface humidity and temperature. Journal of Climate 12:811–828.

Gosling SN, Lowe JA, McGregor GR, Pelling M, Malamud BD (2009). Associations between elevated atmospheric temperature and human mortality: a critical review of the literature. Climatic Change 92:299–341.

Harlan SL, Brazel AJ, Prashad L, Stefanov WL, Larsen L (2006). Neighborhood microclimates and vulnerability to heat stress. Social Science & Medicine 63:2847–2863.

Held IM, BJ Soden (2006). Robust responses of the hydrological cycle to global warming. Journal of Climate 19:5686–5699.

Hoaglin D, Mosteller F, Tukey J (1983). Understanding Robust and Exploratory Data Analysis. New York: John Wiley and Sons.

Huth R, Kysely J, Dubrovsky M (2003). Simulation of surface air temperature by GCMs, statistical downscaling, and weather generator: Higher-order statistical moments. Studia Geophysica Geodaetica 47:203–216.

Kalnay E, Kanamitsu M, Kistler R, Collins W, Deaven D, Gandin L, Iredell M, Saha S, White

G, Woollen J, Zhu Y, Leetmaa A, Reynolds B, Chelliah M, Ebisuzaki W, Higgins W, Janowiak J, Mo KC, Ropelewski C, Wang J, Jenne R, Joseph D (1996). The NCEP/NCAR 40-year reanalysis project. Bulletin of the American Meteorological Society 77:437–472.

Kidson JW, Thompson CS (1998). A comparison of statistical and model-based downscaling techniques for estimating local climate variations. Journal of Climate 11:735–753.

Knappenberger PC, Michaels PJ, and Schwartzman PD (1996). Observed changes in the diurnal temperature and dewpoint cycles across the United States. Geophysical Research Letters 23:2637–2640.

Knowlton K, Rotkin-Ellman M, King G, Margolis HG, Smith D, Solomon G, Trent R, English P (2009). The 2006 California heat wave: Impacts on hospitalizations and emergency department visits. Environmental Health Perspectives 117:61–67.

Knutti R, Furrer R, Tebaldi T, Cermak J, Meehl GA (2009). Challenges in combining projections from multiple climate models. Journal of Climate 23:2739–2758.

Kunkel KE, Changnon SA, Reinke BC (1996). The July 1995 heat wave in the Midwest: A climatic perspective and critical weather factors. Bulletin of the American Meteorological Society 77:1507–1518.

Lanzante JR (1996). Resistant, robust and nonparametric techniques for the analysis of climate data: Theory and examples, including applications to historical radiosonde station data. International Journal of Climatology 16:1197–1226.

Lim Y, Shin DW, Cocke S, LaRow TE, Schoof JT, O'Brien JJ, Chassignet E (2007). Dynamically and statistically downscaled seasonal forecasts of maximum surface air temperature over the southeast United States. Journal of Geophysical Research 112:D24201, doi:10.1029/2007JD008764.

Luber G, McGeehin M (2008). Climate change and extreme heat events. American Journal of Preventive Medicine 35:429–435.

Meehl GA, Tebaldi C (2004). More intense, more frequent, and long lasting heat waves in the 21st century. Science 305:994–997.

Meehl GA, Covey C, Delworth T, Latif M, McAveney B, Mitchell JFB, Stouffer RJ, Taylor KE (2007a). The WCRP CMIP3 multi-model dataset: A new era in climate change research. Bulletin of the American Meteorological Society 88:1383–1394.

Meehl GA, coauthors (2007b). Global climate projections. In: Solomon S, Qin D, Manning M, Chen Z, Marquis M, Averyt KB, Tignor M, Miller HL (eds). Climate change 2007: The physical science basis. Contribution of Working Group I to the Fourth Assessment Report of the Intergovernmental Panel on Climate Change. Cambridge, UK: Cambridge University Press.

Murphy J (1999). An evaluation of statistical and dynamical techniques for downscaling local climate. Journal of Climate 12:2256–2284.

Nakićenović N, Swart R (eds) (2000). Special report on emissions scenarios. Cambridge, UK: Cambridge University Press.

O'Neill MS, Ebi KL (2009). Temperature extremes and health: Impacts of climate variability and change in the United States. Journal of Occupational and Environmental Medicine 51:13–25.

Pan Z, Arritt RW, Takle ES, Gutowski WJ, Anderson CJ, Segal M (2004). Altered hydrologic feedback in a warming climate introduces a "warming hole." Geophysical Research Letters 31:L17109, doi:10.1029/2004GL02528.

Pan Z, Pryor SC (2009). Overview: Hydrologic regimes. In: Pryor SC (ed) Understanding climate change: Climate variability, predictability, and change in the midwestern United States. Bloomington: Indiana University Press, 88–99.

Pryor SC, Schoof JT, Barthelmie RJ (2005). Empirical downscaling of wind speed probability distributions. Journal of Geophysical Research, 110:D19109, doi:10.1029/2005JD005899.

Randall DA, Wood R, Bony S, Colman A, Fichefet T, Fyfe J, Kattsov V, Pitman A, Shukla J,

Srinivasan J, Stouffer R, Sumi A, Taylor K (2007). Climate models and their evaluation. In: Solomon S, Qin D, Manning M, Chen Z, Marquis M, Averyt KB, Tignor M, Miller HL (eds). Climate change 2007: The physical science basis. Contribution of Working Group I to the Fourth Assessment Report of the Intergovernmental Panel on Climate Change. Cambridge, UK: Cambridge University Press.

Robinson PJ (2000). Temporal trends in United States dew point temperatures. International Journal of Climatology 20:985–1002.

Santer BD, Mears C, Wentz FJ, Taylor KE, Gleckler PJ, Wigley TML, Barnett TP, Boyle JS, Brüggemann W, Gillett NP, Klein SA, Meehl GA, Nozawa T, Pierce DW, Stott PA, Washington WM, Wehner MF (2007). Identification of human-induced changes in atmospheric moisture content. Proceedings of the National Academy of Sciences of the United States of America 104: 15248–15253.

Schoof JT, Shin DW, Cocke S, LaRow TE, Lim YK, and O'Brien JJ (2009). Dynamically and statistically downscaled seasonal temperature and precipitation hindcast ensembles for the Southeastern USA. International Journal of Climatology 29:243–257.

Sherwood SC, Meyer CL (2006). The general circulation and robust relative humidity. Journal of Climate 19:6278–6290.

Steadman RG (1984). A universal scale of apparent temperature. Journal of Climate and Applied Meteorology 23:1674–1687.

Trenberth KE, coauthors (2007). Observations: Surface and atmospheric climate change. In: Solomon S, Qin D, Manning M, Chen Z, Marquis M, Averyt KB, Tignor M, Miller HL (eds). Climate change 2007: The physical science basis. Contribution of Working Group I to the Fourth Assessment Report of the Intergovernmental Panel on Climate Change. Cambridge, UK: Cambridge University Press.

Wilby RL, Wigley TML (1997). Downscaling general circulation model output: A review of methods and limitations. Progress in Physical Geography 21:530–548.

Wilby RL, Wigley TML, Conway D, Jones PD, Hewitson BC, Main J, and Wilks DS (1998). Statistical downscaling of general circulation model output: A comparison of methods. Water Resources Research 34:2995–3008.

Willet KM, Gillett NP, Jones PD, Thorne PW (2007). Attribution of observed surface humidity changes to human influence. Nature 449:710–713.

12. Vulnerability of the Electricity and Water Sectors to Climate Change in the Midwest

D. J. GOTHAM, J. R. ANGEL, AND S. C. PRYOR

Energy, Water, and Climate Change

The water and energy sectors exhibit high exposure to climate change and variability, and as discussed in chapters 2 and 17 of this volume, water and energy are also highly interlinked. Water systems use large volumes of energy, and equally, the energy sector is a major consumer of water (see chapter 2). According to some estimates, water supply and treatment consumes 4 percent of the national power supply in the United States, and electricity accounts for a substantial fraction of the cost of municipal water processing and transport (National Assessment Synthesis Team 2000). As described herein, water is essential to electricity production from fossil fuels, and a key tendency that may substantially increase water demand within the Midwest is expansion of ethanol production (see chapter 2 of this volume). Conversion of corn grain and stover to ethanol requires nearly five times as much water to generate fuel to travel one kilometer than is used in conversion of crude oil to gasoline (Scown et al. 2011). In this chapter we introduce some of the primary ways in which climate change may cause changes in the risks realized in the energy and water sectors, the interlinkages between water and energy, and possible methods to reduce vulnerabilities in both sectors.

Electricity and Climate Change

In this section we focus on the electricity industry, while acknowledging that the entire energy sector is at the heart of the climate change policy—both as a major source of greenhouse gas (GHG) emissions (and thus an avenue for mitigation activities) (Metz et al. 2007) and as a component of the socioeconomic system that may experience significant impacts from a changing climate in terms of both supply and demand. As discussed in chapter 2 of this volume, the Midwest has a highly energy-intensive economy, in part because many states are net exporters of electricity. Accordingly, the Midwest is home to a large number of fossil-fuel and nuclear-fueled electricity generating power plants (see Table 12.1 and chapter 2 for maps of the major facilities).

Table 12.1. Electricity generating capacity from fossil-fuel and nuclear facilities in the midwestern states as of December 2008 (data from the EIA).

State	Total			Coal		Petroleum		Natural/other gas		Nuclear	
	Stations	Units	MW	Units	MW	Units	MW	Units	MW	Units	MW
Iowa	137	590	11,620	46	7,052	356	1,112	187	2,776	1	680
Illinois	108	381	46,934	58	16,918	188	1,282	124	16,689	11	12,045
Indiana	47	195	28,951	80	21,456	38	513	77	6,982	0	0
Kansas	101	439	12,185	16	5,472	197	652	225	4,825	1	1,236
Kentucky	28	106	22,700	54	16,771	8	110	44	5,819	0	0
Michigan	94	397	29,828	66	12,612	156	697	171	12,205	4	4,314
Minnesota	95	318	13,247	31	5,511	195	878	89	5,041	3	1,817
Missouri	97	398	21,312	46	11,708	225	1,834	126	6,580	1	1,190
North Dakota	13	36	4,307	12	4,225	22	72	2	10	0	0
Nebraska	65	237	5,704	15	3,204	105	420	117	2,080	0	0
Ohio	95	340	36,014	87	23,250	141	1,187	110	9,340	2	2,237
South Dakota	18	45	1,581	2	481	26	295	17	805	0	0
Wisconsin	70	224	16,839	42	7,337	104	884	75	7,010	3	1,608

Table 12.2. Intersection of electricity sector and climate change events. Bullets indicate aspects of the electricity industry (rows) that could be significantly affected by climate change events (columns).

	Temperature	Precipitation	Storms
Demand	•		
Supply	•	•	•
Delivery	•		•

While the electricity industry is a significant source of GHG in the United States and accounted for over 40 percent of carbon dioxide emissions in 2008 (US Energy Information Administration 2009), it is also susceptible to the effects of climate change in a number of ways. The impact of severe climate change events on the electricity sector can be examined under three broad categories: the demand for electricity, the supply of electricity, and the delivery of electricity through the transmission and distribution networks.

Similarly, there are three types of climate change events that can adversely affect the electricity industry: changes in temperature, changes in precipitation, and changes in the frequency and severity of storm events. Table 12.2 illustrates the areas in which the electricity sector may be vulnerable to climate changes.

IMPACT OF TEMPERATURE
ON ELECTRICITY DEMAND

Electricity demand is determined by a number of factors, such as economic activity, population growth, personal income, and meteorology. A general increase in temperature will affect electricity demand in two opposite ways. Energy used to heat homes and businesses will be reduced if winter temperatures are milder, while energy used for summer cooling and refrigeration will increase if summer temperatures are hotter. The increase in summer demand should be more significant than the decrease in winter demand in the electricity sector in the Midwest. This relationship is expected because almost all buildings in the region are cooled by electricity, but most are heated with another fuel. A similar relationship was seen in a study for the state of Maryland (Ruth and Lin 2006), while in Europe, where electric space heating is much more prevalent, reductions in winter heating loads were most significant for central and northern Europe, and increases in summer cooling loads dominated for southern Europe (Pilli-Sihvola, et al. 2010).

In general, the Midwest experiences its greatest electrical load during the summer, with space cooling requirements being a large component of the amount of peak demand placed on the system. While individual utilities, particularly those serving primarily rural customers, occasionally experience their peak demands in the winter, the demand for the region as a whole peaks in the summer. For example, the forecasts of the Midwest Independent Transmission System Operator, which operates the transmission system and wholesale electricity market for a region covering all or parts of the states of Illinois, Indiana, Iowa, Michigan, Minnesota, Missouri, North Dakota, Ohio, South Dakota, and Wisconsin, projected peak demands of 77,909 MW in the winter of 2009–2010 (Midwest ISO 2009) and 104,288 MW in the summer of 2010 (Midwest ISO 2010). Thus, the total resources that utilities need to have at their disposal

in order to provide for the needs of their customers is impacted by the temperature and humidity of the hottest summer days.

Under global climate change scenarios, the probability distribution of air temperature at a given location may change in many different ways. In the simplest case for a Gaussian distributed variable, (i) The mean of the distribution may shift up (toward higher temperatures) while the variance around the mean may remain the same, (ii) the variance may change while the mean remains constant, or (iii) both the mean and variance may change (Meehl et al. 2000). Accurate simulation of temperature variability is a stringent challenge of climate models, and the relationships between the mean and variance of geophysical parameters are complex (Meehl et al. 2000). In considering the ways in which changing thermal regimes may impact electricity demand, it is useful to consider the probability distribution of near-surface temperature for Indianapolis, Indiana, shown in Figure 12.1. These data are taken from a single Regional Climate Model (RCM) and thus should not be used for system planning purposes, but indicate an illustrative example of the evolution of the wintertime and summertime probability distribution of temperatures between 1979–2000 and 2041–2062. For this RCM, the future simulations do not exhibit a marked change in variability, but rather the change in the distribution is dominated by a shift in the central tendency. In this model, the mean summertime temperature in the historical period is 21°C, which is close to the mean temperature (1971–2000) of 22.8°C recorded at Indianapolis Airport. In the future period the mean summertime temperature is projected to increase by 2.7°C, and the frequency with which temperatures above 35°C (95°F) are observed increases nearly a factor of three. The mean wintertime temperature according to the RCM is −3.8°C, which is lower than the observed value of −1.2°C. In the future period the mean wintertime temperature increases by 2.5°C (close to the regional average increase reported in chapter 2 of this volume), and there is a marked decline in the frequency of subfreezing temperatures. The frequency with which subfreezing (0°C) temperatures are observed in the future projected climate is over 15 percent lower than the historical simulation. Thus it seems likely that at least in the near-term, winter demand may decrease, though there will still be periods of extreme low temperature. It also appears likely that summer temperatures—particularly the right tail of the distribution—will generally increase, potentially leading to increased electricity demand for cooling during the summer.

Climate change is expected to impact not only temperature but the specific humidity as well. The saturation vapor pressure (e_s, i.e., maximum water holding capacity of air) is an exponential function of air temperature. Thus for a temperature of approximately 288 K, each degree of warming increases the e_s by approximately 7 percent (Pan and Pryor 2009). Temperature and humidity indices (e.g., the heat index as manifest in the apparent temperature (Steadman 1984)), which combine temperature and specific humidity, are generally better indicators of human health stress and electricity demand than temperature alone. On days that are hot but not humid, consumers may opt to open windows for natural cooling instead of running air conditioners, while on hot and humid days electricity use increases. Due to positive tendencies in both air temperature and specific humidity, heat indices are generally projected to increase within the Midwest (see chapters 10 and 12 of this volume), thus increasing the summertime demand for electricity.

In addition, the duration of heat waves is also a significant factor in the peak demand for electricity as consumers are less likely to forego some of their cooling needs after a few consecutive hot days. Further, urban areas will experience heat buildup during extended heat waves due to the thermal energy retained by structures such as buildings, roads, and parking lots (see chapters 9–11 in this volume). Therefore, increases in the duration/intensity of heat waves will increase electricity demand (Hayhoe et al. 2010).

The impact of higher temperatures and humidity on electricity demand can be illustrated by examining its impact on load forecasts. The PJM Interconnection, a regional transmission operator that covers parts of the Midwest and Mid-Atlantic regions, analyzes the impact of extreme weather in producing their load forecasts. PJM's base forecast is listed as a 50/50 forecast, which means that it is considered to have an equal 50 percent chance of being too low or too high. Their extreme, or 90/10, forecast is intended to have a 90 percent probability of being too low and only a 10 percent probability of being too high. The 2011 90/10 is 7 percent higher than the corresponding 50/50 for the Commonwealth Edison service territory, which covers much of northern Illinois including Chicago (PJM Resource Adequacy Planning Department, 2010). Given that peak demand for the entire Midwest is about 200 gigawatts (GW), this indicates that the increased demand in the region resulting from higher temperatures could easily exceed 10 GW. Based on estimates of the cost of constructing new combustion turbines (US Energy Information Administration 2010), which are commonly used for meeting the peak demand, it would take over $6 billion just to provide the generation infrastructure needed to meet that increased demand.

As an alternative to constructing new generators, the increased demand for electricity could be countered by using energy more efficiently and with load management programs and price responsive demand that can shift demand from the peak usage period to off peak. Options designed to moderate electrical demand (and particularly peak demand) include time-of-use rates, wherein rates charged vary during different block periods of the day, and interruptible rates wherein users are offered discounts in exchange for a user commitment to reduce demand on request. Such policies offer a wide array of benefits, but these options are not without

cost. For instance, in order to allow customers to adjust their usage based on the price of electricity or the time of day, the metering infrastructure would have to be switched to real-time or "smart" meters.

IMPACT OF TEMPERATURE ON ELECTRICITY SUPPLY

The efficiency with which a number of types of electricity generators convert fuel into electricity is affected by temperature. As ambient temperature increases, the efficiency and power generation of combustion turbines decrease. Combustion turbines operate by combusting a fuel source with compressed air to produce a stream of hot exhaust, which turns a turbine to generate electricity. As ambient temperature increases, the lower density of the hotter air entering the combustion turbine causes the efficiency of the unit to decrease. In the Midwest, summer capacity ratings for these types of generators can be as much as 20 percent lower than their winter ratings.

The efficiency of steam-driven generators is also adversely affected by increases in temperature. In the steam cycle, heat energy is used to turn water into steam. This heat energy can be obtained from a variety of methods, including combustion of fossil fuels, nuclear fission, concentrated solar power, and geothermal energy. The steam passes through a turbine that drives a generator to produce electricity. After passing through the turbine, the exhaust steam is cooled and condensed into water. The condensate is then sent back into the steam generator to complete the steam cycle.

According to Carnot's Principle, the maximum achievable efficiency of a steam engine is a function of only two factors: the temperature of the heat source and the temperature of the heat sink. The Carnot efficiency of a heat engine is:

$$n = 1 - \frac{T_H}{T_C} \qquad (12\text{-}1)$$

where η is efficiency, T_H is the absolute temperature of the heat source and T_C is the absolute temperature of the heat sink. The Carnot cycle is illustrated in Figure 12.2 (U.S. Department of Energy 1992).

Assuming no change in the temperature of the heat source, efficiency decreases as the temperature of the heat sink increases. As T_H is generally a design feature of the plant, it is considered to be constant. T_C is determined by the source of the cooling medium and is often directly related to ambient temperatures. Cooling water methodologies for steam plants can be classified in two general forms: recirculating and once-through. In recirculating cooling the cooling water is passed through a secondary heat exchanger (usually a cooling tower) to lower the temperature before sending it back to the condenser for reuse. For cooling towers, T_C is determined directly by the ambient air temperature. In once-through cooling, the cooling water is drawn directly from an outside source (such as a river, lake, or reservoir) and the warmer water is then returned to that source. Thus, T_C is de-

termined by the water temperature of the cooling water source.

Unlike the impact on electricity demand, temperature increases affect electricity generation in a similar fashion in both the winter and summer seasons. That is, an increase in temperature will cause a decrease in efficiency in both seasons. This means it takes more fuel to produce a given amount of energy and it takes more generating capacity to meet a given amount of power demand. As Figure 12.3 illustrates, about 95 percent of the electrical energy generated in the Midwest in 2009 was produced by generators that are susceptible to ambient temperature–induced efficiency losses.

As long as the Midwest uses steam to produce electricity, the electricity supply will be susceptible to the impacts of high ambient temperatures. The primary option to reduce those effects is to incorporate more renewable energy supplies, such as wind, geothermal, and solar generation, in the overall portfolio.

IMPACT OF PRECIPITATION
ON ELECTRICITY SUPPLY

For plants that use once-through cooling, the availability of cooling water can have a significant impact on operations. If drought conditions become more frequent and severe (see chapter 13 of this volume), the volume of water available to disperse the waste heat will be diminished. Therefore, these facilities may have to reduce output to avoid violating water temperature discharge limitations that are in place

Table 12.3. Percentage of fossil-fueled capacity and generation by cooling system type as of 2005 (data source: EIA Form 767). Columns labeled "Once" use once-through cooling, column labeled "Recirc" use recirculating cooling systems, and columns labeled "None" do not have a cooling system.

	Capacity			Generation		
	Once	Recirc	None	Once	Recirc	None
Iowa	52.6	35.3	12.1	64.1	34.5	1.3
Illinois	50.2	47.6	2.2	34.5	65.3	0.1
Indiana	39.6	52.7	7.7	18.0	76.5	5.4
Kansas	30.4	63.5	6.1	35.9	63.9	0.2
Kentucky	29.1	68.1	2.7	9.1	90.8	0.1
Michigan	70.9	22.8	6.4	95.0	4.3	0.7
Minnesota	28.3	59.0	12.6	7.5	92.2	0.3
Missouri	85.3	10.6	4.1	96.5	3.2	0.3
North Dakota	40.0	59.7	0.3	30.7	69.3	0.0
Nebraska	77.7	13.2	9.1	96.6	2.9	0.5
Ohio	52.4	39.2	8.4	35.0	64.2	0.8
South Dakota	0.0	94.8	5.2	0.0	99.7	0.3
Wisconsin	65.8	22.9	11.3	71.0	28.7	0.3
Total	51.1	42.4	6.4	43.1	55.6	1.3

to protect plants and animals. A further confounding issue is that in the drought of 1988, not only did stream-flow diminish, but water temperatures noticeably increased, leading to a "one-two punch" for addressing cooling needs as temperatures and electricity demand soared.

The Midwest generates a large percentage of its electricity from facilities that use once-through cooling. Table 12.3 shows the percentage of fossil-fueled generating capacity that used once-through, recirculating (i.e., cooling tower), or no cooling system (primarily combustion turbines) as of 2005, which was the last year the data were collected. The percentage of generation from fossil-fueled sources is also reported. Due to the Midwest's heavy reliance on coal, the generators included in the table represent about three-fourths of the electricity generation in the region.

Thus, approximately one-third of the region's electricity is generated from units relying on once-through cooling. A number of units use large bodies of water such as the Great Lakes (this is particularly common for generators in Michigan and Wisconsin). The large volume of the Great Lakes means those units should not be as susceptible to drought-induced operations limitations, though there may be implications for the energy sector from projected reductions in lake levels (see chapters 15 and 17). The majority of the units using once-through cooling, however, rely on rivers, reservoirs, and small lakes. Note that nuclear units were not included in the EIA form; some of them also use once-through cooling.

While the Midwest is not blessed with large amounts of hydroelectric capacity (1.7% of the region's electricity is provided by hydroelectric facilities, compared to 6% for the United States as a whole), much of the Midwest's hydroelectric capacity operates on a run-of-river basis. Run-of-river hydroelectric facilities lack the ability to store excess water behind a dam during times of abundant rainfall and then use that stored water to generate during dry periods. Thus, excessive rainfall can result in unproductive spillage of water that bypasses the generator, and drought conditions would severely restrict generator output.

Options for reducing the impact of changes in precipitation include replacement of existing generators with types that are not susceptible to water availability. Alternatively, cooling towers could be installed at steam-powered plants to reduce the dependence on once-through cooling. Current estimates of the cost to retrofit range from about $35 million to retrofit a 100 MW plant to about $80 million for a 500 MW facility (North American Electric Reliability Corporation, 2010). In addition to those capital expenditures, the plant's output would decrease due to increased internal loads needed to run the cooling system.

IMPACT OF STORMS ON ELECTRICITY SUPPLY

While most sources of electricity supply are not particularly vulnerable to storm events, wind and solar power are notable exceptions. Unlike their fossil-fueled and nuclear counterparts, wind and solar rely entirely on exposure to the elements in order to function. As such, they may be vulnerable to climate change–driven storm events, such as wind, lightning, and icing (see chapter 16 of this volume).

IMPACT OF TEMPERATURE ON ELECTRICITY DELIVERY

The networks used to transmit and distribute electricity from the generators to the customers are made up largely of transformers and power lines. Transmission lines generally consist of a number of aluminum cables reinforced with steel cables for structural strength and strung between poles or towers. As current flows on these lines, heat is produced that is dissipated to the air. Conditions with high ambient temperatures and low wind speeds reduce the amount of heat dissipated and may reduce the ability of the line to transmit power without suffering damage. On a hot summer day with low wind, conductor temperatures can reach 100°C (US–Canada Power Outage Task Force, 2004).

As it heats up, the metal in the line expands. Since the distance between poles does not change, the now longer line will sag toward the ground. This may result in the line coming in contact with vegetation or coming close enough for an arc to form, resulting in a fault. Thus, higher ambient temperatures have the potential to limit power transfer in the network as well as adversely affect its reliable operation. Conductor sag has been identified as a contributing factor in the August 1996 blackout that affected 4 million people in 8 western states, as well as the August 2003 blackout that affected 50 million people in the midwestern and northeastern United

States and Ontario (US–Canada Power Outage Task Force, 2004).

Vegetation management is a common approach to try to avoid sag-related outages. This involves removing vegetation and trimming trees from the line's right-of-way. Additionally, lines may be de-rated in hot conditions to reduce the allowable loading and resistive heating. Design options include constructing additional lines to reduce loading or burying lines so they are not subjected to ambient temperatures.

IMPACT OF STORMS ON
ELECTRICITY DELIVERY

The major threat to electric power delivery system reliability comes from storms. If climate change causes an increase in the frequency or severity of storms with lightning, high winds, or tornadoes, more storm-related outages would be expected.

Winter events, particularly ice storms, can be particularly damaging due to the widespread nature of the effects within the storm region. Restoration of services during winter storm events is especially challenging. Access to damaged facilities may be impossible and lines may be restored only to be knocked out again as more snow and ice accumulates. While the frequency of ice storms and windstorms within the region may not change with climate change, the location where they would be expected to occur could change (see chapter 16). Thus, some locations may experience more frequent ice storms and/or windstorms while others may experience fewer. If a larger region experiences ice during an event, with a corresponding

smaller region experiencing snow, it could be particularly devastating since utilities typically call on crews from other regions of the country to assist in restoration. This would then result in increases in the time needed to restore power.

Water Resources and Climate Change

As discussed in other chapters within this volume, climate change has altered and will alter the hydrological cycle and thus water availability, water quality (both above and below ground), and the intensity and frequency of extreme hydrological events (floods/droughts). At the most fundamental level the atmospheric water content is a (nonlinear) function of air temperature, with an increase of about 7 percent in the water-holding capacity of the air for each one-degree increase in atmospheric temperatures (Pan and Pryor 2009). This increases water availability for precipitation, and observed global precipitation increased by about 2 percent per 1°C warming over the historical period (Pan and Pryor 2009). However, the spatial distribution and timing of precipitation is considerably more complex. Further, the subsequent allocation of the water between infiltration into the soil, runoff, and evapotranspiration is strongly mediated by human decision making regarding land use and land cover. Thus, as discussed below, it is likely that future precipitation, runoff, and soil moisture will exhibit marked differences at the sub-regional level.

The hydrologic system within the United States has been extensively modified by human actions. For example, the United States has over 80,000 dams that greatly regulate flow in streams and rivers (Hightower and Pierce 2008) (Figure 12.4). A few of these dams (approximately 2,400 (Spellman and Bieber 2011)) are operated as hydroelectric plants. Nationally, the total installed capacity of hydroelectric facilities is nearly 100 GW, but only a small fraction of these facilities are located within the Midwest. There are hydropower facilities in North and South Dakota, Minnesota, Wisconsin, Michigan, Illinois, Missouri, and Kentucky, but of these only South Dakota has greater than 5 percent penetration of hydroelectricity in the state electricity supply. As a further example of the extensive human fingerprint in the hydrology of the United States, large areas within the Midwest that are now productive farmland were converted from prairie and seasonal wetlands. To make the land suitable for agriculture, water management in the form of tiling systems and canal development was started in the middle 19th century (Gasteyer 2008). Tile facilitated drainage of excess water, thus enabling crop production. Much of the excess water was carried away by the canals, which in turn lead to the Mississippi or Missouri Rivers and thus act as a conduit for discharge of nutrients to downstream locations such as the Gulf of Mexico. Other engineering modifications to the major river systems include the construction of bridges, dikes, levees, and artificial meander cutoffs, which have substantially altered the geometry and flow dynamics of the river channel and/or floodplains (Pinter et al. 2010).

Making projections for future water demand is a complex function of population, irrigation amounts and effectiveness, and domestic and industrial projections, both in terms of basic need and economic demand (or "willingness to pay"). Thus the adequacy of future freshwater supplies is a complex function of precipitation regimes, land use patterns, water infrastructure, and water demand, use, and management. According to some estimates, by 2025, more than half of the world's nations will face "freshwater stress or shortages, and by 2050, as much as 75 percent of the world's population could face freshwater scarcity" (Hightower and Pierce 2008). An assessment of the water stress in 2000 found that much of the Midwest has a demand per discharge as a function of population that is below the threshold for water stress (Vorosmarty et al. 2000). Nevertheless, the average U.S. citizen uses 200 liters of freshwater per day, which is about one-third higher than comparable figures from Europe (National Research Council 2011), and thus demand for access to freshwater is relatively high within the United States. Data from 1995 indicate some counties within the Midwest (including counties in metropolitan Chicago and parts of Nebraska and Kansas) have freshwater withdrawals several times the water available from rainfall (Hightower and Pierce 2008). One analysis of groundwater over-pumping within the United States suggested that Illinois, Wisconsin, and Nebraska were already experiencing significant impacts from excessive groundwater withdrawals (Scown et al. 2011; see further discussion in chapter 17 of this volume). In a further study Fung et al. (2011) suggest that much of the eastern United States is already showing signs of extreme water stress and that this will amplify in a +2°C warmer world.

The Great Lakes are a key freshwater resource. Indeed, according to some estimates the Great Lakes account for "18% of the world's supply of freshwater and 90% of the United States supply" (Cherkauer and Sinha 2010). As discussed in chapter 15 of this volume, changes in lake levels as a result of climate change may have major impacts on both the ecology and the economy of the Great Lakes. Currently, the Great Lakes and associated waterways support commercial shipping in excess of 175.3 million tons annually (Cherkauer & Sinha 2010). Much of this cargo is international, and in 2001, 49.2 percent of the cargo that was transported through the Montreal–Lake Ontario section of the Great Lakes–St. Lawrence seaway was classified as being of international origin (Millerd 2011). Reductions in lake levels may necessitate reduced cargo loads and thus negatively impact this important economic sector. One analysis suggested that the impact of restrictions on vessel drafts and reductions in vessel cargos varied between a 5 percent increase in vessel variable operating costs for a climate change scenario representing the possible climate in 2030 to over 22 percent for a scenario representing a doubling of atmospheric carbon dioxide (Millerd 2011).

Water supply and quality in the Great Lakes is strongly influenced by water management in the surrounding states. Indeed, approximately 50 percent of the net basin supply of freshwater to the lakes derives from land surface runoff from the land areas surrounding the Great Lakes (Brinkmann 2000), and so water supply and water quality in the Great Lakes are highly dependent on land surface processes in the surrounding states. Thus the hydrology, water quality, and ultimately economic and ecological services offered by the Great Lakes are greatly dependent on management of the land surface. In this context it is noteworthy that the ability to divert waters outside the Great Lakes basin is severely limited by state, federal, and international agreements.

Below we discuss some of the key aspects of water as both a resource within the Midwest and impact sector under a changing climate. Given that extreme conditions—and specifically floods and droughts—are generally of greatest concern to water managers, they are thus the focus of much of the following discussion and the subsequent chapters. It is worthy of note that these phenomena (floods and drought) exhibit marked differences in frequency and intensity in the historical record (see chapters 2, 13, and 14 herein) and that sub-regions within the Midwest may exhibit distinctly different trajectories with respect to these events in the future. This dichotomy was recently illustrated in work that examined historical tendencies linked to increased irrigation in the High Plains region (specifically Nebraska and Kansas) from groundwater that were dynamically coupled to increased precipitation and streamflow in the eastern portions of the Midwest such as Illinois and Indiana (Kustu et al. 2011).

STREAMFLOW AND FLOODING

Runoff (the difference between precipitation and water loss from evapotranspiration and storage below the surface) is ultimately channeled in the natural or anthropogenic channels and is thus referred to as streamflow. It is a key metric of freshwater availability. The response of streamflow to changing precipitation is referred to as the precipitation elasticity (ε_p) (Sankarasubramanian et al. 2001):

$$\varepsilon_p = \frac{dQ}{dP}\frac{P}{Q} \qquad (12\text{-}2)$$

where P is precipitation and Q is discharge.

Precipitation elasticity depends on many factors, including precipitation intensity, evapotranspiration, soil moisture, and water holding capacity, and thus exhibits tremendous spatial variability (Sankarasubramanian et al. 2001). If the soil were saturated, all the increased rainfall would translate into runoff, resulting in a large increase in streamflow. Over the relatively moist midwestern United States, the value of ε_p is approximately 2, meaning that a 1 percent increase in precipitation would result in approximately a 2 percent gain in streamflow (Jha et al. 2004). As discussed in chapter 14 of this volume, streamflow elasticity is a useful rubric in considering climate change impacts, but it is important to emphasize the roles of changing land cover in determining the elasticity, which thus shows tremendous temporal and spatial variability and high potential for management intervention. A recent study of changes in streamflow in the Upper Mississippi River basin over the last 60 years found "that precipitation trends alone cannot explain the direction and magnitude of flow trends" and rather there was a strong influence of land use change even in non-urban watersheds (Kochendorfer and Hubbart 2010).

Rivers provide a wide range of services—including water purification (processing of nutrients and contaminants by plants and microbial activity), food production, sediment control (e.g., by riparian vegetation), and recreation (Palmer et al. 2009). However, rivers are under increasing stressors, just one of which is climate change, but other important drivers of change include urbanization, which changes not only water supply and quality but also key variables such as water temperature (Palmer et al. 2009). Further, some ecosystem services are threatened or impaired due to depletion of water levels from excessive withdrawals. Adaptation to climate change impacts is currently largely reactive—one example being the breeching of levees on the Missouri River (May 2011) to prevent downstream flooding of high value assets. But proactive measures that restore or enhance the capacity of rivers to buffer climate change impacts may ultimately be of great value. Such measures include improved storm water management in highly developed basins and levee setbacks to reduce the exposure of critical infrastructure to flood risk (Palmer et al. 2009).

As described in chapter 2 of this volume, flooding represents a major environmental hazard in the Midwest. In addition to historical floods within the Midwest, such as that during 1993, which resulted in over $3 billion in losses (Rosenzweig et al. 2001), floods have been experienced in the region in 2008, 2010, and 2011. Overall losses resulting from the flooding during the May–June 2008 midwestern floods were estimated to be $15 billion, including about $8 billion in agricultural losses and 24 deaths (Budikova et al. 2010). During the floods of 2008 the Cedar River had a maximum discharge of 4 million liters per second, or 140,000 cubic feet per second (nearly twice the earlier record flow recorded in 1961), and crested at 9.5 m, 1.5 m above the 500-year flood level (Mutel 2010). The flooding affected 14 percent of the city of Cedar Rapids, and city representatives estimated an economic impact on that city of over $5.4 billion.

Precipitation receipts during April 2011 in many locations across the Midwest were greatly in excess of climate normals. For example, by May 1, 2011, Saint Louis, Missouri, had received 150 percent of normal precipitation, and Louisville, Kentucky, had received 170 percent of precipitation normals computed for 1971–2000. As of May 1, 2011, according to data from the NWS, 251 locations across the eastern United States were experiencing flooding, with many of these being located within the Midwest. The extensive flooding that affected the Midwest during spring and summer 2011 was a combined result of:

(i) Melting of an above-average snow pack across the Northern Rocky Mountains combined with above-average precipitation, which caused a breach of the levees of the Missouri and Souris Rivers at multiple loca-

tions across the Upper Midwest (Montana, North Dakota, South Dakota, Nebraska, Iowa, Kansas, and Missouri). This flooding led to over 11,000 people being evacuated from Minot, North Dakota, and the flooding of 4,000 homes. According to data from NCDC, estimated losses exceeded $2 billion (see http://www.ncdc.noaa.gov/oa/reports/billionz.html#chron).

(ii) Extreme sustained rainfall over much of the central and eastern Midwest combined with (i) led to extensive flooding on the Mississippi River. Estimated economic losses from this flooding range from $2–$4 billion (see http://www.ncdc.noaa.gov/oa/reports/billionz.html#chron).

In the 2011 floods, crisis management required that a federal judge provide permission to the U.S. Army Corps of Engineers to deliberately breach some levees along the Missouri River to prevent worse flooding downriver. The breach flooded the Bird Point–New Madrid Floodway, a 130,000-acre area of farmed river bottom designed as a flood-control tool. The floodway is one of three located along the Lower Mississippi River. They were established after a Mississippi flood in 1927 killed nearly 250 people across 10 states, an acknowledgment that under severe conditions, levees alone were unlikely to keep floodwaters at manageable levels (Christian Science Monitor 2011: http://www.csmonitor.com/USA/2011/0429/Midwest-flooding-What-s-at-stake-in-plan-to-blast-open-Missouri-levee).

Naturally, not all of the change in flood risk and impact that has been observed over the historical past or is projected for the future is associated solely with changes in the hydrological cycle. Other factors, such as population growth and exposure, economic development, and changes in infrastructure are at least of equal importance to determining resilience. Nevertheless, given recent evidence of intensification of extreme precipitation events within the Midwest in the historical past (Pryor and Schoof 2008, Pryor et al. 2009) and in climate projections (Schoof et al. 2010), it seems likely that flooding will remain a major natural hazard within the Midwest and indeed that the risk associated with flooding may amplify.

DROUGHT

As discussed in chapter 13 of this volume, drought is a complex environmental impact of climate variability and change. Accordingly, attribution of droughts to human drivers is difficult (Seager et al. 2009). Nevertheless, according to some estimates, the percentage of time spent in "severe, extreme or exceptional drought" during 1895–1995 over the Midwest ranged from a minimum of 5 percent in parts of Indiana, Michigan, Ohio, and Kentucky, to nearly 20 percent in parts of South Dakota (see chapter 13 and the U.S. Drought Monitor: http://www.drought.unl.edu/). Indeed, during the summer of 2011 a region extending from the southwest of the Midwest (Missouri and Kansas) down toward the Gulf Coast exhibited moderate to extreme drought conditions (see chapter 13 for discussion of drought severity indices).

One study of yields of corn and soybeans in two states with low irrigation penetration (Indiana and Illinois) found that over the period 1980–2007, yields were particularly strongly correlated with the occurrence of meteorological drought and maximum daily temperature during the grain filling and reproductive growth period (Mishra and Cherkauer 2010). In such situations, it is clear that the timing of drought in addition to the severity and longevity are critical factors in determining the impacts on the agricultural sector. However, simulating these parameters with accuracy for future periods is a very stringent test of climate models. Nevertheless, it appears that drought is a major risk factor to the agricultural sector in the current and historical climate (see chapter 5) and, based on at least some climate projections (see chapters 2 and 13 herein), it appears to continue to be so in the future.

WATER QUALITY

One consideration in water management to support drinking water supply and other environmental/ecological services is the possible direct and indirect impacts of climate change on water quality. Projected changes in thermal and hydrological regimes may impact water quality both directly and indirectly. For example, increased air temperatures will lead to higher water temperatures, which in the case of large water bodies (e.g., lakes and reservoirs) may lead to greater thermal stratification and increased eutrophication risk, including cyanobacteria blooms (Wagner and Adrian 2009) and oxygen depletion (Jankowski et al. 2006). Indirect impacts may include increased turbidity spikes due to more intense precipitation events and reduced assimilative capacity for contaminants due to prolonged droughts or periods of reduced stream flows.

Nonpoint source pollutant (NPS) loading in midwestern rivers creates water quality problems that range local to national in scope: from locally impaired water for midwestern communities that derive potable water from rivers to hypoxia in the Gulf of Mexico. Indeed, there is evidence that anthropogenic nitrogen (N) in the northern reaches of the Gulf of Mexico primarily derives from agricultural fertilizer and is delivered via the Mississippi River (Bianchi et al. 2010). A recent study showed that nitrate-N loading in the Upper Midwest (Minnesota) has increased in recent decades, and application of the Agricultural Drainage and Pesticide Transport (ADAPT) model determined that discharge and nitrate-N loses have responded more to climate variability during that period than to changes in land use and management (Nangia et al. 2010). Even in the absence of efforts to reduce nutrient discharge from the Mississippi River, eutrophication of the Gulf of Mexico may be amplified by climate change due to the role of climate change in enhancing the stratification of the coastal waters (Rabalais et al. 2009), which may prompt the need for even greater reductions in nutrient efflux from the Midwest.

A further key challenge to water management, particularly in urban areas within the Midwest, is posed by aging water infrastructure, particularly in light of tendencies toward amplification of extreme precipitation events. Sewer design guidelines are frequently based on historical rainfall properties and extreme values therein (Rauch and De Toffol 2006), most often applied assuming climate stationarity. The EPA estimates that roughly 3.2 trillion liters of combined sewer overflow (CSO) wastewater is discharged annually into our nation's surface waters (McLellan et al. 2007). Sewer overflows leading to discharge of untreated water as a result of unanticipated precipitation events represent a major threat to human health (McLellan et al. 2007, Rijal et al. 2009). While not all urban areas within the Midwest have combined sewers (designed to capture both sanitary sewage and storm water) for delivery to wastewater treatment plants, many are, and such systems are vulnerable to CSO during extreme precipitation events. Further, it should be noted that even separated sanitary sewers may also be overwhelmed, resulting in sewer overflow and discharge to receiving waters with no treatment (McLellan et al. 2007). Approximately 770 communities comprising over 40 million people in the United States are served by combined systems, including several cities within the Midwest (e.g., Chicago and Milwaukee) (McLellan et al. 2007).

Since sewer overflow events are strongly linked to high-magnitude but low-probability precipitation events, there is value in understanding how these events have changed in the recent past and in determining likely future characteristics of such events. Analysis of historical data suggests that the intensity of daily precipitation events with return periods in excess of one year have substantially amplified over much of the Midwest (see the example given in Figure 12.5). For example, analysis of data collected over the course of the 20th century indicate that in Chicago the probability of accumulating more than 100 mm in a single day more than doubled, increasing from 2.5×10^{-5} to over 6×10^{-5}, while the ten-year return period precipitation amount increased by over 10 percent (Pryor et al. 2009). Presuming that these historical tendencies toward intensification of extreme precipitation events do not reverse in the future, it appears that sewer overflow will continue to constitute a significant health threat and a critical source of climate change vulnerability for major urban areas within the Midwest.

The Midwest is characterized by a complex and rich ecological system. It is likely that changes in the climate and hydrological cycle may have profound impacts on both land and aquatic ecosystems. These impacts include related commercial activities such as fisheries (Lynch et al. 2010). The economic value of Great Lakes fisheries is strongly mediated by market demands and shifts in societal interests (Rothlisberger et al. 2010), thus confounding attribution of changes in sector income. Under most climate scenarios and a wide variety of fish species, optimal thermal habitat is expected to expand because fish have the opportunity to move both northward (in the longitudinally oriented lakes) or deeper (in the deep lakes) to maintain their preferred temperature.

These expansions of habitat will likely be greatest for warmer-water species, and they may not translate into an increase in fish populations due to confounding influences of anoxia, dispersal ability, and changes in food-web dynamics, in addition to the threat played by invasive species (Lynch et al. 2010).

Concern has also been voiced that changes in hydrologic regimes and/or water quality partially resulting from climate change may cause a substantial shift in health risk both to humans and other organisms. For example, reduced lake level and elevated water temperatures within the Great Lakes have been linked to type E avian botulism outbreaks. In 2002 and 2007, type E botulism outbreaks in the Great Lakes caused estimated annual mortality of over 18,000 and 17,000 birds, respectively (Lafrancois et al. 2011). Since climate change projections for this region generally indicate decreased lake levels and elevated water temperatures (see chapter 15 of this volume), the frequency and magnitude of type E botulism outbreaks in the Great Lakes may increase. Managing freshwater ecosystems to reduce or minimize human and wildlife disease risk is arguably "one of the most significant ecosystem services" (Johnson and Paull 2011) and may need to be modified in the light of expected climate change within the region.

Concluding Remarks

As discussed further in the following chapters, climate change may have substantial impacts on the energy and water sectors within the midwestern United States. These sectors are highly inter-linked, and thus at least some of the impacts may reflect that intersection and key interdependencies. Impacts on the electricity sector will likely derive from shifting demand profiles and from changes in production capacity. However, as in the case of water resources, additional factors are contributing to the vulnerability of the sector, including aging infrastructure and shifts in socioeconomic conditions within the region.

Some of the vulnerabilities and challenges identified herein are amenable to treatment within current management systems. Others may require adoption of new approaches or multi-sectoral analyses and decision-making strategies. For example, there are a number of engineering approaches that can be deployed to reduce the impacts of floods, but adoption of such measures needs to be accompanied by improved quantification of flood probability, reductions in exposure of key infrastructure, and alterations of management strategy. Options for reducing water use by at least one key end-user—the electrical power generation sector—are also readily available and include use of wastewater or reuse of water condensed from cooling towers. Equally, innovative tools are available to dynamically manage electricity demand and to diversify the electrical power generation capacity to increase resilience to some aspects of climate variability and change.

As discussed further in the subsequent chapters, the intersection between substantial changes in the hydrological cycle due to climate change and land use and land cover, coupled with changes in water demand, will necessitate changes in water management. Reduced accessibility to freshwater may characterize future conditions in some parts of the Midwest as competing demands for water grow. A key challenge to adopting improved approaches to water management is the fragmented responsibility. In the United States, over 20 federal agencies have responsibility for different aspects of water policy (Hightower and Pierce 2008), as well as a considerable number of state, regional, and local jurisdictions. Reconciling disparate needs and implementing informed policies to increase resilience to climate change and the other major stressors may require a fundamental change in management of water resources (Gleick 2003). The Chicago Metropolitan Agency for Planning (CMAP) provides an example of how to consider all the factors involved in a water supply/demand plan, including climate change, water supply and quality, and growth in demand (CMAP, 2010).

In the following chapters we identify the major hazards to the energy and water sectors within the Midwest poised by climate variability and change—specifically, droughts, floods, and changes in lake levels. Each is discussed in terms of historical occurrence, future projections, and key stressors that contribute to system vulnerability. We end this section by addressing whether key vulnerabilities to the electricity distribution system deriving from extreme events will likely increase or decline as a result of climate evolution.

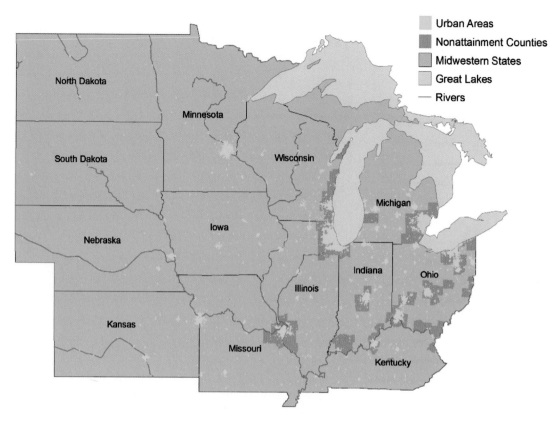

Figure 9.3. Counties in the Midwest in nonattainment status for ozone (based on the MDA 8-hr, (i.e., 8-hour average daily maximum ozone, standard) and particulate matter ($PM_{2.5}$) in 2008. (Data from EPA 2011.)

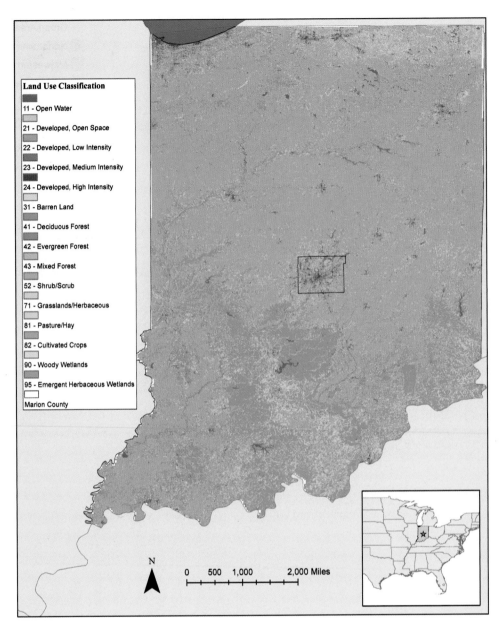

Land Use Classification

11 - Open Water
21 - Developed, Open Space
22 - Developed, Low Intensity
23 - Developed, Medium Intensity
24 - Developed, High Intensity
31 - Barren Land
41 - Deciduous Forest
42 - Evergreen Forest
43 - Mixed Forest
52 - Shrub/Scrub
71 - Grasslands/Herbaceous
81 - Pasture/Hay
82 - Cultivated Crops
90 - Woody Wetlands
95 - Emergent Herbaceous Wetlands
Marion County

N

0   500   1,000   2,000 Miles

Figure 10.1. Location of case study city, Indianapolis, Indiana, and land cover in Indiana.

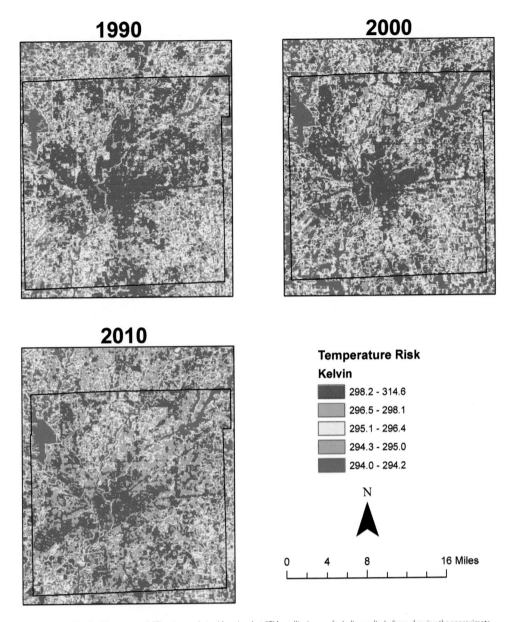

Figure 10.2. Land Surface Temperature (LST) estimates derived from Landsat 5TM satellite images for Indianapolis, Indiana, showing the approximate magnitude of the UHI.

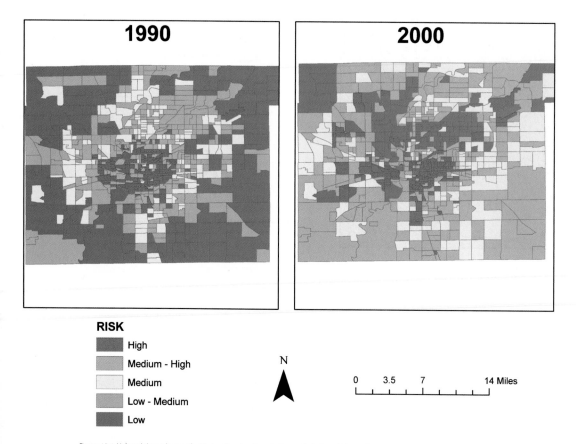

Factor Components Eigenvalue ≥ 1

P
C
A

= Risk

Socioeconomic and
Remotely Sensed Variables
Aggregated at the Block Group Level

Risk Aggregated at the Block
Group Level

Figure 10.3. Schematic overview of the process for determination of risk based on principal components analysis.

1990

2000

RISK

High
Medium - High
Medium
Low - Medium
Low

N

0   3.5   7   14 Miles

Figure 10.4. Vulnerability risk maps for Marion County, where Indianapolis, Indiana, is located.

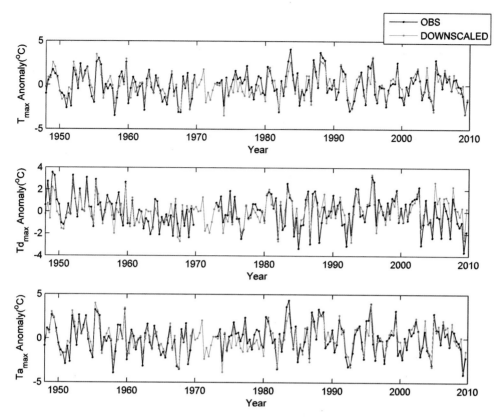

Figure 11.3. An example of the downscaling approach applied to historical data from O'Hare International Airport in Chicago, Illinois. The panels show the observed and downscaled anomalies of T_{max} (top), Td_{max} (middle), and Ta_{max} (bottom). The black line shows the observations, while the red line shows the downscaled values.

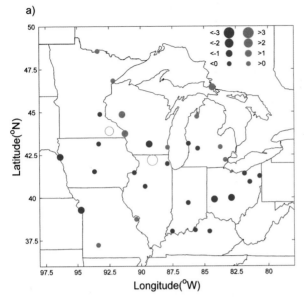

Figure 11.4. Linear trends in the historical period (1948–2009) of summer (JJA) T_{max} (a, b), Td_{max} (c, d), and Ta_{max} (e, f). Results are shown for the mean (a, c, e) and 90th percentile (b, d, f) of each parameter. The size of the symbol denotes the magnitude of the trend. Open symbols represent significant trends ($\alpha = 0.05$).

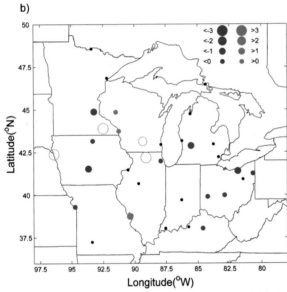

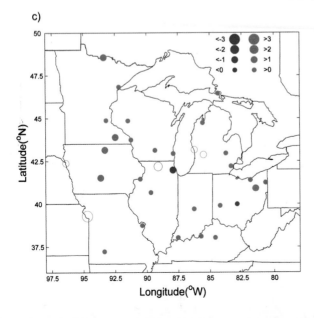

d)

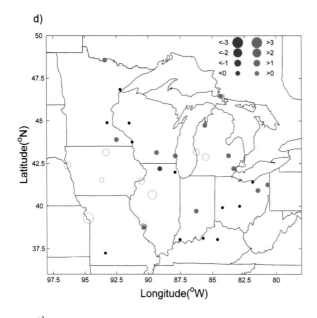

e)

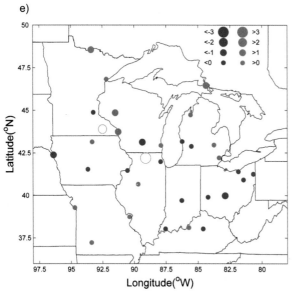

f)

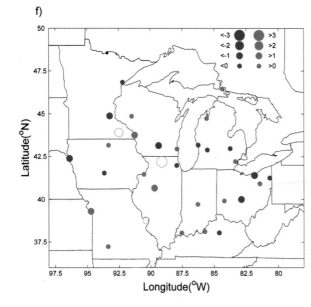

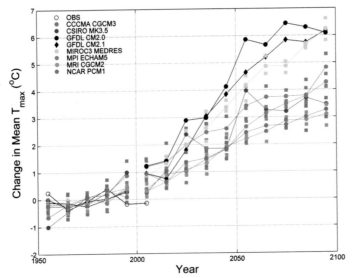

Figure 11.5. Downscaled historical and future (A1B) AOGCM simulations for T_{max} averaged over all 33 stations. As indicated in the legend, each line represents a single AOGCM. For AOGCMs with multiple runs, the squares represent the maximum and minimum values.

a)

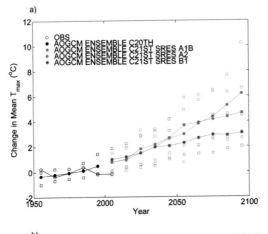

Figure 11.6. Regionally averaged downscaled AOGCM ensemble projections of T_{max} (a, b), Td_{max} (c, d) and Ta_{max} (e, f) averaged over all 33 stations. Results are shown for the mean (a, c, e) and 90th percentile (b, d, f). The line and solid symbol indicate the decadal average of the projection for each greenhouse gas scenario. The open symbols indicate the maximum and minimum values for AOGCM simulations included in the ensemble.

b)

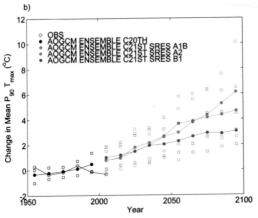

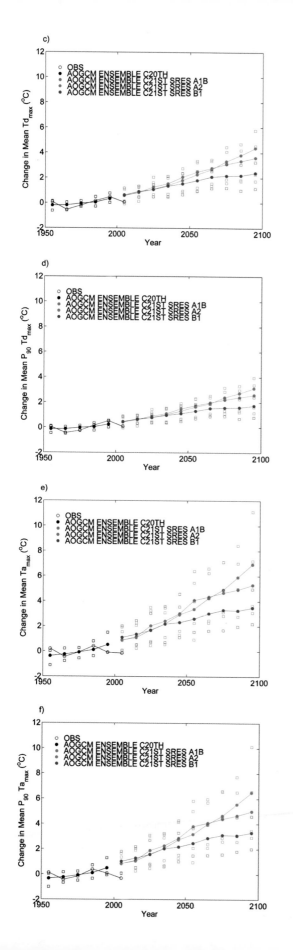

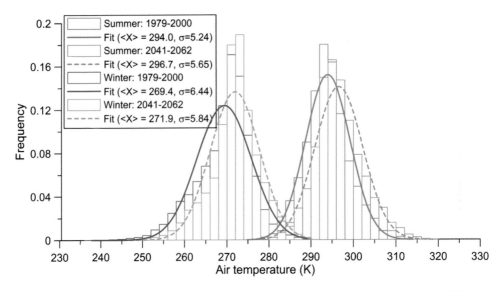

Figure 12.1. Probability distribution of three-hourly air temperature (in Kelvin, where temperature in Kelvin is temperature in Celsius plus 273.15) from climate simulations conducted with the Canadian Regional Climate Model nested within the Canadian Global Climate Model (see chapters 2 and 16 for discussions of these simulations). The data are for the grid cell containing Indianapolis, Indiana. The bars denote the data, and the lines as fits of a Gaussian distribution to data from the two time-periods.

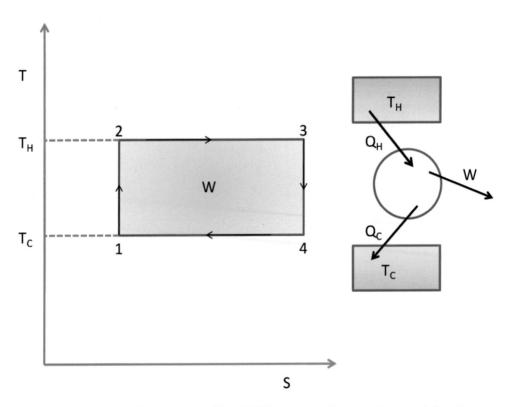

Figure 12.2. The Carnot cycle (redrawn from U.S. Department of Energy (1992)). The temperature of the heat source is represented by T_H, and the temperature of the heat sink is T_C. S is entropy. The area under the line between points 2 and 3 represents the heat input Q_H. The area under the line between points 4 and 1 represents the heat lost Q_C. The net work, W, is the area of the rectangle.

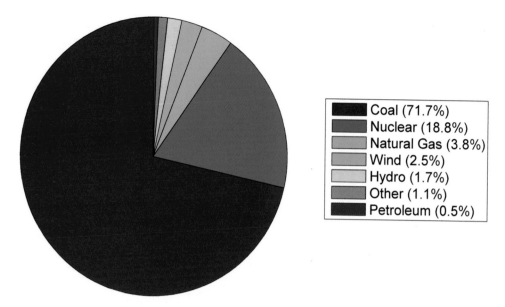

Figure 12.3. Sources of electricity generation in the Midwest in 2009. Generators that use coal, nuclear, natural gas, and oil are likely to operate less efficiently at high ambient temperatures. "Other" includes a number of sources, including biomass, waste products, and solar. The Midwest is defined as the states of Illinois, Indiana, Iowa, Kansas, Kentucky, Michigan, Minnesota, Missouri, Nebraska, North Dakota, Ohio, South Dakota, and Wisconsin. (Data from the EIA.)

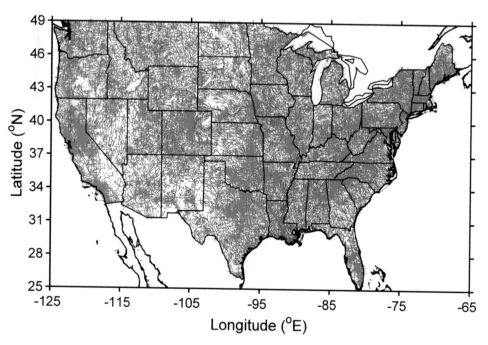

Figure 12.4. Major rivers and streams in the United States (blue lines) and the location of dams (red symbols). (Data from http://www.nationalatlas.gov/.)

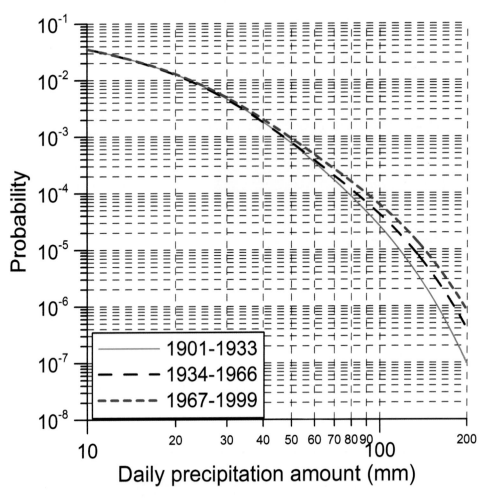

Figure 12.5. The tail of the probability distribution function for wet-day precipitation amounts in the three time-windows (1901–1933, 1934–1966, and 1967–1999) at Chicago University, Illinois. The probability distribution function was derived based on fitting of observations to a mixed-exponential distribution.

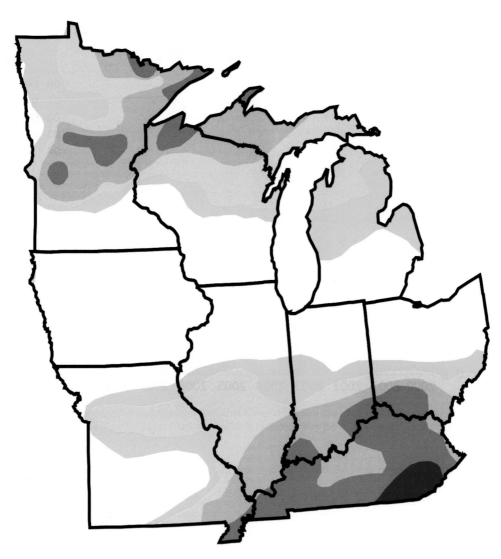

Figure 13.1. The US Drought Monitor map for the Midwest region for data ending September 11, 2007. The drought intensities depicted are D0 ("abnormally dry," in yellow), D1 ("moderate," in tan), D2 ("severe," in orange), D3 ("extreme," in red), and D4 ("exceptional," in dark brown). The D-level categories are roughly based on a percentile ranking system where D0-D4 represent the 30th, 20th, 10th, 5th, and 2nd percentiles, respectively. When possible, the climate inputs, used to subjectively produce the map, have been calculated into percentile rankings. (Data from the National Drought Mitigation Center, U.S. Department of Agriculture, and the National Oceanic and Atmospheric Administration, 2011 (http://drought.unl.edu/.)

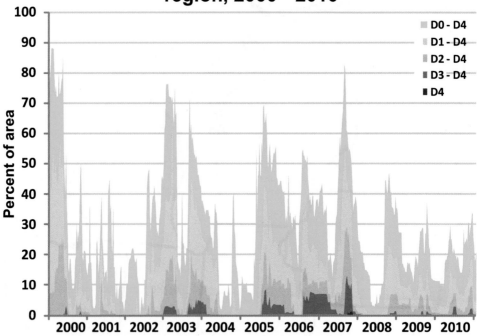

Figure 13.2. The percent of the Midwest region experiencing D0-D4 dryness and drought conditions, according to the U.S. Drought Monitor map between January 2000 and December 2010. The data can be accessed from http://drought.unl.edu/.

Impacts in MRCC region by year, 2005-2010

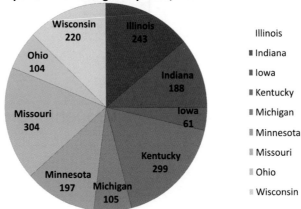

2010 14%
2009 7%
2008 9%
2005 24%
2006 14%
2007 32%

2005
2006
2007
2008
2009
2010

Total number of impacts: 1,721

Impacts in MRCC region by state, 2005-2010

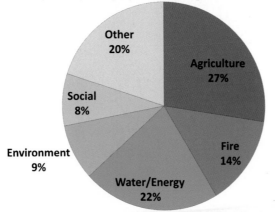

Wisconsin 220
Ohio 104
Missouri 304
Minnesota 197
Michigan 105
Illinois 243
Indiana 188
Iowa 61
Kentucky 299

Illinois
Indiana
Iowa
Kentucky
Michigan
Minnesota
Missouri
Ohio
Wisconsin

Impacts by category in MRCC region, 2005-2010

Other 20%
Social 8%
Environment 9%
Water/Energy 22%
Fire 14%
Agriculture 27%

Figure 13.3. Classification of drought impacts within the Drought Impact Reporter within the Midwest Region (as shown in Figure 13.1 and based on the Midwest Regional Climate Center or MRCC). Data from http://droughtreporter.unl.edu/.

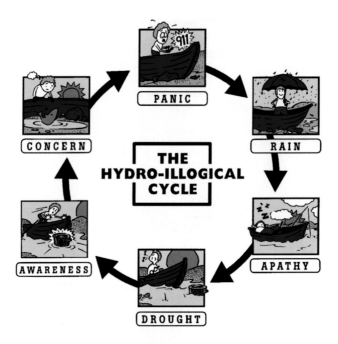

Figure 13.4. The Hydro-Illogical Cycle. Source: National Drought Mitigation Center, 2006, http://drought.unl.edu.

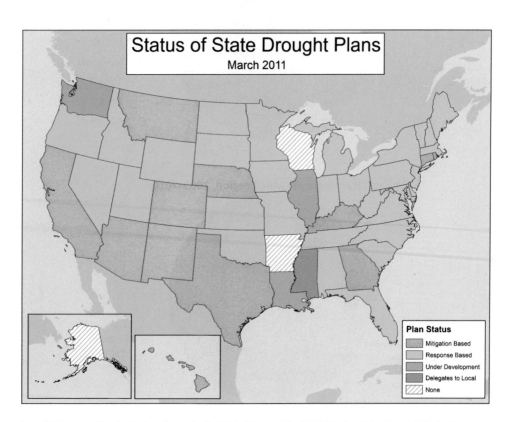

Figure 13.5. The status of drought planning at the state level in the United States as of March 2011. (Data from National Drought Mitigation Center (2011).)

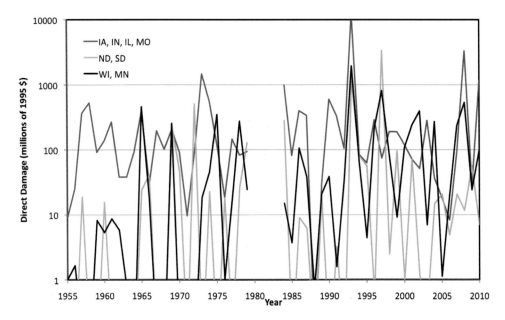

Figure 14.1. Annual direct flood damage 1955–2010, excluding 1980–1983 (2010 values are preliminary estimates and subject to change upon review). Note the y-axis is logarithmic. Units: millions 1995 US dollars. (Data from http://www.flooddamagedata.org (1955–2002) and http://www.nws.noaa .gov/hic (2003–2010); state data available by request.)

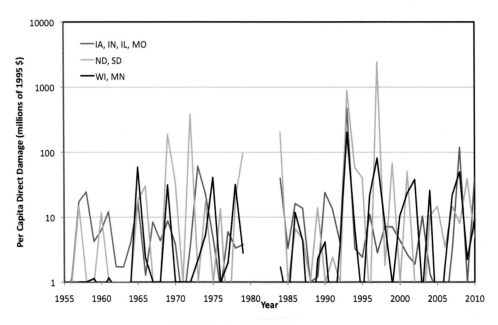

Figure 14.2. Per capita annual direct flood damage 1955–2010, excluding 1980–1983 (2010 values are preliminary estimates and subject to change upon review). Note the y-axis is logarithmic. Units: millions 1995 US dollars. Data from http://www.flooddamagedata.org (1955–2002), http://www .nws.noaa.gov/hic (2003–2010; state data available by request), and http://www.census.gov/ (state population estimate for July 1).

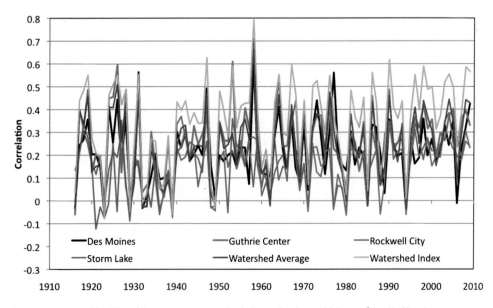

Figure 14.3. Correlation of five daily rainfall metrics using stations within the Raccoon River Basin and daily streamflow at Van Meter, Iowa.

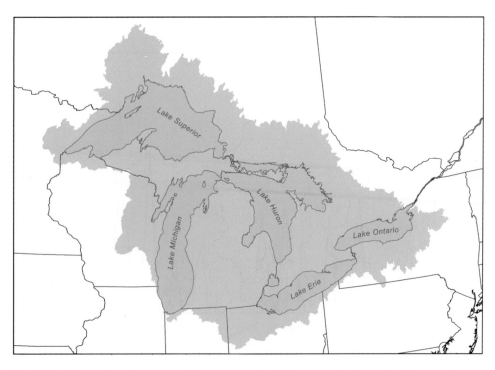

Figure 15.1. Map of the Great Lakes and its drainage basin (shown by the green shading). The gray lines show the boundaries of the states and Canadian provinces that border the Great Lakes.

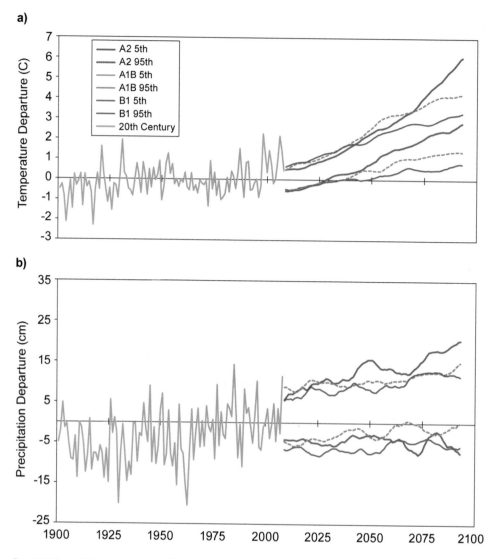

Figure 15.2. Observed 20th-century temperature (°C) and precipitation (cm) departures from the 1971–2000 average, as well as the 5th and 95th percentiles of the temperature and precipitation scenarios, based on the three GHG emission scenarios (B1, A1B, and A2). The 20th century records are unsmoothed, while a 7-year running average was applied to the 21st century projections.

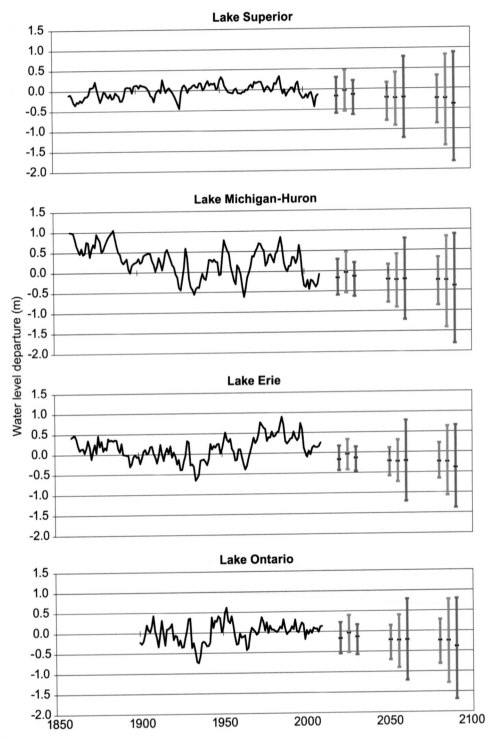

Figure 15.3. The observed departures of annual lake levels (in m) from the long-term mean for the 19th and 20th centuries for the four major lake groups, as well as the twenty-first century modeled lake levels for the B2 (blue), A1B (green), and A2 (red) bars. The three sets of bars are for the 15-year average lake levels at 2020–2044, 2050–2064, and 2080–2094. The bars are slightly offset for legibility. The mark in the middle of the bar represents the median, while the lower and upper ends of the bars represent the 5th and 95th percentiles, respectively, of all the model runs for that period and emission scenario.

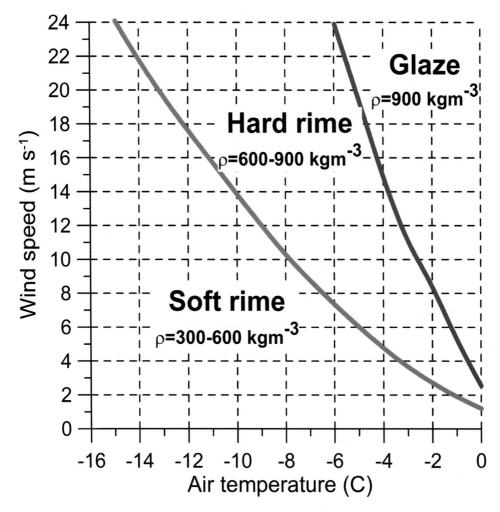

Figure 16.1. Properties and meteorological parameters of accreted atmospheric ice. Adapted from Fikke et al. (2007).

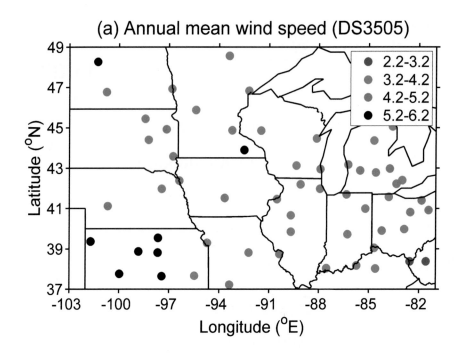

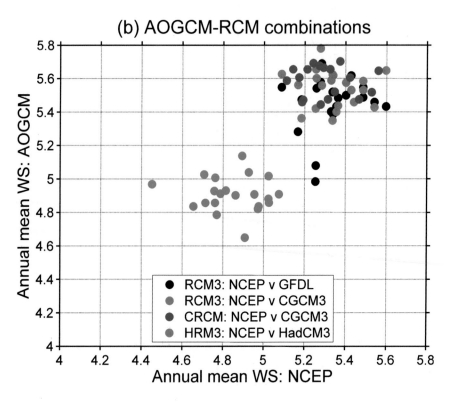

Figure 16.2. (a) Mean annual mean wind speeds for 1979–2000 (m s⁻¹). Data are for a height of 10 m and are drawn from in situ observations in the DS3505 data set (Pryor et al. 2009, Pryor & Ledolter 2010). (b) Scatterplot of the annual mean wind speed at 10 m over the Midwest computed from the different RCMs nested in the AOGCMs versus values from the same RCM nested in the NCEP reanalysis. The individual points show the annual mean averaged over the entire domain for each of the 22 years in the control period (1979–2000).

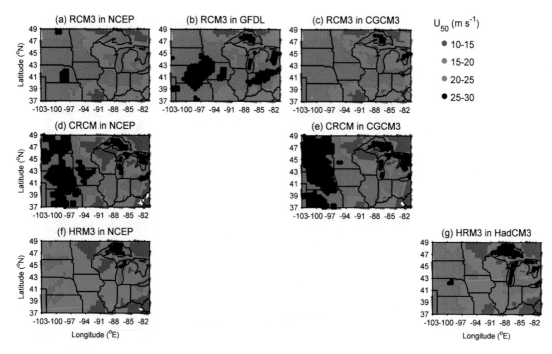

Figure 16.3. Fifty-year return period sustained wind speed (U_{50yr}) (m s^{-1}) over the midwestern United States during the historical period (1979–2000) derived from output from the different RCMs (shown by the rows) and AOGCMs (columns). The frames are arranged in the matrix shown by Table 16.2. The scale used in the images to depict the magnitude of the extreme wind speeds is shown in upper right of the figure.

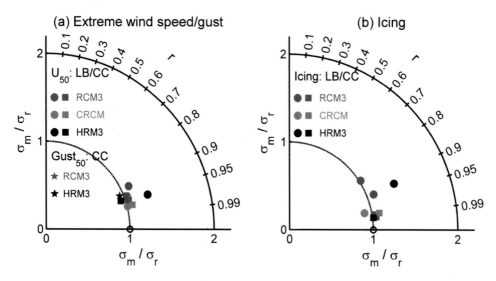

Figure 16.4. Taylor diagram of (a) 50-year return period values extreme wind speeds and gusts and (b) icing frequencies over the Midwest (domain −103 to −81°E, 37–49°N) computed for the different AOGCM-RCM combinations and for the historical climate versus the mid-twenty-first century. The solid circles show comparisons of fields of U_{50yr} and icing from the same RCM with different lateral boundaries (LB) for the control period (1979–2000). The squares show the climate change signal (CC) for 2041–2062 versus 1979–2000 in U_{50} and icing. The stars shown in frame (a) depict the climate change signal in Gust$_{50yr}$ estimates from 2041–2062 versus 1979–2000.

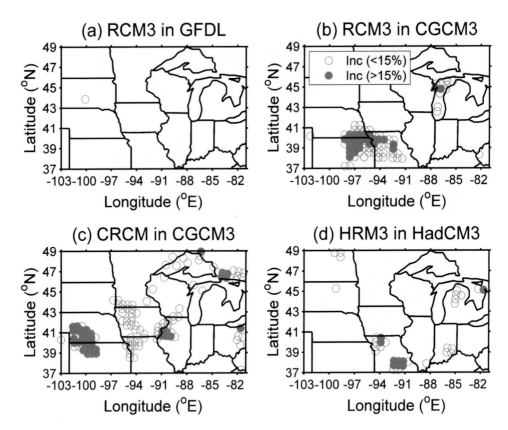

Figure 16.5. Difference in the fifty-year return period sustained wind speed (U_{50yr}) over the midwestern United States for 2041–2062 vs. 1979–2000. The frames show the different AOGCM-RCM combinations. The magnitude of change is only shown for grid cells where the value for the future period lies beyond the 95 percent confidence intervals on the control period. Note: None of the grid cells behind the legend in frame (b) exhibited significant changes.

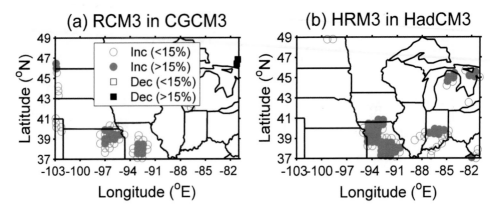

Figure 16.6. Difference in the fifty-year return period wind gust ($Gust_{50yr}$) over the midwestern United States for 2041–2062 versus 1979–2000. The frames show the two AOGCM-RCM combinations. The magnitude of change is only shown for grid cells where the value for the future period lies beyond the 95 percent confidence intervals on the control period. Note; Two grid cells behind the legend in frame (a) exhibited significant changes.

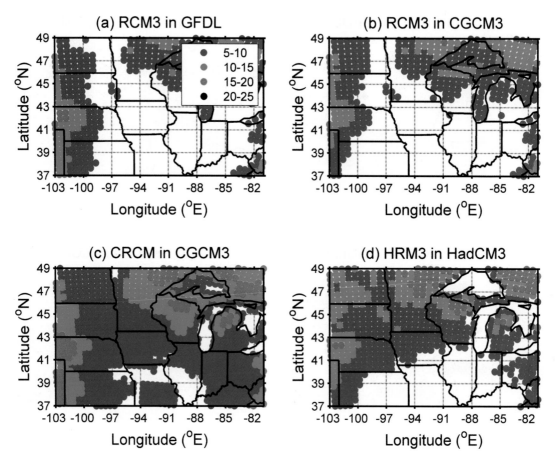

Figure 16.7. Mean icing frequency (percentage of annual hours) in the control period (1979–2000) from (a) RCM3 nested in GFDL, (b) RCM3 nested in CGCM3, (c) CRCM nested in CGCM3, and (d) HRM3 nested in HadCM3.

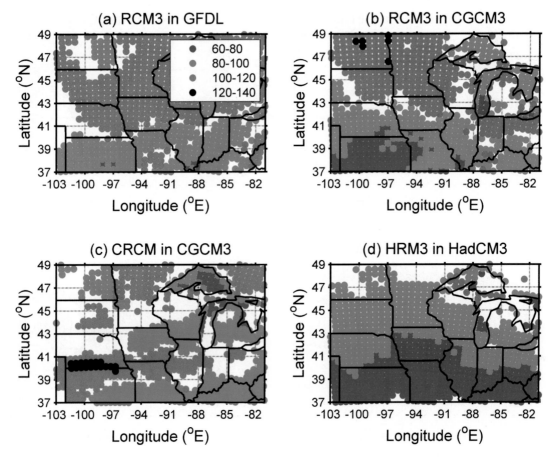

Figure 16.8. Mean icing frequency in 2041–2062 versus the control period (1979–2000) from (a) RCM3 nested in GFDL, (b) RCM3 nested in CGCM3, (c) CRCM nested in CGCM3, and (d) HRM3 nested in HadCM3. The values shown are the fraction of the value in the control period. Thus a value of 110 is a 10 percent increment over the control period. Values are only shown for grid cells where the change in mean annual frequency is greater than 2 times the standard deviation of annual values during the control period.

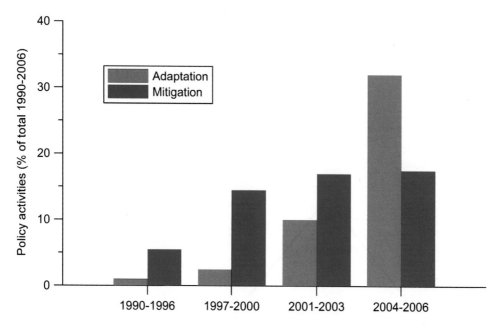

Figure 17.1. Proportion of adaptation and mitigation activities introduced in Europe between 1990 and 2006 expressed as a fraction of the total policy initiatives. Figure redrawn from Neufeldt et al. (2010).

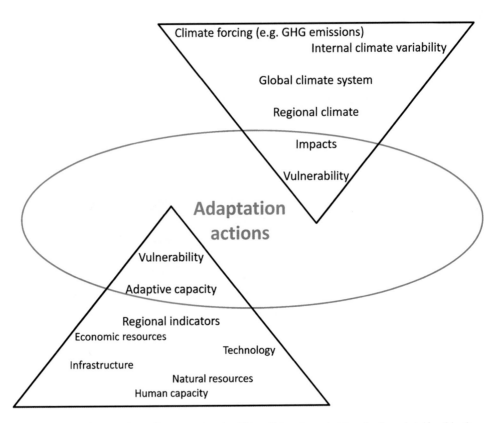

Figure 17.2. Schematic of the approaches used herein to examine vulnerabilities and inform climate adaptation policy. Figure adapted from Cohen & Waddell (2009).

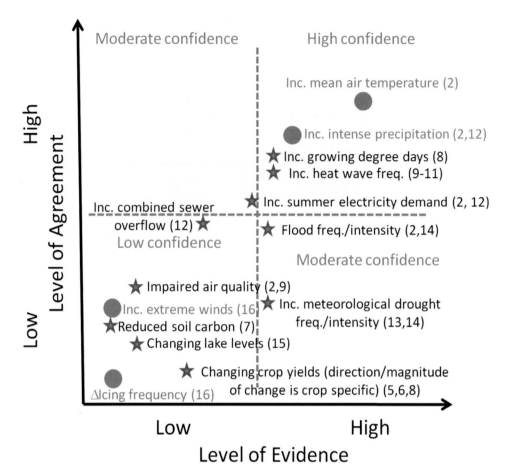

Figure 17.3. Subjective evaluation (i.e., expert judgment) of the level of agreement and level of evidence for possible changes in physical parameters and impacts in the Midwest based on analyses and summaries presented in this volume. This assessment for the Midwest is depicted for physical climate parameters (shown by the red dots) and impact on physical/socioeconomic systems (blue stars). The numbers below each summary label indicate the chapters in which these processes/parameters are discussed and in which relevant analyses and literature are synthesized. Returning to the parlance of the IPCC Fourth Assessment Report as articulated in chapter 1 of this volume, the text in green shows associated confidence statements that might reasonably be applied to projections of these climate parameters and impacts within the Midwest.

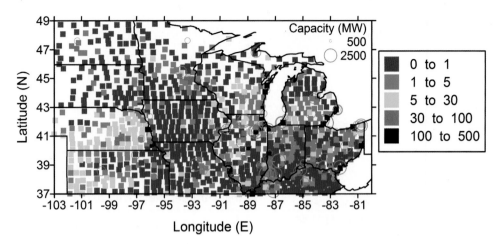

Figure 17.4. Percentage of total freshwater withdrawals relative to water available from precipitation. Data pertaining to freshwater withdrawals are for 2005 (data from http://rd.tetratech.com/climatechange/projects/nrdc_climate_supporting_data.asp), while the precipitation data derive from 1971–2000 and are taken from the PRISM (Parameter-Elevation Regressions on Independent Slopes Model) data set (data from http://www.prism .oregonstate.edu/). The ratio of withdrawals to atmospheric supply for each county is plotted in the population centroid of the county. The overlay shows the location and capacity of major electricity generating facilities (coal and nuclear) within the Midwest (see Figure 2.3 and the associated text in chapter 2 for a description of these data).

REFERENCES

Bianchi TS, DiMarco SF, Cowan JH, Hetland RD, Chapman P, Day JW, Allison MA (2010). The science of hypoxia in the Northern Gulf of Mexico: A review. Science of the Total Environment 408:1471–1484.

Brinkmann WA (2000). Causes of variability in monthly Great Lakes water supplies and lake levels. Climate Research 15:151–160.

Budikova D, Coleman JSM, Strope SA, Austin A (2010). Hydroclimatology of the 2008 midwest floods. Water Resources Research 46:W12524, doi:12510.11029/12010WR009206.

Cherkauer KA, Sinha T (2010). Hydrologic impacts of projected future climate change in the Lake Michigan region. Journal of Great Lakes Research 36:33–50.

Chicago Metropolitan Agency for Planning (2010). Water 2050, northeastern Illinois regional water supply/demand plan, Available from: http://www.cmap.illinois.gov/documents/ 20583/be751083-5476-4eb0-a66f-65b0059241b3.

Fung F, Lopez A, New M (2011). Water availability in +2 degrees C and +4 degrees C worlds. Philosophical Transactions of the Royal Society a-Mathematical Physical and Engineering Sciences 369:99–116.

Gasteyer SP (2008). Agricultural transitions in the context of growing environmental pressure over water. Agriculture and Human Values 25:469–486.

Gleick PH (2003). Global freshwater resources: Soft-path solutions for the 21st century. Science 302:1524–1528.

Hayhoe K, Sheridan S, Kalkstein L, Greene S (2010). Climate change, heat waves, and mortality projections for Chicago. Journal of Great Lakes Research 36:65–73.

Hightower M, Pierce SA (2008). The energy challenge. Nature 452:285–286.

Jankowski T, Livingstone DM, Buhrer H, Forster R, Niederhauser P (2006). Consequences of the 2003 European heat wave for lake temperature profiles, thermal stability, and hypolimnetic oxygen depletion: Implications for a warmer world. Limnology and Oceanography 51:815–819.

Jha M, Pan Z, Takle ES, Gu R (2004). Impacts of climate change on stream flow in the Upper Mississippi River basin: A regional climate model perspective. Journal of Geophysical Research 109:D09105, doi:10.1029/2003JD003686.

Johnson PTJ, Paull SH (2011). The ecology and emergence of diseases in fresh waters. Freshwater Biology 56:638–657.

Kochendorfer JP, Hubbart JA (2010). The roles of precipitation increases and rural land-use changes in streamflow trends in the Upper Mississippi River basin. Earth Interactions 14:1–12.

Kustu MD, Fan Y, Rodell M (2011). Possible link between irrigation in the U.S. High Plains and increased summer streamflow in the Midwest. Water Resources Research 47:W03522 doi: 10.1029/2010WR010046.

Lafrancois BM, Riley SC, Blehert DS, Ballmann AE (2011). Links between type E botulism outbreaks, lake levels, and surface water temperatures in Lake Michigan, 1963–2008. Journal of Great Lakes Research 37:86–91.

Lynch AJ, Taylor WW, Smith KD (2010). The influence of changing climate on the ecology and management of selected Laurentian Great Lakes fisheries. Journal of Fish Biology 77:1964–1982.

McLellan SL, Hollis EJ, Depas MM, Van Dyke M, Harris J, Scopel CO (2007). Distribution and fate of Escherichia coli in Lake Michigan following contamination with urban storm water and combined sewer overflows. Journal of Great Lakes Research 33:566–580.

Meehl GM, Karl T, Easterling DR, Changnon S, Pielke Jr. R, Changnon D, Evans J, Groisman PY, Kutson TR, Kunkel KE, Mearns LO, Parmesan C, Pulwarty R, Root T, Sylves RT, Whetton P, Zwiers F (2000). An introduction to trends in extreme weather and climate events: Observations, socioeconomic impacts, terrestrial ecological impacts, and model projections. Bulletin of the American Meteorological Society 81:413–416.

Metz B, Davidson OR, Bosch PR, Dave R, Meyer LA (eds) (2007). Climate change 2007: Mitigation of climate change. Contribution of Working Group III to the Fourth Assessment Report of the Intergovernmental Panel on Climate Change. Cambridge, UK: Cambridge University Press.

Midwest Independent Transmission System Operator Regulatory and Economic Studies Department (2009). 2009–2010 Winter Reliability Assessment. Available from: https://www.midwestiso.org/_layouts/MISO/ECM/Redirect.aspx?ID=92008.

Midwest Independent Transmission System Operator Regulatory and Economic Studies Department (2010). 2010 Summer Reliability Assessment. Available from: https://www.midwestiso.org/Library/Repository/Study/Seasonal%20Assessments/2010%20Summer%20Resource%20Assessment.pdf.

Millerd F (2011). The potential impact of climate change on Great Lakes international shipping. Climatic Change 104:629–652.

Mishra V, Cherkauer KA (2010). Retrospective droughts in the crop growing season: Implications to corn and soybean yield in the Midwestern United States. Agricultural and Forest Meteorology 150:1030–1045.

Mutel C (2010). A watershed year: Anatomy of the Iowa floods of 2008. Ames: University of Iowa Press.

Nangia V, Mulla DJ, Gowda PH (2010). Precipitation changes impact stream discharge, nitrate-nitrogen load more than agricultural management changes. Journal of Environmental Quality 39:2063–2071.

National Assessment Synthesis Team (eds) (2000). Climate change impacts on the United States—overview report: The potential consequences of climate variability and change, vol. Cambridge, UK: Cambridge University Press. Available from: www.usgrcp.gov/usgrcp/Library/nationalassessment/.

National Research Council (2011). Climate stabilization targets: Emissions, concentrations, and impacts over decades to millennia. Washington, DC: National Academies Press.

North American Electric Reliability Corporation (2010). 2010 Special Reliability Scenario

Assessment: Resource Adequacy Impacts of Potential US Environmental Regulations, Available from http://www.nerc.com/files/EPA_Scenario_Final.pdf.

PJM Resource Adequacy Planning Department (2010). PJM Load Forecast Report January 2010, Available from: http://www.pjm.com/faqs/~/media/CEDC88A734AC4719ADB11AF1CBC8034D.ashx.

Palmer MA, Lettenmaier DP, Poff NL, Postel SL, Richter B, Warner R (2009). Climate change and river ecosystems: Protection and adaptation options. Environmental Management 44:1053–1068.

Pan ZT, Pryor SC (2009). Overview: Hydrological regimes. In: Pryor SC (ed) Understanding climate change: Climate variability, predictability and change in the midwestern United States. Bloomington: Indiana University Press, 88–99.

Pilli-Sihvola K, Aatola P, Ollikainen M, Tuomenvirta H (2010). Climate change and electricity consumption—witnessing increasing or decreasing use and costs. Energy Policy 38:2409–2419.

Pinter N, Jemberie AA, Remo JWF, Heine RA, Ickes BS (2010). Cumulative impacts of river engineering, Mississippi and lower Missouri Rivers. River Research and Applications 26:546–571.

Pryor SC, Howe JA, Kunkel KE (2009). How spatially coherent and statistically robust are temporal changes in extreme precipitation in the contiguous USA? International Journal of Climatology 29:31–45.

Pryor SC, Schoof JT (2008). Changes in the seasonality of precipitation over the contiguous USA. Journal of Geophysical Research 113, doi:10.1029/2008jd010251.

Rabalais NN, Turner RE, Diaz RJ, Justic D (2009). Global change and eutrophication of coastal waters. Ices Journal of Marine Science 66:1528–1537.

Rauch W, De Toffol S (2006). On the issue of trend and noise in the estimation of extreme rainfall properties. Water Science and Technology 54:17–24.

Rijal G, Petropoulou C, Tolson JK, DeFlaun M, Gerba C, Gore R, Glymph T, Granato T, O'Connor C, Kollias L, Lanyon R (2009). Dry and wet weather microbial characterization of the Chicago area waterway system. Water Science and Technology 60:1847–1855.

Rosenzweig C, Iglesias A, Yang XB, Epstein PR, Chivian E (2001). Climate change and extreme weather events: Implications for food production, plant diseases, and pests. Global Change and Human Health 2:90–104.

Rothlisberger JD, Lodge DM, Cooke RM, Finnoff DC (2010). Future declines of the binational Laurentian Great Lakes fisheries: The importance of environmental and cultural change. Frontiers in Ecology and the Environment 8:239–244.

Ruth M, Lin A (2006). Regional energy demand and adaptations to climate change: Methodology and application to the state of Maryland, USA. Energy Policy 34:2820–2833.

Sankarasubramanian A, Vogel RM, and Limbrunner JF (2001). Climate elasticity of streamflow in the United States, Water Resources Research, 37:1771–1781.

Schoof JT, Pryor SC, Suprenant J (2010). Development of daily precipitation projections for the United States based on probabilistic downscaling. Journal of Geophysical Research 115, doi:10.1029/2009JD013030.

Scown CD, Horvath A, McKone TE (2011). Water footprint of US transportation fuels. Environmental Science & Technology 45:2541–2553.

Seager R, Tzanova A, Nakamura J (2009). Drought in the southeastern United States: Causes, variability over the last millennium, and the potential for future hydroclimate change. Journal of Climate 22:5021–5045.

Spellman F, Bieber R (2011). Science of renewable energy. Boca Raton, FL: CRC Press.

Steadman RG (1984). A universal scale of apparent temperature. Journal of Climate and Applied Meteorology 23:1674–1687.

US-Canada Power Outage Task Force (2004). Final report on the August 14, 2003 blackout in the United States and Canada: Causes and recommendations. Available from: https://reports.energy.gov/BlackoutFinal-Web.pdf.

US Department of Energy (1992). DOE fundamentals handbook: Thermodynamics, heat transfer, and fluid flow, Volume 1 of 3, DOE-HDBK-1012/1-92.

US Energy Information Administration (2009). Emissions of greenhouse gases in the United States 2008. Report #DOE/EIA-0573(2008).

US Energy Information Administration (2010). Updated capital cost estimates for electricity generation plants, Available from: http://www.eia.doe.gov/oiaf/beck_plantcosts/updatedplantcosts.pdf.

Vorosmarty CJ, Green P, Salisbury J, Lammers RB (2000). Global water resources: Vulnerability from climate change and population growth. Science 289:284–288.

Wagner C, Adrian R (2009). Cyanobacteria dominance: Quantifying the effects of climate change. Limnology and Oceanography 54:2460–2468.

13. The Drought Risk Management Paradigm in the Context of Climate Change

M. HAYES

Introduction

The 2010 drought and heat wave in Russia's wheat belt sent rippling impacts that were felt worldwide, including civil disturbances such as food riots in Mozambique (CNN 2010).This event is a recent example of how drought and the interconnectedness of issues such as food security, water availability, climate variability and extremes, and the potential of climate change can challenge societies around the world. It is also an example why discussions about potential drought events and the agriculturally rich Midwest (see chapter 2 of this volume) are especially relevant when thinking about the future because of the impacts these events might have both local and global dimensions.

Drought is a natural hazard that can occur at almost any location, causing considerable economic, environmental, and social impacts. For the United States, a compilation by the National Climatic Data Center (NCDC 2011) of weather and climate disasters causing at least $1 billion in losses and damage documents that 14 "billion-dollar" drought/heat wave events

have occurred since 1980, totaling more than $180 billion in losses. This total represents 25 percent of all losses from these billion-dollar weather disasters. The average loss per disaster for droughts and hurricanes (about $13 billion per event) is far higher than for any other disaster (NCDC 2011).

Drought differs from these other hazards in terms of several key characteristics. First, droughts are often referred to as a "creeping phenomenon" because of their slow onset (Gillette 1950). Second, unlike other natural hazards, droughts lack a universal definition, and drought severity is best described by multiple indicators. Heim (2002) provides an overview of various drought indicators representing the variety of ways to depict both drought intensity and the spatial and temporal scales of drought. Third, the impacts of drought are often non-structural in terms of infrastructural damage and are spread over very large areas. Because of these unique characteristics, it is often difficult to focus attention on drought events as they are occurring, and these characteristics have made progress on drought risk management slow (Wilhite et al. 2005a, Wilhite and Buchanan-Smith 2005).

Similar to drought, climate change is long-term, slowly evolving, and difficult to perceive by humans. Drought, therefore, becomes a good proxy for understanding some aspects of climate change. In fact, for some people, particularly for those within the agricultural sector, drought as an issue can be more tangible than climate change because it is something they have had to face in the past and will likely face in the future (Center for Research on Environmental Decisions 2009). Droughts, then, become a good starting point for identifying potential approaches to dealing with some aspects of climate change. Lessons learned and applicable strategies from drought risk management can help regions like the Midwest gain insight on climate change impacts, vulnerability, and adaptation.

In this context, Daniel Connell (2010) of the Australian National University recently described drought as "a force for truth" for Australia in how Australians must look at climate change as a nation. In other words, a thorough examination of drought could reveal important information on how to address climate change. He highlighted three points to support this argument. First, an analysis of drought risk management is the starting point for a comprehensive institutional analysis that is necessary in understanding how to deal with climate change. Second, the stress from a drought highlights both the strengths and weaknesses in how a society deals with types of long-term threats and the political priorities and underlying cul-

tural values revealed by difficult choices in these situations. Third, societies are likely to manage climate change in the same way they will manage drought, for better or worse. This chapter will briefly examine these points from the perspective of the United States, with a focus on the Midwest.

Drought in the Midwest

Agriculture has a major influence on the midwestern economy and lifestyle (see chapter 2 of this volume). More than 50 percent of the land area is in farms, making the region critical for the agricultural production, with 89 and 87 percent of the nation's corn and soybeans, respectively (USDA 1994, Pryor and Tackle 2009). Climate, climate variability, and extremes are all very important for the Midwest, and midwestern droughts can have significant local, regional, and national impacts. In addition, the fact that the United States accounts for 60 and 40 percent of the corn and soybean exports, respectively (ERS 2009), implies that midwestern droughts will also have impacts around the world similar to what was seen for the 2010 drought in Russia.

Table 13.1 shows the crop insurance indemnity payments (payments made for crop losses based on crop insurance policies held by the producers) for the Midwest (those states included within the territory of the Midwest Regional Climate Center) between 1989 and 2009 in comparison to nationwide crop indemnity payments and to midwestern indemnity payments for all losses. During this

Table 13.1. Drought-related crop insurance indemnity payments for the Midwest (the states of Minnesota, Wisconsin, Michigan, Iowa, Missouri, Illinois, Indiana, Ohio, and Kentucky). (Data source: http://www.rma.usda.gov/tools/ accessed on January 31, 2011.)

Year	Indemnities (millions $)	Percentage of total US drought indemnities	Percentage of Midwest indemnities for all losses
1989	185	30.1	73.6
1990	24	4.7	17.4
1991	349	48.8	63.3
1992	20	16.6	13.5
1993	10	3.7	1.2
1994	14	11.4	10.5
1995	63	19.3	18.4
1996	46	8.9	13.4
1997	53	20.4	29.5
1998	45	6.0	14.0
1999	216	29.3	45.9
2000	122	10.0	31.8
2001	207	21.4	33.8
2002	481	19.3	60.4
2003	602	42.2	62.8
2004	26	4.4	2.6
2005	332	48.3	49.5
2006	202	9.6	54.4
2007	604	47.3	59.0
2008	775	31.0	18.1
2009	93	7.4	9.2
Total	4,469	22.9	30.2

period, the Midwest had on average about 23 percent of the drought-related indemnity payments for the nation, and drought accounted for approximately 30 percent of the crop losses covered by insurance each year in the Midwest.

In 1988, a very serious drought struck large parts of the United States, including the Midwest. National agricultural losses for 1987–1989 were estimated at around $15 billion, while federal crop insurance payments and federal drought assistance were estimated at approximately $4 billion and $3.4 billion, respectively (Riebsame et al. 1991; Whittaker 1990). Many of these loss estimates were within the Midwest. Another drought in 2002, which also affected the Midwest, resulted in an estimated $2.5 billion in crop insurance indemnity payments, a $9 billion drop in U.S. livestock cash receipts, and a $9.5 billion drop in U.S. net farm income (Henderson and Novack 2002). Although quantitative economic estimates are difficult to identify for a region and attribute directly to drought, these estimates illustrate that droughts affecting an agricultural region like the Midwest can have significant economic implications.

In 1999, a tool to assess current drought conditions, the U.S. Drought Monitor (USDM), was developed in partnership by the National Drought Mitigation Center (NDMC), the U.S. Department of Agriculture (USDA), and the National Oceanic and Atmospheric Administration (NOAA). The USDM is a composite indicator of both agricultural and hydrological drought conditions developed through expert analysis of a suite of climatic and hydrologic variables and feedback from local experts across the country (Svoboda et al. 2002). Figure 13.1 highlights an example of the USDM map for the Midwest region on September 11, 2007. At this time, drought was occurring across the Ohio Valley, with extreme and exceptional drought covering much of Kentucky. Drought and dryness, with pockets of extreme drought, were also occurring across the northern Midwest.

Using the USDM in a historical perspective between the first maps produced in 2000 through the present time, more than 20 percent of the Midwest experienced moderate drought or worse for large portions of 2000, 2003–2004, 2005–2007, and for a brief period in 2008 (Figure 13.2). The locations of these drought events shifted so that most areas of the Midwest have experienced drought at some point during the decade. Similar graphics for individual states illustrate, for example, the major drought in Kentucky during 2007, with minor droughts early in the decade, at the end of 2005, and in 2010. A major drought occurred in Illinois during 2005, with minor droughts in 2000, 2003, and 2007. Nebraska experienced a series of severe droughts between 2000 and 2006. Wisconsin, meanwhile, recorded more drought coverage between 2004 and 2010 compared to earlier in the decade.

Another method to gain an understanding about the severity of drought is to look at the occurrence of impacts in more detail. In the past, however, it has been very difficult to make comparisons because of the lack of impact-related archives. In 2005, the NDMC developed a tool called the Drought Impact Reporter to collect and display drought impacts. For the Midwest, Figure 13.3 shows a series of pie charts representing drought impacts during 2005–2010. The impacts are categorized by year, state, and category. In keeping with the documented water use within the Midwest (see chapter 2 in this volume), agriculture-related impacts are the most frequently reported impacts for the region, with the energy sector having the second highest number. The temporal variability implied by Figure 13.3 is consistent with the time series shown in Figure 13.2, indicating that 2007 was a year during which drought conditions were particularly intense and widespread. The geographic representation of the impacts reemphasizes that droughts occurred in most areas at least at some point during the period.

While drought is a complex phenomenon, in principal drought projections will critically depend on changes in both thermal and hydrological regimes. With respect to the former, it is likely that much of the region will experience 1°C to 3°C of warming (see Figure 2.13). Future projections of precipitation regimes for the Midwest are considerably less uncertain. It is likely that there will be enhanced seasonal variability in precipitation, and it is expected that there will be more intense periods of rainfall (Mishra et al. 2010, O'Gorman and Schneider 2009, chapter 2 of this volume). The combination of increased temperatures and the seasonal variability in precipitation will likely bring changes in the hydrological cycle, which could lead to the potential for dryness and drought conditions (Mishra et al. 2010). To support this assertion, Karl et al. (2008) describe an expected increase in extreme events with climate change, which would also lead to an increase in drought events. The key point remains, however, that droughts have occurred in the past, and, based on available climate projections, there is no reason to not anticipate them across the Midwest—keeping the region vulnerable to drought impacts in the future.

Drought Risk Management Analysis

A drought risk management analysis is a potential starting point to a more comprehensive institutional analysis for understanding how to approach climate change as an issue (Connell 2010). Historical drought response can be described as crisis management in that the focus has been on impacts during or after a drought event. Not surprisingly, given the characteristics of drought, the crisis management approach has meant that the responses have often been uncoordinated and untimely, with little attention placed on trying to reduce future drought impacts (GSA 2007, Wilhite and Pulwarty 2005). The opposite approach, called drought risk management, requires a new paradigm of preparing for future droughts by improving drought monitoring, planning, and mitigation strategies (Wilhite et al. 2005a). Drought risk management is proactive and directed at identifying who and what are at risk in terms of population groups, sectors, and geographic regions, as well as why and how individuals respond to drought events, and then developing plans to address these vulnerabilities.

Although progress has been slow, there has been some success in moving forward with drought risk management (Wilhite et al. 2005a). In the United States, for example, following a recommendation made at a national drought conference held in Portland, Oregon, in 1994, the National Drought Mitigation Center (NDMC) was formed in 1995 at the University of Nebraska with federal support. The mission of the NDMC is to promote drought

risk management. In 1997, the Western Drought Coordination Council (WDCC) was formed following a meeting the previous year of the Western Governors' Association (WGA). An outcome of the WDCC was a quarterly report named the "Western Climate and Water Status," which was an important precursor to the U.S. Drought Monitor (USDM) product. Momentum continued, and the National Drought Policy Act, which formed the National Drought Policy Commission (NDPC), was passed in 1998. The NDPC issued a final report to Congress in 2000 with multiple recommendations on risk management, preparedness, and mitigation, including that a more comprehensive drought monitoring system be established for the United States.

In 2004, the WGA proposed an idea that would become the National Integrated Drought Information System (NIDIS), passed by Congress in December 2006 (WGA 2004). The NIDIS Implementation Plan was released in 2007 (NIDIS 2007). Drought risk management is a key emphasis of NIDIS and its objectives. Since 2007, NIDIS has moved forward in a variety of ways. Multiple knowledge assessments and workshops have taken place across the country, and working groups have been established to focus on (1) the development of a national drought portal, (2) integrated monitoring and assessment, (3) interdisciplinary research, (4) public awareness and education, and (5) the engagement of the preparedness communities. The approach NIDIS is taking to address these issues across all the local, state, tribal, and federal agencies dealing with drought and water is to establish pilot projects focused on a region with specific drought-related needs. The three pilot projects that have been established at this point include the Upper Colorado River Basin (including parts of Colorado, Wyoming, Utah, New Mexico, and Arizona), the Apalachicola-Chattahoochee-Flint (ACF) River Basin (including parts of Georgia, Alabama, and Florida), and the state of California.

An important next step will be to take the lessons learned from, and the innovative strategies identified by, the pilot projects and implement them across the country, including in the Midwest. This institutional approach taken by NIDIS serves as an important model in several ways critical for the climate change issue. There have been considerable discussions describing how the United States needs to establish a national climate service. One of the examples highlighted by NOAA Administrator Jane Lubchenco (2009) in her presentation on the need for a national climate service was NIDIS. Using the NIDIS approach as a model, it has been emphasized that if the United States cannot "get NIDIS right," it will not be able to "get a national climate service right" either (Redmond 2009). NIDIS will also serve an important role within the National Climate Assessment—a status report on climate science and impacts required by Congress every four years—currently underway. Providing benchmarks to track drought severity and impacts over time will hopefully be an ongoing critical component of the climate assessment process. As these examples show, being able to link drought

and long-term climate variability and change issues within institutions will be of general benefit for both issues across the nation and within the Midwest because of their similar characteristics.

Drought Highlights Societal Values

The stress from drought highlights both the strengths and weaknesses that are usually unrecognized in how a society deals with types of long-term threats, and political priorities and underlying cultural values are revealed by difficult choices in these situations. As just one example, what are the relative roles and responsibilities of the government and the individual in preparing for, and responding to, droughts? Specific to the agricultural sector, how effective are agricultural programs and policies in encouraging a culture of drought risk management? This is a difficult question to answer. Drought risk management tends to encourage a culture of self-reliance and resilience (Wilhite and Buchanan-Smith 2005). In contrast, federal drought relief programs, which have focused mainly on agriculture, have historically responded to drought through crisis management. Such ad-hoc drought responses are expensive and do little to reduce drought vulnerability (Wilhite 2001). In fact, some federal drought responses may increase drought vulnerability, by, for example, encouraging ranchers to "wait and see" whether conditions improve, resulting in overgrazed and degraded rangelands (Thurow and Taylor 1999). In 2006, a *Washington Post* investigation (Gaul et al. 2006) provided a scathing assessment of several national drought relief programs, highlighting the political nature of many of these programs.

An assessment of the agriculture-related drought programs and policies—and whether they are increasing or decreasing self-reliance and the long-term sustainability of American agriculture—both in light of drought and climate change is long overdue. Such an assessment would likely start with the U.S. Farm Bill, the federal government's primary agricultural and food policy instrument. The Farm Bill is usually revised every five years or so. The 2008 Farm Bill included several new policies related to drought issues. This bill recognized the U.S. Drought Monitor as the current "state-of-the-art" drought monitoring tool for the United States, and provided guidelines based on conditions depicted by the weekly USDM maps for several agricultural drought disaster assistance programs, targeted particularly toward livestock producers. Discussions on similar modifications are already ongoing for the next farm bill.

Naturally, future vulnerability of agricultural production systems to drought is not only a function of climate change but also of demographics, technology, land and water use patterns (see Figure 17.4 and the associated discussion in chapter 17), and environmental and recreational preferences, which all could potentially amplify drought vulnerability and increase drought impacts. Once vulnerabilities have been determined, societal priorities will dictate how and whether these vulnerabilities are going to be addressed so that future impacts can be reduced.

In the natural hazards communities, this is called "mitigation," and in the climate change communities, it is referred to as "adaptation." The Centre for Research on the Epidemiology of Disasters (CRED) discussed the importance of mitigation for all disasters. Guha-Sapir et al. (2004) noted that in spite of the understanding that risk management is critical to reducing disaster impacts, the money spent for relief overwhelms that spent for risk management funding. The reasons for this are the absence of convincing, quantitative analyses of estimated losses and impacts and the inability to illustrate the importance of mitigation (Guha-Sapir et al. 2004). Along those same lines, the Council of Governors' Policy Advisors recognized that realizing opportunities for mitigation will remain difficult unless officials understand the economic impacts resulting from disasters and the positive quantitative benefits of mitigation taken to reduce those impacts (Brenner 1997). The Multihazard Mitigation Council Report (2005) noted that "a dollar spent . . . on hazard mitigation . . . provides the nation about $4 in future benefits." The 1:4 ratio needs to be proven for drought, and the only way to do this is to quantify impacts, mitigation actions, and the reduced impacts that result from mitigation. These calls for impact data collection were fundamental in the development of the Drought Impact Reporter tool (http://droughtreporter.unl.edu). The goal for this tool is to help promote understanding and encourage drought mitigation strategies. NIDIS (2007) also emphasizes the importance of a drought impact collection system as a necessary component of reducing future drought impacts. Based on the Drought Impact Reporter example, the NDMC has received inquiries about the feasibility of a climate change impacts collecting tool.

Drought Risk Management as a Model

Some would assert that societies will manage climate change in the same way they will manage drought (Connell 2010). A cartoon representing a typical crisis management approach for drought, called the Hydro-Illogical Cycle, is presented in Figure 13.4. Unfortunately, a similar cartoon could probably be developed for the climate change issue as well. The hydro-illogical cycle demonstrates that drought is frequently occurring for an extended time before awareness, concern, and panic take place—with panic not being the ideal response. It also illustrates that, once precipitation returns, the drought experience is quickly forgotten, and apathy develops. With apathy, those involved do not learn from past experiences and do not prepare for future droughts, leading to another round of crisis responses when the next drought occurs. This type of reaction is common for a number of reasons, including the slow, insidious development of drought, past notions that nothing could be done to prepare for drought, the misconception that the government or the individual can handle any drought situation, the hesitancy of governments to disburse funds until absolutely necessary, a lack of planning foresight, and optimism that

frequently leads a person to believe it will start raining tomorrow. By the time the impacts are severe enough that governments must take action, these actions are mostly too late and too little to be effective (Wilhite et al. 2005b).

Drought planning is one mechanism of drought risk management that can help break the hydro-illogical cycle. The objective of planning is to reduce the impacts of drought by identifying the principal activities, groups, or regions most at risk and developing mitigation actions and programs that address the risks and response actions that can be taken during a drought event. The three key components of a drought plan include: (1) a monitoring component so that the evolving conditions are known and placed into proper context, (2) a vulnerability and impact assessment component to understand who is vulnerable to droughts and why, and (3) a mitigation and response component to develop and implement these actions. Such plans provide an effective and systematic means of assessing drought conditions, developing mitigation strategies that reduce risk in advance of drought, and devising response options that minimize economic stress, environmental losses, and social hardships during drought. The best time to plan for droughts, in reference to the hydro-illogical cycle, is after precipitation has returned and valuable lessons gained from the previous drought are still remembered.

Drought planning can take place at a variety of institutional levels. In the absence of any noteworthy federal-level drought planning, significant progress has been made by individual states during the past three decades. In 1982, only three states (Colorado, South Dakota, and New York) had drought plans. By March 2011, 46 states had some kind of drought plan or had one in development, though the specific focus of the plans varies between states (Figure 13.5). In 1998, New Mexico took an important step of incorporating drought mitigation actions into their drought plan. Since then, a handful of states have followed New Mexico's example and have either revised their existing plans to incorporate mitigation or have developed new plans that include mitigation actions. Progress on drought planning has also been made by Native American tribes, particularly in the southwestern United States. Some of the benefits realized through drought planning across the United States include improved drought monitoring systems and the delivery of this information to decision makers at all levels, better identification of the risks associated with droughts, improved interactions with stakeholders, improved public awareness of drought, and protection of water resources during periods of shortage (Wilhite et al. 2005a).

Progress on drought planning is also taking place more often at the local level, and there are opportunities to link these efforts with progress being made in planning for climate change. For example, there is growing recognition of climate change as an issue among local governments and city planners. The American Planning Association released a Planners Advisory Services Report in 2010,

Planning for a New Energy and Climate Future, helping urban planners understand how climate issues intersect with the plans, actions and regulations that they work with on a daily basis. ICLEI—Local Governments for Sustainability USA—in November 2010 unveiled a Climate Resilient Communities™ program to help its member communities plan for and adapt to climate change. Meanwhile, the NDMC, the Oklahoma Climatological Survey, the Illinois State Water Survey, and the Lower Platte River Corridor Alliance, also in 2010, completed a two-year project working with three pilot communities to develop a "Guide to Community Drought Preparedness" (http://drought.unl.edu/plan/DRC_Guide.pdf). The guide was designed so that communities across the nation could take steps toward understanding and reducing their drought risk. A planning section for communities is included within the guide, along with case studies and an extensive resources section.

At the river basin level, the NDMC and NOAA teamed up with three Natural Resource Districts along the Republican River basin in Nebraska to create the Republican River Basin (RRB) Water and Drought Portal (http://www.rrbdp.org/). This portal was specifically designed for farmers, ranchers, resource managers, and decision-makers both within and outside the basin. Included within the portal is information regarding monitoring water supply and drought, water conservation, management strategies, current research, and planning activities. The portal is expected to serve as an important planning resource for decision makers throughout the basin and as an example or model to follow in creating similar websites for other watersheds across the country.

Drought planning is also possible and needed at the individual agricultural producer level. The NDMC, with support from the USDA's Risk Management Agency, has also partnered with extensive faculty from the University of Nebraska–Lincoln, South Dakota State University, and Texas A&M University, as well as with ranchers and advisors from several states in the Great Plains, to develop a "Managing Drought Risk on the Ranch" website and planning process. The website will be launched soon with the objective to help ranchers better prepare for, and respond to, drought. Information on drought monitoring and risk management will be provided, as well as a step-by-step planning process to help ranchers develop individual drought plans. This effort was developed with the expertise of livestock producers who have previously employed drought planning and mitigation strategies and of experts and advisors who have worked directly with producers during droughts.

This overall emphasis on drought planning is fundamental to drought risk management at any decision-making level. Incorporating planning will assist in the preparedness for multiple hazards, including drought and climate change, and will promote sustainability and natural resources management leading toward greater economic and societal security at all levels (GSA 2007).

Concluding Remarks

Droughts will continue to occur across the Midwest in the years to come, and the impacts from these droughts will present a significant risk to local populations and multiple economic sectors. Given the importance of Midwest agriculture, severe droughts affecting agricultural production in this region can have cascading effects worldwide. Climate change adds another dimension to these complex interactions. This chapter highlighted the drought risk management paradigm and how this paradigm can provide insight for managing a world facing climate change. Because drought and climate change have several similarities and both challenge decision makers to develop strategies to respond to changes on longer timeframes, any actions taken to reduce drought vulnerability that are appropriate for the Midwest region may also be considered as climate change adaptation strategies for the region as well.

ACKNOWLEDGEMENTS

I would like to acknowledge Kelly Helm Smith, Denise Gutzmer, and Ya Ding from the NDMC for their assistance in the preparation of this chapter.

REFERENCES

Brenner E (1997). Reducing the impact of natural disasters: Governors' advisors talk about mitigation. Council of Governors' Policy Advisors, Washington, DC.

Center for Research on Environmental Decisions (CRED) (2009). The psychology of climate change communication: A guide for scientists, journalists, educators, political aides, and the

interested public. Available from: http://cred
.columbia.edu/guide/index.html.

CNN (2010). U.N. agency to hold special meeting over food prices. Available from: http://
edition.cnn.com/2010/WORLD/africa/09/04/
un.food/.

Connell D (2010). Drought past and future:
Developing an auditing framework for the
governance of rivers in federal systems.
International Drought Symposium, Water
Science and Policy Center, University of California–Riverside, March 24. Available from
http://cnas.ucr.edu/drought-symposium/
presentations/Daniel%20Connell.pdf..

Economic Research Service (ERS) (2009). Corn:
Trade. Available from: http://www.ers.usda
.gov/Briefing/Corn/trade.htm.

Gaul GM, Morgan D, Cohen S (2006). No
drought required for federal drought aid.
Washington Post, 18 July, A01.

Geological Society of America (GSA) (2007).
Managing drought: A roadmap for change in
the United States. A conference report from
Managing Drought and Water Scarcity in Vulnerable Environments: Creating a Roadmap
for Change in the United States, Longmont,
CO. Available from: http://www.geosociety
.org/meetings/06drought/roadmapHi.pdf.

Gillette HP (1950). A creeping drought under
way. Water and Sewage Works, 104–105.

Guha-Sapir D, Hargitt D, Hoyois P (2004). Thirty
years of natural disasters 1974–2003: The
numbers. Centre for Research on the Epidemiology of Disasters, Belgium. Available
from http://www.emdat.be/old/Documents/
Publications/publication_2004_emdat.pdf.

Heim RR (2002). A review of twentieth-century
drought indices used in the United States.
Bulletin of the American Meteorological Society 83:1149–1165.

Henderson J, and Novack N (2002). Will rains
and a national recovery spur a rural rebound?
The Main Street Economist, December.

Karl TR, Meehl GA, Peterson TC, Kunkel KE,
Gutowski Jr. KE, Easterling DR (2008). Executive summary. Weather and climate extremes
in a changing climate. Regions of focus: North

America, Hawaii, Caribbean, and U.S. Pacific
Islands. In: Karl TR, Meehl GA, Miller CD,
Hassol SJ, Waple AM, Murray WL (eds), A
report by the U.S. Climate Change Science
Program and the Subcommittee on Global
Change Research, Washington, DC.

Lubchenco J (2009). Written testimony. Hear-
ing on "Expanding Climate Services at the
National Oceanic and Atmospheric Administration (NOAA): Developing the National
Climate Service" before the Subcommittee
on Energy and Environment, U.S. House of
Representatives. May 5. Available from: http://
nwseo.org/pdfs/NOAASciComTes.pdf.

Mishra V, Cherkauer KA, Shukla S (2010). Assessment of drought due to historic climate
variability and projected future climate change
in the midwestern United States. Journal of
Hydrometeorology 11:46–68.

Multihazard Mitigation Council (2005). Natural
hazards mitigation saves: An independent
study to assess the future savings from mitigation activities. National Institute of Building
Sciences, Washington, DC. Available from
http://www.nibs.org/client/assets/files/mmc/
Part1_final.pdf.

National Climatic Data Center (2011). Billion
dollar U.S. weather disasters. Available from:
http://www.ncdc.noaa.gov/oa/reports/
billionz.html.

National Integrated Drought Information System
(2007). NIDIS implementation plan. Available
from: http://www.drought.gov/pdf/NIDIS
-IPFinal-June07.pdf.

O'Gorman PA, Schneider T (2009). Scaling of
precipitation extremes over a wide range of
climates simulated with an idealized GCM.
Journal of Climate 22:5676–5685.

Pryor SC, Takle ES (2009). Climate variability,
predictability, and change: An introduction.
In: Pryor SC (ed) Understanding climate
change: Climate variability, predictability
and change in the midwestern United States.
Bloomington: Indiana University Press, 1–18.

Redmond K (2009). Personal communication. 6th
U.S. Drought Monitor Forum, Lower Colorado
River Authority, Austin, TX, October 7–8.

Riebsame WE, Changnon Jr. SA, Karl TR (1991). Drought and natural resources management in the United States: Impacts and implications of the 1987–89 drought. Boulder, CO: Westview Press.

Svoboda M, Lecomte D, Hayes M, Heim R, Gleason K, Angel J, Rippey B, Tinker R, Palecki M, Stooksbury D, Miskus D, Stephens S (2002). The drought monitor. Bulletin of the American Meteorological Society 83:1181–1190.

Thurow TL, Taylor Jr. CA (1999). The role of drought in range management. Journal of Range Management 52:413–419.

United States Department of Agriculture (USDA) (1994). Major world crop areas and climatic profiles. Agricultural Handbook No. 664. Available from: http://www.usda.gov/oce/weather/pubs/Other/MWCACP/world_crop_country.htm.

Western Governors' Association (WGA) (2004). Creating a drought early warning system for the 21st century: The National Integrated Drought Information System. Available from http://www.westgov.org/wga/publicat/nidis.pdf.

Whittaker GW (1990). Effects of the 1988 drought on farm finances. USDA, Agriculture Information Bulletin 611.

Wilhite DA, (2001). Moving beyond crisis management. Forum for Applied Research and Public Policy 16:20–28.

Wilhite DA, Botterill L, Monnik K (2005a). National drought policy: Lessons learned from Australia, South Africa, and the United States. In: Whilhote D (ed) Drought and water crises: Science, technology, and management issues. Boca Raton, FL: CRC Press, 137–172.

Wilhite DA, Buchanan-Smith M (2005). Drought as hazard: Understanding the natural and social context. Whilhote D (ed) Drought and water crises: Science, technology, and management issues. Boca Raton, FL: CRC Press.

Wilhite DA, Hayes MJ, Knutson CL (2005b) Drought preparedness planning: Building institutional capacity. In: Whilhote D (ed) Drought and water crises: Science, technology, and management issues. Boca Raton, FL: CRC Press.

Wilhite DA, Pulwarty RS (2005). Drought and water crises: Lessons learned and the road ahead. Whilhote D (ed) Drought and water crises: Science, technology, and management issues. Boca Raton, FL: CRC Press.

14. Local Adaptation to Changing Flood Vulnerability in the Midwest

C. J. ANDERSON

Introduction

A new public perspective on Midwest flood hazard is emerging. Midwest flood damage in recent years has elicited debate among citizens, city and regional planners, and state and federal government officials on the role of changing climate conditions, and one aspect of the discussion is whether rebuilding should encompass an additional goal of adapting flood protection measures to withstand higher frequency and greater severity of floods under the anticipation of continued climate change (Laasby 2011, Beeman 2011, Schnoor 2011, Hancock 2010, McAuliffe 2010, Hedin 2010, Kousky and Kunreuther 2010).

Adaptation to reduce exposure to future flood hazard is largely a local decision. While the U.S. Army Corps of Engineers (USACE) is responsible for mediating flood risk through, for example, reservoir management, land use decisions by private landowners and community developers ultimately determine the rate at which rainfall turns into runoff and enters a river system. It is also at the local level that government constrains construction of city infrastructure and development of commercial and private property within flood plains. This means communities and private landowners will bear the cost burden of adaptation, and a critical impetus for adaptation will be the aid provided by federal programs to offset the cost of hazard mitigation activities. At present, the potential characteristics of future floods are not a point of consideration in any of federal mitigation assistance programs (i.e., the National Flood Insurance Program (NFIP), Hazard Mitigation Grant Program (HMGP), or Pre-Disaster Mitigation Grant Program (PDM)).

Time is needed for climatologists and hydrologists to learn how to develop projections of future floods and to communicate these projections effectively within public discourse in order to assist in the assessment of the local cost of adaption and within state and federal agencies to guide the development of new mitigation aid programs. Though expediency is urged by the tone of public debate, reliable knowledge is the key to reducing costs and to maintaining the role scientific information plays in encouraging a rational public discourse. The goals of this chapter are to synthesize the current knowledge on rainfall, streamflow, and flood damage and summarize key building blocks to encourage adaptation. This chapter contains the following information: (1) a historical context for the recent Midwest flood damages; (2) an explanation of the linkages between changes in precipitation, streamflow, and flood damage; (3) a novel metric based upon recent findings in hydrological science that may be useful in examining past and projecting future flood risk from precipitation alone; (4) projections of precipitation and streamflow; and (5) a summary of community processes identified as critical to climate change adaptation.

Table 14.1. Categories of flood damage cost with examples

Flood Damage Cost	Examples
Direct tangible	Destruction of property; destruction of crops; destruction of city and transportation infrastructure
Direct intangible	Destruction of cultural treasures; loss of ecosystem functions
Indirect tangible	Reduced property tax revenue from devaluation of property and relocation of property owners; disruption of public services and commercial activities outside of flood area
Indirect intangible	Economic losses from crops that never went to market; commercial revenue if normal business conditions had not been interrupted; loss of trust in authorities

Historical Flood Damage in the Midwest

I adopt descriptions of flood damage as direct or indirect and tangible or intangible from Downton and Pielke (2005) and Merz et al. (2010) (Table 14.1). Because estimates of direct damage contain fewer assumptions and existing databases include primarily direct costs, my discussion is limited to direct damage estimates.

Estimates from the National Weather Service (NWS) are the longest continuous data source of direct flood damage. Though the NWS procedure uses a coarse categorization and estimates are made from diverse sources, disparities between NWS state-aggregated damage estimates and actual damage are 40 percent or less for damages in excess of $500 million (Downton and Pielke 2005). Thus, NWS

estimates, while an incomplete assessment of total losses, represent a robust and broadly meaningful measure. A comparison of state-aggregated direct damage since 1955 (excluding 1980–1983, when NWS did not report flood damage; adjusted to 1995 $) shows that four Midwest states rank among the top 10 across the nation in both total damage and maximum single-year damage (Table 14.2). Illinois, Iowa, Missouri, and North Dakota account for 71 percent of total direct damage in the Midwest (and 15 percent of the damage across the entire United States), and they combine to have the highest total direct damage of noncoastal regions in the United States. What distinguishes damage in these states from other Midwest states is that over half of the total direct damage has accumulated

Table 14.2. Total direct damage (1955–2010, excluding 1980–1983; values for 2010 are preliminary and subject to change), maximum single-year direct damage, and percentage of total from maximum single year (national rank in parentheses). Units: millions 1995 dollars. (Data source: http://www.flooddamagedata.org (1955–2002) and http://www.nws.noaa.gov/hic/flood_stats/Flood _loss_time_series.shtml (2003–2010; state data available by request).)

State	Total damage	Maximum damage	Maximum/ total (%)
Illinois	5,638 (8)	2,751 (10)	49 (21)
Indiana	3,098 (17)	1,085 (18)	35 (30)
Iowa	11,698 (6)	5,982 (4)	51 (19)
Kansas	2,186 (26)	574 (32)	26 (38)
Minnesota	4,172 (12)	1,004 (21)	24 (41)
Missouri	6,451 (7)	3,574 (6)	55 (16)
Nebraska	1,476 (32)	307 (38)	21 (45)
North Dakota	4,967 (10)	3,286 (7)	66 (9)
South Dakota	2,081 (28)	795 (23)	38 (28)
Wisconsin	2,895 (20)	941 (22)	32 (31)

during the largest single year on record. That is, they have a characteristic suscepti-bility to rare but severely damaging, floods that have national implications.

Midwest floods are caused by both snowmelt and rainfall. I loosely separate damages from both types by examining direct flood damage using three collec-tions of states. Damages are summarized for snowmelt floods with data from North Dakota and South Dakota; for rainfall floods with data from Iowa, Illinois, Mis-souri and Indiana; and for a combination of rainfall and snowfall floods with data from Wisconsin and Minnesota. The southern states where rainfall floods are the primary cause of flood damage have annual direct damage generally between $100 million and $500 million (adjusted to

1995 $), whereas both clusters of northern states have generally less than $100 mil-lion annual direct damages (Figure 14.1). Smaller population in the northern states partially explains this disparity (see chap-ter 2 of this volume), so that direct dam-ages when normalized by state population are comparable across the region and sometimes much higher in the northern states (Figure 14.2). Large inter-annual variability renders application of trend analysis highly speculative, but, for all three state groups, the two costliest years of direct damage (total and per capita) have occurred since 1990.

Historical Precipitation and Streamflow in the Midwest

The concept of streamflow elasticity (Schaake 1990, Sankarasubramanian and Vogel 2001) characterizes streamflow sen-sitivity to changes in precipitation in the absence of anthropogenic influences such as ground water pumping, flow diversion, and land use changes. Streamflow elas-ticity is:

$$\frac{dQ}{Q} = \varepsilon \frac{dP}{P} \tag{14-1}$$

Where Q and P are the long-term averages of annual streamflow and precipitation, respectively, dQ and dP are increments in annual streamflow and precipitation, respectively, and e is streamflow elasticity, sometimes called climate elasticity. For streamflow elasticity greater than one, a 1 percent change of precipitation will produce >1 percent change of streamflow (i.e., streamflow is highly sensitive to precipitation change—that is, elastic). Historical measurements for basins of varying drainage area that are relatively devoid of anthropogenic influences are used to estimate streamflow elasticity across much of the Upper Mississippi River basin (UMRB). The range is 2.0–2.5 (Sankarasubramanian and Vogel 2001), and its variability across the UMRB is related to water storage processes (Sankarasubramanian and Vogel 2003). The high streamflow elasticity within the UMRB means that any change in precipitation receipt will be amplified in streamflow.

Streamflow elasticity alone does not explain connections between changes in rainfall and flood damage, because floods are threshold events (with event-specific thresholds for reasons described below), and streamflow elasticity is derived from annual rather than event data. Precipitation is transformed into streamflow—by the processes of water infiltration into the soil, movement of stored soil water into water channels, and the tortuous path taken by surface water over terrain and through vegetation before entering a water channel. For a given precipitation rate, the fraction of precipitation that becomes streamflow varies over time as the dynamic processes of infiltration, storage, and runoff co-evolve, leading to a time-varying threshold of precipitation that can cause a flood. While it is reasonable to expect the principal meaning of streamflow elasticity to hold for events—that is, the runoff fraction of rainfall increases with rain rate—variations of soil conditions from one event to the next also mean that

elasticity is event dependent. Thus, as illustrated below, explanation of changes in flood damage due to precipitation changes requires a long record of flood occurrence reflecting the range of daily precipitation rates and landscape conditions (e.g., soil moisture, land use) associated with floods.

High daily rainfall events exhibit statistically significant increasing trends in a large fraction of stations across the Midwest, with a steeper trend evident in the last quarter of the 20th century (Karl and Knight 1998, Groisman et al. 2005, Pryor et al. 2009). While significant spatial variability in the temporal trends is evident, the large fraction of stations with increasing trends in the Midwest relative to other regions has led to the recognition that this region contains one of the "clearest trends in the U. S. observational record" (CCSP 2008). However, to relate high daily rainfall to streamflow, it is necessary to consider the contribution of high daily rainfall to seasonal or longer periods. Percentile analysis of station daily precipitation indicates that the frequency of days with high daily rainfall in spring and early summer has increased, and this has led to an increase in the seasonal total rainfall in Iowa and Missouri (Pryor and Schoof 2008). An increase in seasonal rainfall suggests an increase in soil moisture reducing the water holding capacity of the soil. Consequently, the daily rainfall rate may exceed the infiltration rate of the soil more frequently. The expected result is an increase in the fraction of rainfall that becomes surface runoff, consistent with the high streamflow elasticity diagnosed in this region.

Analyses of the streamflow data set compiled by Slack and Landwehr (1992), from a collection of stream gauges within rivers that have been relatively unaltered by watercourse regulation, diversion, groundwater pumpage, or land use change, indicate robust increasing trends of minimum and median daily discharge within Iowa, Missouri, and Minnesota, though a trend was not found in maximum daily discharge (Lins and Slack 1999). The authors conclude that the increasing trend of median and minimum daily streamflow is confirmation of larger volume coursing through rivers due to heavy rainfall. The authors further interpret the lack of trend in maximum discharge as an indication that high-rate rainfall increases do not contain water volume large enough to produce region-wide changes in flood levels. Using the stream gauges selected by Slack and Landwehr (1992), Groisman et al. (2001) evaluate trends for rain gauges and stream gauges within the same basin. Their results show statistically significant correlation for the number of days exceeding 99th percentiles for large, medium, and small basins (Table 14.3), providing clear evidence that high daily rainfall and high daily streamflow have increased in tandem. They further examine whether this conclusion is an apparent contradiction with the results of Lins and Slack (1999) by using a regional averaging procedure. In the regional data set, the correlation becomes insignificant at the 99th percentile. They thus hypothesize the localized nature of high daily rainfall and the small number of stream-

Table 14.3. Correlation between number of days for which precipitation or streamflow exceeded extreme percentiles (adapted from Groisman et al. 2001). Asterisk indicates statistically significant correlation. Upper Mississippi River Basin region consists of Minnesota, Iowa, and Wisconsin. The Missouri River Basin consists of Montana, North Dakota, South Dakota, Wyoming, and Nebraska. Midwest region consists of Missouri, Illinois, Tennessee, Indiana, Ohio, and West Virginia.

Region	Percentiles	Correlation
Large Basins (2590 km² < area < 10000 km²), gauges in same basin	Annual number days > 99th percentile	0.58*
Medium Basins (260 km² < area < 2590 km²), gauges in same basin	Annual number days > 99th percentile	0.66*
Small Basins (area < 260 km²), gauges within the same basin	Annual number days > 99th percentile	0.16*
Missouri River Basin	Annual number days > 90th [99th] percentile	0.3* [0.2]
Upper Mississippi River Basin	Annual number days > 90th [99th] percentile	0.7* [0.3]
Midwest	Annual number days > 90th [99th] percentile	0.6* [0.2]

flow gauges in the central United States may mean regional averages are unrepresentative.

The more complex problem of separating human and climatic effects in dictating the frequency with which flooding is observed is illustrated with results from study of the Raccoon River watershed (9,364 sq. km; categorized as a "large river basin" by Groisman et al. 2001) in west-central Iowa. Over the period 1917–2004, land use within the watershed has resulted in an almost complete displacement of small grain production by corn production (row crop acreage has increased from 40% to 80% of the basin) via application of sub-surface drainage tiles to increase the acreage of agricultural managed land. Annual precipitation and streamflow have increased over the 1917–2004 period of record, but only the streamflow trend is statistically significant (Schilling et al. 2008). A water budget analysis indicates the reduction of evapotranspiration in May–July, when small grains would normally reach maturity whereas corn plants are immature, was largely responsible for streamflow increases (Table 14.4). This has implications when considering region-wide trends since similar land use transformation has occurred over large portions of Iowa and Illinois (two of the Midwest states that rank highest in total and maximum single-year flood damage).

A region-wide examination of the potential to separate human and climatic impacts on streamflow is achieved through examination of annual maximum instantaneous peak discharge (Villarini et al. 2011), a temporal aggregation of discharge over less than a day but more than a few minutes. Sub-daily rather than daily maximum streamflow corresponds more closely to the maximum river depth achieved during the year, and may relate more closely to flood damage than daily maximum streamflow. Villarini et al. (2011) separately analyze step changes and linear trends under the assumption that human changes should have more immediate impacts on streamflow than

Table 14.4. Change of precipitation, evapotranspiration, and streamflow for the Raccoon River Watershed in west central Iowa over the period 1917–2004 (adapted from Schilling et al. 2008).

Water balance variables	2004 minus 1917 estimated from least squares trend line	p-value of least squares trend
Annual precipitation	66 mm	0.18
Ratio of annual evapotranspiration to precipitation	0.1	<0.005
Ratio of annual discharge to precipitation	−0.1	<0.005
Ratio of April evapotranspiration to precipitation	−0.16	0.15
Ratio of May evapotranspiration to precipitation	−0.2	<0.005
Ratio of June evapotranspiration to precipitation	−0.14	<0.005
Ratio of July evapotranspiration to precipitation	−0.21	<0.005
Ratio of August evapotranspiration to precipitation	−0.06	0.05

climate changes. Their results show step changes are the primary signal at most stream gauge stations for which a change is evident. This suggests it may be impossible to identify from empirical evidence alone the impact of climatic changes in streamflow within river basins that have been subject to substantial human modifications. Taken together with the results of Lins and Slack (1999) and Groisman et al. (2001), the conclusion that can be drawn is that sampling uncertainty arising from sparse gauge networks and human impacts on landscape may render empirical analysis an incomplete approach for understanding the contribution of precipitation trends to extremes of streamflow and, ultimately, flood damage, especially for regions that aggregate across basins.

Potential for Reconciling Flood Damage, Streamflow, and Rainfall in Basin Analysis

The previous sections argue that changes are evident in flood damage, precipitation, and streamflow, but explanations of how the trends are interconnected remain imprecise. Below I provide a novel analysis that seeks to demonstrate the linkages between rainfall and streamflow. In order so to do it is necessary to first define the three terms:

(i) Waterway travel time. This term describes the time required for rainfall to move through the river system to its outlet. For example, rainfall occurring near Cedar River basin outlet at Cedar Falls, Iowa, and at its farthest extent in Austin, Minnesota, have waterway travel times of one day and six days, respectively. The time required for water to move through the Cedar River basin may permit rainfall on multiple days to flow into and amplify a flood crest as it moves through the river system, a process termed a waterway "traffic jam" (Krajewski and Mantilla 2008). It is estimated for the 2008 flood (see discussion in chapter 2 of this volume) that an absence of phasing between rainfall and the flood crest traveling through the river system would have reduced the flood amplitude by 75 percent (Krajewski and Mantilla 2008).

(ii) The "traffic jam" concept. Key aspects are (1) the frequency of extreme rainfall is an insufficient measure for explaining the frequency of extreme streamflow, (2) extreme streamflow is a function of frequency *and* timing of rainfall, and (3) extreme streamflow may result from a sequence of well-timed and well-placed moderate rainfall days rather than isolated extreme rainfall days.

(iii) A rainfall index defined in the spirit of waterway "traffic jams," called the Waterway Traffic Index (WTI). WTI is the sum over all stations within a basin of rainfall with lag equal to the waterway travel time, divided by the number of stations.

The Raccoon River basin in west-central Iowa contains four weather stations with rainfall records extending backward more than a century from present, and streamflow measurements since 1916 at its outlet in Van Meter, Iowa. In the Raccoon River basin, WTI is the sum of rainfall one day prior at Des Moines and Guthrie Center, two days prior at Rockwell City, and three days prior at Storm Lake, divided by four. Correlation between daily streamflow and WTI is examined for 1916–2009, using only days in the warm-season period March 1–September 1 to reduce the impact of snowmelt on streamflow. Figure 14.3 shows the annual correlation of daily streamflow with several rainfall metrics: WTI, station average rainfall with a lag of one day, and rainfall at Des Moines, Guthrie Center, Rockwell City, and Storm Lake with lags of one day, one day, two days, and three days, respectively. Among the five rainfall metrics, WTI produces the highest correlation with daily streamflow in nearly every year, suggesting efforts to incorporate this waterway "traffic jam"

Table 14.5. Percentiles of projected percentage change of annual precipitation and streamflow (2040–2069 minus 1950–1999) for the region enclosed by 40.5625 to 43.5625 N and 96.5625 to 90.0625 W. The middle column shows the change in annual precipitation amount from the annual average precipitation for 1950–1999.

Precipitation percent change	Delta-P (mm) (1950–1999 average annual P: 846 mm)	Streamflow percent change (2.0–2.5 streamflow elasticity)
5th percentile: −10.2	−86	5th percentile: −20.4–−25.5
10th percentile: −5.3	−45	10th percentile: −10.6–−13.5
20th percentile: 1.6	24	20th percentile: 3.2–4
25th percentile: 3.4	29	25th percentile: 6.8–8.5
50th percentile: 8.0	68	50th percentile: 16–20
75th percentile: 11.2	95	75th percentile: 22.4–28
80th percentile: 11.8	100	80th percentile: 23.6–29.5
90th percentile: 13.3	113	90th percentile: 26.6–33.9
95th percentile: 16.3	138	95th percentile: 32.6–40.7

concept may improve basin-scale analysis of rainfall-streamflow trend relationships and the predictive capacity for flood damage based on precipitation projections.

Precipitation and Streamflow Projections

Climate projections currently do not directly simulate floods and, given the complexity of expected climate and demographic changes, a methodology to generate flood damage estimates from climate projections is not straightforward. This argues for a simpler approach that preserves the relationship between aggregated precipitation and streamflow as expressed in streamflow elasticity. I use the observation-based range of UMRB streamflow elasticity with projections of mid-21st century precipitation to produce projections of change in streamflow from the 20th century to the mid-21st century. The climate projections are taken from the bias-corrected and spatially downscaled climate projections derived from World Climate Research Programme's (WCRP's) Coupled Model Intercomparison Project phase 3 (CMIP3) multi-model dataset and served here: http://gdo-dcp.ucllnl.org/downscaled_cmip3_projections/, as described by Maurer et al. (2007). This archive contains 112 coupled Atmosphere-Ocean General Circulation Model (AOGCM) projections generated from greenhouse gas emissions scenarios B1 (37 AOGCM projections), A1B (39 AOGCM projections), and A2 (36 AOGCM projections). The spread of the model ensemble represents the quantifiable uncertainty range (Jones 2000) of the projected changes. More than 80 percent of ensemble members project an increase in annual precipitation, and the median projection is similar to the change in annual precipitation that has occurred in Iowa over the past 50 years (Table 14.5). For each AOGCM projection the average annual precipitation for 1950–1999 and 2040–2069 was computed over a region across which streamflow elasticity values are variable and the primary flood mechanism is warm-season rainfall (40.5625°N to 43.5625°N and 96.5625°W to 90.0625°W). That is, this is a region of similar precipitation climatology but varying soil characteristics. The UMRB streamflow change projections were computed from the difference in annual average precipitation (2040–2069 minus 1950–1999) for each AOGCM projection, sorting the result from lowest to highest precipitation change to produce an empirical cumulative distribution function (CDF) and selecting percentiles of the precipitation change CDF for which the precipitation change is multiplied by the range of observation-based streamflow elasticity (Table 14.5). The results indicate that, even in the absence of land use change, basins across the Midwest are likely to experience an increase of annual water yield with a median streamflow change of +16–20 percent (almost double the median change in precipitation).

Some Keys for Adaptation to Alleviate Flood Vulnerability in a Changing Change

Climate adaptation may be defined as "[a]djustment in natural or human systems in response to actual or expected climatic stimuli or their effects, which moderates harm or exploits beneficial opportunities" (IPCC TAR 2001). Floods represent a significant natural hazard within the midwestern United States with more than $45 billion (1995 US$) in direct damage since 1955. Based on the synthesis provided above, I assert that historical rainfall mea-surements show evidence of an increase beyond historical variability of the frequency of high rainfall days in the Midwest, and that the increased frequency of high rainfall days is largely responsible for increase in spring to early summer total rainfall across the region. The response within the Midwest river system is an increase beyond historical variability in the number of moderate to high discharge days.

Although precipitation climatology is changing, the linkage between high rainfall days and high streamflow days, however, does not fully explain documented increases in flood damage. By its nature, flood damage is local rather than regional, and, as discussed previously, the impact of changing climate on maximum streamflow in sub-regional basins requires analysis of not only frequency but also timing of high rainfall days. Additionally, human land use and waterway management decisions can become dominant factors in streamflow changes. In light of the importance of both climatic and societal changes to streamflow, one interpretation of the recent occurrence of unprecedented flood damage is that communities with flood vulnerability may have increased their sensitivity to climate change through the developmental choices they have made without consideration to the potential for climate change.

One key for adaptation to alleviate flood vulnerability is community self-assessment. "The solutions to the nation's flood problems lie not only in a better understanding of the hydrological and climatological aspects of flooding, but also in a better understanding of the societal aspects of flood damage" (Pielke and Downton 1999). This assertion argues strongly for communities with historical flood vulnerability to integrate evaluations of changes in rainfall, waterway management, and demographics to form a complete understanding of factors contributing to its current flood vulnerability.

A second key is the recognition that most communities will not have the wherewithal, knowledge, and expertise to complete a comprehensive assessment of flood vulnerability. Recent empirical analysis of flood mitigation plans indicates that a lack of organizational capacity within a community—the financial resources, staffing, technical expertise, communication and information sharing, leadership, and commitment to flood protection—is the primary deterrent to implementation of flood mitigation plans (Brody et al. 2010). A case study of flood mitigation planning in the Front Range of the Colorado Rocky Mountains demonstrates the need for an approach in which decision makers and information providers combine knowledge and expertise to co-produce publicly available resources by collectively iterating on statements of knowledge gaps, information sharing, tools for information sharing, and evaluation of newly generated information (Morss et al. 2005). Consistent with the Colorado Front Range, Brody et al. (2010) argue for the development of collaborative, public decision-making institutions as a key step in support of climate adaptation.

A third key is to adapt policy that is already effective. A study on the cost effectiveness of hazard mitigation programs estimates that during 1993–2003, society avoided four dollars in losses for every dollar spent on mitigation, with benefit cost ratios ranging 3:1 to 7:1 for individual flood projects (Multihazard Mitigation Council 2005). Additionally, it is estimated the federal treasury avoided $3.64 of future discounted expenditures or lost taxes for every $1 spent on mitigation. In order to identify steps that can be taken to incorporate climate change adaptation and resiliency concepts in hazard mitigation plans, the Environmental Protection Agency has partnered with multiple agencies on a pilot project in Iowa. Pilot project participants include federal, state, county, and city government officials; hydrologists; climatologists; and city and regional planners. Findings from the pilot project report suggest several incentives that could be created within existing mitigation and insurance programs. Suggested incentives include (1) additional Hazard Mitigation Grant Program funds to offset costs for communities willing to incorporate climate projections in hazard mitigation plans, (2) cost-sharing incentive for implementation of hazard mitigation planning by increasing the federal contribution when climate change data are used to adopt more aggressive mitigation steps, and (3) allowing communities to improve their scores in the NFIP Community Rating System, thereby lowering their NFIP rates, for mitigation activities motivated by climate projections.

Concluding Remarks

A concern that recent flood damage will worsen with climate change has created a public debate in many Midwest communities about whether rebuilding should include climate adaptation by mitigating for future rather than past floods. From a synthesis of research on trends in precipitation, streamflow, and flood damage, I conclude the following:

- Infrequent but extremely costly floods are characteristic of flood damage statistics in Iowa, Illinois, Missouri, North Dakota, and, to a lesser extent, Indiana. Recent damage has been unusually severe, as many Midwest states have experienced their top 2 costliest flood damage years since the early 1990s.
- Evidence is clear of an increase beyond historical variability of the frequency of high rainfall days in the Midwest, and the response within well-gauged basins that have been relatively unaltered by humans is an increase beyond historical variability in the number of moderate to high discharge days.
- The connections between changes of rainfall, streamflow, and flood damage are imprecisely known for many basins and for the region as a whole. Ambiguity in trend detection and attribution in streamflow arises from large changes in land use and waterway management as well as sparse gauge networks for precipitation and streamflow.

Climate projections suggest a high likelihood of increases in annual rainfall in the Midwest by the mid-21st century, and the streamflow elasticity of this region means that should a precipitation in-crease occur it would be amplified in annual river discharge. Current climate projections indicate an increase in annual streamflow by the mid-21st century of similar magnitude to what has occurred during the past 50 years. Considering that the cost of adapting to potential flood consequences will fall upon communities despite the national economic impact of Midwest floods, there is considerable incentive for climatologists and hydrologists to develop methods for future streamflow scenarios. Sociological research suggests, however, that these estimates must be developed within a broader community of experts and decision makers in order to link directly to economic losses, local policy options, and hazard mitigation plans.

ACKNOWLEDGEMENTS
We acknowledge the modeling groups, the Program for Climate Model Diagnosis and Intercomparison (PCMDI), and the WCRP's Working Group on Coupled Modelling (WGCM) for their roles in making available the WCRP CMIP3 multi-model dataset. Support for this work was provided by from the Iowa State University Bioeconomy Institute and the Iowa Flood Center.

REFERENCES
Beeman P (2011). Lawmakers propose flood-fighting plan. Des Moines Register. Available from: http://www.desmoinesregister.com/apps/pbcs.dll/article?AID=2011101200351.

Brody SD, Kang JE, Bernhardt S (2010). Identifying factors influencing flood mitigation at the local level in Texas and Florida: The role of organizational capacity. Natural Hazards 52:167–184.

CCSP (2008). Weather and climate extremes in a changing climate. Regions of focus: North America, Hawaii, Caribbean, and U.S. Pacific

Islands. In: Karl TR, Meehl GA, Miller CD, Hassol SJ, Waple AM, Murray WL (eds) A report by the U.S. Climate Change Science Program and the Subcommittee on Global Change Research. Department of Commerce, NOAA's National Climatic Data Center, Washington, DC.

Downton MW, Pielke Jr. RA (2005). How accurate are disaster loss data? The case of U.S. flood damage. Natural Hazards 35:211–228.

Groisman PY, Knight RW, and Karl TR (2001). Heavy precipitation and high streamflow in the contiguous United States: Trends in the twentieth century. Bulletin of the American Meteorological Society 82:219–246.

Groisman PY, Knight RW, Easterling DR, Karl TR, Hegerl GC, and Razuvaev VN (2005). Trends in intense precipitation in the climate record. Journal of Climate 18:1326–1350.

Hancock J (2010). Culver calls Ames floods "the new normal," scientists agree. Iowa Independent. Available from: http://iowaindependent.com/41139/culver-calls-floods-the-new-normal-scientists-agree.

Hedin J (2010). An almanac of extreme weather. New York Times. Available from: http://www.nytimes.com/2010/11/28/opinion/28hedin.html?_r=1.

IPCC (2001). Climate change 2001: Impacts, adaptation and vulnerability. IPCC third assessment report. , Cambridge, UK: Cambridge University Press.

Jones RN (2000). Managing uncertainty in climate change projections: Issues for impact assessment. Climatic Change 45:403–419.

Karl TR, Knight RW (1998). Secular trends of precipitation amount, frequency, and intensity in the United States. Bulletin of the American Meteorological Society 79:231–241.

Kousky C, Kunreuther H (2010). Improving flood insurance and flood risk management: Insights from St. Louis, Missouri. Natural Hazards Review 11(4):162–172.

Krajewski WF, Mantilla R (2008). Why were the 2008 floods so large? In: Mutel CF (ed) A watershed year: Anatomy of the Iowa floods of 2008. Ames: University of Iowa Press.

Laasby G (2011). Northwest Indiana region voices hoping astute planning helps slow climate change. Indiana Economic Digest, Available from: http://www.indianaeconomicdigest.net/main.asp?SectionID=31&SubSectionID=136&ArticleID=57809.

Lins HF, Slack JR (1999). Streamflow trends in the United States. Geophysical Research Letters 26:227–230.

Maurer EP, Brekke L, Pruitt T, Duffy PB (2007). Fine-resolution climate projections enhance regional climate change impact studies. Eos Transactions American Geophysical Union, 88(47):504.

McAuliffe B (2010). Getting real about a warmer, wetter Minnesota. Minneapolis Star Tribune, Available from: http://www.startribune.com/local/103011049.html.

Merz B, Kreibich H, Schwarze R, Thieken A (2010). Assessment of economic flood damage. Natural Hazards Earth System Science 10:1697–1724.

Morss RE, Wilhelmi OV, Downton MW, Gruntfest E (2005). Flood risk, uncertainty, and scientific information for decision making: Lessons from an interdisciplinary project. Bulletin of the American Meteorological Society 86:1593–1601.

Multihazard Mitigation Council (2005). Natural Hazard Mitigation Saves: An Independent Study to Assess the Future Savings from Mitigation Activities. National Institute of Building Sciences, Washington, DC. Available from: http://www.nibs.org/MMC/mmcactiv5.html.

Pielke Jr. RA, Downton M (1999). U.S. Trends in streamflow and precipitation: Using societal impact data to address an apparent paradox. Bulletin of the American Meteorological Society 80:1435–1436.

Pryor SC, Schoof JT (2008). Changes in the seasonality of precipitation over the contiguous USA. Journal of Geophysical Research 113: doi:10.1029/2008JD010251.

Pryor SC, Kunkel KE, Schoof JT (2009). Did precipitation regimes change during the twentieth century? In: Pryor SC (ed) Understanding climate change: Climate variability, predictability and change in the midwestern United States. Bloomington: Indiana University Press, 100–112.

Sankarasubramanian A, Vogel RM (2001). Climate elasticity of streamflow in the United States. Water Resources Research 37:1771–1781.

Sankarasubramanian A, Vogel RM (2003). Hydroclimatology of the continental United States. Journal Geophysical Research Letters 30:1363, doi:10.1029/2002GL015937.

Schaake JC, (1990). From climate to flow. In: Waggoner PE (ed) Climate change and U.S. water resources. New York: John Wiley.

Schilling KE, Jha MK, Zhang YK, Gassman PW, and Wolter CF (2008). Impact of land use and land cover change on the water balance of a large agricultural watershed: Historical effects and future directions. Water Resources Research, 44: doi:10.1029/2007WR006644.

Schnoor J (2011). Climate change is upon us; Iowa must adapt. Daily Iowan. Available from: http://www.dailyiowan.com/2011/01/17/Opinions/20662.html.

Slack JR, Landwehr JM (1992). Hydro-climatic data network: a U.S. Geological Survey streamflow data set for the United States for the study of climate variations, 1874–1988. United States Geological Survey Open-File Report.

Villarini G, Smith JA, Baeck ML, Krajewski WF (2011). Examining regional flood frequency in the midwest U.S. Journal of the American Water Resources Association 47:447–463.

15. The Response of Great Lakes Water Levels and Potential Impacts of Future Climate Scenarios

J. R. ANGEL

Introduction

The Great Lakes contain one-fifth of the world's fresh surface water and 84 percent of the North America surface water supply (U.S. EPA 2011). The Great Lakes basin (Figure 15.1) is home to some 34 million people (Great Lakes Information Network, 2011), with a multi-billion-dollar economy and a rich variety of ecosystems. However, the impacts of future climate change on society and the environment in the region are of great concern. The Great Lakes are currently experiencing (among other things) warmer air and water temperatures, decreases of lake ice, longer onset of lake stratification, and more variable water levels (Hinderer et al. 2010). Accordingly, "stakeholders throughout the Great Lakes are beginning to plan for and implement adaptation measures that will help prepare for and diminish these impacts" (Hinderer et al. 2010).

These impacts are not hypothetical. Drought conditions in the last decade have given some insight into the kinds of issues related to low Great Lakes water levels. The National Drought Mitigation Center's Drought Impact Report (NDMC 2010) noted 17 incidences of impacts of low water levels since 1999. Many of the reports dealt with impacts on the operation of marinas and small boats. One incident in 2000 noted that the sustained dry weather caused lake levels to drop between 28 and 33 cm, forcing ships to lighten loads in order to avoid running aground. An official with the Lake Carriers' Association was quoted as saying that this "light loading" costs about $200,000 in cargo per shipment. Another incident in 2000 noted that the wild rice beds dried up in the Kakagon Sloughs, a coastal wetland off of Lake Superior. In a 2007 incident, the report noted that the Edison Sault Electric power plant in Sault Sainte Marie was operating below 50 percent capacity due to low water levels. At the time, Lake Superior was at its lowest point in 81 years.

This chapter examines the response of the Great Lakes water levels to future climate change scenarios and compares them to historical lake levels. The potential impacts of those changes in lake levels are substantial. Some of these impacts are examined here as well.

Lake Superior is the uppermost lake in the basin, as well as the deepest, with an average depth of 147 m. According to historical records (Great Lakes Environmental Research Laboratory (GLERL) 2010) for 1860–2009, annual lake levels in Lake Superior have ranged from 0.33 m above to 0.45 m below its 1860–2009 average. This is the smallest range of annual lake levels of any of the Great Lakes. Record low levels appeared in 1927 and again in 2007, while the highest level was in 1986. Levels have been consistently below average since 1998.

Lakes Michigan and Huron, considered as one hydrologic unit because water flows freely between the two, has an annual range of lake levels from 1.05 m above to 0.62 m below its 1860–2009 average. Lake levels were remarkably high in the 19th century. Record low levels appeared in 1964. Like Lake Superior, levels have been consistently below average since 1999.

Lake Erie is the southernmost and shallowest (average depth of 19 m) of the Great Lakes. Its range of annual lake levels is from 0.89 m above to 0.66 m below its 1860–2009 average. Record low levels appeared in 1934, with record high levels appearing in 1986. Unlike the upper lakes, Lake Erie has experienced average to above-average lake levels since 1967.

Lake Ontario is the lowermost lake in the basin, with an average depth of 86 m. Record low levels appeared in 1935, a year after Lake Erie, and record high levels in appeared 1952. Like Lake Erie, Lake Ontario has experienced above-average lake levels since 1966.

Water flow and hence water levels in the Great Lakes are subject to considerable management. For example, Lake Superior and Lake Ontario have been directly regulated since 1921 and 1958, respectively, so in addition to the resistance to variability of water levels due to the high volumes of the lakes, there is also resistance to significant lake level changes due to management. Accordingly, recent lake-level variability is relatively modest (Lenters 2001). Paleoclimate evidence suggests that Great Lakes water levels have been much lower in the past. Croley and Lewis (2006) reviewed the paleo evidence when the Great Lakes were believed to have been closed (i.e., non-flowing) during an extremely dry period around 7,900 BP. Using a hydrological model and several possible combinations of higher temperatures and lower precipitation, they found that Lake Superior became closed when either air temperatures increased more than 13°C above present or precipitation dropped 60 percent or more below present. The other lakes required similar drastic temperature and precipitation changes. The lakes closed in the order of Erie, Superior, Michigan-Huron, and finally Ontario for increasingly warmer and drier climates.

IMPACTS OF LAKE LEVEL
VARIABILITY

A study by Hartmann (1990) identified several possible impacts from declining water levels in the Great Lakes. The impacts range from environmental (e.g., loss of wetlands, changes in the shoreline) to socioeconomic (e.g., loss of hydropower, increased navigation challenges, loss of shipping, reduced marina access). Her discussion on power production reveals the complexity of these impacts. The Great Lakes are a major source of hydroelectric power in the region, with facilities on the St. Marys, Niagara, and St. Lawrence Rivers. Lower lake levels would lead to decreased flows through these facilities. For example, instances of low flows in the 1960s resulted in hydroelectric power generation losses of 19–26 percent on the Niagara and St. Lawrence Rivers. Any losses in generation would have to be made up by other facilities such as coal-fired power plants, which in turn may be impacted by higher shipping costs and availability of coal as a result of lower lake levels. Finally, the expected increases in summertime temperatures will likely increase power demands at the same time that hydroelectric power generation falls.

One of the most comprehensive studies of potential impacts of future low lake levels was performed by Changnon (1993) along the Illinois shoreline of Lake Michigan. Changnon examined the impacts of the record low levels of the 1964–1965 and conducted structured interviews with 29 lakeshore experts. Most of the Illinois shoreline is covered by Chicago and its suburbs, reflecting valuable lake property typical of most metropolitan areas along the Great Lakes including Milwaukee and Cleveland. He discovered that the record low levels of the 1964–1965 period were too short-lived and not well documented, limiting the period's usefulness as an

analogy for future changes. Therefore, the study included interviews with experts in the private sector (e.g., shipping, engineering) and public sector (e.g., water management, environmental sciences, and harbor maintenance), using scenarios from several sources of 0.9 m, 1.0 m, 1.3 m, and 2.5 m below the 1951–1980 average level of Lake Michigan. The estimated costs from Changnon (1993), adjusted here to 2011 dollars, for the lowering of Lake Michigan by 1.3 m below the historical mean and 2.5 m below that level are shown in Table 15.1. In general, a drop in average lake level from 1.3 m below the average to 2.5 m below the historical mean nearly doubles the resultant costs. The costs of maintaining commercial and recreational harbors were considerable, combining for approximately $1 to $1.3 billion dollars under a 2.5 m drop. However, those costs were overshadowed by the considerable cost on the Chicago River Diversion. As Changnon (1993) outlined, lower lake levels on Lake Michigan would require deepening of all the channels in the Chicago River as well as constructing new bulkheads (walls) all along the shores in the highly urban area. It would also require major changes to the Chicago Sanitary and Ship Canal, including new locks, as well as major changes in the city's sanitary treatment system. Taking into consideration these factors, the cost was approximately $28 to $65 billion for a 1.3 m drop and $56 to $140 billion for a 2.5 m drop. These costs are about two orders of magnitude larger than all the other impacts.

Parry et al. (2007) summarized several other impacts of lower lake levels in the

Table 15.1. Estimated costs associated with lowered Lake Michigan levels of 1.3 m and 2.5 m from Changnon (1993), adjusted to 2011 dollars. Note that all estimates are in millions of dollars, except for the Chicago River diversion, which is in billions of dollars.

Category	Costs due to a decrease in lake level of 1.3 m	Costs due to a decrease in lake level of 2.5 m
Recreational harbors (dredging, bulkhead, docks)	$122 to $196 million	$281 to $439 million
Commercial harbors (dredging, bulkhead, docks)	$352 to $439 million	$707 to $916 million
Water supply (extending intakes, adding new intakes)	$67 to $84 million	$120 to $150 million
Beaches	$9 to $19 million	$9 to $19 million
Storm water (extending and modifying outflows)	$7 to $11 million	$15 to $22 million
Subtotal	$557 to $750 million	$1131 to $1546 million
Chicago River Diversion	$28 to $65 billion	$56 to $140 billion

Great Lakes–St. Lawrence system. Many of these impacts may have considerable economic and environmental costs, some of which may not be fully realized until several years of lower lake levels. The impacts listed include:

• Fisheries: loss of fish species, loss of habitat, contamination
• Industry and energy: less potential for hydropower, less water for industrial uses
• Municipalities: increased water quality problems, potential water supply problems
• Health: increased illness from water contamination and water quality, beach closures

On the other hand, there are always winners and losers in changing lake levels. For example, Changnon (1993) noted that railroad companies gained market share over the Great Lakes shipping companies in shipping raw materials and that dredging companies and consulting engineers benefited from an increased demand for their services.

Higher lake levels bring their own set of impacts. Changnon (1987) examined the cause and impacts of record-high levels of Lake Michigan during the mid-1980s. He found that the primary cause for the high levels was an exceptionally wet 15-year period through 1985. The impacts of these record-high levels were both positive and negative. In general, higher lake levels benefited shipping (allowing heavier loads) and hydropower (higher flows in the outlets of the lower Great Lakes). However, impacts on recreational boating were mixed, with more water for boats in harbors and marinas but more damage to those same facilities. Environmental impacts were mixed as well. For example, shoreline flooding helped some species while harming others. The impacts on the shoreline were decidedly negative and included beach and bluff erosion; destruction of piers, breakwaters, and shoreline property; submersion of docks; and undermining of sewer and drainage lines. The damage to Illinois alone was estimated in excess of $100 million (2011 US$). Furthermore, Changnon found that the International Joint Commission as well as local, state, and federal agencies in the United States were slow to respond and many times were faced with limited options.

The options for controlling Great Lakes water levels are limited. Water flows can be adjusted to a limited extent at the St. Marys Rapids (outlet for Lake Superior), the St. Clair and Detroit Rivers (outlet for Lake Huron), the Niagara River (outlet for Lake Erie), and the St. Lawrence River (outlet for Lake Ontario), as well through the Chicago River and other diversions. However, changes may be limited by the U.S. Supreme Court, as in case of the Chicago River diversion, or by international treaties between the United States and Canada. Furthermore, while changing the flow at a point may be beneficial to upstream concerns, it may have detrimental impacts downstream.

PREVIOUS STUDIES ON POTENTIAL FUTURE LAKE LEVELS

Several previous studies have developed projections of future water levels in the Great Lakes under scenarios of greenhouse gas–induced climate change. These studies relied on a small number of Global Climate Models (GCM) and scenarios of future emissions, most often a doubling of CO_2 concentrations. Cohen (1986) used the results of two GCMs to estimate future changes in water supply and found large reductions in the net basin supply (NBS = the sum of precipitation over the lakes and runoff into the lakes minus evaporation from the lake surfaces) in several instances. However, one scenario yielded a slight increase in NBS. Croley (1990)

applied output of three GCM simulations to a hydrologic model, finding reductions in NBS that ranged from 23 to 51 percent. Hartmann (1990) applied the NBS results of Croley (1990) and determined that Great Lakes water levels declined by 0.13 to 2.5 m, depending on the lake and the scenario. Lofgren et al. (2002) examined changes in Great Lakes water levels using scenarios from two GCMs and a hydrologic model. One GCM yielded sharp drops in lake levels, while a second GCM yielded moderate increases in lake levels. In general, the small set of scenarios used in these studies yielded mixed results of both increased and decreased Great Lakes water levels. In the following section, I present results of lake level analyses under a wider range of climate projections.

Methodology

Angel and Kunkel (2010) examined potential future Great Lakes water levels using a much larger number of climate scenarios. However, that work was focused on Lakes Michigan and Huron. Here the results are examined for all lakes and compared to historical water levels.

Potential future climate states over the Great Lakes region were derived from the suite of GCM simulations produced for the Intergovernmental Panel on Climate Change (IPCC) Fourth Assessment Report (AR4) (Randall et al. 2007). Model data for the Great Lakes region was extracted for the 20th and 21st centuries. Simulations for three emission scenarios (Nakicenovic et al. 2000) were used. The first is a moderately high emission scenario (A2) that yields CO_2 levels of 855 ppm by 2100. The second is an intermediate emission scenario (A1B) that yields CO_2 levels of 705 ppm by 2100. The third is a low emission scenario (B1) that yields CO_2 levels of 535 ppm by 2100. Between 18 and 23 GCMs were used in this project, the number varying depending on their availability for each particular emission scenario. In many cases, multiple runs were made for each model with slight adjustments in their initial conditions. A total of 160 model runs were used for the A2 emission scenario, 211 for the A1B emission scenario, and 194 for the B1 emission scenario. Because there is no universally accepted methodology for evaluating the relative quality of GCMs with regard to their skill in predicting the future (Bader et al. 2008), the model simulations are considered in this study as having an equal likelihood of occurrence.

The GLERL Advanced Hydrologic Prediction System (AHPS) was used to calculate final lake levels under each climate scenario. AHPS is a system of integrated models to estimate lake levels, lake heat storage, and water and energy balances (Croley, 2005). Additional models are employed for channel routing (Hartmann 1988), lake regulation (International St. Lawrence River Board of Control 1963), diversions, and water consumption (International Great Lakes Diversions and Consumptive Uses Study Board 1981). AHPS has been used to make probabilistic hydrologic outlooks of the Great Lakes based on long-range outlooks of temperature and precipitation (GLERL 2008) as well as several studies of climate change

impacts (e.g., Lofgren et al. 2002, Croley and Lewis 2006).

To downscale the results of the GCM simulations for AHPS, change functions were calculated for each of the 565 GCM simulations for all grid points near the basin. The change function represented the change in a climate variable between a future period and the base period built into AHPS (1970–1999) for each month and was expressed as either ratios or differences, depending on the variable. Change functions were computed for maximum, minimum, and mean temperature; precipitation; humidity; wind speed; and solar radiation for three periods (2005–2034, 2035–2064, and 2065–2094).

These change functions were introduced into the GLERL model to compute the expected water levels for each of the periods. The first 15 years of the 30-year period were used to spin up the AHPS model to the new climate state. Then averages were taken of the second 15 years of the period and used here. Lake-level departures were computed between the AHPS run using observations for 1970–1999 and each following period.

Results and Discussion

Historical annual temperatures in the Great Lakes basin have varied by ±2°C since 1900 and were generally cooler in the first half of the 20th century (Figure 15.2). GCM simulations of potential future temperatures over the Great Lakes basin exhibit upward tendencies and an increase of between +0.5°C and +6°C by the end of the current century. In keeping with the modest differences in GHG concentrations (see chapter 2 of this volume), the temperature increases show little difference between emission scenarios or from the historical record through 2025. By 2050, nearly all simulations produced above-average temperatures, with the upper bounds approaching the upper range of the historical levels. By 2075 and beyond, major differences are seen between the emission scenarios. As expected, the high emission scenario A2 yielded the highest temperature changes, followed by the A1B and B1 scenarios. Much of the model distribution of temperatures was above anything found in the historical record by the end of the 21st century. All simulations show temperatures above the 1971–2000 mean by 2075 and beyond.

Historical annual precipitation over the Great Lakes basin varied by as much as ±20 cm relative to the 1971–2000 period. In general, the period before 1965 was considerably drier than the 1971–2000 average. Wetter conditions have prevailed since 1965. Unlike the steady increase in temperatures with time, the precipitation projections for the 21st century show less change over time and only small differences between the emission scenarios. Further, the projections are not consistent in terms of the sign of the tendency. Many GCM simulations showed generally wetter conditions in the future and slight increases at the 95th percentile toward the end of the 21st century. However, several of the simulations showed drier than average conditions over time until the end of the 21st century. In general, the drier scenarios are less severe than what was

experienced in the 20th century. The wetter scenarios are at or slightly above the wettest conditions experienced in the 20th century.

The results of the lake level changes for all four lake groups (Superior, Michigan–Huron, Erie, and Ontario) for all three emission scenarios (A2, A1B, and B1) and for three periods in the future (2020–2034, 2050–2064, and 2080–2094) are shown in Figure 15.3. Also included are the historical lake level departures for the 19th and 20th centuries (GLERL 2011) for comparative purposes.

As shown in Figure 15.3 the range of lake level projections under the various climate projections is large. Further in keeping with the climate projections shown in Figure 15.2, which indicate that the range of projected changes in precipitation and especially temperature increased with simulation time, the range in resulting lake levels also widens over the course of the 21st century (Figure 15.3). A common feature to all lakes, all emission scenarios, and all time periods is that the median projection is for declining lake levels. However, as described in detail below, the range from 5th to 95th percentile in lake level projections always spans zero for all three emission scenarios and time periods considered.

For Lake Superior, the median lake level departures at 2020–2034 for all three emission scenarios are close to zero. However, the range of the model results, as represented by the 5th and 95th percentiles, is already larger than the historical variability in Lake Superior water levels. Historical water levels on Lake Superior vary by only 0.8 m, much less than the other Great Lakes. By 2050–2064, the median lake level departures from model simulations for all three emission scenarios are about 0.2 m below average. The range of lake levels for the A1B and A2 scenarios is wider, compared to 2020–2034, and extends beyond the range of historical water levels. By 2080–2094, the range in potential change in lakes levels is much larger than anything experienced in the historical record. The A2 scenario in particular yielded levels from 0.8 m above to 1.8 m below average.

For Lakes Michigan–Huron, the median lake level departures at 2020–2034 for all three emission scenarios are close to zero, and the range in model results is within the range of the historical lake level departures. Unlike Lake Superior, historical water level departures are double in range on Lakes Michigan–Huron, varying by 1.6 m from 1865 to present. By 2050–2064, the median lake level departures of all three scenarios are below average by about 0.2 m. The range of lake level projections for the middle of this century under the A1B and A2 scenarios increased compared to 2020–2034. All three scenarios produced lake levels below anything experienced in the historical record. By 2080–2094, the potential change in lakes levels at the high end of the distribution is comparable to historical levels. Levels at the low end of the distribution are far below the historical levels, especially at the A1B and A2 scenarios. The A2 scenario yielded levels from 0.9 m above to 1.8 m below average.

For Lake Erie, the median lake level departures at 2020–2034 for all three emission scenarios are close to zero, and the range in model results is within the range of the historical lake level departures. By 2050–2064, the median lake level departures of all three scenarios are below average by about 0.2 m. The range of lake levels for the A1B and especially the A2 scenarios increased compared to 2020–2034. Only the A2 scenario produced lake levels below the historical record. By 2080–2094, the potential change in lake levels at the high end of the distribution is comparable to historical levels. Levels at the low end of the distribution are much below the historical levels for the A1B and A2 scenarios. The A2 scenario yielded levels from 0.6 m above to 1.4 m below average.

For Lake Ontario, the median lake level departures at 2020–2034 for all three emission scenarios are close to zero, and the range in model results is within the range of the historical lake level departures. By 2050–2064, the median lake level departures of all three scenarios are below average by about 0.2 m. The range of lake levels for the A1B and A2 scenarios increased compared to 2020–2034 and produced lake levels below the historical record. By 2080–2094, the potential change in lake levels at the high end of the distribution is comparable to historical levels. Levels at the low end of the distribution are much below the historical levels for all scenarios. The A2 scenario yielded levels from 0.7 m above to 1.7 m below average.

As implied by the detailed description of each lake, the lake level results are sensitive to the greenhouse gas emission scenario principally because there are sizeable differences in the magnitude of temperature increases with time among the three emission scenarios. There are also some differences in the range of precipitation changes, although this is a lesser effect. Furthermore, while the temperature scenarios show consistent warming, the precipitation scenarios show a wide range of both wetter and drier conditions. Thus, the range of resulting lake levels is large, varying from sizeable increases to large declines. The A2 high emission scenario produced larger temperature increases and a slightly greater range of precipitation changes than either the A1B or the B1 emission scenarios. Therefore the A2 emission scenario resulted in the widest range of lake levels of the three greenhouse gas emission scenarios.

Concluding Remarks

In general, the climate change projections presented herein and the modeled results for future lake levels indicate that future water levels in Lake Superior are likely to be close to the range of results found in the historical record. For the remaining lakes, the upper ranges of modeled results are similar to the historical records. However, the lower ranges are about a meter lower than the historical records. This suggests that possible increases in lake levels, if realized, would be within the range of past experience on the Great Lakes. However, the possible decreases in lake levels could be well outside the range of past

experience, requiring much different and more significant responses and adaptations than in past experience.

The review of impacts from the historical variability of lake levels shows that there are significant issues with both high and low lake levels on the Great Lakes. As Changnon (1993) indicates, the costs can increase rapidly for larger departures of lake levels—in some cases doubling from a 1.5 to 2.5 m drop. While the results here provide no clear indication of which way future lake levels will go, Hinderer et al. (2010) correctly demonstrates that the time to begin planning for and adapting to a wider range of lake levels is now.

ACKNOWLEDGMENTS
This work was supported by the state of Illinois and the Illinois State Water Survey. I would like to thank Thomas Croley II for providing the GLERL model software. Any opinions, findings, and conclusions or recommendations expressed in this publication are those of the author and do not necessarily reflect the views of the Illinois State Water Survey.

REFERENCES
Angel JR, Kunkel KE (2010). The response of Great Lakes water levels to future climate scenarios with an emphasis on Lake Michigan–Huron. Journal of Great Lakes Research, 36: doi:10.1016/j.jglr.2009.09.006.

Bader DC., Covey C, Gutowski Jr. WJ, Held IM, Kunkel KE, Miller RL, Tokmakian RT, Zhang MH (2008). Climate models: An assessment of strengths and limitations. A report by the U.S. Climate Change Science Program and the Subcommittee on Global Change Research, Department of Energy, Office of Biological and Environmental Research, Washington, DC.

Changnon SA (1987). Climate fluctuations and record-high levels of Lake Michigan. Bulletin of the American Meteorological Society 68:1394–1402.

Changnon SA (1993). Changes in climate and levels of Lake Michigan. Climatic Change 23:213–230.

Cohen SJ (1986). Impacts of CO_2-induced climatic change on water resources in the Great Lakes basin. Climatic Change 8:135–153.

Croley II TE (1990). Laurentian Great Lakes double-CO_2 climate change hydrological impacts. Climatic Change 17:27–47.

Croley II TE (2005). Using climate predictions in Great Lakes hydrologic forecasts. In: Garbrecht J, Piechota T (ed) Climatic variability, climate change, and water resources management. American Society of Civil Engineers, Arlington, VA .

Croley II TE, Lewis CFM (2006). Warmer and drier climates that make terminal Great Lakes. Journal of Great Lakes Research 32:852–869.

GLERL (Great Lakes Environmental Research Laboratory) (2008). Probabilistic outlooks of Great Lakes hydrology and water levels. Available from: http://www.glerl.noaa.gov/wr/ahps/curfcst/curfcst.html.

GLERL (NOAA Great Lakes Environmental Research Laboratory) (2011). Great Lakes water level observations. Available from: http://www.glerl.noaa.gov/data/now/wlevels/levels.html.

Great Lakes Information Network (GLIN) (2011). Peoples of the Great Lakes. Available from: http://www.great-lakes.net/envt/flora-fauna/people.html.

Hartmann HC (1988). Historical basis for limit on Lake Superior water level regulations. Journal of Great Lakes Research 14:316–324.

Hartmann H (1990). Climate change impacts on Laurentian Great Lakes levels. Climate Change 17:49–67.

Hinderer J, Haven C, Koslow M (2010). Climate change in the Great Lakes: Advancing the regional discussion. Great Lakes Commission. Available from: http://glc.org/climate/pdf/Climate-Change-in-the-Great-Lakes-Advancing-the-Regional-Discussion.pdf.

International Great Lakes Diversions and Consumptive Uses Study Board (1981). Great Lakes diversions and consumptive uses. International Joint Commission, Washington, DC.

International St. Lawrence River Board of Control (1963). Regulation of Lake Ontario: Plan 1958-D., Washington, DC.

Lenters JD (2001). Long-term trends in the seasonal cycle of Great Lakes water levels. Journal of Great Lakes Research 27:342–353.

Lofgren BM, Quinn FH, Clites AH, Assel RA, Eberhardt AJ, Luukkonen CL (2002). Evaluation of potential impacts on Great Lakes water resources based on climate scenarios of two GCMs. Journal of Great Lakes Research 28:537–554.

Nakicenovic N et al. (2000). Special report on emissions scenarios: A special report of Working Group III of the Intergovernmental Panel on Climate Change. Cambridge, UK: Cambridge University Press. Available from: http://www.grida.no/climate/ipcc/emission/index.htm.

National Drought Mitigation Center (2010). Drought impact report. Available from: http://droughtreporter.unl.edu/.

Parry ML, Canziani OF, Palutikof JP, van der Linden PJ, Hanson CE (eds) (2007). Climate change 2007: Impacts, adaptation and vulnerability. Contribution of Working Group II to the Fourth Assessment Report of the Intergovernmental Panel on Climate Change, Cambridge University Press, Cambridge, UK.

Randall DA, Wood RA, Bony S, Colman A, Fichefet T, Fyfe J, Kattsov V, Pitman A, Shukla J, Srinivasan J, Stouffer RJ, Sumi A, Taylor KE (2007). Climate models and their evaluation. In: Solomon S, Qin S, Manning M, Chen Z, Marquis M, Averyt KB, Tignor M, Miller HL (eds) Climate change 2007: The physical science basis. Contribution of Working Group I to the Fourth Assessment Report of the Intergovernmental Panel on Climate Change. Cambridge, UK: Cambridge University Press.

US Environmental Protection Agency (2011). Great Lakes basic information. Available from: http://www.epa.gov/glnpo/basicinfo.html.

16. Vulnerability of the Energy System to Extreme Wind Speeds and Icing

S. C. PRYOR AND R. J. BARTHELMIE

Introduction

EXTREME WIND SPEEDS AND
ICING AS SOURCES OF RISK
AND VULNERABILITY

The economies and ecosystems of North America tend to be much more sensitive to extremes than to average conditions. However, "incomplete understanding of the relationship between changes in the average climate and extremes . . . limits our ability to connect future conditions with future impacts and the options for adaptation" (Field et al. 2007). Here we examine two climate extreme events that are of particular importance to the energy, infrastructure, transportation, forestry, and insurance industries in the midwestern United States: extreme wind speeds and icing. Below we briefly introduce the metrics used, provide examples of risks posed by these phenomena, and indicate the availability of adaptation strategies to reduce current—and possible future—vulnerability. In the following sections we evaluate the current vulnerability within the Midwest using a range of climate simulations and possible changes in the risk under a range of climate change projections.

"Extreme wind speeds" describe the right tail of the probability distribution of sustained wind speeds, typically averaged over time periods of 10 minutes to one hour. "Wind gusts" are by definition transient phenomena and are typically averaged over a 3-second period. Both parameters are used in design standards in the context of ensuring structural integrity under extreme loading cases (Pryor and Barthelmie 2012), and extreme values of these parameters have been linked to failures in the electricity distribution network (Reed 2008, Yu et al. 2009, Banik et al. 2010). Table 16.1 summarizes recent economic losses across the continental United States associated with extreme wind events *not* attributable to thunderstorm-derived downbursts or tornadoes. Despite their importance to regional fatalities and economic losses (Black & Ashley 2010), we explicitly exclude events associated with deep convection (thunderstorms) because the resolution and characteristics of the Regional Climate Model (RCM)

213

Table 16.1. Annual summaries of human health impacts and economic costs from high wind events in the continental United States normalized to 2010 dollars. (Data source: http://www.economics.noaa .gov/?goal=weather&file=events/storm&view=costs.)

Year	Fatalities	Injuries	Property damage (millions of dollars)	Crop damage (millions of dollars)
2004	26	68	3,876	398
2005	7	43	66	25
2006	26	133	215	17
2007	16	76	275	1.3
2008	42	122	1,274	179
2009	25	68	204	0.1
2010	18	63	60	1.2

simulations used herein preclude characterization of such phenomena. The RCM simulations analyzed herein likely have substantially higher skill in capturing strong wind events associated with synoptic-scale phenomena (such as cold front passages) (Browning 2004, Lacke et al. 2007, Pryor et al. 2012a). Further, extreme winds associated with synoptic scale phenomena comprise 70 percent of damaging wind events in the Midwest and are likely to be manifest on larger (regional) spatial scales (Changnon 2007, Changnon 2009). Comparatively few studies have focused on possible evolution of extreme storm climates and extreme wind speeds in the context of infrastructure damage and insurance losses (Schwierz et al. 2010). However, such changes, if realized, may also have implications for multiple economic sectors.

"Atmospheric icing" describes accretion of ice on structures and/or other objects due to freezing precipitation (which gen-

erally leads to accretion of glaze) and/or freezing fog (or ground-based cloud) (which leads to accretion of rime) (Fikke et al. 2007). As indicated by this brief précis, icing is a complex phenomenon (Degaetano et al. 2008, Farzaneh 2008, Thorkildson et al. 2009). Ice storms are typically associated with solid precipitation that falls through a warm layer, causing melting of the precipitate, which subsequently refreezes on contact with a surface that has a temperature below 0°C. Riming from deposition of smaller cloud droplets is less dramatic but can dominate icing events in some locations (Thorkildson et al. 2009). The probability of icing and the density of the ice formed are nonlinear functions of prevailing meteorological conditions (Figure 16.1). The mass of ice accumulated, and therefore the likelihood of infrastructure impact, are thus also highly nonlinear functions of the atmospheric conditions (Farzaneh 2008). Across the United States as a whole, between 1990 and 1994, ice storms caused an average of 10 fatalities and 528 injuries, and were associated with economic losses of $380 million each year (Irland 2000). A prominent example of this type of event was the ice storms of January 1998 that caused over 3 million people to lose power in eastern Canada, New York, and New England, but such events are also common within the Midwest (Changnon 2003, Jones et al. 2004a). Herein we use a simple index of icing probability, and although it should be acknowledged that icing coupled with high wind speeds can yield substantial negative consequences for infrastructure (Farzaneh 2008), here we treat these phenomena in isolation.

RISK AND VULNERABILITY OF THE ENERGY AND OTHER SECTORS IN THE MIDWEST

We focus here on the risk and vulnerability of infrastructure in the Midwest to extreme winds and icing with a particular focus on the energy system and specifically the distribution network. The North American power network comprises over 10,000 power plants, many of which lie within the Midwest (see chapters 2 and 12 of this volume), and hundreds of thousands of miles of transmission lines and distribution networks. In 2000 the North American power network was estimated to have a total worth of over US$800 billion, with the transmission and distribution valued at US$358 billion (Massoud 2003). While herein we focus on the climate component of the vulnerability of the energy sector to icing and extreme winds it is worth noting that the exposure of the sector is also likely to evolve. From 1988 to 1998 the electricity demand in the United States rose by 30 percent, while the transmission system capacity increased by only 15 percent (Massoud 2003), potentially leading to increased vulnerability of the system to cascading failures. Historically, power outages in the United States have lead to economic losses of US$30–$130 billion annually (LaCommare & Eto 2004). While not all power supply failures are weather related, from 1994 to 2004, fourteen U.S. utilities experienced 81 non-

hurricane storms, which cost an average of US$49 million per storm (Johnson 2005).

The United States has just over 200,000 miles of transmission cable, only about 5,000 miles of which are underground (Abel 2009). In the Midwest an even smaller fraction of transmission lines are underground (<1%). Large-scale blackouts are comparatively infrequent in the Midwest, but icing events and windstorms are the two dominant meteorological causes of historical failures (Hines et al. 2009). Although the primary focus here is the energy sector, major icing and windstorm events also cause a range of impacts and economic losses across a range of sectors (e.g., forestry (Rebertus et al. 1997, DeWalle et al. 2003) and aviation (Ratvasky et al. 2010)). The electricity transmission system within the midwestern region is operated by a number of Independent Transmission System Operators. The two largest are the Midwest ISO (which covers most of Illinois and Indiana along with North Dakota, Minnesota, Wisconsin, Iowa, Michigan, and parts of Missouri and Ohio), and the PJM Interconnection (which covers parts of Illinois, Indiana, and Ohio, along with most of Pennsylvania, Virginia, and other eastern states). The Midwest ISO Transmission Expansion Plan 2009 calls for $903 million of investment in new transmission infrastructure to (1) support several state renewable portfolio mandates and other activities designed to facilitate increased harnessing of the regions renewable energy resources (e.g., wind power), (2) reduce the risk of demand exceeding transmission capacity, and (3) provide economic benefit by increased efficiency via facilitating transmission of power by the lowest cost source. Currently MISO has over 55,000 miles of transmission lines and experienced peak demand of 136,520 MW in summer 2009 and 87,207 MW during the winter season 2009–2010 (Midwest ISO 2010). The 2009 Transmission Expansion Plan calls for approximately 3,350 miles of new or upgraded transmission lines by 2019 (Midwest ISO 2009).

Nonconvective high wind events are defined by the NWS as comprising sustained wind speeds of at least 18 ms^{-1} (40 mph) for at least one hour and/or a wind gust of at least 26 ms^{-1} (58 mph). Such events are fairly rare in the states bordering the Great Lakes (comprising less than 0.05% of observations) (Lacke et al. 2007), but caused 21 percent of weather related deaths and property damage in the region (Knox et al. 2008). Further, in states bordering the Great Lakes, nonconvective high winds caused "more property and crop-related damages than did winds produced by either convective storms or tornadoes from 2000 to 2004" (Lacke et al. 2007). Structures and the electricity transmission network can be designed to withstand the dynamic loading that results from high and gusty wind events, but over-engineering can be costly. Thus robust climate projections of such phenomena are of tremendous value in system design, management, and maintenance.

Ice accumulation on components of the aboveground electricity distribution network (including overhead power transmission and distribution lines and associated poles and towers) can change the aerodynamics of the transmission lines, causing short circuits (Farzaneh 2008). If enough ice forms, the weight can cause the lines to collapse, causing loss of distribution capacity and thus a failure to supply consumer demands for electricity. The results of such events are extremely costly to repair and can cause disruption to supply over many days. The ice storm in December 2002 caused power interruptions to over 1.5 million Duke customers in the southeastern United States that in some instances lasted over a week (Degaetano et al. 2008). The southern portions of the Midwest also experienced significant icing during this event, with ice accumulations of over 5 mm (radial ice thickness) in some locations (Jones et al. 2004a). During the December 2002, power outages were caused primarily by ice-covered trees and branches falling on power lines. This level of damage occurred for radial ice thicknesses as small as 8 mm (Jones et al. 2004a). As context for these accumulations, ice storms are defined by the NWS as resulting in 0.25 inch (6.4 mm) of ice on exposed surfaces.

A further growing impact sector for icing within the Midwest is the wind energy industry (see chapter 2 of this volume). Ice accumulation on wind turbines can degrade turbine performance (due to changes in the blade aerodynamics and thus the "lift" experienced on the blade) and durability (due to increased mechanical stresses on components) (Frohboese & Anders 2007, Hochart et al. 2008). Further, icing can even lead to safety concerns if ice is thrown from the rotating blades (IEA 2008).

Engineering solutions to icing both on electrical distribution infrastructure and wind turbines exist. For example, in the case of wind turbines, either passive methods, such as modifications to blade design to reduce ice accumulation, or active methods, such as blade heating, may be deployed to ameliorate the risk (Maissan 2001, Makkonen et al. 2001, Hochart et al. 2008). Equally, prevention of damaging ice accumulation or melting of accumulated ice is possible for electricity distribution lines using load and short-circuit currents (Merrill & Felttes 2006, Peter et al. 2007). If icing is sufficiently frequent, or costly when it occurs, an underground power distribution system can be deployed (Bumby et al. 2010), or support structures can be reinforced (Farzaneh 2008). The efficacy of such measures needs to be carefully evaluated in the context of the incremental costs and benefits of such adaptation options (de Bruin et al. 2009) and thus will benefit from the climate projections developed and presented herein.

Based on the prior discussion, the questions that must be posed are as follows: is the current vulnerability sufficient to merit deployment of measures to reduce the risk associated with icing and/or extreme wind events, and in light of our best climate projections, are these or other adaptation mechanisms cost-effective and/or necessary to overcome likely future risk? As part of efforts to quantify the risk and identify robust adaptation options, herein we consider a range of current and possible future climate scenarios as manifest in different RCM simulations.

CHARACTERIZING UNCERTAINTIES IN CLIMATE PROJECTIONS

Any effort at developing climate projections for climate risk, vulnerability, and impact assessments should be conducted in a manner consistent with end-user needs and predictor skill (Leary et al. 2007). Such efforts should also incorporate assessment and attribution of uncertainty (Meehl et al. 2009). One analysis of different uncertainty sources in coupled Atmosphere-Ocean General Circulation Model (AOGCM) projections of decadal-mean global-mean surface air temperature in the 21st century found that for the first decade, internal (inherent) variability was important, model uncertainty dominated out to a 50-year lead time, and subsequently, emission scenario—and thus radiative forcing—dominated (Hawkins & Sutton 2009). A further study proposed the following ranking of sources of projection spread for intense and extreme wind speed projections for the 21st century over Scandinavia: model formulation (AOGCM and RCM), initial conditions, internal variability, emission scenario and stochastic influences within an AOGCM (Pryor and Schoof 2010). While a comprehensive assessment of uncertainty is beyond the scope of the current work, herein we analyze output from a suite of AOGCM-RCM simulations and apply a range of statistical tools in an attempt to quantify at least part of the uncertainty in the climate projections of the variables derived herein. Specifically, given that different models incorporate different techniques to discretize the equations and to represent sub-grid effects, we use a multi-model data set to investigate model uncertainty. We analyze simulations from RCMs nested within lateral boundary conditions from three AOGCMs and one observationally derived data set (the NCEP-DoE reanalysis (Kanamitsu et al. 2002)) to examine the sensitivity of extreme winds and icing frequency that derives from the model used to provide information to the RCM about conditions outside the RCM model domain. Further, we compare and contrast the spatial fields and climate change signal that derives from variations in the RCM used to conduct the simulations.

OBJECTIVES

Projection of future impacts of climate is particularly challenging in the case of extreme events. Thus, the research described herein was undertaken with the objectives of addressing the following key research questions:

- How skillful are RCMs in simulating the near-surface wind climate, including extreme wind speeds and gusts, and the parameters that dictate the intensity and frequency of icing?
- Is there evidence for possible evolution of these phenomena?
- How certain/uncertain are the climate projections? For example, does the climate change signal exceed differences in simulations of the variable during the control period?
- Are the changes of sufficient magnitude to present a significant change in risk?

Herein we use the most inclusive definition of the midwestern United States

as described in chapter 2 of this volume (Figure 16.2). Simulations of 1979–2000 are analyzed to represent the historical climate (referred to herein as the control period). Simulations of 1979–2000 are thus used to quantify the current frequency and intensity of extreme winds and icing. These results provide information pertinent to current vulnerability/risk and a context for considering the climate projections. The future time period (2041–2062) is selected to represent a temporal window that encompasses the possibility of a discernible climate change signal, but is sufficiently "close-at-hand" to be of value in current planning processes. For example, both current and planned wind farms will still be within their operational lifetimes.

Data and Methods

MODEL SIMULATIONS

The RCM simulations analyzed herein are drawn from the North American Regional Climate Change Assessment Program (NARCCAP) (Mearns et al. 2009). Herein we used a subset of those simulations taken from three AOGCMs, one reanalysis data set (the NCEP-DoE reanalysis data (Kanamitsu et al. 2002)), and three RCMs (Table 16.2).

The future simulations are for the A2 emissions scenario (Nakicenovic & Swart 2000). This emission scenario is at the higher end of those considered by the IPCC. It equates to global greenhouse gas emissions of approximately 80 Gt CO_2-eq per year (twice the rate in 2000) by approximately 2055, but given

Table 16.2. Matrix of coupled atmosphere-ocean general circulation model (AOGCM, or NCEP reanalysis) and regional climate model (RCM) simulations used here. For each model combination, the metric calculated (fifty-year return period wind speed (U_{50}), fifty-year return period gust ($Gust_{50}$), or icing frequency (Icing)), and time windows for which the simulations were analyzed are shown in the appropriate grid cell. The AOGCMs are: GFDL = Geophysical Fluid Dynamics Laboratory model (CM2.1) (Delworth et al. 2006), CGCM3 = Canadian model (Scinocca et al. 2008), HadCM3 = Hadley Centre model (Pope et al. 2000). The RCMs are: RegCM3 = Regional Climate Model 3 used by the University of California–Santa Cruz (Pal et al. 2007), CRCM = Canadian regional climate model (de Elia & Cote 2010), HRM3 = third-generation Hadley Centre RCM (Jones et al. 2004b).

AOGCM $\longrightarrow$ RCM $\downarrow$	NCEP	GFDL	CGCM3	HadCM3
RCM3 (RegCM3)	Icing, U_{50} (1979–2000)	Icing, U_{50} (1979–2000, 2041–2062)	Icing, U_{50} and $Gust_{50}$ (1979–2000, 2041–2062)	
CRCM (MRCC)	Icing, U_{50} (1979–2000)		Icing, U_{50} (1979–2000, 2041–2062)	
HRM3 (HadRM3)	Icing, U_{50} and $Gust_{50}$ (1979–2000)			Icing, U_{50} and $Gust_{50}$ (1979–2000, 2041–2062)

the future period considered is relatively near-term, variations in climate forcing between the different emission scenarios is rather modest (Solomon et al. 2007). Thus, results presented herein are likely representative of a broad suite of possible future greenhouse gas emissions and atmospheric concentrations.

The climate sensitivities (i.e., global temperature response to a doubling of CO_2) of the AOGCMs used are 3.4°C, 3.4°C, and 3.3°C (Mearns et al. 2009), and thus differences in the climate projections derived using the three AOGCMs for the lateral boundaries likely differ due to differences in the climate model physics rather than the global temperature sensitivity of the models. The RCM simulations were conducted at a grid resolution of approximately 0.44 × 0.44° (~ 50 × 50 km). The temperature, specific humidity, and wind speed data used herein were archived at a 3-hourly interval, while the gust represents a once-daily maximum wind gust.

METHODS AND METRICS

We compute two metrics of extreme wind speeds key to dictating extreme loads on structures: the 50-year return period values of both the 10-minute sustained wind speed (U_{50}) and 3-second gust wind speed ($Gust_{50}$). With respect to the latter, RCM3 and HRM3 include a parameterization of wind gusts based on the concept that if the mean turbulent kinetic energy of deep eddies exceeds the buoyant energy between the surface and any parcel height within the planetary boundary layer, that parcel can be brought to the surface. Thus, the wind gust close to the surface is the maximum wind speed at any level for which that criterion is fulfilled (Brasseur 2001, Brasseur et al. 2002).

Fifty-year return period wind speeds and gusts are derived herein under the assumption that the tail of the probability distribution of wind speeds (and gusts) is exponential, the accumulated probability of extreme winds is double exponential (Cook 1986, Mann et al. 1998), and the wind speed for a 50-year return period can thus be determined from:

$$U_T = \frac{-1}{\alpha} ln \left[ln \left(\frac{T}{T-1} \right) \right] + \beta \qquad (16-1)$$

where U_T is the wind speed for a given return period ($T = 50$ years) and the distribution parameters (α and β) are derived by the method of moments (Bury 1975, Abild et al. 1992).

Assuming a Gaussian distribution of U_T, then 95 percent of all realizations will lie within $\pm 1.96\sigma$ of the mean, and thus $s(U_T)$, can be used to provide 95 percent confidence intervals on the estimates of extreme winds with any return period:

$$\sigma\left(U_T\right) = \frac{\pi}{\alpha} \sqrt{\frac{1 + 1.14 k_T + 1.10 k_T^2}{6n}} \qquad (16-2)$$

where

$$k_T = -\frac{\sqrt{6}}{\pi} \left(ln \left[ln \left(\frac{T}{T-1} \right) \right] + \gamma \right)$$

and γ is Euler's constant.

Although icing is a complex phenomenon, herein we use a simple index of icing probability, in which icing is assumed to occur when the simulated surface air temperature in a given RCM grid cell is below freezing (T < 0°C) and the relative humidity (RH, computed based on

the modeled specific humidity) exceeded 95 percent (Claussen et al. 2007). The accumulated ice is assumed to persist as long as the air temperature remains below freezing (Claussen et al. 2007).

We present results of climate change projections in the context of the historical (control) period and show percent changes in the parameters of interest only when the estimate for the future period for a given grid cell lies beyond the 95 percent confidence intervals computed for the control period. We also use Taylor diagrams (Taylor 2001) as a mechanism for synthesizing a comparison of the climate change signal with sensitivity to lateral boundary conditions. Taylor diagrams are a concise summary of how well two fields match each other. They depict three components of the degree to which patterns are similar: the correlation (r) of the spatial patterns (shown by the azimuthal angle), the ratio of the standard deviation in the fields (σ_m/σ_r, shown by the radial distance from the origin on the x-axis at a ratio of the standard deviation of the two fields—from the model and a reference field (σ_m/σ_r) = 1), and the root mean square difference (RMSD) in the fields (shown by the distance from the origin, on the x-axis at $\sigma_m/\sigma_r=1$).

Results

HOW SKILLFUL ARE RCMS IN REPRODUCING THE WIND CLIMATE OF THE MIDWEST?

Regional Climate Models typically exhibit lower skill in reproducing wind climates than many other parameters (Pryor et al. 2009), and RCMs tend to closely follow the driving AOGCMs in their representation of the large-scale circulation (and thus flow fields). However, the skill with which RCMs simulate wind climate is increasing, and output from RCM is increasingly being used to examine possible evolution of wind regimes, including extremes (Della-Marta et al. 2009, Pinto et al. 2009, Pinto et al. 2010, Pryor and Barthelmie 2011, Pryor et al. 2012a, Pryor et al. 2012b).

Prior to application of the RCM output to derive extreme metrics of the near-surface wind speeds, output from each RCM simulation of the control period was used to compute the annual mean wind speed and interannual variability for comparison with observationally derived estimates. The results indicate that at the regional level all of the RCMs generate realistic mean wind climates and have an interannual variability similar to that in the DS3505 observational dataset (Figure 16.2). They also indicate that, irrespective of the lateral boundary conditions, HRM3 simulated mean wind speeds are biased low compared to the other two RCMs.

As a further evaluation of the wind climates as simulated by the RCMs analyzed herein, the wind speeds from 1979–2000 were extrapolated from a nominal height of 10 m above ground level (a.g.l.) to 50 m a.g.l. following the procedure in Pryor and Barthelmie (2011) used to compute an energy density and compared with an independent evaluation of the "power in the wind" derived from the National Renewable Energy Laboratory (NREL) (Elliott et

Table 16.3. Degree of agreement between wind resource estimates from NREL and those derived from the RCM simulations used herein. The wind energy density in the analysis of Elliott et al. (1984) was expressed in wind power classes where 2 = "marginal," wind energy density = 200–300 W m^{-2}; 3 = "fair," 300–400 W m^{-2}; 4 = "good," 400–500 W m^{-2}; 5 = "excellent," 500–600 W m^{-2}; 6 = "outstanding," 600–700 W m^{-2}; and 8 = "superb," 700–800 W m^{-2}. Thus the degree of agreement is shown as the fraction of grid cells within the entire contiguous United States and the Midwest domain (i.e., 103–81°W, 37–49°N) in each of the RCM simulations of 1979–2000 that exhibit an annual mean wind energy density at a height of 50 m equal in or above wind power class 2 and falls in the same class as the NREL estimated wind power. See Figure 2.4 for a depiction of the wind resource over the Midwest as described using the NREL wind power classes.

RCM-AOGCM	Contiguous United States: Fraction of grid cells "correct" class (%)	Midwest: Fraction of grid cells "correct" class (%)
RCM3-NCEP	30	41
CRCM-NCEP	14	17
HRM3-NCEP	16	33
RCM3-GFDL	29	37
RCM3-CGCM3	29	33
CRCM-CGCM3	11	9
HRM3-HadCM3	15	31

al. 1984, http://www.nrel.gov/gis/wind.html) (see Figure 2.4). Thus spatial patterns of average annual mean energy density for the historical period (1979–2000) from the four RCM-AOGCM combinations were re-mapped onto the gridded energy density estimates, and the number of grid cells that showed the same wind power class was computed. The results indicate that although the RCM-derived fields of energy density exhibit a high degree of qualitative similarity with those derived from observations by NREL (Pryor and Barthelmie, 2011), the absolute magnitudes show considerable discrepancies. Simulations from the HRM3-HadCM3 model chain are negatively biased relative to NREL over the Midwest, while simulations with CRCM tend to be positively biased. RegCM3 (RCM3) nested in NCEP, GFDL, or CGCM3 exhibits greatest accord with the U.S. Wind Resource Maps over the Midwest (Table 16.3).

ARE EXTREME WIND SPEEDS GOING TO CHANGE?

Figure 16.3 shows the spatial patterns of extreme wind speeds arranged in the matrix of the RCM-lateral boundary conditions shown in Table 16.2. Spatial patterns of extreme wind speeds derived from the RCM output are reasonably consistent with those manifest in observations (Lacke et al. 2007) and, consistent with physical reasoning, are highest over the lakes. It is relatively difficult to evaluate the estimates of extreme wind speeds from RCM. However, one recent evaluation of U_{50yr} derived from the NARCCAP RCM output for the historical period (1979–2000) relative to extreme wind speed estimates computed from station-observed daily maximum fastest mile speeds at 35 stations across the contiguous United States found that estimates from the RCM exhibit some skill in capturing the macro-scale variability of extreme wind speeds. However, there is a clear negative bias in the spatially averaged extreme wind speeds from the RCM relative to the station estimates (Pryor and Barthelmie 2012). This raises the following question: to what degree might the climate change signal in extreme wind speeds also exhibit scale dependence?

As in the case of the mean wind speeds, HRM3-derived extreme wind speeds are typically lower than those from the other two RCMs for both sets of lateral boundary conditions. Conversely, extreme wind speeds derived from simulations with CRCM tend to be higher than those for the other two RCMs, particularly in the western portion of the domain.

Analysis of the spatial patterns of extreme wind metrics (50-year return period sustained wind speeds and gusts) indicates that differences due to variations in the lateral boundary conditions are of similar magnitude to the climate change signal (Figure 16.4a). Fields for the historical (control) and future periods from a given AOGCM-RCM combination exhibit a higher correlation and smaller RMSD than fields for the control period derived for simulations with a given RCM nested in an AOGCM versus NCEP reanalysis.

Spatial patterns of changes in the extreme sustained wind speed and gust values generally indicate that although there is something of a tendency toward increased magnitude of extreme wind speeds, the changes are generally not statistically significant (Figures 16.5 and 16.6). Results for some AOGCM-RCM combinations and some grid cells do show statistically significant differences in both $Gust_{50yr}$ and U_{50yr}, and notably the RCM-AOGCM combination that exhibits highest U_{50yr} estimates in the control period also shows the most well-defined tendency towards increased values in the future. Simulations with CRCM nested in CGCM3 indicate a substantial number of grid cells (14% of the total number of grid cells in the midwestern domain) that exhibit estimated U_{50yr} that is up to 20 percent above the values from the control period, oriented in a SW–NE swath that is consistent with (but displaced north of) the current prevailing storm track for Colorado low systems (Mercer & Richman 2007). This is consistent with the northwest shift of the dominant Atlantic storm track in CGCM3-CRCM simulations under climate change projections (Long et al. 2009).

IS ICING FREQUENCY GOING TO CHANGE?

The Automated Surface Observing System (ASOS) deployed by the NWS includes an instrument used to report freezing rain via the resonant frequency of a vibrating rod, but relatively few climatologies of icing frequency and intensity have been undertaken for the United States. However, estimates of icing frequency based on observational data indicate strong north–south gradients with high frequencies in and around the Great Lakes and declining frequencies south and west of the Great Lakes (Young et al. 2002). Somewhat similar patterns are also evident in estimates for the control period from the RCMs, though all the simulations also indicate a secondary maximum in the west of the region (Figure 16.7), in a region previously identified as being characterized by a high frequency of freezing rain (Irland 2000). Thus, although quantitative evaluation of RCM derived icing fre-

quency is not possible; the spatial patterns of icing occurrence as estimated using the simple approach used herein appear realistic relative to prior estimates based on observational data.

Variations in derived icing frequency with lateral boundary conditions appear to exceed the regional climate change signal (Figure 16.4b). In all cases, fields for the past and future periods from a given AOGCM-RCM combination exhibit a higher correlation and smaller RMSD than fields for the control period derived for simulations with a given RCM nested in an AOGCM versus NCEP reanalysis. Thus the climate projections must be viewed as uncertain and treated with caution. Nevertheless, some of climate change signal appears consistent in the four simulations, which might indicate some confidence in the projections. Changes in icing frequency derived from all four RCM-AOGCM combinations indicate reduced icing frequencies in the southeast of the study domain in a region characterized by low icing probabilities in the control period (Figure 16.7). Three of the four AOGCM-RCM combinations also indicate increased icing frequency in the north of the domain (Figure 16.8) in the region of highest icing frequency in the control period (Figure 16.7). Icing probabilities in Minnesota and Wisconsin in these simulations are up to 20 percent higher in the mid-century simulations than in the control period, wherein annual icing frequencies at the surface were estimated to be in the range of 5–15 percent. Thus these simulations indicate that regions that currently have a 10 percent probability of icing may see an increase to 12 percent by the middle of the current century. These changes are likely causally related to changes in ice cover over the Great Lakes due to warming temperatures and hence higher water vapor availability. Icing frequencies during 1979–2000 are highest in simulations from CRCM-nested in CGCM3. This model combination exhibits a complex pattern of change in the climate projection period—with decreased icing frequencies over the Great Lakes and increased frequencies in a region extending from along the Nebraska–Oklahoma border into central Illinois. The cause of this change is currently uncertain but may be related to alteration of storm tracking as described above in the context of extreme wind speeds.

Concluding Remarks

Research to assess the current and possible future vulnerability of midwestern infrastructure to extreme events is nascent, and more is warranted. Analyses presented herein must be considered preliminary, pending improvements in model skill and exposure assessment. The NARCCAP suite of RCMs exhibits some skill in reproducing the historical mean wind climate over the Midwest, but the different simulations exhibit large variations in the magnitude and spatial patterns of extreme wind conditions. The results further indicate that for much of the midwestern region, sustained extreme wind speeds and wind gusts with long recurrence intervals (50 years) are not likely

to evolve out of the historical envelope in the near-to-medium term (i.e., by the middle of the current century). There is some evidence of a slight tendency toward increased extreme wind speeds and gusts in some areas, but the magnitudes are rather modest (typically < 15%), and the climate change signal is of the same order of magnitude as the uncertainty that derives from variations in the lateral boundary conditions used in the RCM simulations. If the magnitude of such changes is confirmed, they are likely within the conservative design standards used for structures such as wind turbines. However, when changes of similar magnitude were applied in a storm loss model over Germany, they were associated with mean increases in annual insurance losses of −4 percent to +43 percent relative to the end of 20th century (Pinto et al. 2010). Thus changes in extreme wind climates of the magnitude of those reported herein may have the potential to be associated with substantial increases in insurance losses.

Several caveats should be applied to the estimated climate change signal in extreme winds. The current formulations of RCMs and the application at a 50 km grid-spacing precludes treatment of phenomena such as severe thunderstorms that may be associated with damaging winds. Although extra-tropical cyclones are generally well described by the quasi-geostrophic equations, future high-resolution simulations conducted using non-hydrostatic formulations may exhibit different sensitivity to greenhouse gas forcing (Bengtsson et al. 2009). Further, given the high internal climate variability of storm and wind climates, a given 22-year period may not be reflective of the long-term tendency or "climate normals" in the future.

Icing frequencies computed herein using a simple methodology are sufficiently similar to those that have previously been derived using observational data to imply some skill in the methodology used. Variations in the icing frequency with lateral boundary conditions appear to exceed the regional climate change signal; hence, the climate projections must be viewed with caution. Nevertheless, there is evidence of decreased icing probabilities in the south of the midwestern domain in the middle of the 21st century, with some evidence for increased icing frequency (of up to 20%) in the north. Several caveats should be applied to these findings. First, the index for icing used herein is a greatly simplified abstraction of the actual processes that lead to icing. Additionally, the ability of AOGCMs and RCMs to simulate humidity conditions is substantially lower than other variables (Sanderson et al. 2010).

Deployment of anticipatory adaptation may be a key component of optimal response to climate change, particularly for critical infrastructure within the Midwest. There is some evidence that such measures may be much less expensive than relying on reactive adaptation only, even in the face of relatively high uncertainty in the climate projections (Fankhauser et al. 1999). The Midwest currently exhibits climate-related disaster risk that derives in part from icing and extreme wind events. As described herein adaptation mecha-nisms are available that could be used to reduce these risks in both the current and projected future climate. Based on analyses presented herein, parts of the region may exhibit increased vulnerability to these events due principally to increased infrastructural development and to a lesser degree to the evolving climate. There may be substantial value in implementing measures to reduce that vulnerability even in the absence of climate change, particularly given increased risk due to infrastructure development.

ACKNOWLEDGMENTS

Financial support was supplied by the National Science Foundation (grant 1019603), the International Atomic Energy Authority, and the Center for Research in Environmental Science at Indiana University. We wish to thank the North American Regional Climate Change Assessment Program (NARCCAP) for providing RCM output used in this paper. NARCCAP is funded by the National Science Foundation (NSF), the U.S. Department of Energy (DoE), the National Oceanic and Atmospheric Administration (NOAA), and the U.S. Environmental Protection Agency Office of Research and Development (EPA).

REFERENCES

Abel A (2009). Electric transmission: Approaches for energizing a sagging industry. In: Kaplan SM, Sissine F, Abel A, Wellinghof J, Kelly SG, Hoecker JJ (eds). Smart grid. Modernizing electric power transmission and distribution; Energy Independence, Storage and Security Act of 2007 (EISA); improving electrical grid efficiency, communication, reliability and resiliency; integrating new and renewable energy sources. Capitol.Net Inc., Alexandria, VA.

Abild J, Mortensen NG, Landberg L (1992). Application of the wind atlas method to extreme wind-speed data. Journal of Wind Engineering and Industrial Aerodynamics 41:473–484.

Banik SS, Hong HP, Kopp GA (2010). Assessment of capacity curves for transmission line towers under wind loading. Wind and Structures 13:1–20.

Bengtsson L, Hodges KI, Keenlyside N (2009). Will extratropical storms intensify in a warmer climate? Journal of Climate 22:2276–2301.

Black AW, Ashley WS (2010). Nontornadic convective wind fatalities in the United States. Natural Hazards 54:355–366.

Brasseur O (2001). Development and application of a physical approach to estimating wind gusts. Monthly Weather Review 129:5–25.

Brasseur O, Gallee H, Boyen H, Tricot C (2002). Development and application of a physical approach to estimating wind gusts—Reply. Monthly Weather Review 130:1936–1942.

Browning KA (2004). The sting at the end of the tail: Damaging winds associated with extratropical cyclones. Quarterly Journal of the Royal Meteorological Society 130:375–399.

Bumby S, Druzhinina E, Feraldi R, Werthmann D, Geyer R, Sahl J (2010). Life cycle assessment of overhead and underground primary power distribution. Environmental Science and Technology 44:5587–5593.

Bury KV (1975). Statistical models in applied sciences. New York: John Wiley and Sons.

Changnon SA (2003). Characteristics of ice storms in the United States. Journal of Applied Meteorology 42:630–639.

Changnon SA (2007). Catastrophic winter storms: An escalating problem. Climatic Change 84:131–139.

Changnon SA (2009). Temporal and spatial distributions of wind storm damages in the United States. Climatic Change 94:473–482.

Claussen NE, Lundsager P, Barthelmie RJ, Holttinen H, Laakso T, Pryor SC (2007). Wind power. In: Fenger J (ed.) Impacts of climate change on renewable energy sources. Copenhagen: Norden.

Cook NJ (1986). The designer's guide to wind loading of building structures. Part 1: Background, damage survey, wind data and structural classification. London: Butterworths.

de Bruin K, Dellink RB, Ruijs A, Bolwidt L, van Buuren A, Graveland J, de Groot RS, Kuikman PJ, Reinhard S, Roetter RP, Tassone VC, Verhagen A, van Ierland EC (2009). Adapting to climate change in the Netherlands: An inventory of climate adaptation options and ranking of alternatives. Climatic Change 95:23–45.

de Elia R, Cote H (2010). Climate and climate change sensitivity to model configuration in the Canadian RCM over North America. Meteorologische Zeitschrift 19:325–339.

Degaetano AT, Belcher BN, Spier PL (2008). Short-term ice accretion forecasts for electric utilities using the weather research and forecasting model and a modified precipitation-type algorithm. Weather and Forecasting 23:838–853.

Della-Marta PM, Mathis H, Frei C, Liniger MA, Kleinn J, Appenzeller C (2009). The return period of wind storms over Europe. International Journal of Climatology 29:437–459.

Delworth TL, Broccoli A, Rosati A, Stouffer RJ, Balaji V, Beesley JA, Cooke WF, Dixon KW, Dunne J, Dunne KA, Durachta JW, Findell KL, Ginoux P, Gnanadesikan A, Gordon CT, Griffies SM, Gudgel R, Harrison MJ, Held IM, Hemler RS, Horowitz LW, Klein SA, Knutson TR, Kushner PJ, Langenhorst AR, Lee H-C, Lin H-J, Lu J, Malyshev SL, Milly PCD, Ramaswamy V, Russell J, Schwarzkopf MD, Shevliakova E, Sirutis JJ, Spelman MJ, Stern WF, Winton M, Wittenberg AT, Wyman B, Zeng F, Zhang R (2006). GFDL's CM2 global coupled climate models—Part 1: Formulation and simulation characteristics. Journal of Climate 19:643–674.

DeWalle DR, Buda AR, Fisher A (2003). Extreme weather and forest management in the mid-Atlantic region of the United States. Northern Journal of Applied Forestry 20:61–70.

Elliott DL, Holladay CG, Barchet WR, Foote HP, Sandusky WF (1986). Wind energy resource atlas of the United States. Washington, DC: AWEA CSN. Available from: http://rredc.nrel.gov/wind/pubs/atlas/ (Solar Technical Information Program. U.S. Department of Energy, Washington, DC).

Fankhauser S, Smith JB, Tol RSJ (1999). Weathering climate change: Some simple rules to guide adaptation decisions. Ecological Economics 30:67–78.

Farzaneh M (ed) (2008). Atmospheric icing of power networks. Berlin: Springer.

Field CB, Mortsch LD, Brklacich M, Forbes DL, Kovacs P, Patz JA, Running SW, Scott MJ (2007). North America. In: Parry ML, Canziani OF, Palutikof JP, van der Linden PJ, Hanson CE (eds), Climate change 2007: Impacts, adaptation, and vulnerability. Contribution of Working Group II to the Fourth Assessment Report of the Intergovernmental Panel on Climate Change. Cambridge, UK: Cambridge University Press.

Fikke S, Ronsten G, Heimo A, Kunz S, Ostrozlik M, Persson PE, Sabata J, Wareing B, Wichura B, Chum J, Laakso T, Säntti K, Makkonen L (2007). COST 727, Atmospheric icing on structures measurements and data collection on icing: State of the Art. Zurich: MeteoSwiss.

Frohboese P, Anders A (2007). Effects of icing on wind turbine fatigue loads: The science of making torque from wind. Journal of Physics: Conference Series. Copenhagen: IOP Publishing, doi:012010.011088/011742-016596/012075/012061/001206.

Hawkins E, Sutton R (2009). The potential to narrow uncertainty in regional climate projections. Bulletin of the American Meteorological Society 90:1095–1107.

Hines P, Apt J, Talukdar S (2009). Large blackouts in North America: Historical trends and policy implications. Energy Policy 37:5249–5259.

Hochart C, Fortin G, Perron J (2008). Wind turbine performance under icing conditions. Wind Energy 11:319–333.

IEA (2008). IEA Wind energy annual report 2007. Available from: http://www.ieawind.org/annual_reports_PDF/2007.html.

Irland LC (2000). Ice storms and forest impacts. Science of the Total Environment 262:231–242.

Johnson BW (2005). After the disaster: Utility restoration cost recovery. Prepared for Edison Electric Institute, Available from: http://www.eei.org/ourissues/electricitydistribution/Documents/Utility_Restoration_Cost_Recovery.pdf.

Jones KF, Ramsay AC, Lott JN (2004a) Icing severity in the December 2002 freezing-rain storm from ASOS data. Monthly Weather Review 132:1630–1644.

Jones RG, Noguer M, Hassell DC, Hudson D, Wilson SS, Jenkins GJ, Mitchell JFB (2004b). Generating high resolution climate change scenarios using PRECIS. Met Office Hadley Centre, Exeter, UK.

Kanamitsu M, Ebisuzaki W, Woollen J, Yang SK, Hnilo JJ, Fiorino M, Potter GL (2002). NCEP-DOE AMIP-II reanalysis (R-2). Bulletin of the American Meteorological Society 83:1631–1643.

Knox JA, Lacke MC, Frye JD, Stewart AE, Durkee JD, Fuhrmann CM, Dillingham SD (2008). Non-convective high wind events: A climatology for the Great Lakes Region AMS 24th Conference on Severe Local Storms. Available from: http://ams.confex.com/ams/24SLS/techprogram/paper_141684.htm, p 13B.15.

Lacke MC, Knox JA, Frye JD, Stewart AE, Durkee JD, Fuhrmann CM, Dillingham SM (2007). A climatology of cold-season nonconvective wind events in the Great Lakes region. Journal of Climate 20:6012–6022.

LaCommare KH, Eto JH (2004). Understanding the cost of power interruptions to U.S. electricity consumers. Ernest Orlando Lawrence Berkeley National Laboratory, Berkeley, CA.

Leary N, Averyt KB, Hewitson B, Marengo J, Moss B (2007). Crossing thresholds in regional climate research: synthesis of the IPCC expert meeting on regional impacts, adaptation, vulnerability, and mitigation. IPCC TGICA Expert Meeting: Integrating Analysis of Regional Climate Change and Response Options Vol. Available from: http://www.ipcc.ch/pdf/supporting-material/tgica_reg-meet-fiji-2007.pdf. Intergovernmental Panel on Climate Change (IPCC).

Long Z, Perrie W, Gyakum J, Laprise R, Caya D (2009). Scenario changes in the climatology of winter midlatitude cyclone activity over eastern North America and the northwest Atlantic. Journal of Geophysical Research 114: D1211 doi:10.1029/2008JD010869.

Maissan JF (2001). Wind power development in sub-arctic conditions with severe rime icing. Northern Review 24:174–183.

Makkonen L, Laakso T, Marjaniemi M, Finstad KJ (2001). Modelling and prevention of ice accretion on wind turbines. Wind Engineering 25:3–21.

Mann J, Kristensen L, Jensen NO (1998). Uncertainties of extreme winds, spectra, and coherences. In Larsen A, Esdahl S (eds) Bridge aerodynamics. Rotterdam: Balkerna.

Massoud A (2003). North America's electricity infrastructure: Are we ready for more perfect storms? IEEE Security and Privacy 1:19–25.

Mearns LO, Gutowski W, Jones R, Leung R, McGinnis S, Nunes A, Qian Y (2009). A regional climate change assessment program for North America. EOS 90:311–312.

Meehl GA, Goddard L, Murphy J, Stouffer RJ, Boer G, Danabasoglu G, Dixon K, Giorgetta MA, Greene AM, Hawkins E, Hegerl G, Karoly D, Keenlyside N, Kimoto M, Kirtman B, Navarra A, Pulwarty R, Smith D, Stammer D, Stockdale T (2009). DECADAL PREDICTION: Can it be skillful? Bulletin of the American Meteorological Society 90:1467–1485.

Mercer AE, Richman MB (2007). Statistical differences of quasigeostrophic variables, stability, and moisture profiles in North American storm tracks. Monthly Weather Review 135:2312–2338.

Merrill HM, Felttes JW (2006). Transmission icing: A physical risk with a physical hedge. IEEE Power and Energy Systems General Meeting 2006. Institute of Electrical and Electronics Engineers, Montreal.

Midwest ISO (2009). MTEP 09: Midwest ISO Transmission Expansion Plan 2009, Midwest ISO, Available from: www.midwestiso.org.

Midwest ISO (2010). Delivering value to the heartland: Annual report 2009, Midwest ISO, Available from: www.midwestiso.org.

Nakicenovic N, Swart R (eds) (2000). Emissions scenarios, vol. Cambridge, UK: Cambridge University Press.

Pal JS, Giorgi F, Bi XQ, Elguindi N, Solmon F, Gao XJ, Rauscher SA, Francisco R, Zakey A, Winter J, Ashfaq M, Syed FS, Bell JL, Diffenbaugh NS, Karmacharya J, Konare A, Martinez D, da Rocha RP, Sloan LC, Steiner AL (2007). Regional climate modeling for the developing world—The ICTP RegCM3 and RegCNET. Bulletin of the American Meteorological Society 88:1395–1409.

Peter Z, Farzaneh M, Kiss LI (2007). Assessment of the current intensity for preventing ice accretion on overhead conductors. IEEE Transactions on Power Delivery 22:565–574.

Pinto JG, Neuhaus CP, Kruger A, Kerschgens M (2009). Assessment of the Wind Gust Estimate Method in mesoscale modelling of storm events over West Germany. Meteorologische Zeitschrift 18:495–506.

Pinto JG, Neuhaus CP, Leckebusch GC, Reyers M, Kerschgens M (2010). Estimation of wind storm impacts over western Germany under future climate conditions using a statistical-dynamical downscaling approach. Tellus Series a-Dynamic Meteorology and Oceanography 62A:188–201.

Pope V, Gallani M, Rowntree P, Stratton R (2000). The impact of new physical parameterizations in the Hadley Centre climate model: HadAM3. Climate Dynamics 16:123–146.

Pryor SC, Barthelmie RJ (2011). Assessing climate change impacts on the near-term stability of the wind energy resource over the USA Proceedings of the National Academy of Sciences of the United States of America 108:8167–8171.

Pryor SC and Barthelmie RJ (2012). Assessing the vulnerability of wind energy to climate change and extreme events. Climatic Change, in review.

Pryor SC, Barthelmie RJ, Clausen NE, Drews M, MacKellar N, Kjellstrom E (2012a). Analyses of possible changes in intense and extreme wind speeds over northern Europe under climate change scenarios. Climate Dynamics, 38:189–208

Pryor, Nikulin G., Jones C. (2012b). Influence of spatial resolution on Regional Climate Model derived wind climates. Journal of Geophysical Research 117: D03117, doi:10.1029/2011JD016822.

Pryor, Barthelmie RJ, Young DT, Takle ES, Arritt RW, Flory D, Gutowski WJ, Nunes A, Roads J (2009). Wind speed trends over the contiguous United States. Journal of Geophysical Research 114:D14105, doi:110.11029/12008jd011416.

Pryor SC, Ledolter J (2010). Addendum to: Wind speed trends over the contiguous USA. Journal of Geophysical Research 115:D10103, doi:10.1029/2009JD013281.

Pryor SC, Schoof JT (2010). Importance of the SRES in projections of climate change impacts on near-surface wind regimes. Meteorologische Zeitschrift 19:267–274.

Ratvasky TP, Barnhart BP, Lee S (2010). Current methods modeling and simulating icing effects on aircraft performance, stability, control. Journal of Aircraft 47:201–211.

Rebertus AJ, Shifley SR, Richards RH, Roovers LM (1997). Ice storm damage to an old-growth oak-hickory forest in Missouri. American Midland Naturalist 137:48–61.

Reed DA (2008). Electric utility distribution analysis for extreme winds. Journal of Wind Engineering and Industrial Aerodynamics 96:123–140.

Sanderson BM, Shell KM, Ingram W (2010). Climate feedbacks determined using radiative kernels in a multi-thousand member ensemble of AOGCMs. Climate Dynamics 35:1219–1236.

Schwierz C, Koellner-Heck P, Mutter E, Bresch DN, Vidale P, Wild M, Schaer C (2010). Modelling European winter wind storm losses in current and future climate. Climatic Change 101:485–514.

Scinocca JF, McFarlane NA, Lazare M, Li J, Plummer D (2008). Technical Note: The CCCma third generation AGCM and its extension into the middle atmosphere. Atmospheric Chemistry and Physics 8:7055–7074.

Solomon S, Qin D, Manning M, Chen Z, Marquis M, Averyt KB, Tignor M, Miller HL (eds) (2007). Climate change 2007: The physical science basis. Contribution of Working Group I to the Fourth Assessment Report of the Intergovernmental Panel on Climate Change. Cambridge, UK: Cambridge University Press.

Taylor KE (2001). Summarizing multiple aspects of model performance in a single diagram. Journal of Geophysical Research 106:7183–7192.

Thorkildson RM, Jones KF, Emery MK (2009). In-cloud icing in the Columbia basin. Monthly Weather Review 137:4369–4381.

Young GS, Brown BG, McDonough F (2002). An inferred icing climatology—Part I: Estimation from pilot reports and surface conditions 10th AMS Conference on Aviation, Range, and Aerospace Meteorology. American Meteorological Society, Portland, OR, CD-ROM, J1.5.

Yu W, Jamasb T, Pollitt M (2009). Does weather explain cost and quality performance? An analysis of UK electricity distribution companies. Energy Policy 37:4177–4188.

17. Climate Change Impacts, Risks, Vulnerability, and Adaptation in the Midwestern United States: *What Next?*

S. C. PRYOR AND R. J. BARTHELMIE

The Context

A recent study attempted to measure the priorities placed by Americans across a range of "problems" confronting society. When respondents were asked "What do you think will be the most serious problem facing the world in the future if nothing is done to stop it?" 25 percent replied with either "global warming" or "the environment" (Yeager et al. 2011). Variants in the wording of the questions greatly influenced the responses, but nevertheless this study suggests that the general public views anthropogenic forcing of climate as a serious problem. This finding is emphasized by another cross-sectional survey in the United States that found that "of 771 individuals survey, 81% (n = 622) acknowledged that climate change was occurring, and were aware of the associated ecologic and human health risks" (Semenza et al. 2011).

The widespread acknowledgement of anthropogenic forcing of climate—as well as the rapidity with which some aspects of the climate system are changing—means it is imperative that effective climate policy be developed and implemented. Effective responses to climate change will likely incorporate components of both mitigation and adaptation, though interestingly, there has been a marked shift in the relative importance of policy activities in these arenas over the last two decades (see the example provided in Figure 17.1) as recognition of the inevitability of climate change and the presence of an "adaptation gap" (see chapter 1) has grown.

In this volume we have identified and quantified key vulnerabilities to climate variability and change within the Midwest and provided robust projections of relevant climate parameters to assess future risk. We present analyses to address the regional-scale human-environmental system components and interactions in the Midwest in response to climate change and related stressors. Using the schematic framework shown in Figure 17.2, this volume documents the regional indicators of possible climate change vulnerability and the climate change scenarios for the region and thus provides a basis for considering adaptation actions. The research summarized is thus intended as a tool for

230

use by the scientific and decision-making communities to explore regional mitigation and adaptation decisions, constraints, and opportunities under alternate climate policy and climate change futures.

The analyses presented here are sector-specific and use only vertical integration, wherein impacts of future climate change are traced from climate projections through sectoral analysis. It is acknowledged that doubly integrated approaches—wherein the assessment design not only includes vertical integration but also incorporates horizontal integration (i.e., interactions and feedback between biophysical and socioeconomic components, common stressors, and common responses between impact and adaptation sectors)—will ultimately provide a more holistic and effective approach to adaptation (Miles et al. 2010). Such approaches typically employ Integrated Assessment Models (IAM) (Rosenberg and Edmonds 2005, Ciscar et al. 2011) or integrated Global and/or Regional Earth System Models (ESM) (Collins et al. 2011, Rice et al. 2010), with the former generally placing greater emphasis on the socioeconomic components. Application of IAM and or ESM is challenging and costly to undertake, and thus applications are typically less spatially explicit and include fewer climate scenarios, sectors, and impact metrics than is possible with a vertically integrated assessment such as those presented in this volume. We assert that there is much to be learned from vertically integrated impact assessments, particularly in terms of developing plausible scenarios and probabilistic statements that can be disseminated to stakeholders to begin the process to articulating informed decision support systems.

Climate Change Risk and Vulnerability: Charting Paths toward Effective Adaptation Strategies

We intend for the research presented in this volume to provide a basis for local and regional decision making in designing, assessing, and implementing climate change adaptation measures. However, it is important to acknowledge that, as discussed below, many activities are underway in the Midwest to develop effective climate policy. In the following sections, we briefly describe some adaptation and mitigation activities that have been initiated in the Midwest, discuss some specific sectoral vulnerability as illuminated by research presented herein, and conclude by presenting a series of recommendations regarding the foci for future actions.

CLIMATE CHANGE ADAPTATION AND MITIGATION IN THE MIDWEST: CURRENT STATUS

Within the rubric of climate "governance," there are two key elements: (1) capacity building to create the information and conditions necessary to develop effective policy measures and (2) delivering those actions. Steps are already underway on each of these elements within the nation as a whole and sub-regions thereof (e.g., Washington state, Miles et al. 2010). For example, at the national level, the U.S. Department of Agriculture is already funding projects to collect data that can be used to inform adaptation measures (USDA 2011). In all such analyses there is increased recognition of the different scales of response that are required. Further, there is an increased acceptance of system complexity and the need for an overall strategy, planning, and coordination at a regional scale and for management actions for individual sites, all contextualized within a framework of multiple interacting stressors (Palmer et al. 2009).

There are several regional umbrella organizations in the Midwest that are working on issues related to climate change mitigation and issues pertaining to energy security. In November 2007, the governors of Illinois, Indiana, Iowa, Kansas, Michigan, Minnesota, Missouri, Nebraska, North Dakota, Ohio, South Dakota, and Wisconsin along with the premier of Manitoba signed to all or part of the Energy Security and Climate Stewardship Platform for the Midwest that concentrates on four policy areas: energy efficiency, bio-based products and transportation, renewable electricity, and advanced coals with carbon capture and storage (Midwestern Governors Association Advisory Group 2009). Related projects have already yielded significant achievements. For example, energy efficiency improvements in Iowa, Minnesota, and Wisconsin have achieved levels equivalent to 0.7 percent of annual retail energy sales (Energy Center of Wisconsin 2009).

Development, evaluation, and implementation of adaptation strategies within the region have tended to be somewhat more fragmented, although even in the absence of a unified national, regional, and/or state adaptation, planning, and implementation process, some cities, counties, and other decision-making entities have engaged in assessment of key vulnerabilities to climate change impacts. Some have even commenced the processes of building resilience to current and projected climate conditions. To facilitate the process of making informed and effective responses to climate change, many of the midwestern states have adopted climate action plans or formed advisory groups (see http://www.climatesciencewatch. org/2009/06/29/climate-change-impacts -in-our-backyards-the-midwest/). Examples from individual states include:

- Illinois established a Climate Change Advisory Group in 2006 that has drawn up an action plan comprising 24 strategies mainly related to mitigation to meet the governor's goal to reduce emissions of greenhouse gas (GHG) emissions to 1990 levels by 2020 (Illinois Climate Change Advisory Group 2008).

- Iowa established the Iowa Climate Change Advisory Council, designed principally to focus on reducing GHG emissions via improved energy efficiency, use of sustainable materials in all state government offices, and increasing use of biofuels (http://www.iaclimatechange.us/).

- Minnesota has an Interagency Climate Adaptation committee focused on both mitigation and impact quantification and adaptation issues (Interagency Climate Adaptation Team 2010). Key actions undertaken by state agencies include the following:

  • The Minnesota Department of Agriculture has initiated biological control on weeds, pest identification, and integrated pest management education for fruit growers and has increased noxious weed education.

- The Minnesota Department of Commerce–Office of Energy supply has aggressively promoted Minnesota's Renewable Portfolio Standards to increase the penetration of renewable energy sources.

- The Minnesota Department of Health has established a climate change adaptation working group that is charged with developing a five-year strategic plan and is undertaking a mapping analysis of vulnerable populations for flooding and other extreme events.

- The Minnesota Department of Natural Resources established climate change mitigation and adaptation as one of eight agency strategic priorities.

- The Minnesota Pollution Control Agency established revised approaches to reduce storm water runoff through low impact development.

Virtually all state agencies have also engaged in efforts to prompt information dissemination and stakeholder engagement.

A number of cities have also undertaken assessments of climate change impacts and adaptation. Here are two examples:

- Chicago, Illinois: In 2007, the mayor of Chicago launched an initiative to quantify the role of the city in generating GHG emissions and the vulnerability of the city to climate change. This initiative led to a comprehensive analysis of the risks to the city and identifi-

cation of possible adaptation options (Coffee et al. 2010, National Research Council 2010, Wuebbles et al. 2010). Adaptation strategies include education and engagement of stakeholders, including businesses and the public, and a number of initiatives to manage storm water and to reduce the impacts of urban heat issues by protecting green spaces and using urban design to reduce cooling demand.

- Milwaukee, Wisconsin: City planners have commenced activities designed to reduce storm water overflows to reduce water pollution outflow to Lake Michigan. Activities undertaken to date include increasing storm water storage and encouraging development of green spaces that can act to increase infiltration rates (National Research Council 2010).

SYNTHESIS OF MATERIALS
PRESENTED IN THIS VOLUME

Most of this volume is focused on assessing the impacts and risks posed by climate change—the sensitivity, exposure, and vulnerability of key sectors within the Midwest—and thus providing a sound basis for mapping a path toward adaptation options for the Midwest. However, as a counterpoint to the Midwest, after discussing the backdrop for climate change impact analyses and the regional context for this regional climate change assessment, we start by considering vulnerability and adaptation in the southeastern United States with a specific focus on the agricultural sector (chapter 3). Although the climate of the southeast has not shown major changes in the historical record due to global climate change, there are strong relationships between seasonal variation in climate across this region and a key mode of internal climate variability: El Niño–Southern Oscillation. Thus the Southeast Climate Consortium uses a two-pronged strategy to both provide downscaled climate information on medium to long time scales and engage with stakeholders in the context of near-term climate variability. This strategy provides a clear mechanism by which immediate stakeholder needs for improved seasonal and interannual forecasts can be addressed and a framework put in place to allow dialogue regarding longer-term climate evolution. Using an economic framework, Zhao (chapter 4) outlines difficulties in forming strategies that can be shown to be positive in terms of net future benefits and, in particular, the roles of uncertainty and a lack of information in impacting the decision-making process. Both chapters indicate the need for coupled modeling to link physical changes with stakeholder decision making and for more accessible information to be provided by stakeholders to the research community and vice versa. The remainder of the volume focuses on assessing the historical and future climate over the Midwest and the major vulnerabilities to possible changes in extreme events. The sectors considered herein are as follows: agriculture, human health, infrastructure, energy, and water. These sectors represent socioeconomic systems that exhibit climate sensitivity and for which data have indicated vulnerability to historical climate variability. They are also diverse and complex systems that include multiple players and are also sectors that

are strongly interconnected and occasionally compete for resources.

THE ADAPTATION CHALLENGE

As documented herein, the scientific evidence for anthropogenic forcing of climate is overwhelming, and climate change due to human activities is increasingly manifest at global, regional, and local scales. Key tendencies and projections for physical climate parameters for the Midwest are as follows:

- Mean annual air temperature across the Midwest increased by approximately $0.67°C$ ($> 1°F$) over the 20th century (i.e., the rate of change over the entire century is $0.067°C$ decade^{-1}). In keeping with the recent increase in the rate of accumulation of GHG gases in the atmosphere, as with the global mean temperature, the rate of warming across the Midwest increased to $0.23°C$ decade^{-1} toward the end of the century (1979–2010, chapter 2). Projections for the current century indicate a continuation of the regionally averaged temperature increase and the asymmetric warming trends with greatest warming in the winter (chapter 2). The degree of regionally averaged warming to the middle of the current century is fairly independent of the precise GHG emission scenario, but the temperature projections diverge substantially by the end of the 21st century according to the GHG emissions scenario and the climate model used (see chapters 2 and 11). Indeed, although the A2 SRES exhibits highest GHG concentrations (and thus greatest warming) by the end of the century, because of the trajectory of GHG emissions, the A1B SRES exhibits highest warming at both the global and regional scale for the middle of the current century. The mean regional warming for the three SRES (B1, A1B, and A2) averaged across ten AOGCMs are 3.1°C, 4.3°C, and 4.8°C by the end of the 21st century, although the upper range for warming is over 7°C (chapter 2). Projected changes in thermal regimes, both from RCMs and statistical downscaling of AOGCMs (see chapters 2 and 11), indicate a clear tendency toward increased frequency of conditions that have been associated with "heat waves" in the historical period (chapter 9). Summertime apparent temperature (a metric of heat stress) across the region is projected to increase by 3.5°C, 5.3°C, or 6.9°C by the end of the 21st century, depending on whether GHG emissions follow a low, medium, or high trajectory (the B1, A1B, and A2 SRES), indicating that the combined roles of increased air temperatures and humidity will lead to enhanced heat stress relative to estimates based solely on air temperature (chapter 11). Despite the overall tendency toward increasing temperature, it is important not to confuse short-term meteorological extremes (e.g., the winter storm that affected the eastern United States in early February 2011) with long-term trends. Further, cold-air outbreaks and other extreme cold spells will still occur in the Midwest but with reduced likelihood (chapters 2 and 8).

- Precipitation regimes exhibit large spatial variability across the Midwest. Annual total precipitation varies by a factor of three along a gradient from northwest to southeast, and the fraction of precipitation that derives from the annual ten wettest days of the year (intense "downpours") follows a similar gradient spanning from nearly 60 percent in the west of the domain to less than 40 percent in the southeast (chapter 2). Temporal trends in historical data

have generally indicated an intensification of high-magnitude precipitation events (chapters 2 and 12). This tendency is also evident in future projections, though in the western states (including Nebraska, South Dakota, and North Dakota), there is evidence that annual total precipitation may decline (chapter 2). Key current environmental hazards in the region associated with the water sector are floods and droughts (chapters 2, 13, and 14), and these are likely to continue to represent major concerns in the current century. Indeed, there is evidence to suggest a bifurcation of future precipitation projections with increased interannual and intraannual variability of precipitation receipt and thus increased probability of both droughts and floods, as was experienced during 2011 (chapter 2).

- Modes of internal climate variability (e.g., teleconnection patterns such as ENSO, PDO, NAO, and PNA) play a key role in historical climate variability and will continue to do so in the future (chapters 2 and 6). Thus there should not be an expectation of a single linear trend in climate parameters over the region.

- The Midwest exhibits a high frequency of climate hazards in the historical record, and indeed, many of the impacts on socioeconomic systems have historically derived from extreme events including floods, droughts, and windstorms and ice storms (chapters 2, 12–14, and 16). Although not a focus of this volume, it is worth reemphasizing that extreme events such as heavy precipitation and ice storms have historically had major impacts on supply chains and resources that many commercial operations rely upon. Increases in the frequency of some of these events are projected (e.g., icing in the northern states and around the Great Lakes; chapter 16) and may have significant implications for commerce within the Midwest.

CLIMATE CHANGE VULNERABILITY AND IMPACTS

Agriculture is a dominant sector within the region in terms of land use and economic activity and is uniquely sensitive to multiple stressors in the climate system, including changes in both central tendency and extremes of temperature and precipitation that influence the growing season, pest prevalence, and yield. One study of cropland net primary productivity (NPP) over the Midwest found that "NPP for counties in Iowa (yields) varied among years by a factor of 2, with the lowest NPP in 1983 (which had an unusually wet spring), in 1988 (which was a drought year), and in 1993 (which experienced floods)" (Prince et al. 2001). As described in chapter 5, agricultural yields of two key crops within the Midwest—soybean and corn—have increased dramatically (by factors of 3 to 5) over the last century, primarily due to technological innovation. However, interannual variability of yields is still largely dictated by climate conditions (chapter 2). Future yields are likely to be a complex function of climate changes, water resource availability and quality, crop variety, weeds and pests, technological innovation, and atmospheric composition change, along with the rates of change of those parameters (chapter 5). Resilience in agricultural communities is tied closely to crop yield susceptibility to drought or flood, so government insurance programs have been put in place to prevent drought- or flood-induced losses and to aid rapid economic recovery. The efficacy and sustainability of these programs may be challenged as a result of climate change, and thus there is a need to establish future needs for flood/drought emergency management and mitigation planning. Key themes pertaining to climate change vulnerability within the agricultural sector that may be drawn from analyses presented in chapters 5–8 are as follows:

(i) Crop yield responses to changing climate conditions are highly nonlinear, indicating the need for robust climate change projections. When modest changes in temperature and precipitation are coupled with increased CO_2, model simulations indicate either no change or slight increases in average yields of key row crops within the region. However, projections for the end of the current century that encompass larger changes in thermal and hydrologic regimes generally indicate decreased yields of critical crops such as corn (chapters 5 and 6). For the Great Lakes region, increasing CO_2 concentrations did not compensate for decreased corn yields as a response to changes in water availability and temperature, while for wheat simulations, CO_2 enhancement led to major increases in yields for all climate scenarios (chapter 6). As a caveat, it is important to note that the confounding influence of weeds, diseases, insect pests, and other stressors could potentially change the magnitude or even sign of changes in yields. Further, as discussed in chapter 5, it appears that crops other than corn exhibit higher yield sensitivity to heavy precipitation and waterlogging of soils.

(ii) The timing of extreme temperatures and presence of water shortages or excess water (flooding) relative to vegetative "stage" is critical to determining the magnitude and indeed the sign of crop yield changes (chapters 5 and 8). Commercial fruit production in the Midwest is a relatively small portion of total agricultural production. However, fruit production represents a sector for which climate variability is particularly critical to yields, both in terms of the requirement of some fruits for long winter chilling periods and the sensitivity to the occurrence of freezing temperatures at specific phonological development stages. Thus, this is an industry that has particular, specific vulnerability to climate evolution. Although temperatures across the Midwest are likely to increase on average, as shown by Figure 2.14 and discussed in chapter 8, cold air outbreaks are likely to continue to be a feature of the climate of the Midwest, and the vulnerability of tart cherries and other fruits to springtime freezes may actually be enhanced by early development of the crop as a result of the gradual increase in temperatures. Assessing this type of climate sensitivity places a stringent requirement on future climate projections—and reemphasizes the importance of simulating changes in seasonality and extreme events in agricultural impact assessments.

(iii) Soils are critically important to global carbon balance and productivity. The soil carbon pool is more than three times the size of the atmospheric pool and more than four times the biotic pool (Lal 2004). Soil carbon across the Midwest has been greatly reduced by land use change post–European settlement (chapter 7). Because the Midwest contains 35 percent of U.S. cropland, there is huge potential for carbon sequestration or carbon loss from soil to the atmosphere dependent on precise climate conditions and management practices. Potential losses of soil carbon under reasonable climate projection scenarios are large, but the soil organic carbon responses to climate change are strongly mediated by management practices (chapter 7), indicating a clear need for information dissemination to key stakeholders in the agricultural sector to manage soil carbon reserves in a fashion consistent both with objectives to maximize crop yields and to mitigate GHG emissions.

The majority of the population of the Midwest is designated as urban dwelling (chapters 2 and 9). Climate change poses some key threats to urban infrastructure and urban populations, including (Hunt & Watkiss 2011):

- A range of extreme events impact on built infrastructure (chapters 12 and 16)
- Increased temperature and disease changes on health (chapters 9–11)
- Changing energy use (chapter 12)
- Water availability and resources (chapters 12–15)

Cities within the Midwest are already under significant stress, and adaptation of those cities to climate change may be made particularly challenging by aging in situ infrastructure and the changing demographics of the urban landscape. Nevertheless, some cities have taken strides to increase resilience (see discussion above). Key themes pertaining to the challenges presented by climate change in the context of urban environments are as follows:

(i) The most direct impacts of climate on human health are heat-related morbidity and mortality due to elevated air temperatures and humidity. These impacts are particularly severe in urban areas due in part to amplification of air temperatures by the urban heat island effect (chapter 9). Using statistically downscaled climate projections from ten AOGCMs to assess likely changes in the occurrence and intensity of heat waves, Schoof (chapter 11) found that heat stress in the Midwest increased across all the GHG emission scenarios and all climate simulations over the course of the 21st century. These types of climate impacts may lead to growing welfare inequalities, as demographic vulnerability is critical to dictating heat exposure and the risk posed by elevated temperatures (chapter 10).

(ii) Climate change effects on air quality and exposure to vector-borne and other diseases are not specific to urban environments but may be particularly important to cities (chapter 9). Many of the major metropolitan areas within the Midwest fail to comply with current air quality standards, leading to preventable mortality and morbidity (chapters 2 and 9). It appears likely that projected regional climate conditions will tend to make it more challenging for counties in the Midwest to meet air quality standards. However, the benefits of doing so are substantial. As discussed in a recent editorial, "Curing cancer, which is among Americans' highest health-related priorities, would increase average life expectancy by about 3 years. But it is far easier to clean up air pollution, and data suggest that doing so in some of America's dirtiest cities would increase life expectancies by about the same 3 years" (Chamedies, 2011). Further, there may be symbioses to be realized between measures to reduce air pollution levels and contribute to climate mitigation or adaptation policy (Smith and Haigler 2008, Shindell et al. 2012).

(iii) The stability, viability, and economic prosperity of cities rely on vast infrastructure networks to supply essential service such as wastewater removal and treatment and mass transportation/communication. Given projections for intensification of extreme precipitation events (chapter 2) it seems likely that one key risk that will increase across much of the Midwest is the threat of waterborne disease due to more overflows from coupled sanitary and storm sewer systems (chapters 9 and 12).

The midwestern states are among the highest energy consumers and the highest GHG emitters in the United States. Thus, there are major opportunities within the energy sector for mitigation of climate change (chapter 2). The energy sector and particularly the electricity sector also exhibit changing risk profiles under climate change, such as:

(i) Shifting demand profiles under an evolving climate. Specifically, hotter summers may lead to increased summer demand for electricity (e.g., increased air conditioning use) (chapter 12).

(ii) Reduced efficiency of conventional (fossil-fuel) electricity generation facilities as a result of increased air temperatures and potential changes in the availability of cooling water (chapter 12). Water use in the Midwest is dominated by withdrawals for thermoelectric power or irrigation, leading to complex cross-sectoral vulnerabilities.

(iii) Shifting vulnerabilities of the distribution network to extreme events (chapters 12 and 16). The expression of these changes may be highly variable across the Midwest, and while some regions may see decreased risk of the occurrence of icing or extreme wind events that are currently associated with major interruptions to electrical power distribution, other parts of the region may see, for example, increased risk of icing due to increased number of occasions when air temperatures cross the freezing point (chapter 16).

The Midwest has substantial freshwater water resources, including the Great Lakes and a number of major rivers. These rivers (including the Missouri and the upper reaches of the Mississippi) are extensively managed and provide a suite of goods and services to the region, including navigation for transport of industrial goods and pleasure craft, habitat for a wide array of organisms, and water for agricultural, industrial, and domestic purposes (Palmer et al. 2009). However, at least some of the services offered by the rivers are being put under increasing strain due both to climate change and, specifically, climate extremes (such as the floods of May 2011) and to human modification both of the rivers themselves and the surrounding landscapes. Based on assessments provided herein, management of the water sector faces the following key challenges with respect to climate change:

(i) Water shortages. Droughts are complex phenomena driven by multifaceted factors. However, historically, meteorological droughts have had major economic consequences via reduced agricultural productivity (chapter 5) and lake levels (chapter 15). Drought awareness and preparedness in the region, like climate change adaptation policy, are still nascent, though much progress has been made in disseminating information about drought conditions and impacts and in developing drought plans. The majority of states within the Midwest have state drought plans in place, but overwhelmingly, these are response based rather than mitigation based (chapter 13). Thus they are reactive rather than proactive in terms of risk management. Projections of hydrological and thermal regimes indicate the possibility for decreased soil moisture and thus possible increases in agricultural drought (chapter 2). According to some analyses, yield losses of crops such as soybeans due to enhanced evapotranspiration can potentially be compensated for by enhanced use of irrigation. However, as documented in this chapter, at least some counties within the Midwest are already experiencing excess water demand and withdrawals. While the Midwest is not currently characterized by persistent physical water scarcity, managing competing demands for these resources and establishing optimum resource allocation to avoid economic water scarcity will require careful negotiation across multiple stakeholders.

(ii) The Midwest has experienced extensive and repeated flood damage during the historical record (chapters 2 and 14). Historically, these events have been concentrated in Illinois, Iowa, Missouri, and North Dakota, but each state in the Midwest region has experienced flood losses totaling tens of millions of dollars since 1955. Using concepts of streamflow elasticity, projected increases in precipitation over much of the region are estimated to increase median streamflow by 16–20 percent (almost double the median change in precipitation) (chapter 14). As demonstrated by the historic flooding of 2011 (chapter 12), there is an urgent need to develop and implement strategies to alleviate flood vulnerability and to revise flood mitigation plans.

(iii) Changes in water levels in the Great Lakes as a result of climate change may have major impacts both on the ecology and the economy of the Great Lakes. Combining thermal and hydrologic regime projections with potential changes in management practices gives a wide range of predictions for levels of water in the Great Lakes over the current century. Hydrologic modeling of climate scenarios from 23 AOGCMs results in lake level projections for each of the Great Lake basins that on average indicate declining levels in the future but span both positive and negative

values (chapter 15). With the exception of Lake Superior, the upper ranges of modeled results are similar to the historical records. However, the lower ranges are about a meter lower than the historical records. Lowering of Lake Michigan by 1.3 m, which has approximately a 1 in 20 chance of occurrence by the middle of the current century in simulations using the A2 SRES, is associated with the possible need to divert the Chicago River. If realized, this major infrastructure project would require investment in excess of $50 billion (chapter 15). Despite uncertainty in the precise trajectory of lake levels over the Great Lakes, given the importance of the Great Lakes (to critical energy infrastructure, freshwater provision, agriculture and transport, and ecosystem services), stakeholders throughout the region are already beginning to plan for and implement adaptation measures that will diminish the impacts of reduced ice cover and possible declines in lake levels (see chapter 15 and Hinderer et al. 2010).

As discussed in chapter 1 of this volume, assigning confidence to climate change projections and impacts is tremendously challenging, as are the twin challenges of detecting and attributing causes of change. In general, the presence of multiple lines of high-quality evidence and agreement is associated with "high confidence" in any climate scenario, even in the absence of comprehensive analysis/quantification of the entire uncertainty space. Thus, Figure 17.3 synthesizes major findings of research presented herein in one framework for depicting the confidence in projected changes in climate parameters and impacts on related physical systems. This synthesis for the Midwest is articulated in terms of the level of agreement and level of evidence and is depicted for possible changes in physical climate parameters (red dots) and derived climate index or impact on selected physical/socio-economic systems (blue stars). (The numbers below each label indicate the chapters in which these processes/parameters are discussed and relevant analyses and literature are synthesized.) The matrix thus shows two components that might be integrated to underpin statements regarding level of confidence and is drawn from the foci of this volume. In this diagram the two axes denote:

• Ordinate: Level of agreement. Denotes the degree of convergence of scenario projections.
• Abscissa: Level of evidence. Denotes a qualitative assessment of the number and quality of independent analyses of possible direction/magnitude of changes in given parameter.

This analysis is a subjective "expert judgment" of the authors but is provided as one mechanism that can be usefully employed to convey the relative confidence with which key projections for regional vulnerabilities might be articulated. This synthesis also illustrates some key aspects of making and using climate change projections/scenarios in the context of assessing risks, impacts, and vulnerabilities:

• First, the degree of confidence in our climate projections for differing parameters shows wide variations with the parameter or impact of interest. Items denoted as having

a high level of agreement are generally parameters or processes for which we have a high degree of process-level understanding of how and why global climate is evolving in response to increased greenhouse gas concentrations, and how that is dynamically linked to a change in regional physical climate metrics (e.g., mean air temperature) and impacts (e.g., increased demand for electricity during the warm season) (i.e., there is a relatively high degree of detection and attribution). This level of physical understanding and our ability to both measure and develop robust simulations of future conditions is generally highest for thermal regimes. Thus, there is typically greater consistency in projections of physical climate parameters (than in derived indices or impacts), specifically for thermal parameters.

• Second, the level of confidence implicit in Figure 17.3 does not scale with potential impact/risk, since risk is a product of consequence and probability. As discussed in detail in chapter 15, the economic consequences of even modest changes in lake level are substantial, but as elaborated upon in that chapter, our ability to simulate lake levels under historical and potential future climate scenarios remains incomplete, and projections of lake levels developed from different climate models and scenarios are highly divergent (in sign and magnitude). Further, changes in extreme wind events may have enormous economic consequences for the insurance industry (and beyond) (Schwierz et al. 2010), but our current ability to accurately describe the mechanisms that generate these events and thus to simulate them under current and possible future climate conditions remains nascent. To undertake a comprehensive analysis of possible economic losses requires not only accurate assessment of the hazard magnitude (i.e., intensity of the winds of a given integration interval and return period), but also an assessment of vulnerability (e.g., a conditioned relationship between wind intensity and mean damage ratio based on historical data) and the value distribution and cover conditions (e.g., the sums that are insured, cover limits, etc.) (Schwierz et al. 2010).

• Third, the impacts described in Figure 17.3 are described under the presumption that no adaptive action is undertaken. Clearly, actions described in this volume can be undertaken to reduce the risks implicit in the projected increases in, for example, heat wave frequency or to manage or reduce the energy demand response to increasing temperatures.

• Fourth, it should be emphasized that this synthesis is specific to the Midwest and to the state of knowledge in mid-2011. Any such assessment is a function of location and spatial scale of integration and is a statement of the current state of the art with respect to scientific understanding.

CLIMATE CHANGE ADAPTATION AND MITIGATION IN THE MIDWEST: RECOMMENDATIONS

Recommendations derived from the research presented in this volume are outlined below in three contexts. First, we articulate some guiding principles for appropriate methodological approaches to undertaking regional climate change impacts assessments. Second, we identify critical impacts sectors within the Midwest that exhibit high exposure to climate change and/or high sensitivity and thus warrant priority in future actions. Third, we

articulate just a few of the options available to increase resilience to climate change.

Methodological recommendations for making regional climate change impact assessments. Many resource management systems are still designed around expectations of climate stationarity (i.e., that the past is an adequate analogue of the future). This assumption is no longer tenable. Thus there is increasing interest in regional modeling and analyses of climate change and associated decisions regarding mitigation and adaptation that highlight the need to address uncertainties in projecting future climate states and socioeconomic conditions. Decision makers need tools and information to evaluate the implications of uncertainty for decisions that must be made before uncertainties can be reduced or resolved. Our recommendations are as follows:

(i) Climate change methodologies and scenarios used to inform impact assessments should be (a) evaluated using independent data to demonstrate at a minimum some level of skill in the historical period using standardized metrics (see examples in chapters 11 and 15) and (b) of sufficient duration (optimally 20 to 30 years in length) to build credibility in capturing variability and to avoid confusion of internal climate variability and climate change signals. The evaluation of climate projections (from AOGCMs and/or downscaled therefrom) should be made relative to high-quality, robust, and homogenized observational records.

(ii) Not all models or downscaling techniques will be equally skillful in all regions or all parameters. Thus documentation of model credibility in simulating climate processes of importance in the given study region must be conducted in that region (i.e., skill is not universally transferable) and for the parameters relevant to the impact assessment under consideration.

(iii) It is critically important to explicitly consider uncertainty in making both climate projections and vulnerability assessments. This uncertainty derives both from limitations in the ability of climate simulations to fully capture the phenomena of interest and also difficulties in making robust projections of key socioeconomic indicators, including demographic projections. There are a number of interlocking spatial scales and influences inherent in climate, land use, and socioeconomic processes and parameters. The level of detail and confidence in climate, land use, and socioeconomic processes, parameters, and projections generally declines with increasing spatial resolution and with increasing time horizons. Acknowledgement of these realities must underpin all impact analyses. Quantification of uncertainty if properly explained and contextualized will also enhance and inform dialogue with stakeholders.

(iv) Climate change projections should be presented in the context of (a) skill in the evaluation period, (b) historical variability in the climate parameter, (c) uncertainty in the projection, and (d) sensitivity of the impact sector to changes in the climate parameter. Skill in the historical period does not per se guarantee robust projections (Macadam et al. 2010); however, discussion of the ability of the tools used to develop

climate projections to simulate the past conditions provides both a mechanism to introduce end-users to a discussion of confidence or certainty. For some parameters, it may be necessary to de-bias climate model output to make it suitable for use in impact analyses. Further, thorough investigation of performance in historical conditions will allow development of more carefully chosen and useful ensemble climate projections, which continues to be a subject of considerable interest despite expanding computational resources (Kendon et al. 2011).

(v) It is useful to make climate projections from a suite of climate models, downscaling tools, and climate forcings. A major focus of the research presented herein is based on multi-model ensembles and the derivation of projection spread. Large suites of climate projections (e.g., ENSEMBLES in Europe and NARCCAP in North America) are increasingly available to facilitate such analyses. While it is likely that any suite of climate projections will under-sample the full uncertainty space, analysis of output from a suite of models, emission scenarios, and downscaling techniques allows for informed discourse about the range of possible future conditions, and given a sufficiently large projection suite, it may ultimately be possible to provide some information about probabilities of certain outcomes. Stakeholders and decision makers from many sectors (e.g., the insurance industry) are fully versant with probabilistic approaches and operate within risk frameworks that explicitly incorporate probabilistic information. Thus while some level of education and communication may be required to clearly convey complex climate projections, this information is a critical component of informed decision making.

(vi) Depending on the specific application, there is merit in using either medium-term (e.g., mid-century) and longer-term climate scenarios. For other applications, as discussed in chapter 3 of this volume, stakeholder decision making is based on the near-term. Many of the analyses presented herein focus on conditions in the middle of the current century. This future time period is selected to represent a temporal window that encompasses the possibility of a discernible climate change signal but is sufficiently near-term to be within the lifetimes of most stakeholders. Other analyses have focused on conditions at the end of the century to examine conditions over the entire course of the operational lifetime of infrastructure projects (which may be 50 to 100 years or more). Where possible, continuous time horizons should be considered to allow decision makers to examine change across a range of time scales and to evaluate interannual and interdecadal variability.

(vii) Multiple factors shape vulnerability to climate change. Thus, the risks and opportunities posed by climate change may exhibit a high degree of spatial variability even within a region. Likewise, climate projections are unlikely to be uniform across regions. Hence, assessment exercises such as those presented herein should be informed by data regarding the characteristics of past events and should incorporate sub-regional components.

(viii) There is a need to engage with stakeholders early in the process to ensure that climate projections are produced in a man-

ner consistent with their use. Such coupling of "producers" of climate information and "consumers" thereof will great enhance the likelihood of generating actionable information. Further, when climate projections are disseminated to stakeholders or other end users who may conduct independent impact assessments, there is a critical need to provide logistic support and full documentation (chapter 8) to facilitate correct use and interpretation by non-specialists. This capacity-building will be a key component of developing effective climate policy, mitigation, and adaptation processes.

Although not an explicit outcome of the research presented herein, we also recommend use of the most recent climate science products in all impact assessments. The skill and voracity of the latest generation of climate models (both global and regional), the resolutions at which they are being applied, and the sophistication of statistical techniques for downscaling and extreme value simulation are evolving rapidly (see the suite of assessment reports from the IPCC).

Based on research presented herein, the primary **systems/sectors of concern for climate change impacts** in the Midwest are:

- Management of water resources. These include both building resilience to flooding (as in Cedar Rapids) and addressing issues pertaining to water levels in the Great Lakes and the implications for commerce, water supply, tourism, ecosystem services, and the energy and agricultural sectors. For example, Illinois has approximately 27 water supply intakes, and lower lake levels would increase energy costs to pump the water to the plants (Rice et al. 2010). Other key issues pertain to the results of changing precipitation regimes and the implications for flooding and urban infrastructure and health as a result of combined sewer overflows (CSO). Further, there is increased evidence of localized water shortages due to rising demand. According to some estimates, water demand from the Great Lakes may increase by 20–50 percent between 2005 and 2050 (Angel & Kunkel 2010). Major changes to infrastructure may be necessary to adapt water supply and management systems and point to the key importance of providing (1) improved fidelity projections of extreme events such as 5-, 10-, and 100-year return period precipitation amounts at high resolution and (2) seasonal, annual, and decadal variability of lake levels.

• Urban infrastructure and health. Several of the major cities within the Midwest (e.g., Chicago and Milwaukee) are served by combined sewer and storm water systems. Sewer overflows leading to discharge of untreated sewage as a result of unanticipated precipitation events represent a major threat to human health. Indeed, the EPA estimates that roughly 3.2 trillion liters of CSO wastewater is discharged annually into our nation's surface waters (McLellan et al. 2007). One study examined changes in extreme precipitation associated with CSO into Lake Michigan and found the frequency of these events is expected to rise by 50 percent to 120 percent by the end of this century, which may negatively affect drinking water quality and use of recreational beaches (Patz et al. 2008). In addition to CSO, intense precipitation over urban areas such as Chicago has led to major property and insurance losses

(Changnon 1999) due in part to basement flooding (Rice et al. 2010). Increased resilience to extreme precipitation could be achieved by increasing water storage capacity, but this has not generally been the historical trajectory of regional flood planning (Changnon 1999). There are also major challenges confronting urban populations, including increased frequency and intensity of heat waves. Significant steps have been taken in some cities (notably Chicago), but additional measures are likely to be necessary.

• Agriculture. The Midwest serves as the "bread basket" for the United States and indeed significantly contributes to global production of key crops such as corn and soybeans. The annual yields of these and other crops are crucially determined by conditions during multiple phases of crop development. Further, demand for increased biofuel production may cause significant increases in water demand and competition for land with crops intended for food supply even in the absence of climate change. Drought constitutes a major natural hazard over much of the Midwest and, given predictions of reduced water supply from the atmosphere and soil moisture under many climate projections, must be considered a real threat in the future. Conversely, over parts of the United States, major recent yield deficits have been associated with floods. Thus increasing resilience to both extremes would greatly enhance the stability and predictability of yields.

• Energy and other critical infrastructure. Reduced water levels in the Great Lakes in the historical period have had have profound impacts on commerce and transport of goods. Transportation of goods by land and rivers are also impacted by climate extremes. As described in chapter 2 of this volume, major disruptions to freight transport in the past have been caused by extreme precipitation and flooding. Given climate projections and the importance of transportation to the regional competitiveness and economic well-being, this sector may warrant special attention with respect to implementation of measures to enhance resilience to extreme events. Climate change will also influence supply and demand for energy and the ability of critical distribution networks to deliver electricity to consumers, and thus the energy sector must be a key and continuing focus for measures to reduce vulnerability to climate change, variability, and extreme events.

A further key recommendation that derives from research presented herein is the need for cross-sectoral approaches to impact analyses and adaptation assessments. This need is evident in multiple locations and sectors within the Midwest, but nowhere is it more evident than in the energy-water-land nexus. To illustrate the tight coupling of these sectors, one metric of population pressure on freshwater supplies was computed based on the ratio of estimated annual total freshwater withdrawals by county for 2005 to mean annual precipitation totals for 1971–2000 (i.e., water supply by precipitation for each county in the Midwestern states) following the approach of Hightower and Pierce (2008). This index is thus the percentage of total freshwater withdrawals from available rain and snowfall, where a higher number indicates excess water demand relative to local supply from rain and snowfall. The results indicate that water

withdrawals in some western parts of the Midwest are quantitatively similar to supply from atmospheric sources, while generally counties in the east of the region indicate that atmospheric supply currently exceeds water withdrawals. However, even within states where withdrawals are generally substantially below precipitation receipt, there are counties with the percentage of total freshwater withdrawals greatly exceeds supply from the atmosphere (Figure 17.4). In the western states that compose the Midwest, the highest withdrawals appears to be linked to irrigation use (Table 2.3), while in the east many counties that have an index greatly in excess of 100 percent are home to large electricity power plants (Figure 17.4). This further reemphasizes the interconnected nature of the water and energy sectors, as does a recent analysis of the vulnerability of coal-fired electricity-generating power plants in the United States that indicated 126 of these facilities in the Midwest exhibit vulnerability to water supply (Table 17.1) (Elcock & Kuiper 2010). The state-to-state variability in this analysis and the high implied vulnerability of these facilities to water shortages reflects both access to water and also the prevalence of "once-through" cooling systems (see chapter 12 in this volume, Table 12.3).

The vulnerabilities to water supply shortfalls described above may be amplified by climate change within the region in addition to increasing water demands from other sectors. As just one example, groundwater serving 8.2 million people in the Chicago-Milwaukee area has declined by over 250 m from pre-development levels

Table 17.1. Number of coal-fired electricity generating stations within each state as of December 31, 2008 (data supplied by D. Gotham) and the number coal-fired electricity generating stations that exhibit vulnerability to the availability of water for cooling purposes (data from Elcock & Kuiper (2010)

State	Coal		"Vulnerable" coal-fired power plant units
	Units	MW	
Illinois	58	16,918	15
Indiana	80	21,456	18
Iowa	46	7,052	8
Kansas	16	5,472	7
Kentucky	54	16,771	15
Michigan	66	12,612	7
Minnesota	31	5,511	10
Missouri	46	11,708	15
Nebraska	15	3,204	5
North Dakota	12	4,225	6
Ohio	87	23,250	15
South Dakota	2	481	0
Wisconsin	42	7,337	5

and continues to decline at a rate of about 5 m per year (http://www.sandia.gov/energy-water/docs/121-RptToCongress-EWwEIAcomments-FINAL.pdf). Possible increased water use in the agricultural sector, and specifically development of biofuels as a climate mitigation tool, further confound development of climate policy. Increased production and use of biofuels may help to achieve climate change mitigation goals but may infringe on efforts to build climate resilience due to the relatively high demand for water. Even in the absence of substantial changes to hydrologic regimes, there may be benefits to modifying water use and management by explicitly incorporating considerations linked to the energy sector, particularly given that growing scarcity of freshwater

supplies may lead to rising prices and adverse competition between end users (Hightower and Pierce 2008).

Adaptation options will require adjustments in physical, ecological, and socioeconomic systems to compensate for the climate impacts documented herein in order to make human (and natural) systems within the Midwest more resilient to the impacts of climate change and to make it possible to take advantage of opportunities provided. The most appropriate adaptation options are likely to be highly dependent on the region and sector under consideration. The process of considering and ultimately adopting adaptation measures will be enhanced by participation of all decision makers in activities to identify key vulnerabilities to climate change and critical impediments to adoption of climate change adaptation strategies, in addition to assessing measures that could be enacted to increase resilience. The chances of successfully responding to and ameliorating climate change–related risks and vulnerabilities will be greatly enhanced both by increasing the confidence in (and understanding of) climate projections and by engaging affected stakeholders in multiple realms, including at the enterprise level (i.e., the scale of the activity that might be impacted either negatively or positively by climate change/variability).

Given the scale and frequency of major environmental disasters (many linked to climate extremes) within the Midwest, it is asserted that anticipatory adaptation to climate change is a highly desirable risk-management strategy. This type of approach offers the possibility to reduce costs associated with current extreme conditions and thus potentially avoid (or reduce) catastrophic impacts in the future. As documented above, the majority of actions and measures that have already been undertaken within the region to explore methods to enhance resilience and adapt to a changing climate (1) may be characterized as reactive rather than proactive (Easterling et al. 2004) and (2) have tended to have been undertaken in an incremental way (i.e., using marginal changes in existing systems). However, it may be that some of the challenges presented by climate change will require transformation of management practices or other systematic change (Howden et al. 2007). Thus it may be necessary to transition adaptation activities from incremental to transformational in scale and scope. Preparing for and undertaking such responses to the risk posed by climate change are complex and challenging tasks. Infrastructure assets have long operational lifetimes, and thus they are sensitive not only to the climate at the time of construction, but also to climate variations over the decades of their use. As illustrated in the following discussion of the U.S. electricity supply network, a substantial proportion of infrastructure built in the next five years will still be in use long after 2030. Thus this sector is useful in illustrating some of the key questions that confront climate change policy making:

(i) What measures can or should be put in place to facilitate progress in adapting infrastructure to impacts of climate change? How can/should economic and regulatory systems be modified to accommodate and facilitate adaptation to climate change?

(ii) How can the adaptive capacity of both private and public agencies/companies be enhanced to enable robust (and cost-effective) decision making in the context of climate change (and multiple uncertainties)?

(iii) How can the potential economic opportunities that adapting infrastructure to climate change be optimally realized?

(iv) How can infrastructure modifications or developments be built in a way that maximizes flexibility so infrastructure assets can be modified in the future without incurring excessive costs?

Based on the major vulnerabilities within the Midwest illuminated herein, below we provide suggestions of policy measures that could form the focus for possible adaptation actions. Many available adaptation and mitigation strategies are inherently "no regrets" solutions. For example, increased energy conservation and efficiency lead to economic benefits, while also reducing climate forcing as part of a portfolio of mitigation measures. The measures that could or should be implemented to address key climate change vulnerabilities and risk and to increase resilience in the face of climate evolution and variability span a range of scales (and costs) from large-scale massive infrastructure development down to actions by individuals. Examples of policy options available to enhance resilience to climate change and variability within the Midwest are given below:

Enhancement of electricity infrastructure and management. As described above, the energy sector (and specifically the electricity sector) exhibits key vulnerabilities to climate evolution in terms of changing demand and supply. Developing an energy infrastructure (as in the water and transportation sectors) that is resilient to today's natural hazards and changing demand and supply options and is prepared for the future changing climate is considered by many to be a necessity to help protect the economy and its future growth. It is worth noting that climate-related factors are not the sole cause of vulnerability in critical infrastructure such as the electricity supply and transmission system. On August 14, 2003, electricity supply to over forty million people was disrupted. A major cause was that "one power plant in Ohio had shut down, elevated power loads overheated high-voltage lines, which sagged into trees and short-circuited. Like toppling dominoes, the failures cascaded through the electrical grid, knocking 265 power plants offline and darkening 24,000 square kilometers" (Grant et al. 2006). This example demonstrates how failure of a single piece of infrastructure can have widespread repercussions. So what actions could be undertaken to enhance the resilience and reliability of the electrical grid? The U.S. electrical grid has evolved in piecemeal fashion over the past 100 years. World War I saw a rapid rise in the demand for electrical power and increase in transmission capacity across the United States (Hughes 1983). In 1935, President Roosevelt established the Rural Electrification Administration as part of the New Deal but it was not until the 1950s that almost all U.S. farms had access to electricity (Davis 1986). Now the $1 trillion infrastructure comprises millions of kilometers of wire operating at up to 765,000 volts (Grant et al. 2006). A comparably ambitious project to the initial electrification of the nation may be necessary to address to challenges that confront the energy sector, and specifically electricity sector, in the 21st century. Concerns over the security of electric supply, combined with increasing pressure to tackle climate change, have forced many European countries to urgently reevaluate their energy strategies and to propose a huge, pan-European electricity "super grid" to act as a transmission network, enabling the secure spread of electricity between countries and to facilitate large-scale harnessing of the massive wind resource in the northern seas (Macilwain 2010). It should be emphasized that wide-area power generation (as proposed in a super grid approach) is highly complementary with decentralized power generation (Battaglini et al. 2009) and thus may also facilitate flexibility in electricity generation and supply management. However, adoption of policies to integrate, strengthen, and modernize the transmission and supply network in a super-regional or national context in the United States would face many challenges with respect to jurisdiction and management. Despite the critical importance of the electricity grid, operation and management of the grid is currently highly fragmented. Thus substantial changes may need to be made to the oversight and management responsibility of this critical infrastructure. However, if implemented, a national 'super grid' would not only provide energy security/reliability benefits, but also address the following two climate-relevant policy issues:

- It would facilitate enhanced penetration of renewable and other intermittent generation supplies by allowing greater flexibility of demand-supply management. It is often argued that introduction of large-scale wind or solar power will lead to excessive demand for spinning reserve due to intermittency of supply. However, given the spatial scales of synoptic scale weather systems, the spatial autocorrelation function for wind is only a few hundreds of kilometers (Pryor et al. 2006), and thus a distributed network exhibits much smaller temporal variability. Therefore, development of a U.S. super grid could play a key role in development and implementation of effective climate mitigation policy by enhancing the opportunities for use of non-carbon-based generation sources.

- It would allow for greater resilience to be built into the system and thus could be used to reduce the outages associated with natural hazards. For example, if drought occurrence requires reduced operation of power plants as a result of shortage of cooling water in a given region, supply could be provided from facilities outside the affected region. Thus the enhanced grid could enhance resilience to extreme events such as droughts. Further, during heat waves, there is a massive increase in electricity demand. It may not be possible to address that demand locally, but given that such events are typically regional rather than national in scale, it may be possible to manage such a system to deliver the needed power.

Enhancing the distribution network both to facilitate integration of renewable energy supplies and to increase resilience to extreme events such as icing and extreme windstorms would yield tremendous economic benefits to the region. Such policies could also be coupled with local actions such as deployment of increased smart-metering systems that, coupled with dynamical (real-time) pricing regimes, allow consumers (private and commercial) to determine usage based on price (Zhang and Nuttall 2011). This type of system can be managed to reduce peak demand for electricity and is increasingly being considered or deployed by electricity providers to assist with system management and operation. Although refinements may be necessary for full-scale operation, this mechanism has been shown to be effective in moderating peak demand in small-scale deployments (Strengers 2010).

The year 2012 provides an illustrative example of how drought combined with high air temperatures during summer may enhance electricity demand while compromising some generator capacity. Record-breaking heat led to a new all-time record for electricity demand and peak load in the MISO region (July 23, 2012), during a period when some nuclear plants across the Midwest (e.g., Broidwood, IL) were curtailed due to cooling water temperature above regulated levels.

Enhancement of infrastructure and management policies to address extremes of water availability. Recent flooding due to extreme precipitation events (and possible changes in dam failures) coupled with increased water demand, and possibilities for increase meteorological droughts indicate a need to rethink water management. Flooding within the Midwest during 1993 was associated with $30 billion in total costs, while the 2008 floods caused losses in excess of $15 billion. It is important to recall that a principal mechanism driving up flood disaster damages is development in high-risk areas such as floodplains (Pinter et al. 2010). However, tendencies in precipitation regimes (both historical and projected) appear to indicate increased likelihood of flooding. Possible transformative adaptation tools that could be employed to address these and other issues include increasing water storage by strengthening reservoirs to reduce the risk of dam failure and possibly covering reservoirs during summer to reduce water loss by evaporation. These approaches could be coupled with the retrofitting of dams to upgrade or introduce hydroelectric power generation turbines and thus also contribute to climate change mitigation efforts. The catastrophic flooding within and down-river of the Midwest during 2011 will doubtlessly trigger renewed interest in flood risk issues and renewed calls for reinforcing some of the century-old levees that act as cornerstones of flood prevention measures and the development and application of new, innovative techniques to map floodplain inundation and thus flood risk and hazard in the face of changing climate and socioeconomic contexts. Some have called for large-scale floodplain reconnection to parent rivers to reduce flood risk. Such efforts are already underway in parts of the Mississippi River basin, where

the Ouachita River is being reconnected to its floodplain. Proponents argue that such activities will reduce flood risk in two ways. "First, land use within reconnected floodplains will move toward activities compatible with periodic inundation. Flood-tolerant land uses (described below) will be much less vulnerable to flood damages and therefore less likely to require disaster relief payments. Second, reconnection increases the area available to store and convey floodwaters and can reduce flood risk for nearby areas" (Opperman et al. 2009).

Enhancement of agricultural management systems. The agricultural sector has historically shown tremendous flexibility and adaptability to the direct effects of short-term climate stress. Use of innovative technology has led to massive increases in agricultural yields across the Midwest and beyond. Extension of existing mechanisms such as changes in cropping, planting, harvesting, and seed programs may provide key components of a comprehensive adaptation strategy to secure food and other services. Breeding approaches to mitigate the effects of increased heat and drought in crop production are already being implemented (Trethowan et al. 2010). However, external factors may limit the feasibility of some adaptation measures in the long run due to, for example, competition for resources, multiple stressors (e.g., flood and droughts, coupled with increased disease burdens (Evans et al. 2008)), and international trade policies (Easterling 1996). Further, some traditional approaches are less appropriate to long-lived crops (e.g., fruit trees). A key way in which future conditions may differ from the historical variability to which agricultural systems have adapted is the possible rapidity of change and the possibility that climate shift may be associated with substantial increases in pest and disease prevalence (Hellmann et al. 2010). Thus there may be great value in development of disease warning systems that might reasonably have a format similar to those described herein for drought (and floods). Where possible, adaptation mechanisms should be coupled with other goals such as reduced water demand (e.g., use of irrigation techniques that are more efficient in delivering water to plants). Ultimately, however, there is increasing recognition that cessation of agriculture may be necessary in some regions (National Research Council 2010).

Enhancement of urban infrastructure. As discussed herein, urban areas frequently exhibit high vulnerability to climate change. For example, a recent study extrapolated data from historical observations of heat-waves and mortality and found that in the absence of large-scale mitigation efforts, the city of Chicago "could experience between 166 and 2,217 excess deaths per year attributable to heat waves" by 2081–2100 based on temperature projections from seven GCMs (Peng et al. 2011). However, some measures that have already been implemented to adapt to the risks posed by climate change. At least some of the measures designed to reduce the impact of heat waves will lead to reduced energy consumption in urban areas within the region and improve livability. For example,

the city of Chicago has implemented a "cool roofs" program focused on both increasing the albedo of the city and thus reducing the intensity of the UHI (Krayenhoff and Voogt 2010) and installing of green roofs to reduce the associated air pollution. Indeed, Chicago is the U.S. city with greatest installed area of green roofs (Yang et al. 2008). Heat wave–related mortality and morbidity can also be reduced through public health campaigns and community mobilization. Heat wave warning systems have already been put in place inlocations across the United States and have been credited with reductions in heat-related mortality and morbidity (Ebi et al. 2004). "For example, emergency medical services use was reduced 49% in Milwaukee, Wisconsin during a 1999 heat wave compared to one in 1995, in part due to improved prevention efforts" (O'Neill et al. 2010). However, triggering of alert days and ultimately the initiation of emergency responses by a heat-health warning system varies significantly across approaches adopted (Hajat et al. 2010), and the effectiveness of such systems needs to be continuously evaluated. Also, there is a continued need adapt those systems as new information becomes available (Kalkstein et al. 2009). A recent survey of representatives from 76 cities to assess actions to reduce heat vulnerability found that 26 considered excessive heat events a significant issue for the local government. Thirty had established preventive programs, but baseline information was reported to be lacking (O'Neill et al. 2010). The need for such programs was re-emphasized by a recent study that found "heat waves have indeed become more common, on average, in the nations heartland over the last six decades" (Perera et al, 2012). Cities and surrounding areas within the Midwest are already experiencing substantial health burdens associated with CSO events. Given increasing demands on water removal systems, increased urbanization of the midwestern population, and climate projections that indicate intensification of extreme precipitation events, remediation measures to limit the occurrence of CSO must be the cornerstone of urban adaptation and indeed are already being implemented in some of the region's major metropolitan areas.

Concluding Remarks

As discussed in chapter 1 of this volume, Article 2 of the United National Framework Convention on Climate Change (UNFCCC) requires that dangerous interference with the climate system be prevented. Agreements at the 2010 meeting in Cancun included a goal of limiting global temperature rises to ≤ 2°C. However, "emissions reductions pledged by countries at the same conference would actually result in a 50 percent chance of global temperatures rising by 3–4°C" (Mabey et al. 2011). Thus there is a pressing need for all regions and countries to adopt measures to adapt to the risks posed by climate change.

At least some of the possible approaches to adaption mentioned above would require government intervention (at the national, state, or local level) to address a number of possible obstacles to adoption, including the following:

- Behavioral barriers that may delay complex decisions. This is an issue in particular for adaptation due to the uncertainty over the exact impacts of climate change (see chapter 4).
- Institutional, financial and regulatory barriers.

Further, as discussed in the recent National Research Council reports, a national or at least regional strategy based on effective institutional arrangements for implementation that includes tools such as incentives, standards, requirements, metrics, and coordination mechanisms (across jurisdictions) would promote consistency and coordination across adaptation activities (National Research Council 2010). However, the private sector must also be a leading player due to its roles as investors, owners, operators, insurers, etc.

As we move forward, it is also critical to ensure that the policies designed to respond to climate change are promulgated within a coupled adaptation and mitigation framework to ensure that measures taken to adapt to climate change are not detrimental to mitigation efforts, and vice versa. It is therefore important to provide better understanding of the interlinkages, trade-offs, and synergies of adaptation and mitigation and to maximize the degree to which the different actors engaged in these domains are cognizant of other activities. Thus consultation and partnerships across sectors and between federal, state, and local governments with the private sector and nongovernmental organizations may be key cornerstones of a successful regional climate change management policy. Further, sustained leadership is required to ensure that climate change policy development does not follow "the hydro-illogical cycle" described in chapter 13, wherein individual extreme events cause "panic" and responsive action in the short-term, but subsequent strategic planning is stymied by the apathy that evolves at the end of the event.

The complexity of the challenges posed by climate change should not be understated. However, the scientific basis for making informed decisions about adaptation and mitigation options and thus designing effective responses to the threats and opportunities that will arise from climate change is sound, and resources for decision support are increasingly available. Doubtless, there will continue to be substantial improvements quantifying likely, probable, and possible future climate states at scales coherent with stakeholder needs. Additionally, the socio-economic context for, and operational systems used to formulate, decision analyses will continue to evolve. Nevertheless, as documented herein, there is already robust science in place to:

(i) Identify the impacts, opportunities, and risks posed by climate change;

(ii) Provide plausible climate scenarios to decision makers;

(iii) Form the basis of participatory scenario planning and provide input to impact analyses; and

(iv) Facilitate the process of adapting to climate change.

In closing, it is worth recalling that analyses based on an IAM by the Organization for Economic Cooperation and Development (OECD) (de Bruin et al. 2009) indicated that one dollar spent on climate change adaptation delivers four times its value in terms of potential damage avoided. Further, while the economic losses from climate change are likely to be comparatively modest in the short term, total costs are lowered by implementing adaptation and mitigation options sooner rather than later (de Bruin et al. 2009). Additionally, developing new technologies and skills required to implement effective adaptation strategies within the Midwest may lead to transferable expertise that can be used within the region and exported elsewhere to exploit economic opportunities.

ACKNOWLEDGEMENTS

Funding for the work presented herein was provided by the Indiana University Center for Research in Environmental Science (CRES). The authors gratefully acknowledge discussions with Gary Yohe regarding the analysis framework employed in Figure 17.3.

REFERENCES

Angel JR, Kunkel KE (2010). The response of Great Lakes water levels to future climate scenarios with an emphasis on Lake Michigan-Huron. Journal of Great Lakes Research 36:51–58.

Battaglini A, Lilliestam J, Haas A, Patt A (2009). Development of SuperSmart Grids for a more efficient utilisation of electricity from renewable sources. Journal of Cleaner Production 17:911–918.

Chamedies WL. (2011). Editorial: EPA in the crosshairs. Science 332:397.

Changnon SA (1999). Record flood-producing rainstorms of 17–18 July 1996 in the Chicago metropolitan area. Part III: Impacts and responses to the flash flooding. Journal of Applied Meteorology 38:273–280.

Ciscar JC, Iglesias A, Feyen L, Szabo L, Van Regemorter D, Amelung B, Nicholls R, Watkiss P, Christensen OB, Dankers R, Garrote L, Goodess CM, Hunt A, Moreno A, Richards J, Soria A (2011). Physical and economic consequences of climate change in Europe. Proceedings of the National Academy of Sciences of the United States of America 108:2678–2683.

Coffee JE, Parzen J, Wagstaff M, Lewis RS (2010). Preparing for a changing climate: The Chicago climate action plan's adaptation strategy. Journal of Great Lakes Research 36:115–117.

Cohen SJ, Waddell MW (2009). Climate change in the 21st century. Montreal: McGill-Queen's University Press.

Collins WJ, Bellouin N, Doutriaux-Boucher M, Gedney N, Halloran P, Hinton T, Hughes J, Jones CD, Joshi M, Liddicoat S, Martin G, O'Connor F, Rae J, Senior C, Sitch S, Totterdell I, Wiltshire A, Woodward S (2011). Development and evaluation of an Earth-system model—HadGEM2. Geoscience Model Development Discussions 4:997–1062.

Davis KS (1986). FDR: The New Deal Years, 1933–1937. New York: Random House.

de Bruin K, Dellink R, Agrawala S (2009). Economic aspects of adaptation to climate change: Integrated assessment modelling of adaptation costs and benefits, OECD Environment Working Papers, #6, OECD publishing, Available from: http://dx.doi.org/10.1787/225282538105.

Easterling D, Hurd B, Smith J (2004). Coping with climate change. The role of adaptation in the United States. Pew Center on Global Climate Change, Arlington, VA.

Easterling WE (1996). Adapting North American agriculture to climate change in review. Agricultural and Forest Meteorology 80:1–53.

Ebi KL, Teisberg TJ, Kalkstein LS, Robinson L, Weiher RF (2004). Heat watch/warning systems save lives—Estimated costs and benefits for Philadelphia 1995–98. Bulletin of the American Meteorological Society 85:1067–1073.

Elcock D, Kuiper JA (2010). Water vulnerabilities for existing coal-fired power plants. Report No. DOE/NETL-2010/1429, Department of Energy/National Energy Technology Laboratory, Argonne National Laboratory.

Energy Center of Wisconsin (2009). A review and analysis of existing studies of the energy efficiency resource potential in the Midwest, Energy Center of Wisconsin, Madison.

Evans N, Baierl A, Semenov MA, Gladders P, Fitt BDL (2008). Range and severity of a plant disease increased by global warming. Journal of the Royal Society Interface 5:525–531.

Grant PM, Starr C, Overbye TJ (2006). Power grid for the hydrogen economy. Scientific American 295:76–83.

Hajat S, Sheridan SC, Allen MJ, Pascal M, Laaidi K, Yagouti A, Bickis U, Tobias A, Bourque D, Armstrong BG, Kosatsky T (2010). Heat-health warning systems: A comparison of the predictive capacity of different approaches to identifying dangerously hot days. American Journal of Public Health 100:1137–1144.

Hellmann JJ, Nadelhoffer KJ, Iverson LR, Ziska LH, Matthews SN, Myers P, Prasad AM, Peters MP (2010). Climate change impacts on terrestrial ecosystems in metropolitan Chicago and its surrounding, multi-state region. Journal of Great Lakes Research 36:74–85.

Hightower M, Pierce SA (2008). The energy challenge. Nature 452:285–286.

Hinderer J, Haven C, Koslow M (2010). Climate change in the Great Lakes: Advancing the regional discussion, Great Lakes Commission, Available from: http://glisa.umich.edu/great_lakes_climate/docs/Climate-Change-in-the-Great-Lakes-Report-Advancing-the-Regional-Discussion.pdf.

Howden SM, Soussana JF, Tubiello FN, Chhetri N, Dunlop M, Meinke H (2007). Adapting agriculture to climate change. Proceedings of the National Academy of Sciences of the United States of America 104:19691–19696.

Hughes TP (1983). Networks of power: Electrification in western society, 1880–1930. Baltimore: Johns Hopkins University Press.

Hunt A, Watkiss P (2011). Climate change impacts and adaptation in cities: A review of the literature. Climatic Change 104:13–49.

Illinois Climate Change Advisory Group (2008). Report of the Illinois Climate Change Advisory Group: Executive summary, Illinois Environmental Protection Agency.

Interagency Climate Adaptation Team (2010). Adapting to climate change in Minnesota. Preliminary report of the Interagency Climate Adaptation Team. Report No. p-gen4-07, Minnesota Pollution Control Agency.

Kalkstein LS, Sheridan SC, Kalkstein AJ (2009). Heat/health warning systems: Development, implementation, and intervention activities. In: Ebi K, Bruton I, McGregor (eds) Biometeorology for adaptation to climate variability and change. Berlin: Springer.

Kendon EJ, Jones RG, Kjellstrom E, Murphy JM (2011). Using and designing GCM-RCM ensemble regional climate projections. Journal of Climate 23:6485–6503.

Krayenhoff ES, Voogt JA (2010). Impacts of urban albedo increase on local air temperature at daily-annual time scales: model results and synthesis of previous work. Journal of Applied Meteorology and Climatology 49:1634–1648.

Lal R (2004). Soil carbon sequestration impacts on global climate change and food security. Science 304:1623–1626.

Macilwain C (2010). SUPERGRID. Nature 468:624–625.

Mabey N, Gulledge J, Finel B, Silverthorne K (2011). Degrees of risk: Defining a risk management framework for climate security. E3G, report available from the Pew Charitable Trust. Available from: http://www.pewclimate.org/publications/degrees-risk-defining-risk-management-framework-climate-security.

Macadam I, Pitman AJ, Whetton PH, Abramowitz G (2010). Ranking climate models by performance using actual values and anomalies: Implications for climate change impact assessments. Geophysical Research Letters 37: L16704 doi:16710.11029/12010GL043877.

McLellan SL, Hollis EJ, Depas MM, Van Dyke M, Harris J, Scopel CO (2007). Distribution and fate of Escherichia coli in Lake Michigan following contamination with urban stormwater and combined sewer overflows. Journal of Great Lakes Research 33: 566–580.

Midwestern Governors Association Advisory Group (2009). Midwestern energy security and climate stewardship roadmap, Midwestern Governors Association, Lombard IL.

Miles EL, Elsner MM, Littell JS, Binder LW, Lettenmaier DP (2010). Assessing regional impacts and adaptation strategies for climate change: The Washington Climate Change Impacts Assessment. Climatic Change 102:9–27.

National Research Council (2010). Adapting to the impacts of climate change. Washington, DC: National Academies Press.

Neufeldt H, Jochem E, Hinkel J, Huitema D, Massey E, P. W, McEvoy D, Rayner T, Hof A, Lonsdale K (2010). Climate policy and interlinkages between adaptation and mitigation. In: Hulme M, Neufeldt H (eds) Making climate change work for us. Cambridge, UK: Cambridge University Press.

O'Neill MS, Jackman DK, Wyman M, Manarolla X, Gronlund CJ, Brown DG, Brines SJ, Schwartz J, Diez-Roux AV (2010). US local action on heat and health: are we prepared for climate change? International Journal of Public Health 55:105–112.

Opperman JJ, Galloway GE, Fargione J, Mount JF, Richter BD, Secchi S (2009). Sustainable floodplains through large-scale reconnection to rivers. Science 326:1487–1488.

Palmer MA, Lettenmaier DP, Poff NL, Postel SL, Richter B, Warner R (2009). Climate change and river ecosystems: Protection and adaptation options. Environmental Management 44:1053–1068.

Patz JA, Vavrus SJ, Uejio CK, McLellan SL (2008). Climate change and waterborne disease risk in the Great Lakes region of the US. American Journal of Preventive Medicine 35:451–458.

Peng RD, Bobb JF, Tebaldi C, McDaniel L, Bell ML, Dominici F (2011). Toward a quantitative estimate of future heat wave mortality under global climate change. Environmental Health Perspectives 119:701–706.

Perera EM, Sanford T, White-Newhouse JL, Kalkstein LS, Vanos JK, Weir K. 2012. Heat in the Heartland: 60 years of warming in the Midwest, Union of Concerned Scientists. Cambridge, MA, pp. 36.

Pinter N, Jemberie AA, Remo JWF, Heine RA, Ickes BS (2010). Cumulative impacts of river engineering, Mississippi and lower Missouri Rivers. River Research and Applications 26:546–571.

Prince SD, Haskett J, Steininger M, Strand H, Wright R (2001). Net primary production of US midwest croplands from agricultural harvest yield data. Ecological Applications 11:1194–1205.

Pryor SC, Barthelmie RJ, Schoof JT (2006). Interannual variability of wind indices across Europe. Wind Energy 9:27–38.

Rice J, Moss R, Runci P, Anderson K (2010). iRESM initiative: Understanding decision support needs for climate change mitigation and adaptation: US Midwest Region, Pacific Northwest National Laboratory, Oak Ridge.

Rosenberg NJ, Edmonds JA (2005). Climate change impacts for the conterminous USA: An integrated assessment Climatic Change 69:1–6.

Schwierz C, Koellner-Heck P, Mutter E, Bresch DN, Vidale P, Wild M, Schaer C (2010). Modelling European winter wind storm losses in current and future climate. Climatic Change 101:485–514.

Semenza JC, Ploubidis GB, George LA (2011). Climate change and climate variability: personal motivation for adaptation and mitigation. Environmental Health 10: doi: 10.1186/1476-1069x-1110-1146.

Shindell D, Kuylenstierna JCI, Vignati E, van Dingenen R, Amann M, Klimont Z, Anenberg SC, Muller N, Janssens-Maenhout G, Raes F, Schwartz J, Faluvegi G, Pozzoli L, Kupiainen K, Hoeglund-Isaksson L, Emberson L, Streets D, Ramanathan V, Hicks K, Oanh NTK, Milly G, Williams M, Demkine V, Fowler D (2012). Simultaneously mitigating near-term climate change and improving human health and food security. Science 335:183-189.

Smith KR, Haigler E (2008). Co-benefits of climate mitigation and health protection in energy systems: Scoping methods. Annual Review of Public Health 29:11–25.

Strengers Y (2010). Air-conditioning Australian households: the impact of dynamic peak pricing. Energy Policy 38:7312–7322.

Trethowan RM, Turner MA, Chattha TM (2010). Breeding Strategies to Adapt Crops to a Changing Climate. In: Lobell D, Burke M (eds) Climate Change and Food Security: Adapting Agriculture to a Warmer World. Springer, 155–174.

USDA (2011). Climate change, mitigation, and adaptation in corn-based cropping systems. Report No. 3605-13000-004-11. United States Department of Agriculture: Agriculture Research Service.

Wuebbles DJ, Hayhoe K, Parzen J (2010). Introduction: Assessing the effects of climate change on Chicago and the Great Lakes. Journal of Great Lakes Research 36:1–6.

Yang J, Yu Q, Gong P (2008). Quantifying air pollution removal by green roofs in Chicago. Atmospheric Environment 42:7266–7273.

Yeager DS, Larson SB, Krosnick JA, Tompson T (2011). Measuring Americans' issue priorities: A new version of the most important problem question reveals more concern about global warming and the environment. Public Opinion Quarterly 75:125–138.

Zhang T, Nuttall WJ (2011). Evaluating government's policies on promoting smart metering diffusion in retail electricity markets via agent-based simulation. Journal of Product Innovation Management 28:169–186.

List of Contributors

G. Alagarswamy is a senior research associate with the Department of Geography and the Center for Global Change and Earth Observations at Michigan State University.

C. J. Anderson is research assistant professor of agronomy at Iowa State University. His research emphasis is climate adaptation for water resource and natural resource management.

D. B. Andrade is a doctoral student at Saint Louis University in the Department of Earth and Atmospheric Sciences.

J. A. Andresen is associate professor in the Department of Geography at Michigan State University. He also serves as state climatologist for the state of Michigan and conducted research on the impacts of weather and climate on agriculture.

J. R. Angel is state climatologist for the state of Illinois at the Illinois State Water Survey with the Prairie Research Institute University of Illinois Urbana–Champaign.

W. L. Bartels is a post-doctoral research associate with the Southeast Climate Consortium and the Florida Climate Institute. She engages agricultural and water management stakehold-ers as they prepare for and adapt to climate variability and change.

R. J. Barthelmie is a professor of atmospheric science and sustainability at Indiana University. Her research focuses on the climate change mitigation potential of renewable energy sources and climate change impacts thereon.

J. M. Bisanz served as the project manager for the Pileus Project and coordinated the development of web-based tools for stakeholders.

N. E. Breuer is an interdisciplinary ecologist at the University of Miami and the University of Florida. He focuses on human dimensions of agroecology, including decision making, adaptation, and resilience in light of climate variability and change in human-ecological coupled systems.

J. Clark is a graduate student studying atmospheric physics at Howard University. He currently is involved with the modeling of mesoscale convective systems in West Africa.

C. Fraisse is a climate extension specialist at the University of Florida. His extension and research programs focus on developing and providing climate information and decision support tools for agricultural producers.

N. Gosselin is a master's student in the Department of Earth and Atmospheric Sciences at Saint Louis University in Saint Louis, Missouri.

D. J. Gotham is director of the State Utility Forecasting Group at Purdue University, with which he has worked in various capacities since arriving at Purdue University in 1992.

S. C. Grady is an assistant professor at Michigan State University. She is a medical geographer and a scholar with Building Interdisciplinary Research Careers in Women's Health.

G. Guentchev is a project scientist at NCAR RAL CSAP. Her research interests focus on the impacts of regional climate variability and change on human and natural systems.

M. Hayes is the director of the National Drought Mitigation Center and a professor within the School of Natural Resources at the University of Nebraska–Lincoln.

K. T. Ingram is coordinator of the Southeast Climate Consortium. He conducts research on crop-environment interactions and scaling-up crop simulation models to regional agricultural outlooks.

D. P. Johnson is an assistant professor at Indiana University–Purdue University Indianapolis. His primary research interests include modeling vulnerability to extreme weather events including heat waves and floods.

J. W. Jones is a distinguished professor at the University of Florida and director of the Florida Climate Institute. His fields of study are mathematical modeling of plant growth

and environmental interactions, decision support applications, and climate effects on cropping systems.

D. Letson is a professor at the University of Miami. He studies the economics of extreme weather and climate variations and specifically the value of predictions from the geosciences and how those predictions are interpreted and used.

V. Lulla is a postdoctoral research assistant at Indiana University–Purdue University Indianapolis. His primary research interests are in computational geography and hyperspectral remote sensing.

V. Mishra is a post-doctoral fellow in the Department of Civil and Environmental Engineering at the University of Washington.

H. K. Min is a web architect at Google. She received her MA in telecommunication, information studies, and media with a concentration on digital media art and technology from Michigan State University.

D. Niyogi is the state climatologist for Indiana and a university faculty scholar/associate professor with appointments in the Department of Agronomy, Crops and Earth System Sciences, and the Department of Earth and Atmospheric Sciences at Purdue University.

J. Nugent is the former coordinator of the Northwest Michigan Horticultural Research Station and the district horticulturalist Michigan State University Extension. He is also a tart cherry grower.

J. J. O'Brien is the Robert O. Lawton professor of meteorology and oceanography at Florida State University. He founded the Center for

Ocean Atmosphere Prediction Sciences and cofounded the Southeast Climate Consortium.

Z. Pan is an associate professor in the Department of Earth and Atmospheric Sciences at Saint Louis University. He works principally in the field of regional climate change and land-surface interaction.

Perdinan is a PhD student and Fulbright scholar in the Department of Geography at Michigan State University.

K. Piromsopa is an assistant professor of computer engineering at Chulalongkorn University in Thailand. His research focuses on computer architecture and computer security.

A. Pollyea is a master's student in the Department of Geography at Michigan State University. He also serves as the Enviro-Weather Technical Specialist for the Michigan State Climatologist's Office.

H. Prawiranata is a transportation and air quality modeler at Tri-County Regional Planning Commission in Lansing, Michigan. He received his MS in environmental engineering and was a web/database programmer for the Pileus Project.

S. C. Pryor is provost professor of atmospheric science at Indiana University. Her research focuses on regional climate variability and change. She is a member of the US National Climate Assessment and Development Committee and the editor of this volume.

M. C. Roncoli is adjunct professor in the Department of Anthropology at Emory University. Her research focuses on integration of farmers' knowledge, risk perceptions, and

information processing habits into the development of science-based decision support systems.

N. Rothwell is the coordinator of the Northwest Michigan Horticultural Research Station and District Extension horticulture educator. Her research interests include tree fruit training systems and pest management strategies.

J. T. Schoof is an associate professor of Geography and Environmental Resources at Southern Illinois University. His research focuses on regional manifestations of climate variability and change.

A. C. Stanforth is a graduate student at Indiana University–Purdue University Indianapolis focusing on modeling social and environmental vulnerability.

J. van Ravensway is a GIS and remote sensing research associate at the Center for Global Change and Earth Observations at Michigan State University.

J. A. Winkler is a professor in the Department of Geography at Michigan State University. Her research focuses on synoptic and applied climatology and regional climate variability and change.

C. Zavalloni is a postdoctoral fellow at the Department of Agriculture and Environmental Sciences at the University of Udine. Her research interests include climate impacts on fruit phenology and yield.

J. Zhao is a professor in the Department of Economics and the Department of Agriculture, Food and Resource Economics, and the director of the Environmental Science and Policy Program at Michigan State University.

D. F. Zierden is the Florida state climatologist based at Florida State University. He conducts research on climate variability and prediction, especially for the southeastern United States, and development of climate information products for decision support.

Index

Irrigation, 19–23, 26, 35–36, 52, 54, 59, 62, 74, 76, 167, 168–171, 239, 246, 252

Lakes, 20, 164, 171, 173. *See also* Great Lakes
Lake levels, 23, 164, 168, 173, 203–211, 239–240, 241, 244–245, 245–246
Land cover/land use, 13, 54, 166, 169, 174
Livestock, 20, 22–23, 180, 184, 187

Maize (corn), 17–19, 21, 24, 34, 35–36, 53, 65–66, 69–72, 73–74, 82–83, 84, 86–88, 95, 96, 100, 171, 179, 195, 236–237, 245
Maladaptation, 4, 38
Midwest Independent Transmission System Operators (MISO), 14–15, 160, 215–216, 250
Mitigation. *See* Climate change mitigation; Drought: mitigation; Flood: mitigation; Heatwave mitigation
Modes of climate variability, 30, 51, 53, 235
Morbidity, 24, 37–38, 117–121, 125, 129–130, 142–143, 154, 238, 252
Mortality, 24, 37–38, 117–121, 129–130, 142–143, 146, 154, 238, 252

National Ambient Air Quality Standards (NAAQS), 23–24, 122
Net Basin Supply (NBS), 168, 207
North American Regional Climate Change Assessment Program (NARCCAP), 218, 243

Palmer Drought Severity Index (PDSI), 29
Pathogens, 35
Photosynthesis, 24, 69, 72, 92
Pileus project, 105–106
Planned v. autonomous adaptation, 4, 22
Pollution. *See* Air pollution; Air quality; Water: quality; Combined Sewer Systems and Combined Sewer Overflow (CSO)
Power plants, 36, 130, 158–159, 205, 215–217, 246, 249
Precipitation, 14, 19, 26, 27–29, 31–36, 54, 69–70, 84–89, 94–97, 99–100, 107–108, 125, 159, 163–165, 166–173, 181, 191–198, 207, 209, 214, 235–237, 240, 245–246, 250–251
Probabilistic analyses, 28–29, 50, 52, 208, 231, 243–244
Projections of climate. *See* Climate projections

Radiative forcing, 1, 147, 217
Rainfall. *See* Precipitation
Reanalysis data, 30, 108, 149–150, 218–219
Regional Climate Models (RCM), 26, 39, 160, 213–214, 217–220, 221–222, 235
Remote sensing, 134, 138–139
Renewable energy, 15–17, 129, 150, 163, 215, 233, 250
Resilience, 5, 6–8, 20, 55, 171, 174, 183, 232, 236, 238, 244–246, 247–248, 249, 250
Respiration, 92, 93, 95, 97–101
Risk (defined), 6
River discharge. *See* Streamflow

Sensitivity (defined), 6–7
Skill (model skill), 7, 94, 150–152, 208, 217, 220–222, 242–244
Snow. *See* Precipitation
Social Vulnerability Index (SoVI), 135–136, 142
Soil: carbon, 77, 92–101, 237; management, 17, 75–76, 84, 92–101, 237; moisture/water, 19, 26, 34–35, 73, 84, 94, 125, 166, 169, 193, 237
Southeast Climate Consortium (SECC), 48, 49–55
Soybean, 17–20, 21, 24, 35–36, 65–66, 70–76, 83, 95–100, 171, 179, 236, 239, 245
SRES scenarios. *See* Emission scenarios
Stakeholders, 50, 55, 57, 64, 105, 108, 112–113, 186, 203, 231, 233, 234, 237, 240, 243–244, 247, 254
Storms, 32, 33, 38–39, 55, 159, 165–166, 213, 214–223, 250
Streamflow, 34–35, 56, 125, 168, 169–172, 191–200, 240
Surface air temperature. *See* Temperature

Taylor diagrams, 220
Temperature: air, 25–27, 30, 35, 105–108, 138, 139–141, 160–162; apparent, 118–120, 146–153, 154; dew point, 37, 121, 148–153; diurnal temperature range, 26; historical trends/ variability, 1, 25–27, 53–54, 208, 234; projections, 2, 26–27, 36, 54, 70–73, 84–86, 94–97, 109–111, 123, 146–153, 234–235, 252; upper-air, 28
Thresholds, 4, 56, 66, 106, 108, 109–110, 167, 193
Tillage, 17, 93–96, 101